Saudi Bodyguard

Copyright © 2010 by Mark Young

The moral right of Mark Young to be identified as the author of this work has been asserted in accordance with the Copyright, Designs and Patents Act 1988.

ISBN: 978-1-4675-0243-6
Published by LLamekuf LLC USA

Acknowledgements

Sue, Stacey and Wayne

They supported me throughout the years regardless of the 'trials' and tribulations we faced. I wish I could turn back the clock and save them the suffering they endured.

Foreword

My brief is extreme—I must protect my charge at all costs. I am by profession a 'Bodyguard': I work at the upper echelons of personal protection. I am willing to place myself in the firing line at the critical moment and to sacrifice my life for that of my charge. Should the situation occur, I am prepared to intercept without hesitation the bullet meant for them.

As a youngster, I saved my younger brother Scott from a beating and this sowed a seed in me. From this seed grew my strong desire to protect others my dream of becoming a bodyguard.

I received martial arts training from arguably the best Karate coach in the world. My career has revolved mainly around the Saudi royal family, with other Arab royals and a couple of celebrities thrown in for good measure. I witnessed sexual perversion, greed, corruption and physical brutality—all incidents that have left their mark on me for life.

As I know these people for 'what they are', it instils a caution not to reveal too much personal information because it may put my family at risk from the dangers lurking behind the scenes. Over the years, I've watched and suffered as I wrestled with my daily duties battling against my core beliefs and morals.

Initially, I couldn't wait to become involved with the Saudi royals. After my experiences, I never want to be involved with them again. I observed as their cheating, double standards and hypocrisy—which knew no bounds—were used against their own people and the people who served them. Money flowed before me as readily as the oil flowed from the oilfields in Saudi Arabia. British Government officials fell over themselves to get in favour with the ruling family, lying and cheating their way to untold riches. I couldn't speak out, as the power these people hold would have been used to destroy me without hesitation. An example of a politician's involvement with the Saudis became known when the *Guardian* newspaper and *Granada* television faced a libel action in June 1997, brought by Jonathan Aitken, Member of Parliament. Aitken's case collapsed when evidence showed that he, his family and friends had lied to the court. He was a puppet of the Saudi Government for years, and they pulled his strings at will.

My experiences brought me to the conclusion that it is not the Saudi royal family that needs protecting from the people; it is the people that need protecting from the Saudi royal family.

So here begins my story. I know it sounds controversial. Some of it may even seem beyond belief. Nevertheless, this was my experience. So please, read on.

Chapter 1

My Early Years

My early life was hard. At five years old, my three brothers and I were taken into care by the social services. They claimed we suffered cruelty and neglect at the hands of our mother. I found the separation from my parents traumatic and was a little boy lost. I pined daily for Mum and Dad. The Council run home we were placed in was large and set in sprawling grounds. It housed thirty or so other children.

On my seventh birthday, I received a visit from my parents who had bought me a new toy, a shiny red fire engine. It had a siren and bells, which rang loudly—I loved it dearly. That evening the staff took it away, saying it made too much noise. I never saw it again. At mealtimes they took pleasure in forcing us to eat our greens and vegetables to the point of throwing up. It wasn't a good place to be in. The staff, I found cruel—crueller than our mother was supposed to have been! Mind you, they never had a chrome-tipped riding crop like the one Mum had used on us liberally when her mood dictated. Those lashes smarted and raised welts on our bodies.

After two years, the social services returned us to our parents. We found Mum drinking too much and having an affair with our father's best friend, a man named Derek. This led to our parent's separation, and ultimately to their divorce. On the day Mum left Dad, she took my younger brother Scott and me with her to London, but for some reason she left our two older brothers behind. I was seven years old, Scott was six. Our older brothers, Billy and Tony, were nine and ten. I never found out why Mum left my brothers but guessed she thought it fair, if she took the two younger boys then Dad could have the two older ones!

In one day, I lost my father and older brothers. My life was never the same. Dad was a strong and fearless character, having served in the special forces of the British Army and later in MI6, part of the British Secret Services. When he discovered Mum's affair he had gone after Derek who ran and hid from him. Derek enjoyed bullying us boys even though he knew that if our Dad ever heard of it he would be in serious trouble.

If Derek thought we had misbehaved he would often go to the tree at the bottom of the garden and break off a thick, long twig, and if it had buds breaking out on it, so much the better. A few lashes with that would make him feel better and us much worse. I often wondered why Derek had become involved with my mother given that he was so afraid of my father. Mum moved us around all the relatives' houses and after exhausting that avenue, she then moved us from one rented house to another. After some time passed, we finally settled down in a house in Brixton Hill, South London.

By now I had toughened up and was always involved in some fight or other. Once while playing cricket, I got into an argument with the batsman. He threatened to hit me with the bat so I dared him to. He hit me so hard I went to hospital with concussion! From then on, I never dared anyone to do anything again.

Even after we had settled in Brixton, I still missed my older brothers. So, it was with great joy when I heard that one of them, my brother Billy, was coming to live with us. However, my joy was short-lived as within a few weeks, Mum and Derek sent all three of us off to St Vincent's Convent in Mill Hill, North London. I was now eight years old. This was another home and the nuns ran this one from the Sisters of Charity of St. Vincent de Paul to the Lazarist Fathers.

At nine and a half years old, I was back at home with my two brothers in Brixton. Within weeks, I stood in front of my mother and stepfather as two Criminal Investigations Department Police Officers interviewed me. Along with six other young boys in the area, I'd been sexually abused by a woman living nearby. As the police officers asked me their searching questions on what had taken place, I wished the ground would swallow me up. The woman concerned pleaded guilty to all charges against her and was jailed.

Shortly after this I lost my brother, Billy, once again, as he was taken off by the social services to another council home. They said he was unruly and uncontrollable: a juvenile delinquent. It was years before he came home as he was moved around various homes in the

2

Lambeth area of London. By this time, he had become seriously institutionalised and would be in and out of prison for years to come.

My formative years were spent in despair. The only upbeat moment that I remember was when Mum gave birth to a daughter, my half-sister, Lisa. Mum's drinking got worse and I found myself taking on the responsibility of caring for my younger brother and sister.

At the age of ten, I found Mum slumped on her bed drunk and with an empty bottle of sleeping pills next to her.

I telephoned for an ambulance and the operator told me to keep Mum walking, making sure she didn't fall asleep. I struggled to rouse her and tried my best to move her with her help of course. I wasn't strong enough and while I shouted at her to move, tears streamed down my face. Finally, I had to sit her down in a wooden chair. Then to my horror, I noticed a puddle of blood forming on the floor beneath her. I screamed at my Mum not to die—I thought I had let her down by not moving her and that because of my failure she was now bleeding to death. Only when I was older did I find out that she had been having a heavy period at the time. The image of her sitting there in that chair wearing red trousers, which highlighted the colour of the blood, haunts me to this day.

At eleven, I was taken into hospital with a tumour in my back. I was suffering from Eosinophilicgranuloma. The illness also affected my left hip joint. I recovered after undergoing surgery and a long convalescence.

From a young age, I always found myself siding with the underdog. At fourteen years old, I attended Tulse Hill Secondary School in Lambeth. On the morning my younger brother Scott started at the school, I told him if he had any trouble, I would take care of it. On the first break of the morning my brother came running round a corner and over to me.

"They're coming!" he screamed.

"Don't worry, I'll sort them out," I replied, just as half a dozen kids came flying round the corner. I grabbed two of them in headlocks, Scott, laid into another one. The rest ran off, and then school prefects broke up the fight. Minutes later, my brother and I stood outside Mr Shelley's office. He was the deputy head of the

3

school. Mr Shelley stood before us wearing his black mortarboard hat and long black cloak. With a cane in his hand, he looked daunting. Satisfied that my brother had been set on, he let him go. Not satisfied with my explanation, I suffered six of the best from his cane. Three lashes were given across the palm of each hand. I held in the tears as my palms smarted with the pain.

* * *

At fifteen, I decided to develop my fitness and fighting skills. At school, I had been a brawler and enjoyed a good tear up, and then I had developed a keen interest in Karate and decided to join a local club. It wasn't long before I became obsessed with Karate and was training every night. I pushed myself hard and progressed through the lower ranks rapidly.

One problem at the club tortured me both mentally and physically: a 25-year-old brown belt named Alan. He stood about six feet tall, and was athletic and muscular. I, on the other hand, was slim and stood about five feet eight at the time. Alan was the best fighter in the club and was looked up to by the other high grades. I think Alan saw the potential I had and didn't like it, so he punished me, hoping I would give up. He had taken a dislike to me and often sent me home battered and bruised. It became so bad that I started looking for his car in the car park and if I saw it, my heart would race and thoughts of skipping the training session and going home would emerge.

I fought myself harder than I ever fought anyone in Karate. My tenacity won through and I carried on training.

The beatings from Alan became more frequent. I suffered, but persevered and improved with every training session and every sparring match. I was sixteen years old.

Life carried on as usual until one evening I was cajoled by my brother and his friends into going to a local pub with them. That night changed my life. There were six of us guys, and a few girls, too. One strikingly attractive girl named Sue was going out with a close friend of mine called Gerry. I wondered if they were serious about each other. She had noticed me, too. The evening ended with

4

no further developments. Over the next few months, I continued training and looking after Lisa. I also left school and worked at the local artist's factory. On New Year's Eve I went out with friends. As we walked into the pub, I was surprised to see Sue there, too.

She no longer went out with Gerry. Sue approached me and we started chatting. We welcomed in the New Year of 1973 together and arranged to meet a week later. Over the coming months, our relationship grew stronger and we became more of an item.

Within weeks of celebrating the New Year, trouble brewed at home, as I found myself taking more and more responsibility for my younger sister. Mum was comatose daily from the drink and Derek had started beating her, although she denied it. She would not let me confront him and said I was wrong. One evening, as I was getting ready for Karate, Derek and I got into a row. I already gave him and Mum nearly all of my salary for board but he wanted more to supplement the cost of Mum's drinking. The argument ended and I walked to the bottom of the stairs to call Sue, who was upstairs in the house at the time.

As she appeared halfway down the stairs, Derek said, "If I can't get you, then I'll get her."

He knew that if he tried to get at me in some way he would come off much the worse so like the coward he was he threatened to get Sue instead. I flew towards him but Mum got between us. I never managed to hit him but stormed out of the house taking Sue with me. His words rung in my head, then he shouted from the front door after me:

"The police will be here when you get back. I'm going to tell them how you attacked me."

I had to get out of there. Guilt would follow me for years to come over my decision to leave. Sue's parents allowed me to stay at their house and the council gave me a place to live within a few weeks.

* * *

At seventeen, I trained hard for another club grading. This was a brown belt exam. This time Graham Mitchell, a Second Dan Black Belt and finalist in the European Karate Championships of that year was going to be the examiner. During the grading, I had to fight him. Alan sat watching. The fight began and Graham Mitchell did a one-step roundhouse kick (*surikomi-mawashigeri*) to my head as I did a leg sweep (*ashi-barai*) and down he went. As he hit the floor, I punched at his head—a full-point technique which was enough to win a fight in competition then. His response was to punch me straight in the face! Praising my fighting spirit, Mitchell told me I had passed my grading. I was so proud when I told Sue about the exam. Our relationship had by this time developed to the point where we had decided to get married during September, just after I reached the age of eighteen.

By this time, I had become obsessed with my Karate. I knew that before trying out for my black belt, I would have to gain two further brown belt grades. One day my club instructor told me that he had entered a team and some individuals in a Karate competition. I was named as a team member and an individual fighter. Marvellous, I thought—until he told me the date of the competition. It was the 29th September 1973, my wedding day! I went home to break the news to Sue.

"You must be joking," she said

"No, I'm not. I'm going to bring the wedding forward a week."

"I don't believe it. You want to change our wedding day for a Karate competition?" Sue asked incredulously.

After much discussion and several tears, it was finally agreed. I would fight and the wedding moved forwards a week. Sue, as usual, supported me fully throughout. How lucky I was, considering how stupid I was being!

I fought in the competition and won my fights in both the team and individual events. My prize for this was a small plastic plaque and a hug from my new wife, Sue. The week prior to the competition had found our wedding day going off without a hitch. Apart from Sue and me, there was just one of her brothers and one of mine as witnesses. We were so poor we couldn't afford anything more extravagant. Leaving the register office building, I looked at my new wife in her borrowed wedding dress and thanked God for how lucky I was. Just as this thought crossed my mind, two old women walked past.

To our amazement and amusement, the comment "I wonder how long that will last?" greeted us as we neared them. I was now eighteen years old, a married man, a Karate champion, and my wife was expecting our first child.

My last brown belt grading was in Bristol in the South-West of England. Sensei's Peter Spanton, Dave Wheatley and Alan Flook would take it. I passed and then Alan Flook took me aside.

"You did well," he said, "but we think that before you try for your black belt you should take some specialist training, from either Sensei Spanton or 'Ticky' Donovan."

I was sailing along on a high, especially so after Sue gave birth to our first-born son, Stacey, in March 1974. My responsibilities were greater, so I worked harder. I wanted to provide for them as best I could. I wanted to give Stacey all that I could, even though money was short. I wanted, above all, to be a good husband and a good father.

* * *

'Ticky' Donovan was arguably the best Karate exponent in Britain. He had been British Champion in 1973, '74, '75 and a World and European Karate Team Champion. He was twenty-nine years old and stood about five feet nine inches tall. He had blond hair, but his eyebrows were dark; he was a formidable character, strong and charismatic. I think he was the best, and he expected the best from his students. I telephoned 'Ticky.' A man answered the phone and I asked, "Is that 'Ticky' Donovan?"

"Yes, what can I do for you?"

"I've been advised to call you about some private lessons. I recently graded under Sensei Spanton. It was suggested I take some lessons with you," I said.

'Ticky' replied, "I don't give private lessons—where do you live anyway?"

"I live about thirty-five miles away from you."

"Do you have a car?"

"No," I replied.

After telling him this, he asked me, "You would be happy to travel so far for a one-hour lesson?"

"Yes, I would be more than happy to do so."

With that 'Ticky' said, "Come and see me next Thursday at noon and we'll take it from there."

'Ticky' took me under his wing and trained me hard. I improved dramatically, and as a result graded for my black belt under his guidance. When I was ready, I arranged to attend the next black belt grading, which was to be held in Digbeth, Birmingham. I had just turned twenty. There were seven examiners on the panel led by a senior grade Japanese instructor, Toru Takamizawa. Out of sixteen candidates, only I and one other person passed.

When I watched 'Ticky' teaching, it was as though someone had turned on a bright light. I knew then what a real teacher was.

Around May 1976, I became a Karate instructor and under 'Ticky's guidance opened three Karate schools. Meanwhile I continued my training with the aim of converting to 'Ticky's style of Karate, which was called *Ishinryu* (meaning *'all of one heart'*). My aim was to become a professional Karate instructor. I had given up on becoming a bodyguard some time previously, since I had no idea where or how to get into the business. I taught Karate four times a week at my various schools. As I progressed in my teaching and training, my future seemed assured. I also continued working at the paint factory. I was stretching myself too far, but needed the money to support my family. Even with these jobs, I still found money tight.

Out of the blue, I received a phone call from Lisa, my younger sister. She was now eleven years old and it had been six years or so since I had last spoken with her. I felt guilty and responsible that she had gone into a foster home. Our mother's deepening depressions and alcoholism had taken their toll and with Derek being so weak, they would leave Lisa alone as they went out drinking into the small hours. Only a few weeks after I had left the family home, Lisa was found wandering the streets in the early hours of the morning and social services were brought in to take care of her. I had tried to contact her, but the social services would not give me details of where she was living. She asked her foster parents if I could visit her and they agreed. Lisa said I had been sorely missed and wanted to meet up again. Feeling the same and still protective of her, I set up a meeting with her for the following week.

On a bright sunny morning in November 1976, I made my way over to Charvil near Twyford in Berkshire. Apprehension engulfed me as I wandered up to the front door of the house. Lisa was waiting and threw her arms around me as I neared her. Tears flowed as I said, "I'm so sorry that I left you behind, had I been able to, I would have taken you with me."

She hugged me and whispered in my ear, "You didn't have a choice; I know that and never blamed you in any way. It was my Mum and Dad's fault that I was taken into care."

I would not lose contact with her again. She invited me into her new home and introduced me to Bill, her foster father, and Rene, her foster mother. Bill was tall, taller than I was. He stood about six feet three inches. He was balding and had a Mexican style moustache. He was athletic in build and wore a blue sweater and dark trousers. Rene had black hair, was about five feet six inches in height, and had dark brown eyes. She wore a flower print dress. I struck up a good rapport with Bill and found out that he worked with the Saudis doing chauffeuring and personal protection work. A friend of his named Terry had introduced him into the business. He had been stuck for a driver and had asked Bill if he could drive a Saudi prince around London for a month. Bill took the job, the prince took a shine to him, and Bill never looked back. As we sat chatting, Lisa listened intently. It was so good to see her again. I asked more about Lisa's welfare. Bill and Rene then left Lisa and me to catch up. We reminisced about our upbringing and the way in which our lives had changed. After half an hour, Bill returned and I asked him who his charge was.

"His full name and title is HRH Prince Khalid Bin Talal Bin Abdul Aziz Al Saud." Just hearing the prince's name conjured up memories of the movies I used to watch as a boy with the Arabian princes in them. "I've just returned from a trip to Cannes in the South of France. I stayed with the prince at the Hotel Martinez. Do you know it?"

"No, no I don't," I replied.

9

He spoke of his times with the family, and I listened, envious and fascinated. His tales rekindled the desire I'd had as a youngster to become a bodyguard, after I saved my younger brother Scott from a beating.

"Bill, is there any way you can help me get into the business?" I asked.

"Well, I can open a few doors but you will be responsible in getting yourself through them." Fair enough, I thought.

When I left Lisa, I felt as though I was flying on a magic carpet. My mood soared—I had renewed contact with my little sister and there was the possibility that a new career beckoned me.

I couldn't wait to tell Sue. She was happy for me and pleased it had gone well. The next time I arranged to see Lisa, both Sue and Stacey would go with me.

I telephoned Bill a few days later asking if he had contacted anyone yet. His reply was more subdued than his earlier animated conversation with me.

"I haven't called anyone yet but I will get around to it shortly," he said.

I felt uncomfortable with his reply. This, I thought, was going to be more difficult than I imagined. I telephoned Bill daily. Many times, he was overseas and so I found myself telephoning around Europe and the USA. Bill had not accounted for my tenacity.

That December—it was 1976—I started working occasionally for a security company based in Kent. They specialised in photographic, video and audio surveillance. At the same time, I continued teaching Karate, building up several students at each club. I had thought Bill would make it easy for me to enter the personal protection business, but I now felt he was doing little, if anything, to help me.

* * *

1979

A little over two years later, Bill gave me a telephone number. I was now twenty-three and had the telephone number for a man named Reg Black.

Sue was pregnant with our second child, due in May. I trained and worked hard and looked forward to the birth. I tried to find out about the company that Bill had told me about, but it proved impossible. They were so secretive they didn't even advertise. What did I have to lose?

I dialled Reg Black's number. The ring tone echoed in my ear as I waited for him to answer. "Hello, how can I help you?" said a man with an English public school accent.

"Good afternoon, can I speak to Mr Black?"

"Speaking" he answered. I gave him my name and said, "Bill gave me your number."

"Oh yes, my name is Reg and I have been expecting your call, can we meet at a pub near to your home which would be suitable?"

"Would you be happy to visit my home?" I enquired.

"That would be fine," he said, and we set a time and date for the meeting. Sue told me she would visit her sister when Reg dropped by. Once the meeting had been scheduled, I telephoned Bill out of courtesy to let him know.

"That's good," he said. "By the way I've also spoken to a guy named Ziad about you. He works for Khalid's sister Rima and they may be interested in taking you on too."

"Thanks for that. I will let you know how I get on with Reg Black first." I replied.

On the day of our meeting, Reg arrived driving a new Jaguar motor car. As we spoke, my telephone began to ring. I apologised and answered it. It was a wrong number but this call would prove to be fortunate for me.

As Reg left he said he would speak with his partner about me. This sounded ominous and wondered if I had lost my chance.

As soon as Sue got back from visiting her sister, I filled her in on all the details. She appeared genuinely happy this opportunity had arisen; however, only time would tell if it was the heaven-sent chance that I had been waiting for.

The following week, I received a telephone call from Reg. He said I had impressed him when I had taken the wrong number call during our meeting. He offered me a job as a telephone debt-collector. I turned it down. A week later, I received another offer, as a static guard at the home of Sir James Goldsmith; the billionaire financier (now deceased). I turned down that offer as well as I didn't relish the idea of standing around looking like a lemon and being treated with contempt. I was determined instead to go straight into personal security.

At the end of January, Reg telephoned and said that he had enrolled me on several of the company's in-house training courses. I couldn't believe my luck.

I wasn't aware that this company was arguably the best in Europe. I would have to undertake several courses. Each night I travelled home exhausted and there as usual I would find my rock, my wife. She was now in the later stages of her pregnancy. The thought had crossed my mind that she was only hanging on until my courses had finished so I could be with her.

Sure enough, once I was back at home and settled into our usual routine, Sue went into labour. I called the ambulance and waited with her for it to arrive. Sue's sister Doreen came over to look after Stacey. Even though I had gone through the experience once before, I still felt incredibly anxious and stressed. On the way to the hospital, I held her hand and felt useless. I wished I could take away the pain of her contractions. After eight hours of labour, our second son decided to join us. We called him Wayne. We also gave him the middle name of Paul after one of Sue's brothers.

When the time came I picked up Sue and Wayne from the hospital and brought them home. Sue must have still been feeling low for as soon as she saw how well I had coped without her, she started to cry. It was unusual for her to show her feelings in this way so it concerned me. I prayed she wasn't going to suffer any post-natal depression. Within a day or two Sue settled down. I had taken a week off from work to help her. I even stopped my Karate sessions for the week, which was previously unheard-of. The time flew by and I went back to work at the paint factory and resumed teaching Karate. Not knowing how the position with Reg Black and his security company was going to progress, I decided to keep quiet about my recent escapades to my friends.

One day late in August, Reg called me from the office and told me that they were pleased with my progress. My thirst for knowledge did not go unnoticed, and now Reg asked, "How would you like to take a place on the team going out to Greece?"

This was music to my ears; hardly containing my excitement I replied, "I would like that, sir."

"Right then, we will give you a try out, but remember—you will be under supervision always and evaluated constantly." This was to be my moment and I did not give a shit who would be watching me. Gaining this position with the team working for HRH Prince Talal Bin Abdul Aziz, the brother of the Saudi Arabian King Khalid Bin Abdul Aziz was a dream come true. I believed this was to be the start of an incredible journey. For over two years, I had been killing time waiting for this break, and now it was unfolding before my eyes. We were about to leave for Athens in Greece—I wanted to shout out to the world to let them know I was on my way.

Putting the phone down, I rushed out to the garden where Sue was sitting. "Guess what, guess what," I said to her excitedly.

"What do I have to guess about?" she replied.

"That was Reg Black on the phone, he said they are going to give me a try out, what do you think about that then?"

"Marvellous," she said as she reached out and hugged me. She knew how hard I had worked for this moment. "Sue, there's something else I have to tell you."

"What's that then?" she replied.

"The job is in Athens, Greece. Reg says it will only be for a few days, a week at most. Will that be fine with you?"

"Of course it will. I told you that if you're sure that it's what you want, then you must give it a try." I walked over to the local library and got out a couple of books about Saudi Arabia. I wanted to get an idea on how the country and its people had evolved.

* * *

My charge, His Royal Highness Prince Talal Bin Abdul Aziz Al Saud, had been a controversial figure in Saudi Arabia during the early 1950s. He had emerged as the leader of a group of liberal princes who wanted political reform in the kingdom. By the end of the decade, the Arab media was rife with reports of a new constitution drafted by Prince Talal. However, King Saud rejected the proposals and the Saudi clerical establishment issued a *fatwa* condemning them as a violation of Islamic law. In 1961, the government withdrew Prince Talal's passport and began trying to silence him, prompting him to leave for exile in Egypt the following year. During his stay in Cairo, he broadcast anti-Saudi radio propaganda, earning the nickname 'The Red Prince'. Prince Talal made up with the royal family two years later and was allowed to return to Saudi Arabia on condition he did not express his political views. Over the next two decades, he became very wealthy from construction contracts and real estate trading.

Prince Talal was a forthright person, his own man, and he wasn't averse to upsetting people. He reneged on a deal to provide almost $18 million towards building a hotel. But it was not until the case of two British nurses accused of murder some fourteen years later that he came to the English newspapers' attention: He was bold enough to make a statement prejudging the verdict in their trial. The nurses were charged with the Yvonne Gilford murder on 12th December 1996. Yvonne Gilford, an Australian nurse, was found dead in her room in the nurses' hostel at King Fahd Medical Complex in Dhahran. She had been stabbed four times, hit with a hammer and smothered. Yvonne Gilford was 55 years old, a senior theatre nurse who was halfway through a 12-month contract at the military hospital. By the end of May 1997, new claims were being made: that the nurses had been physically mistreated and threatened with rape to persuade them to sign the confession statements.

The *London Times* ran headlines on the 9th August 1997 saying, "Saudi Prince says there will be no beheadings in nurse's case." The piece went on to say that the threat of execution for the two British nurses had receded after a leading member of the Saudi royal family declared that the nurses did not deserve to face the executioner's sword. Prince Talal also stated firmly in an interview with the *Washington Times*: "I am telling you that in this case there will be no beheadings." It was unprecedented for a member of the royal family to go out by himself and make such a declaration. It appeared that he was overruling the Court and his family. This made him either a very brave or a very stupid man. It was my belief he was the former.

* * *

In my own life, I carried on training hard and was fit—fit for anything, or so I thought. Sue had asked me many times if I was sure that this was what I wanted. I had replied, "Yes, I must try it. If I fail, at least I can say I gave it a go. My main concern will always be for you and the boys, but if you don't want me to go, I will stay home." Seeing how excited I was, Sue supported me fully and even encouraged me to go. Only later would I find out that she never wanted me to leave her or the boys. She had kept quiet so as not to spoil my dream.

As I prepared for departure, I experienced mixed emotions of excitement and anxiety. I had decided to say goodbye to Sue and the boys at home. I didn't want to suffer any emotional goodbyes while standing in an airport lounge.

On Saturday 1st September 1979, I waited to depart with the other members of the team at Heathrow Airport. I wondered what adventures might lay ahead in Athens. I was the new boy. All the other members of the team had served the prince on many occasions before. I wasted no time trying to gain as much information as I could. I asked so many questions about anything and everything that I could think of. What the principals looked like, how they dressed, what they liked, what peculiarities if any in their customs did I need to know? I soaked up the information like a sponge, always knowing there was so much more to learn.

On arrival at Athens, we met with the local police commander who was to aid us throughout Prince Talal's visit. The Prince expected a low-key arrival and departure from the airport. Reg was at pains to ensure good relations between the local authorities and us. Danka, a member of our team fell at the first hurdle not making it through immigration as he was of Yugoslavian nationality and his visa wasn't in order.

On completing the formalities, we made our way to the hotel and waited for the arrival of 'the family' the following morning. That evening Reg conducted a briefing. Reg said to me, "Whatever happens you will stay close to me and follow my lead. Are you clear on that?"

"Yes Boss," I replied.

That evening I phoned home. "Are you good? Are the boys all right?" I asked Sue as soon as she picked up the receiver.

"We're all good, what about you?"

"Yes, I'm doing well. We are staying at a small hotel tonight but we are transferring to the Prince's hotel tomorrow. As soon as I have the telephone and room number of where I'm staying, I will call you."

"Make sure you do," Sue replied.

"It's gorgeous here, from what little I've seen that is. I will get off now and call you tomorrow."

"Maybe you'll be able to talk for longer then?"

"Of course I will. There will be more to tell you about. I want you to know what is going on. I'll call tomorrow, love you."

"I love you, too," Sue whispered back to me.

A little subdued, I made my way to find the other guys. What I didn't know was Sue had burst into tears back home in England the moment she had put down the phone.

* * *

The following day as we assembled at the airport, two of Prince Talal's cars arrived from England. The first was a sparkling white Mercedes Benz Pullman 600. The second was also sparkling white, but a Rolls Royce Corniche convertible, with a white hood and a gleaming milky white leather interior. Other cars we needed were picked up locally. The Rolls Royce belonged to the prince's fifteen-year-old son, Turki. His Royal Highness would arrive on his own private Boeing 727 jetliner. The aircraft nose cone had the princes father's name, King Abdul Aziz Al Saud, painted on it.

I waited expectantly for the arrival. Reg decided that I would be backing him. Reg wanted to keep an eye on me. Notice of the aircraft's approaching descent came through. We took up our respective positions. Reg and I stood at the bottom of the aircraft steps waiting for them to be positioned against the aircraft fuselage when it finally stopped. Gryf, another of the team, stood by the open rear door of the Mercedes Pullman 600. Others stood guard at each corner of the car facing out toward any incoming threat. Danka's position was sitting in a detention room while the Greek authorities sorted out what they would do with him.

The aircraft taxied up towards us at a location away from the terminal buildings. As the aircraft approached, we suddenly found to our amazement four armoured personnel carriers (APCs) shadowing the plane. Lights flashed everywhere. On top of the APCs were soldiers with automatic weapons. They encircled the plane as it taxied to a standstill. *This was a low-key arrival?* What His Highness would make of the welcoming committee, I wondered. This was my first experience of a Saudi royal family arrival, but I would lose count of how many I witnessed over the years. Little did I know that in addition to the prince, I had a surprise heading my way as well!

Chapter 2

September 1979

The aircraft door opened and Prince Talal Bin Abdul Aziz Al Saud emerged, standing majestically at the top of the stairs adorned in his Arabian robes. A large, thickset man about five feet ten inches tall, he had a prominent Arab nose and a black moustache. He exuded wealth and power and commanded respect as his piercing eyes cut straight through you like a red-hot knife.

As soon as Prince Talal's feet touched the tarmac, he was greeted by the Saudi Arabian officials sent from their embassy. The prince then told the police commander greeting him to liaise with his, the prince's, own security team. Now, for the first time, I heard the distinctive, gruff voice that I had been told about by the other guys. I detected Prince Talal was angry, as the tone of his voice was enough to make his feelings clear. His intense gaze hit the police commander between the eyes; giving the effect the officer had been physically assaulted. The commander apologised for the excessive show of force during the arrival as he held on to the open door of the waiting Mercedes for the prince. We drove over to the airport VIP lounge to complete the passport, immigration and customs formalities. After this, we headed off at speed for the hotel at which we'd all be staying.

Two of the team were already on an inspection tour of the new hotel. On our arrival, we were expecting a quick briefing on the layout of the hotel.

We had a 25 kilometre drive to the Arion Astir Palace Hotel, which is 22 kilometres outside Athens and overlooks the Saronic Gulf. I found myself in a heightened state of awareness as I imagined a threat of some sort lurking behind every bush and tree. Showing my inexperience, I searched out every driver and passenger in any nearby vehicles, causing my adrenaline to surge. My heart burned as the blood coursed through it, adrenaline seeping into my veins. I wondered if anyone else could hear my pounding heart as it raced in line with my thoughts. Experiencing a real assignment, I soon found out, released different emotions to the ones I had noted during the training courses I had attended.

We paced across the lobby to the elevator—Prince Talal and three of his children, Turki, Sarah, and Nora; the general manager of the hotel; Reg, and me.

No one came to brief us, and my mind played tricks with me; I had wanted to talk briefly with them. This caused me some concern, and I felt uneasy.

The doors of the elevator closed and instead of rising, it descended. My heart raced, the adrenaline pumped; it gushed! I thought we were heading to certain ambush in the basement.

'Game on', I thought, nearly shitting myself in reality. My palms were sweating, and my knees wobbled. I took slow deep breaths; steeled myself and tried to keep control. The elevator stopped, the doors opened, and there before me stood six or seven people. I nearly died on the spot, I went to make a move and then it dawned on me—I was looking into a huge mirror!

The hotel was designed so the lobby was on the top floor and the lower floors descended toward the Vouliagmeni Bay. Fortunately, I had kept control of myself. My reaction, though, had reminded me of my vulnerability—a tough lesson learned.

Often I would recall that incident with hilarity remembering how 'green' I had been on my first assignment.

Reg called me over. "Don't you think the arrival went well?" he asked. Lying through my teeth I replied, "I thought it went well," deciding to keep the inner turmoil I felt under wraps.

Reg then asked, "You're a good swimmer aren't you?"

"Yes I am, why?"

"Because I'm deploying you to keep watch over Prince Talal when he swims in the morning," he said.

Of course, while I watched over Prince Talal, Reg would watch over me. The pressure was on yet again.

This new revelation concerned me, as Prince Talal was no lightweight—he was a big man indeed. I thought if he got into trouble, he'd bloody well drown! I wouldn't be able to help him but of course I would try.

The following morning Prince Talal appeared, and everyone around, including me, jumped to attention. He was wearing a towelling robe and matching swimming shorts and over his arm, he carried a towel. Could the prince swim, and if so, how well, I wondered. Maybe I was in for a soaking. An entourage accompanied Prince Talal, and Reg in turn accompanied me. This was a normal scene for any of the rich high-powered princes. On our arrival at the pool, I put all of my valuables in my jacket pocket and placed the jacket over my arm, ready to drop it in a hurry if I needed to. I smiled as I surveyed the scene. Reg and I stood by the poolside while some of the prince's entourage stood behind us. Mob-handed, we waited on His Royal Highness as we tried in vain to keep a low profile.

Through the corner of my mouth, I asked Reg, "Can Prince Talal swim?"

"We'll soon find out, won't we?" he answered, playing me like a well tuned violin, "Just make sure you're ready when he gets in, just in case he gets into trouble."

Standing even closer to the pool I mentally rehearsed my heroic saving of the prince as I imagined him foundering in the water. I even whispered a few words to the good Lord asking his help should the prince get into difficulty. Watching closely as the prince walked up to the pool, I steeled myself as he dived in. Entering the water with a perfect dive, he propelled himself through the water like a torpedo. I was sure the prince could have swum back to Saudi Arabia if he was of a mind to. I wondered if anyone near me had heard the huge sigh of relief I must have given. Nonetheless, I kept a close eye on him but in my mind, it was 'job done'.

After his dip and sunning himself, it was off back to his suite. Meanwhile, Prince Turki had headed off in a speedboat round the bay area. He tried his hand at paragliding and some bright spark noticed him soaring above the waves and decided to point it out to Prince Talal. He raised his voice; speaking in Arabic he gestured wildly—I thought he was going to murder someone.

20

The same fellow who had noticed Turki paragliding said in English, "Your Royal Highness, Turki will be fine, he has the English guard and the Greek policeman with him!"

This calmed Prince Talal not a bit. He continued his diatribe again in Arabic, and then commanded Reg in English, "I want Turki back in this suite within ten minutes."

Members of his entourage ran in all directions. I wasn't able to make out if they were running to get Turki or trying to get away from Prince Talal! The Greek police officers tried to contact their colleagues on the boat, as did we. The walkie-talkies did not rouse any response. I asked Reg for permission to go down to the bay area to see if there was anything I could do. With his blessing, off I went. I was happy just to be out of it all and sauntered off down to the bay. As I reached the landing stage, I saw Turki, who was just getting out of the boat. Being a young teenager, he had the body of a youth progressing through puberty. His hair was black like a raven's wing, and his body was slim and lithe as he moved from the boat to the landing stage with ease. I guessed his height at five and a half feet, but knew he would get taller as puberty progressed.

"Turki, your father has ordered you to be in his suite within ten minutes," I said.

He smiled and set off for the hotel. I strolled back myself, and still arrived before Turki. Walking up to Reg I said, "I've managed to get hold of Turki and he's on his way back now. Should someone let Prince Talal know that we've contacted the boy and that he's on his way?"

Reg replied, "I wouldn't bother." It seemed that no one dared knock the door of the prince's suite, preferring to stay out of the way and keep their heads down.

In my naiveté, I knocked the door. The prince called out in his distinctive deep gravelled voice, "Come in."

"Your Royal Highness, I've spoken to Prince Turki. He's on his way back to you as we speak," I said.

"Thank you," he replied.

I turned and walked back out into the corridor as Turki arrived and went in.

We waited expectantly for the fireworks, but there wasn't a thing. The door was open, and we heard Prince Talal talking calmly in Arabic, probably asking Turki to be more careful in future. Looking around the corridor and the nearby rooms, I found it surprising how many people waited at the prince's disposal.

That evening we set off for a seafood restaurant in the port of Piraeus, 25 kilometres from the hotel. The setting was picturesque with the restaurant set on a quayside looking out to sea: its lights reflecting on the water sparkled, and it was a beautiful scene. Prince Talal and his party took their seats and then we sat down on a nearby table. We searched out the surroundings and took note of the people nearby.

On leaving the restaurant, the prince decided he wanted to take a stroll along the harbour. It was a pleasant evening; the sky was bright, it was warm, and the stars were shining. It was magical. At the end of the quayside floated a magnificent yacht. Prince Talal had hired it for a cruise around the Greek Islands at night. Only Terry his driver and the security guys were allowed to escort the prince and his family. That night was special and would stay with me always. I spent most of the time at the bow speaking with Terry, once again gaining as much information as I could. As it was, Terry was a mine of information about their customs, likes and dislikes, and much more besides. I came to respect him, as he was happy to share his knowledge, which I would later find out was something several guys on the circuit would never do. He was happy to guide me along the right path—a path which I've followed throughout my career.

* * *

We stayed at the Arion Astir Palace Hotel for four days. His Royal Highness had decided to move on to London. This was a surprise as we hoped the prince would extend his stay in Greece. Ahead of the prince's departure on the morning of the 5th September, I left for London with an inspection team. We had several checks to perform before the arrival of the main party later in the afternoon.

It was a different world to that I'd previously known—a facet of the world not seen by many. In fact, it was a facet best not seen by the average person over a long period as it can easily cause psychological problems. Just as an example, talk had surfaced about Prince Talal slapping his secretary, Nicolas Abboud, across the face while aboard the aircraft. Abboud had left the prince the moment the aircraft doors had opened after it had landed.

Not thinking about any of this, once we had carried out our checks, we left two of the inspection team at the apartment block. The rest of us went to the Alcock and Brown VIP suite (now renamed the Hillingdon suite) at Heathrow airport to await the prince's arrival. We knew his aircraft was already airborne.

About half an hour later, a call came through telling us the aircraft had diverted. It was on course back to Riyadh, the capital of Saudi Arabia, as the prince needed to sign some papers. As the visit was delayed by a day, we stood down. This was the first time I saw how they use their personal aircraft—that is, just as most people use their cars!

Grabbing this heaven-sent opportunity, I made my way home. Keeping my door keys in my pocket, I knocked on my front door. A few seconds later, the door opened and there stood my beautiful wife. She lunged at me, kissing and hugging me as though I'd been away for a year. Taking me by the hand, she led me through to the boys who were contentedly playing with their toys on the living room floor. Scooping them up in my arms, I kissed them. Sue embraced us all, our little family unit complete once again.

"I only have the night free and then I have to go back to London for a few days."

"That's fine," Sue replied, not letting on that she had loathed every minute we had been apart. I noticed she kept staring at me and wondered if I had grown another nose or something.

"What's wrong, why do you keep staring at me?"

"I just want to look at you as much as I can before you have to go back, that's all." Being a typically obtuse man, I did not notice the signs, which would have told me that my being away had obviously upset her. I was too busy playing at Superman to notice her pain. Therefore, it was in complete oblivion to my wife's feelings that I set off on the Thursday 6th of September to the Alcock and Brown VIP suite to await the arrival of the prince and his family. This time, the arrival would go meticulously. The cars were back from Greece and soon the convoy was on its way out to the aircraft and the adrenaline flowed once more.

* * *

Prince Talal appeared at the open door of his Boeing 727 aircraft, this time wearing a black Savile Row suit. He looked a million dollars. It was a bright, sunny day. We went to work and after completing the formalities, we left the Alcock and Brown suite and Heathrow airport.

The drive into London by the M4 motorway proved uneventful. We escorted Prince Talal to his apartment in Roebuck House on Palace Street in Westminster, just behind Buckingham Palace. This apartment was one of a few he owned in this block. We stayed at a hotel in Carlisle Place.

One of Prince Talal's friends, Adnan Khashoggi, the arms dealer, also had an apartment in the block. Khashoggi's wife, Soraya, had an affair with the MP Jonathan Aitken, which had resulted in her becoming pregnant with Aitken's child. She gave birth to a daughter named Petrina. Soraya also had an affair with the prince—although it lasted all of one day and night despite her having gone to the trouble of dyeing her hair blonde because she knew Prince Talal was partial to blonde women. Soraya, like Jonathan Aitken (the 'Commons Casanova' as he was widely known), played the field. She had also had a five-year affair with the former Conservative MP Winston Churchill (grandson of Britain's wartime Prime Minister) whom she called a "super lover."

Prince Talal was stopping in London for three or four days. The first evening the family spent quietly at home. I struck up a rapport with the prince's valet, Joseph, and we got on well. The next day as I waited, Joseph approached me and slipped a note discreetly into my hand. This intrigued me. When I was alone in the foyer, I took the note from my pocket and read it. He told me he was gay, and he wanted to go out with me. I let him down gently, explaining that I

24

was strictly a lady's man! He fired a look of disappointment at me but accepted my response with good grace. I had spurned his advance but it did not affect our working partnership.

The following afternoon, Friday 7th September, the prince went to meet Sammy, a friend in Belgravia. Then we set off for Haya 1, an expensive women's dress store on Grafton Street in Mayfair. The owner, Leila Khaled, supplied prostitutes to the princes. Leila was in her mid forties, of medium build and about five feet seven inches tall. She dressed well and was classy. Her shops were a front for prostitution and the *News of the World* newspaper ran a story in 1982 about her and the prostitutes she supplied in the United Kingdom.

We checked the shop before the prince entered. The drivers, as usual, stayed with the cars so no undesirables could tamper with them. Leila greeted Prince Talal and introduced him to three gorgeous young women. Two had dark hair while the third was blonde. Each girl was about five feet nine inches tall. The blonde girl had piercing blue eyes, which sparkled brightly. She had large breasts and a tiny waist. Long legs and small hips accentuated her beauty. Her long hair hung loosely but swirled in soft curls. Pink, shiny lipstick glistened on her lips. Knowing Prince Talal preferred blondes, it was obvious which girl he would choose to escort him. Sammy would have to make do with one of the other sex goddesses, I thought. These girls had long dark flowing locks of hair. One had dark brown eyes; the other, green eyes. They, too, had large breasts. I smiled, thinking it must be a man thing. One of the girls was slim while the other was more generously covered, not large but a little more buxom. One wore bright red lipstick. As they smiled, I could see their beautifully white polished teeth. I wondered which woman would escort Sammy and which girl would not be going to the ball.

The dresses in the shop were beautiful and expensive—well over a thousand pounds each. The prince bought a dress for each of the young women. The women would wear these dresses later that evening. By now, it was three o'clock in the afternoon.

After placing the prince safely in his car, we set off. Everywhere we went, the prince's car drew attention. The Mercedes was twenty-odd feet long and nearly six and a half feet wide—it was massive! It was left-hand drive and its front seats were covered in navy-blue leather. The passenger compartment had navy-blue deep-buttoned velvet covered seats and a colour television, videocassette recorder, a large cocktail cabinet, and a telephone.

We followed in a high-powered security car. We returned to the apartment and found it quiet—the prince's children were out. I went to the kitchen to find Joseph and we got chatting.

"What's Prince Talal so happy about?" he asked.

"Joseph, I don't know, I was hoping you were going to tell me that."

"Anyway, Prince Talal is going to take a short nap to charge his batteries for the evening ahead," Joseph said.

On that note, I thought I would take a break too and went to a quieter area of the apartment. Checking my watch, it showed 4pm. With luck, I would get about two hours before being roused again.

I dozed off in an armchair until I felt a nudge on my shoulder at six thirty. We would soon be on the move.

The drivers prepared the cars and the prince emerged from his suite smartly dressed in a navy-blue suit. The hairdresser had done his hair and Joseph had prepared his clothes. We emerged from the apartment block to a lovely summer's evening—the night to come had all the hallmarks of being an interesting experience, at least for the prince. Off we went to meet with Sammy. On entering the hallway of Sammy's house, we were told to wait for the young women. It wasn't long before they showed up. They were something to look at before, but now they were indescribable. Was it my imagination, or could I hear the prince's heartbeat speed up? I was sure I could hear it thumping clearly—or was it my own?

Prince Talal ordered Terry to drive to Mr Chow's Chinese restaurant in Knightsbridge. On the way, you could feel the atmosphere distinctly changing, as the excitement and expectations filled the air yet again. I tucked into my Peking duck with pancakes, cucumber batons and hoisin sauce as Michael Chow came to check that the service met with Prince Talal's approval. Reassured, Mr Chow left the prince to enjoy the rest of his meal. After dinner, I walked out to check the immediate vicinity. It would not do for the prince or his guests to wander into a group of drunks or suchlike.

Terry was then ordered to drive on to Annabel's nightclub in Berkeley Square. As we arrived, Mark Thatcher, the son of the British Prime Minister, Margaret, was cussing at his police bodyguard just as he was leaving. Ignorant pig, I thought. Once inside, Reg and I melted into the crowd, blending into the background. Several 'celebrities' were milling about.

We tuned into the surroundings paying particular attention to the people around the prince. Sammy danced with both the dark haired young women. Prince Talal sat chatting with his blonde escort and drunk his Johnny Walker Black Label whiskey. They watched Sammy and the women on the dance floor. I had my eyes on the prince! Within minutes, the prince gestured for Reg and called for his car. He looked to be in some distress, so we left—in a hurry.

Sammy and the women were left behind. We went straight to Roebuck House. The prince was in a foul mood. This turn of events had surprised us. We were then dismissed for the night. Being perceptive, I wondered what it was that I had missed. Before retiring, I decided to go to the kitchen and get a Coke. As I did so, Joseph came in smiling. He grabbed himself a Coke and we sat talking together. Then as he laughed, Joseph told me what had happened at the club. "The woman sitting next to Prince Talal moved up close to him and started stroking his thigh under the table. Then she started whispering in his ear, and as she fondled him he couldn't contain his excitement and ejaculated down his leg!"

"You're joking?" I said, laughing with him. I felt this explanation was dubious to say the least but it would help to explain the sudden departure of the club.

"Not to worry though," Joseph said laughing, "Prince Talal will try again tomorrow night!"

* * *

On the Saturday morning, I was sent out with Turki, as his bodyguard hadn't arrived. He was going to visit his sister in Belgravia. Graham, Turki's driver, drove down into Lowndes Close and I could see a few people standing by a classic Mercedes convertible car outside a mews house directly in front of us. Princess

27

Rima, I noted, stood by the driver's side of the car. She was about five-feet three inches tall and had long dark hair. I noticed a hint of red in it, no doubt from the henna she must have had applied. She carried a little weight but wasn't fat. She had a large nose, which was commonplace for many Arabs. As she noticed us, she smiled. Her teeth were bright, white and straight. Hugging Turki, she appeared happy to see him.

Princess Rima invited us into her home and asked if I would like a drink while I waited, I thanked her and accepted. Graham waited outside with the car. The princess took Turki into the lounge and called for her husband. As he bounded down the stairs, I couldn't help staring. Prince Walid Bin Saud, was slim and had film star looks. He was a handsome devil, and he knew it.

He had money, good looks, and several expensive cars. I imagined he must have had all the women falling over him. He was polite, and spoke with an ex-public school accent. One of the late King Saud's many sons; Prince Walid had received his education at Millfield Public School in England. The prince's fag (a student at a British public school who has to perform menial tasks for a student in a higher class) had been Major James Hewitt, who years later had a widely publicised affair with Princess Diana. Major Hewitt would call on the prince for help towards the end of the Gulf war when news broke of the affair and it became public knowledge.

Prince Walid's driver was English. The couple's cleaner came from South America, their secretary was from Lebanon, and other staff came with them from Saudi Arabia. I smiled inwardly—the place was like a United Nations convention! I made conversation with Ziad, Princess Rima's secretary, as I waited. It wasn't long before Turki appeared and the prince and princess said their goodbyes. Turki was in good spirits as he told Graham to take him back to Roebuck House. An hour after arriving safely back at the apartment, I watched as Turki mimicked Terry's actions as he explained the rudiments of the parachute roll. They then went over the motions together.

Turki's bodyguard had arrived by this time. We got into the normal routine, which was 'hurry up and wait'. We spent vast amounts of time waiting. One moment everything would be quiet, the next everything would be hectic. This would be the stop-start routine that would go on for years to come. Often the only excitement we got was when an unexpected visitor arrived and we would conduct a thorough search.

That evening, Princess Rima visited her father and asked if she could take Turki and her two younger sisters, Sara and Nora, to the movies. Permission was given and she asked that just one security man escort them. I was the person she wanted. What I wanted was to see the prince's second round performance with the escorts, but Reg had to let me go.

We left for the cinema in two cars. In the foyer, Princess Rima asked casually, "What work do you have planned when my father leaves?"

"I have nothing planned, Your Highness," I replied.

"Can I have your telephone number as I might have something for you?"

"Of course," I said, and wrote down my number for her. She in turn gave me hers. It crossed my mind whether this would be considered suitable behaviour in the eyes of the royal family.

"Please make sure you call me once my father leaves."

"Of course I will," I assured her.

Sunday came and went. Apart from dinner at the Elephant on the River, we spent a boring day at the apartment. Talk had centred on the proposed departure, which was scheduled for Tuesday 11th September. I was warned the principals often changed their minds about anything and everything. Sometimes they changed the days of departure; sometimes they changed the times, but always they changed their minds—minute by minute. Therefore, it came as a surprise when we found ourselves on the way to the Alcock and Brown VIP suite at Heathrow Airport on the Tuesday as planned. On entering the lounge, I noticed Princess Rima was there to see her family off. She reminded me to telephone her. After her family had boarded their aircraft, Princess Rima left. We on the other hand had to wait for half an hour after the aircraft was airborne to check there weren't any problems or indeed whether Prince Talal had decided to return for some reason. On several occasions, we had aircraft take off and then return as the principals changed their minds and had decided to stay longer! We marvelled once more at how they used their aircraft like other people use their cars.

Chapter 3

1979-1980

On the 15th September 1979, I was having a bath and had just doused my hair in shampoo when the phone rang. Sue answered it and brought the receiver to me: "I think you had better take this. It sounds like an Arab man to me," she said. Cursing inwardly, I took the call. It was Ziad, Princess Rima's secretary. It had been four days since Prince Talal's departure and the time had passed quickly.

"Why haven't you called the princess?" he asked.

"Ziad, you must have been reading my mind, I was just thinking about calling her," I lied.

"The princess wants to see you now. Can you come into London right away?"

"I can be there in about an hour's time if that's all right?" I said.

"Yes good, I will wait for you too, try not to be too long." I hung up the phone.

"It was Ziad, Princess Rima's secretary. He wants me to go and see her."

"Will you be long?" Sue asked.

"I shouldn't think so. About three hours at most." As I kissed Sue goodbye, she whispered in my ear. "Good luck." I smiled at her and set off for London.

I should have been dancing with delight. Instead, I felt a little put out. This feeling stayed with me. Why I felt like this was a mystery to me. Perhaps my mind and body were still winding down from the prince's visit.

I was apprehensive as I arrived at Lowndes Close. It was strange, as earlier; I had not felt at all uneasy around the princess or any of her staff. My gut instinct was telling me I should not have bothered going. I didn't listen to it.

I rang the doorbell of the Belgravia mews house and Ziad answered it. He shook my hand vigorously and invited me in.

We sat at the large round table near the bottom of the staircase.

On the wall next to the table was a large mirror, which I noticed Ziad look into several times. As we waited for the princess, Ziad opened the conversation with a question. "How did you meet Bill?"

I told him about my previous visit to Bill and how I had said that I wanted to work in close protection.

"Yes, Bill mentioned it to me. I spoke to Princess Rima about you. When you turned up with Prince Turki, she became more interested in you, as she was then able to put a face to your name."

So Bill had been true to his word and spoke of me, I thought. I took stock of Ziad, noticing the grey striped suit he wore complemented his greying hair and moustache. His build was on the medium to small side and his hair was thinning, too. He had the sallow skin that many Lebanese have and I noticed a crucifix round his neck telling me he was of the Christian faith. I could tell he had a confident personality and that he was a vain man. He was forever preening himself and looking in the nearby mirror. I got on fairly well with him but he was a cunning and slippery man.

Within a minute or two, the princess appeared from the lounge. She wore a white long-sleeved blouse and a long black skirt with black shoes. I stood up immediately. "Please come into the lounge," she said and as I followed her, I noted that Ziad followed me. The princess gestured to a large black leather sofa and said, "Please sit down." I was struck by what I considered a garishly decorated room. Bright reds, black and chrome assaulted me from every angle. Later I found out the room had been professionally designed by Zarach's of Mayfair.

"Can you tell me—are you under any obligation to continue working for my father?"

"No, Your Highness, I'm a free agent and can work for whomever I want."

"I would like to be sure that if you come to work for me that it will not cause any problems."

"Your Highness, rest assured there will be no problems," I replied.

"I will need you to drive me, too, is that acceptable to you?"

I felt uneasy about the driving bit, but knowing the job would provide more security for me and my family I said, "I'm happy with that."

Princess Rima asked Ziad to call her husband, Prince Walid for her. Prince Walid said, "You must consider that we are nowhere near being in the financial league of Prince Talal, Princess Rima's father. Therefore we cannot pay you the same salary as His Highness."

"I understand," I replied, accepting his statement without question. It was true, they were not in Prince Talal's league but they were multimillionaires in their own right. The prince was 23 years old, the princess 21. He thought I was suitable for the job. Meeting over, I left.

I arrived home around nine thirty and opened the front door of my house quietly so as not to disturb the children. Greeted with a hug from Sue, she asked, "How did it go?"

"Well I got the job, but the money isn't up to much. At least working in London, I will be able to come home every night. I'll see how it goes, I suppose." Sue noticed I seemed unsure.

"If you don't want to do it, then don't."

"I've a week before I start, so I'll think about it," I replied, although I knew that I wasn't in any position to turn the offer down.

Over the next few days, I felt decidedly uneasy about starting the job. However, a week after meeting with the princess, despite my reservations, I went to work.

* * *

Ziad took me to the car park underneath the Intercontinental Hotel in Park Lane, Mayfair, where the prince and princess kept their cars. He pointed out each car in turn and told me who owned it. They had ten cars, including a few Ferraris!

At that moment, it crossed my mind what they had said about Prince Talal being in a different league to them. The value of their motorcars alone was immense, and that was apart from everything else they may have owned. So how was it that my salary wasn't up to much? I should have seen the warning signs then. A month later,

33

the princess bought a white BMW 635 CSI sports coupe: not bad for the poor relations of the family!

What a load of crap. I felt conned on my £100 a week salary. It was now October and I was working six days a week, twelve hours or more a day, with no overtime payments. When I finally asked for a pay rise, they offered twenty-five pounds a week extra if I worked the Sunday as well!

*   *   *

Throughout 1979, I suffered irritation from my left ear. Twice I'd been prescribed medication for an ear infection, but the problem persisted. Six weeks after starting work with the princess the problem intensified. This time, I was admitted to hospital as an emergency case. The infection and pain were severe and I had to undergo stag doses of penicillin every six hours, day and night. The injections in the backside hurt like hell. Even after swapping the shots alternately, they soon ran out of fresh sites to inject.

Sue visited every day after arranging for her sister to baby-sit the boys. I looked forward to her visits, as I missed her a lot. The hours passed so slowly. Lying in the hospital bed, I continuously felt guilty about not being at work. I felt I was letting the princess down. Because of the infection, the surgeons couldn't act immediately and it took more than a week for the infection to subside. The surgeon performed a mastoidectomy and after the procedure, my eyes danced independently of each other. My balance was shot and I had difficulty sitting up. Each time I tried, I would throw up. My head was swathed in bandages. I looked a state and I felt terrible too. I had no idea the procedure would cause so much pain, sickness and dizziness. Sue was beside herself with worry. She questioned the doctors about the wild movements of my eyes. She wanted to know why they now moved independently of each other. The surgeon reassured her that they would settle as my balance improved. Nonetheless, she worried about me continuously and nursed me constantly when she visited.

A week after the operation I received a visit from Princess Rima and Bill, who was taking care of her while I recovered. She stayed for a short while, and my condition shocked her. My head was still swathed in bandages and blood still seeped through them even though they were regularly changed. My balance was still off, and I needed support to sit up in the bed. Gripping the handrail on my bed, I sat up abruptly to greet the princess. The dizziness hit me and caused me to throw up. I was in a pitiful state.

Other visitors would come and go and as much as I wanted to get out of hospital, I had to stay put. Two weeks after the operation, I was allowed home. It would be a further two months before my balance would improve sufficiently to enable me to return to work.

I was pleased to be home with Sue and the boys, but I still suffered badly. I couldn't walk anywhere without help. If I tried to walk unaided, I would bump into chairs, tables, and even walls. My eyes slowly settled down and began to work with one another. Slowly over the next few weeks, my health improved. Ziad phoned me a few times mainly to ask when I would be returning to work. This pissed me off, as I had never been one to take time off from work needlessly. As it was, because of this pressure, I returned to work earlier than I should have.

It was now the middle of March, 1980, and within two weeks of returning to work, I worked all the hours God sent. It was a buzz driving around in the cars. I enjoyed going to get a McDonald's burger and would sit outside the take away in the Rolls Royce Corniche convertible with the hood down. As people walked by they often looked twice when they noticed the 3 HRH registration plate.

I was serving what was to become a valuable apprenticeship. I learned how temperamental the Saudi royals could be—they have a different mentality: their very being revolves around saving face and they will do almost anything to avoid confrontation. They always get a third party to do their dirty work, too—and even if they owned companies, they usually hid behind front men.

The pettiness between co-workers often reared its head, too, and never failed to surprise me. There was plenty of competition between Ziad and the prince's driver, Michael, for instance. And there were plenty of other issues that I would have to face along the way.

One particular evening, I took the princess to visit her mother-in-law, Princess Um Mansour, a former wife of King Saud and mother of the old King's favourite son, Mansour. Princess Um Mansour was on vacation in England and had a house about thirty miles outside London in Farnham Common. These trips became a regular feature, as Princess Um Mansour stayed longer and longer in England. While driving back into London late one evening the princess spoke with me. She said how she thought this entire princess and prince thing was "shit." Going on to say no one is any better than anyone else; everyone is equal. She made her views on that clear. Ten days later, I made the mistake of calling Prince Walid by his first name. Princess Rima did not speak with me for three weeks because of it, and only then after I had apologised. What a load of bollocks, I thought.

The job affected me both physically and mentally, but I persevered. I was too loyal for my own good. I would never put up with that nonsense today.

One afternoon in late March, Prince Walid sent me out to get a music tape from the glove box of his car. As I looked for it, I found an open envelope containing a large sum of money. I took the envelope in as well as the tape and gave that to Prince Walid for safekeeping. He hardly noticed it. Later, I told Ziad what happened.

"It could have been a test; the royal family often test their staff in this way."

"That's good of them—maybe I should test them sometime?" I said.

"There was four thousand pounds in that envelope, did you know that?" Ziad asked.

"No, I didn't."

Sent out to the car again some days later I came across a loaded .38 snub nose revolver and some 'ganja'. I left both the gun and the drugs where they were. Some years later, Prince Walid and one of his brothers, Prince Mashour, were prosecuted for drug offences. This came as no surprise to me. Prince Mashour served a prison sentence after negotiations were carried out through the UK Foreign Office and the Government of Saudi Arabia over his diplomatic status. The King, at the time, subsequently waived any diplomatic status the princes may have held to make an example of them to the other young members of the royal family. On his release, Prince Mashour went immediately back to Saudi Arabia where they confiscated his passport.

* * *

On 9th April 1980, the shit hit the fan big-time. Britain screened a programme called 'Death of a Princess'.

This programme was about the public execution of a Saudi princess and her lover. The Saudi government tried to stop it from being aired and banned its importation into Saudi Arabia. However, it was being viewed sneakily in Saudi Arabia within 24 hours of its transmission in Britain. The dramatization told the true story of an execution that had taken place in July 1977. Princess Mishaal Bint Fahd Bin Mohammed and her lover Khalid Mahallal were the subjects of that slaying. The dramatization caused an international uproar around the world. The Saudi government tried everything they could to pressure the British government to either censor or block any screening of the programme in the UK. They even threatened to tear up contracts worth millions of pounds if the screening went ahead.

An estimated ten million people tuned in to watch it. Princess Rima videotaped the programme and then had copies made for her friends. She whooped aloud as the programme aired and ran between rooms in excitement. The status of women in Saudi Arabia was shown in its entirety. It showed the women veiled and segregated. It told the world how their women were unable to drive or vote in Saudi Arabia. They even told how the women were unable to marry without approval from a male family member.

On April 11th, the Saudi Embassy in London called 'Death of a Princess' "an unprincipled attack on the religion of Islam and its 600 million people, and on the way of life in Saudi Arabia, which is the heart of the world of Islam."

All Saudi's stopped visiting Britain and the guys who worked seasonally found themselves without work. Luckily, my permanent meagre salary kept the wolf from the door. On the 23rd April, the

37

government of Saudi Arabia sought the withdrawal of the British Ambassador to Jeddah, James Craig. During the weeks following the screening in Britain, new limits were placed on visas issued to British company executives in Saudi Arabia. The Saudis brought more pressure to bear as they ordered a large United States construction company not to subcontract to the British.

Additionally, supersonic flights over Saudi Arabia were banned, which wiped out the profits from Concorde's London to Singapore route.

Several Members of Parliament and other British officials verbally attacked the television station that had aired the programme. They also called on the government to "apologise to the Saudi government and Royal Family for the film." At the end of May, Lord Carrington, then Foreign Secretary, remarked that the programme was "deeply offensive" and said that he "wished it had never been shown." Asked whether his statement should be regarded as an apology, Lord Carrington said it was "a statement of what Her Majesty's Government thinks."

In July, the British Ambassador was once again in his position in Jeddah. Within a few months, normal privileges were back in place for British businesses working there.

For now, it was back to business as usual. Most days worked rolled into the early hours of the following morning and this went on for six days of the week. Often they called me in on Sundays, too. My nature wouldn't allow me to refuse their demands. However, slowly my confidence and self-respect became eroded; little tasks or favours, out of my normal brief, mounted up. Over time the favours became larger and I felt obliged to help and so on it went. As with many people who worked for the Saudis, it seemed that I warranted no respect from them: if you worked for them you were just another object they felt they owned. No one had a job description because as soon as you started work for them you were asked to do all sorts. You became, in essence, a slave—although a paid one.

Sue wanted me to give up the job. We spent so little time together and the boys missed me. She could also see the toll the long hours were taking on me. She noticed how rarely I smiled and was becoming worried about my confidence.

I struggled by. Then I had an object placed in my care which put their wealth into perspective. I believe it was the beginning of the end for me with Princess Rima and Prince Walid, as I couldn't take the way they claimed that they couldn't afford to give me a pay rise, yet flaunted their immense wealth in front of me with no shame.

* * *

One morning, Princess Rima asked me to prepare the car. When she got into it, she told me to drive to the National Westminster Bank on the corner of St. James' Square and Charles II Street.

I parked the car on double yellow lines, a no parking zone, and went in with the princess. She then went through to the safety-deposit boxes on her own.

When she came out, she passed me a small suede pouch and said, "Keep it with you." I put it in my pocket. We set off to go shopping from there. I've never seen anyone shop as these people do. At times, you would go into the clothes shop when it opened in the morning and stay there all day. Even then, the storekeeper would stay open longer for their special client. Sometimes this would go on six days a week for three or four months at a time. I'm sure it caused me brain damage of some kind! To this day, I cannot stand any form of shopping and have to dart in and out of the shops as quickly as possible.

After our day-long shop, the princess told me to drive to Cartier, the jewellers in Old Bond Street. I parked the car on double yellow lines as usual as she would always kick up a fuss if the car were not parked directly outside the shop. They thought they could do whatever they liked. Most of the time, it seemed as though they could. I escorted the princess into Cartier's and once inside, an assistant who expected her approached. Tipping his head and extending his hand to shake hers he spoke.

"Your Royal Highness, it is so good to see you once again. Please step through to the conference room." I followed her closely. The 'assistant' spoke with a posh upper-class accent and was dressed in a sharp, dark pinstriped suit. He was more than an 'assistant', I deduced.

"Your Highness, please take a seat," said the man. I noticed the seat he gestured her towards wasn't at the head of the table. That seat he reserved for himself and I wondered if this was some power play on his part. I walked down towards the other end of the table and sat down a distance away from the princess, offering her a token amount of privacy. The jeweller asked to look at the stone.

"Of course, at this stage I am only looking for a value on it and would like to know if it could be sold easily." she replied.

Turning to me the princess said, "Can I have the pouch I gave you earlier, please?"

I passed it to the princess, who in turn passed it to the jeweller. He took the object out of the pouch and started to examine it. He looked at the papers Princess Rima had given him, and then back to the object he held in his hand. He did this a few times, no doubt making sure the two married up.

"Your Highness, I am sure we could find a buyer for it," said the jeweller as he valued it for her.

I was in danger of falling asleep on the chair I sat on, but not for long.

"I think we will have no problem in realising $2,500,000," the jeweller said. I nearly fell off the bloody chair—I couldn't believe it. I had been wandering around with a $2,500,000 'stone' in my pocket! In 1980, especially, that was a *hell* of a lot of money.

That caught my attention. The princess passed the object and the pouch back to me. I noted the ring was gold and the 'stone' cut into a heart shape. The 'stone' was a pink diamond! It was about one inch by one inch and about half an inch or more thick and was indescribably beautiful. The princess had received the ring as a gift from her father. I placed the ring back into its pouch and put it into my pocket. We left Cartier's and went directly to the bank. When the ring was secured again in the safety-deposit box, I could relax. I couldn't wait to unload it as the responsibility of it being in my possession weighed heavily.

* * *

Around the end of July, Princess Rima got round to having her nose reshaped. I had often caught her looking at her profile in the large mirror, which hung over the dining table at the bottom of the stairs. The princess had the typical Arab hooked nose and wanted a more streamlined European look. After the initial examinations, she was soon deposited in a suite at the London Clinic for her surgery. Four days later, I picked the princess up and brought her back to the house in Lowndes Close. Her face sported the usual plaster cast one would expect to see after such surgery. The swelling and bruising was obvious too as Princess Rima's eyes were nearly closed.

Each day I went to the house although the princess never went anywhere. I used to sit for hours doing nothing—it drove me up the wall sitting round the small dining table at the foot of the stairs. There was no television or radio to amuse myself with. Finally, the day came when the princess was to have the cast removed. We were all ordered by Ziad to express our surprise at how well she looked as we assembled to await the princess. They had done a great job and her nose looked good. Perhaps it was the money it cost and the attention she had received that made the difference. Whatever it was, her newly shaped nose complemented her features. With her newfound confidence, Princess Rima now set about trying to kill me!

By the first week of September, the bruising and swelling had all but disappeared. Princess Rima decided it was now time to show off her new nose to her mother-in-law, the Princess Um Mansour. Driving down to Farnham Common proved uneventful and no doubt everyone at the princess's house had made the right noises when they had seen Princess Rima's new nose.

Told of Princess Rima's impending departure, I brought the Rolls Royce around to the side door from which she would leave the house. I went to open the front passenger door for her but she said, "I'll drive."

"Do you have a licence and insurance?" I asked her.

"Yes, I have a Kuwaiti licence and I am on the car policy."

That's a first, I thought. As we drove off, I found myself in more danger from Princess Rima than from any other source. As we approached a right-handed bend on the Chiswick flyover, the princess mounted the central reservation. I almost had a heart attack—both the offside front and rear wheels mounted the kerb. The car must have tipped at just such an angle that it just missed the central reservation crash barrier. I had just mentioned how deceiving this bend was; perhaps she wanted to find out for herself if I were telling the truth!

Later I found Princess Rima did indeed have a Kuwaiti driving licence. The fact was she hadn't been to Kuwait to take a driving test, a member of her staff had gone to get it for her! This raised my confidence no end. On our next visit to Farnham Common the following week, I noticed Bassam, Princess Um Mansour's driver, wasn't around, so I asked his whereabouts. I was told that neither he nor the princess's Rolls Royce was about. This was because a few nights earlier Bassam had been out in the car without the princess's permission. After a few drinks, he had introduced the Rolls Royce to a bright yellow rubbish skip. The skip was full of bricks and rubble. The side of the car crumbled, leaving debris all over the street. One of the number plates, which read, 777 HRH also lay on the road. In his drunken state, Bassam had jumped out of the car and run off into the night. Within a week or so he was back working for the princess. For some reason, he—like me and the guys who trained me—felt compelled to get the job done. There was something in our nature which made us feel we must protect and stay loyal to our charge, however our charge behaved.

I continued working all the hours that God sent. After the time I spent travelling and sleeping, I only had a couple of hours each day to spend with Sue and the boys. I couldn't afford to take my family on holiday—not that it mattered, as I wasn't given any holiday time anyway. I couldn't even afford my own car. My life centred on the princess or so it seemed. Sue and the boys were just fed the crumbs of time that were left over. It wasn't long before Christmas 1980 loomed up. I would be lucky to get Christmas day off, I thought.

Even though money was tight, Sue and I went shopping for Christmas presents for the household. On Christmas Eve, I arrived at the princess' mews house with presents for everyone. I could tell from their expressions that no one was pleased with their gifts. I was sure they thought I was being mean and that scrooge had visited

42

them. What the staff didn't know was how little I earned and that I couldn't afford to spend much on them.

The staff probably also didn't know how much the petty bickering and backstabbing that had become the norm between Ziad and Michael bothered me—especially as I was often caught up in the middle of it. They definitely suffered from a clash of personalities. There appeared to be an underlying fight going on as to who would be the 'top dog'. I thought that this was just the case in this particular household but was to find out later that all the Saudi households suffered from the same type of problem. It was quite surreal how people allowed themselves to be degraded and threw their self-respect out of the window in order to fawn over the prince or princess that employed them. I am sorry to say that I also found myself caught in this trap and the real danger that I never realised at the time was that the prince and princess were steadily eroding both my confidence and whatever was left, if any, of my self-respect. I was on a long slippery slope into subservience.

Chapter 4

1981

One night in January, Princess Rima ordered me to take Princess Dalal Bint Saud and her female companion home. It was 11pm, the sky was clear and bright, and the stars shone brightly. Princess Dalal was staying at her mother, Princess Um Mansour's home in Farnham Common, while on vacation. The journey would take roughly an hour, which pissed me off, as I wanted to get home myself. As an aside, I noticed that Princess Dalal and her friend were both attractive.

"Good evening, Your Highness," I said. "What a wonderful night for a drive under the star-filled sky," I said sarcastically—although the sarcasm was lost on her.

"Good evening," Princess Dalal answered as she wafted by and climbed into the car. I hadn't even managed to get out of Lowndes Close before the princess and her friend had lit up some cannabis 'spliffs'. Within minutes, the car filled with smoke; it swirled all around and it soon seemed as though I were driving through a dense, foggy night. Drug and alcohol addiction is rife throughout the Saudi royal family. I don't smoke, but I was obviously inhaling the stuff. Princess Dalal and her friend were giggling and carrying on. After finishing their spliffs, they lit another and by this time, even I was feeling happy! Initially not wanting to take them, I suddenly felt fine! Not having learned any Arabic by that time, I wasn't privileged enough to understand their merriment.

Princess Dalal's husband was Prince Al-Walid Bin Talal, who would be rated the fourth richest person in the world by *Forbes* magazine in 2004. However, his marriage to Princess Dalal was now nearing collapse. During her visit, Princess Dalal would meet with her husband to try to work out their differences.

I was driving the Rolls Royce Silver Wraith belonging to Princess Rima, but whether I was driving it well was another question. The only experience of illegal drugs I ever had was from inhaling them when the Arabs used them.

I didn't know what, if any, long-term effect they were having on me. The fact the princess and her companion didn't care about that showed their irresponsibility.

Throughout the journey, my passengers lit up one joint after another. The car was filled with the cannabis smoke and God knows what would have happened if we had been pulled over by the police. I had visions of opening the car door and the smoke swirling round the police officers rendering them as high as we no doubt were!

I managed to negotiate the dark winding roads that led up to the house without a problem—or so I believe. After dropping them off, I made my way home.

The next day saw me back in Belgravia with Princess Rima. Within the week we visited Princess Um Mansour at Farnham Common yet again. I spent hour after hour at this place. Bassam was back on the scene and spending time with him would kill the boredom. Sometimes after our usual shooting match, we would clean the cars for something to do and chat away as we did so. Princess Um Mansour's Rolls Royce was finished in a metallic green with a gold-plated 'Flying Lady' mascot and side trims; it looked spectacular. It held the registration number 777 HRH. As I was admiring the repairs made to the Rolls after its fight with the rubbish skip, I slammed the driver's door shut. What I hadn't realised was that Bassam had his fingers wrapped round the wing beside the door. When I looked closer, I saw his fingers had disappeared between the door and the wing and I feared the worst.

Opening the door, I was amazed to find Bassam's hand intact. There was no blood and no fainting from either of us, but I was in danger of Bassam throttling me as I danced around pissing myself with laughter. Bassam wasn't amused!

A couple of days later, Princess Rima and I left her house in Belgravia to visit Princess Dalal who was now ensconced in the Dorchester Hotel with her husband Prince Al-Walid Bin Talal, who also happened to be Princess Rima's brother. This visit proved more than interesting. When we entered the lobby area, Princess Dalal was already waiting. Immediately both princesses started talking. I caught the attention of Princess Rima and motioned to her that I would be sitting in a chair across the lobby. Princess Dalal beamed a smile my way. I wasn't aware that they were waiting for Prince Al-Walid to return to the hotel.

As the princesses chatted, two men walked in paying a little too much attention to my charges for my liking. I checked them out and my gut instinct told me that something was about to happen. I rose from the chair and walked across the lobby. Princess Rima looked towards me with a startled expression, just as Prince Al-Walid came through the doors and flew into a rage. 'Game on,' I thought.

The prince lunged at one of the men. He threw a cut glass ashtray at the other, and pieces of glass flew over the floor as the ashtray shattered. A brass litter bin followed. Another ashtray and bin flew across the lobby as I stepped in the middle, grabbed both of the men by their collars and pushed them out through the revolving doors. As they were exiting, I felt a really hard nudge in my back—Prince Al-Walid had grabbed hold of the doors and spun them around, catching me from behind. The prince ran out of the hotel and tried to get at the two men once again. I forcefully threw the men, Americans, towards a taxi—but even before they reached it, another cut glass ashtray flew through the air, shattering as it hit the ground nearby. The chips of glass shimmered and sparkled like diamonds as the beams of light reflected off them in the front car park, and Prince Al-Walid's white stretched Lincoln limousine was lucky not to have been showered with shards of glass. The car was so long it stretched across most of the hotel forecourt. A polished brass wastepaper bin followed the ashtray. The doorman must have thought war had broken out as everything exploded in a fraction of a second. I pushed the men into the taxi and off they went.

I walked in to the hotel with the prince. He was fuming. Inside the lobby, the concierge, doorman, and porters were in shock at what had taken place. But the prince was in no mood to notice them or their concerns.

I escorted the prince and princesses up to his suite and they engaged in animated conversation. After a while, the princesses emerged from the suite ready to go out to dinner. In the lift they giggled about the incident; they told me the two men had thought they were prostitutes 'looking for business'. At the moment the prince entered the hotel, I had seen exactly what he was like. Although slight in build, his temper was ferocious. 'It' was all about him; his ego was bruised and he had lost face. He thought he could behave in any way he liked and I am shamed to say it appeared that he could: no one stopped him.

As the years passed, Prince Al-Walid became increasingly powerful in the business and financial sectors. He bought shares in several companies throughout the world and at one time bought 4.85 percent of America's second largest bank, Citicorp, costing a cool $585 million. Even so, he refused to honour charges run up by his family and friends in Saudi Arabia on cards issued to them by Citicorp, which totalled $30 million. Despite this behaviour, he went on to become one of the richest men in the world.

Two days after the debacle in the Dorchester Hotel, Prince Al-Walid and his wife departed. They divorced shortly afterwards.

* * *

A week later, Ziad called me at Princess Rima's house and told me that we had to go to Heathrow airport. Princess Rima's mother, Princess Mona el-Solh was arriving and Princess Rima had expressed a wish to go and meet her. Only Princess Rima, Ziad and I would go to the airport. I conjured up a vision of what Princess Mona might look like.

I had not met her before but I knew that she was the ex-wife of my first charge, Prince Talal Bin Abdul Aziz Al Saud. I did not know how old she was and thought that she might be middle-aged and dumpy. Maybe she would be swathed from head to foot in black robes, and perhaps she would be wearing the traditional Muslim yashmak (a long narrow face screen) with little slits for her eyes. My mind wandered, as this was normal dress for most of the older princesses. On the way, Ziad said don't go to the VIP suite, as Princess Mona doesn't bother using it.

Waiting for Princess Mona to clear customs, we made ourselves comfortable. I kept looking for the short, dumpy black blob I was expecting. Suddenly, Ziad positively leapt from his chair as he made his way over to greet Princess Mona. The princess was about 40 years old, and surprisingly slim, attractive, and wearing jeans. In fact, she was Lebanese, and a stunner. As I greeted her, she reached out and gave me a gift, a heavy 18-carat gold ring with a strip of pink coral running through it. Some time later, I gave the ring to my oldest son. I've never been materialistic and didn't consider selling any gifts to make up for the poor wages that I received. Instead, I got a buzz out of giving them to members of the family who held the romantic view that I was some highflying bodyguard.

Princess Mona's father had been the first prime minister of the Lebanon. His Excellency Riad el-Solh had been assassinated in Amman, Jordan on the 16th July 1951. Princess Mona had married Prince Talal, one of the King's brothers, on the 22nd October 1954 in Beirut, Lebanon.

Throughout her stay, Ziad fell over himself trying to ingratiate himself with Princess Mona as she originated from one of the most respected Lebanese families, whereas he did not. He would run errands for her and make all her arrangements—no job was too big or too small.

As a result, I never had much to do with Princess Mona on her visit: Ziad spun his silky web around her. He really couldn't do enough for Princess Mona—he positively revelled in being around her. This involved keeping me away from her so he could be the centre of attention, which was fine by me, as I knew if I were around it would only involve more work for me. As it was, I took Princess Rima to see Princess Mona every day at the Dorchester Hotel in Park Lane Mayfair, where I always waited outside the suite.

One day, we arrived at the Dorchester Hotel at nine o'clock in the morning. As Princess Rima and Ziad got out of the Rolls Royce, the princess told me to stay with the car.

They didn't emerge until eleven o'clock at night! I was furious: Princess Rima's house was only five minutes away, so I could easily have gone back there, waited, relaxed, and returned when she was ready to leave. So it was with great relief that after a few days Princess Mona moved on and I could say goodbye to the Dorchester Hotel once more.

Time passed slowly until the end of October that year, and I was getting to the point where I couldn't put up with all the backstabbing and bickering of the household staff. Day-to-day I was being worn down by Princess Rima, too, as she became increasingly snappy. The atmosphere in the house had become atrocious. Many days I felt as though I were in a war zone. So it was a nice surprise when in early November, Princess Rima bounded down the stairs with a beaming smile on her face. She was ready for another of her dreaded shopping trips. This time we went to Brown's in South Moulton Street. She appeared happier than usual, perhaps because she was about to engage in some retail therapy. As she walked towards the shop, I gave her some space. As we neared Brown's, I noticed an Arab-looking man running up towards her, fast. I had never seen this man before.

Was he going to run past? What was he up to? As he got closer to the princess, I couldn't risk doing nothing so I launched myself at him with the same intent as a laser guided-cruise missile bearing down on its target. As he neared the princess, the man stretched his arms out. It looked as though he was going to put his hands over her eyes. I grabbed him and spun him round just as the princess let out a shout, "Stop! It's my brother-in-law, Prince Isa'dene!" I had just managed to repel his 'attack' and quickly apologised for my actions. Prince Isa'dene in turn apologised to me.

I visited Prince Isa'dene in his apartment in Hanover Gate Mansions a couple of times with Michael. The prince had twice faced armed robbers at gunpoint, once having been woken with the barrel of a shotgun pushed into his face. He had a lot of cash and jewellery stolen. Not long after, he contracted AIDS.

He died of the illness. On his death, the Embassy wheels were put into motion, which was normal when a member of the royal family died. The prince's body was removed and flown out almost immediately so he could be home and buried within twenty-four hours as their religion dictates. No post mortems ever take place on the royals and if there were any controversy surrounding the death then a heart attack would be assigned as the cause. If you traced the number of the royal family that had passed on because of heart attacks, they would probably find that Saudi Arabia has the highest incidence of cardiac failure in the world!

In my first eighteen months or so of being a bodyguard there had been some lighter and happier moments, but now there were none; I didn't think life could get much worse at the house, but it did: at one point, I was even told to stop drinking the Coca-Cola. Ziad told me the princess couldn't afford it. What a load of bollocks! Just the 'stone' she owned was worth $2,500,000 and she couldn't afford to supply the staff with Coca-Cola; pull the other one! Generally, too, life there was becoming harder and harder with ever more controls coming into effect and being enforced. For instance, while previously I had taken the cars home after a late finish, now if I finished by eleven at night I had to find my own way home by public transport. As I lived thirty miles outside London, this proved to be a real nuisance—especially as it became commonplace for the princess to send me home at five to eleven most evenings so she saved on the petrol.

*   *   *

On one sunny morning in late November, I arrived at Lowndes Close to have the door answered by a man I had not met before. Inside, sitting at the dining table, was this man's brother. Michael told me that from now on Mohammed, who had opened the door, would go everywhere with the princess and me, while his brother would go everywhere with Prince Walid. Ziad told me that both Mohammed and his brother had been brought up with Prince Walid. They were essentially his companions, charged with making sure he was never lonely as a child. Both of them had been his human toys, his playthings.

Prince Walid rented a three-story maisonette above some shops in the Fulham Road as a base for Mohammed and his brother, and I often visited it with either Ziad or Michael. The place became a drugs haven and a hideaway where Prince Walid took his girlfriends for sex. He was a wild playboy and very often when I arrived I also found the house full of cannabis and cocaine—being used liberally.

Every day, Princess Rima cried. I thought she was suffering from depression or perhaps some hormonal imbalance as life had become so unbearable at the household. That night when I got home, I told Sue that I couldn't take the stress any longer and that I wanted to put in my notice. She saw the vast strain I'd been under and agreed that it was best not just for me but also for the sake of our family that I leave. The next morning I gave them my notice to quit. Prince Walid accepted it; Princess Rima said nothing. I had no idea what had been going on behind the scenes, but was soon to find out.

After working for the family for two years, I felt cheated and deceived by them. Looking back, it was a mistake; I should never have taken the job. I had suffered low wages long working hours and poor working conditions. Mind you it wasn't all one way traffic as I then found out they were to divorce. Prince Walid may well have put the blame on her for the divorce—perhaps even saying that she had not produced any children, but that would be pure assumption on my part. Whatever the reasons given, the prince was going to stay in London and doubtless carry on with his promiscuous, drug-fuelled lifestyle.

By the end of 1981, the princess had returned to Saudi Arabia. That would mean a great loss of freedom, and I couldn't help feeling sorry for her. She had lived such a westernised lifestyle and now she would be subjected once more to the harsh disciplines that women face in Saudi Arabia. I felt no woman should be subjected to the inquisition-like repression under which they live—an example of which is that some face segregation even inside their own homes, as some rooms have separate entrances for men and women.

Ziad lost his job and went on to open a travel agency. Michael stayed with the prince, no doubt continuing to be as manipulative as he had always been.

During my time with them, my reputation had spread. Prince Walid gave me a glowing reference, which I put to good use as I'd managed to set up other contacts during my time with his family. Therefore, I was on my way once again. The problem was, my first port of call wasn't one that I had expected.

Chapter 5

Start of 1982

This wasn't the start to the New Year I'd envisaged, and a worrying time followed as I signed on at the unemployment office. I knew I'd have a small income now, but at least my National Insurance stamp would be paid. I was determined not to allow this situation to continue for long, so I set off to visit the contacts I had made while working for Prince Walid's family. However, many of the Saudis only visited the UK during the summer months. Therefore, unless I was lucky, my working life would dissolve into temporary jobs for them.

The blessing from the free time I had while waiting to find a new job, though, was that I could spend it with my family. And, while playing the waiting game, I kept the Karate going.

As luck would have it within a few weeks of signing on a new job came in. My next port of call was a place I attended regularly—the Intercontinental Hotel on Park Lane, Mayfair. When I arrived, I reported to the duty manager and the hotel security. Introducing myself was important, as they'd then be aware of who I was and what I was doing there: it could save a lot of hassle at times. The hotels were never too happy having outside security staff on their property. Nonetheless, even if they didn't like it, they appreciated being notified.

Many times, the royal family took up entire floors with their entourages and the resulting revenue was vast. The hotels would have been foolish to turn away such a profitable income for what was really rather a minor inconvenience to them. We were careful not to upset any guests and we behaved ourselves. We often had our own rooms and used the hotel facilities as well—thereby adding to their profits still further.

The office told me Princess Munira Al Faisal was due in and would be staying for some time. Martini, from the embassy, was to take care of the arrangements. He assigned one of his drivers, Sammy, to drive the princess and be Martini's eyes and ears throughout the visit. Martini escorted Princess Munira to her suite on her arrival, and introduced me and the team to her. Two of her escorts were Egyptian sisters who lived in England. They took care of the princess's day-to-day arrangements. Two other young women attended the princess; both of them were beautiful and had tremendous figures. They were in their early twenties and dressed in fine silk dresses. Princess Munira wasn't such a pretty picture.

A thin Arab guy named Mohammed was the tea maker, and over the coming weeks, his tea making caused quite a few problems. Another matter that came to dismay the hotel management was the daily incense burning ritual. Both the tea making and burning of incense constantly set off the fire alarms, which in turn caused the evacuation of the other guests and the attendance of the local fire brigade.

The women loved to flirt, and we would indulge them, of course. The women always took care of us, which was cool. They made sure we were fed and watered and had a constant supply of mint tea. When Princess Munira went out, we escorted her. When she was in her suite, we sat in the corridor outside her door, and we always accompanied any hotel staff entering the suite. Behind the suite door was a cupboard which the women had a habit of leaving open. Inside was an open briefcase, full to the brim with bundles of fifty-pound notes. We advised them several times to put the case into the hotel safe-deposit box, but they ignored us. In fact, they never even closed the lid. Some hotel staff noticed the case and we wondered how many other people now knew of its existence.

Soon after the princess's arrival, we found ourselves in an uncomfortable position. Princess Munira would call us into her suite now and again and as we walked in she would be sitting there with her breasts on show. She did not care whether we saw her or not.

Peter, my colleague, went out of his way to entertain the women. I got on with Peter and felt comfortable with him, although years later he let me down badly. In contrast, Sammy was sly and untrustworthy. We felt we had to watch our backs with him. Sammy was dangerous to us.

When all was quiet, Peter and I sat on the floor in the corridor outside the suite and threw dice. This was a way of killing time and relaxed some of the other guests. Although we got friendly with some of them, we still kept our guard up. We expected interest, but skilfully fended off any prying questions. We also paid careful attention to what people said. If more than simple curiosity was shown, we would find out who they were, where they came from, where they were going, how long they were staying, which room or rooms they occupied and suchlike. When we switched on, we must have produced more power than a two hundred and fifty thousand volt electricity pylon.

Princess Munira loved to take the women shopping and she loved buying them colourful, expensive and figure hugging clothes. She got a buzz from watching the men eye up her women.

The younger women laughed and giggled at us, obviously finding the attention hilarious. One day Princess Munira emerged from her suite, walked down the corridor, and entered one of the younger women's rooms. I walked along behind her and then waited outside the room. I noticed a hotel cleaner entering the princess' suite and Peter followed her. Peter had been teasing this hotel cleaner for a couple of weeks. She was attractive, and I guessed about twenty-five years old.

Princess Munira opened the door and asked me to fetch her some cream from her suite. I wasn't happy about this, but as her suite was only a couple of doors away, I made a dash for it. I entered the suite and got a surprise: Peter and the hotel cleaner were in a state of undress. The cupboard was open and so was the briefcase. What would have happened if Princess Munira had been the one to walk in? Maybe she would have dropped dead with shock, maybe not. I couldn't believe Peter had been so stupid. I grabbed the cream and walked out. I returned to the other room, still stunned by what I had seen.

I knocked on the door and was called in. I put the cream down on a side table turned on my heels and walked out, listening to the princess and her aide laughing behind me. I was sure they had set me up in some way. Between Peter and them, I did not know if I was coming or going. Then, when the princess returned to her suite,

I pulled Peter to one side and asked what he thought he was doing. He said it was exciting and just harmless fun. I said it would not have been fun if he'd been caught. But he said he got off on the risk: they had been flirting and it progressed to a dare. So, I realised, it was just a childish game.

That evening we were throwing the dice yet again, when one of the guests we spoke with each night returned to his room. We'd heard this guest was a Libyan arms dealer. Immediately we were on alert. Whilst appearing sociable enough to him we would make it our business to find out all that we could about him. The Saudis and the Libyans are not the best of friends. The last thing we needed was a Libyan taking out our charge. So for the moment it was in our interests to placate him. Therefore, when he asked to throw the dice with us, Peter was up for it. The game progressed to the Libyan betting Peter his maroon Rolls Royce that he could throw a higher number with two dice. Peter confessed he had nothing of value to bet. The Libyan, not perturbed by this, said he would still bet his Rolls. The Libyan threw first and Peter followed. Peter threw a higher score. The Libyan passed the keys for his Rolls Royce to Peter: he was as good as his word. Peter, however, gave back the keys, saying he couldn't take it and that it had just been a sportsman's bet. As a result, the Libyan kept his car and Peter made a friend. Perhaps it was a smart move on Peter's part not to take the car, as it would not do to make an enemy out of a Libyan arms dealer. I think I would have taken the Rolls Royce!

During the game, I took the opportunity to evaluate the Libyan. He was about 6 feet tall and of medium build. His hair was greying on the sides and his moustache matched his hair. He did not wear glasses and was about 45 years old. His manners were perfect and he came across as a pleasant enough fellow. Being an arms dealer, I was sure the Libyan had another side to him, one which no doubt was much more sinister. But so long as we didn't catch sight of it, I thought we'd be all right.

The following day Princess Munira went shopping and the clothes shops, as usual, suffered a hammering. In one of them, I stood next to the princess as her aide tried on some clothes. I accidentally caught sight of the aide as she did not close the curtain properly. I averted my eyes quickly and if Princess Munira noticed, she didn't show it. I kept my back towards the cubicle and surveyed the surroundings. Occasionally, as we walked along the street, a comment or gesture was directed at us. I wasn't concerned so long as the comments were not abusive, but a few times it was necessary to whisper in someone's ear.

We then went on to Kutchinsky, the jewellers on Brompton Road, Knightsbridge. I had often visited this store and was well known there. The princess and the women examined the jewellery closely, while I checked the surroundings as well as any comings and goings. Princess Munira bought Peter and me a watch each. They were not expensive ones, or so I believed, and along the line, I gave mine away. It was a Rado watch and I didn't much like the look of it anyway.

Back at the Intercontinental, the women set about lighting their incense burners. They fanned the smoke over themselves and then stood over the burner, fanning the smoke between their legs. The smoke detectors set off the fire alarms. The fire doors in the corridors closed automatically. Guests and staff started to evacuate the hotel and the hotel security rushed up to see from where the fire was emanating.

The duty manager arrived and what could we say? Apologies can only go so far. The fire brigade arrived and we made our apologies to them as well. When the fire alarms activated in the hotel it was a big deal, and for some reason everyone looked at us bodyguards as though it was our fault. We had warned the princess and her aides on many occasions about their incense burning, but they took no notice. They were not in the least perturbed by these events and their nonchalance annoyed me. Apart from the obvious, their carelessness disturbed many people. It would not have been so bad if it only happened once—but it happened five times overall. The hotel manager called Martini in to see him. He was told that if they did not stop causing a disturbance, the hotel would evict the princess and her entourage.

In response, the women covered the smoke detectors with towels, which the hotel cleaners in turn reported to management.

Hotel security arrived and told us to remove the towels because they breached fire regulations. We got the incense affair under control and Martini then gave an envelope of cash to the management to help smooth matters over. A few hours later, the fire alarms sounded again. This time, I knew the women were not burning incense and thanked the heavens we were not to blame. The alarms wailed and the fire doors closed. Guests and staff started to evacuate. The hotel security arrived and said, "It's you fucking lot again!"

"Not us," I said, "Not this time; no incense burning today."

He took the smile off my face when it was proved Mohammed brewing the tea had set the detectors off. The management called Martini once again—and if it had not been so serious, it would have been funny. I looked to see if there was anyone filming another 'Carry On' movie, because what a carry on it was!

During Princess Munira's visit, we had more problems from the hotel fire alarms than from anything else. A smile crossed my face as I thought that even though the young women's figures had sent plenty of temperatures soaring, even they had not set off the fire alarms.

Another envelope landed on the manager's desk and a grovelling apology followed it. If Princess Munira were to return to England, would she stay at the Intercontinental Hotel again? More to the point, would they let her? I wondered. I was sure they would remember her—I knew I would. Her apparent love of sounding off the fire alarms would linger in my mind for some time, of that I was sure. The other thing that would stay in my mind was the fact that the princess reminded me of my older brother. He is an ugly sod and so was she, but then again many of the older princesses looked rough, and this one was no exception. Not having to do anything apart from shopping all day must wear them down. Many of the younger princesses, on the contrary, took good care of themselves. Perhaps this was because they travelled more widely and were more aware of their appearance. In addition, they did like to attract attention from the men.

As we prepared to leave, I'm sure I heard a round of applause from the hotel management and security staff, and who could blame them? Martini and Bill arrived from the office. They probably thought money was going to change hands and if so, they wanted some of it. It appeared the Saudi royals robbed their people and that Martini and Bill robbed the Saudi royals in turn, I mused. I was becoming sick of money. I needed an amount to provide for my family but I would not stoop low enough to lie, cheat and steal like others did to get it. But little did I know then that a relatively small amount of money would cause such terrible problems for me and my family later on in my life, as I too would be branded with those terms, which would cut me to my core. For now though, I was just happy that the princess was on her way home, and so was I.

Chapter 6

April 1982

No sooner had I got home to spend a few days with my family than another assignment drew me back to London. April of 1982 had dawned as I rushed into the city to aid the son of the Military Attaché. He thought someone was trying to abduct his Filipino servant. On my arrival, he begged me to search the attic. He said he heard noises coming from up there and that people were trying to get in through the roof.

Cautiously, I made my way up the several flights of stairs towards the attic opening. For all I knew, the unseen 'offender' could have left the attic space and be lurking around on one of the floors above me. I didn't fancy the idea of having some antique clock or other such object rapped around the side of my head. They could even be armed with something much more substantial, I thought. Stealthily, I opened the attic door and moved inside. I warily checked the darkened space, leaving no box, bag or suitcase in a position that would afford any cover to anyone hiding behind it. Finding nothing untoward, I made my way down to the principal waiting below.

As soon as I got near to him he said, "Do you know who I am? Do you know who my father is? Do you know how important we are?"

"Of course I do. I've been fully briefed about your important status," I lied. In reality, I didn't care how important he said they were. I had a job to do and wanted to get on with it.

As he waffled on, I made my way over to a basement stairwell. I checked it out—no problems there. I looked in the kitchen and in one of the cupboards found what I was looking for. I tried out the torch to see if it was working; it was, so I decided to make my way up to the landing just beneath the attic again. I could feel it in my bones. Something wasn't right about this place. What I had decided to do was search the house thoroughly from top to bottom without interruption.

Feeling a little anxious, I made my way into the attic. With the torchlight beaming brightly, I searched the attic yet again. I found nothing there. Making my way down to the landing beneath me, my gut instinct roared at me to keep looking. Carefully, I made my way through the upper floor. I could hear the voices of the principal and his companion downstairs. Their speech was highly animated. I had previously noted their pupils were dilated and their eyes bloodshot: combined with their animated speech, it was as though they were on speed or some other drug.

As I combed the building, my mind ached. I knew something glaringly obvious was eluding me but I couldn't figure out what it was. So intense was my train of thought, the obvious had passed me by.

Room by room, floor by floor, I scoured the building. Reaching the lower floor, I spoke with the principal and his companion again.

"Did you find him? What have you done with him? Have you killed him? What will you do with his body?" the principal asked me.

"I haven't found anything yet," I replied, wondering now just how nuts this guy was. Did he think I was James Bond or something like that with a licence to kill, I wondered. He obviously wasn't the full ticket. Perhaps he was a result of the inbreeding that dogged the Saudi royals, I casually thought, before remembering that he wasn't of royal blood.

"Please let me continue my search," I said diplomatically. When what I wanted to say was, "Piss off and leave me alone."

I made my way toward the kitchen again. Meticulously, I searched through the large cupboards and between the shelves of the stainless steel industrial units. Then I came across a large solid door at the far end of the room.

I could hear a muffled sound emanating from the other side but when I tried to open the door, I found it was locked. Quickly, I made my way back to the principal and asked him if he knew where the key to this storeroom was. He passed it to me and I spun round to make my way back to the kitchen, but before I had taken three steps, he called to me.

"Shall I come with you?"

"No, stay out of the way," I said, just as the torch died on me. One moment it was fine the next, it was fucked. Bloody marvellous, I thought. On reaching the door, my heart raced. The thumping was so loud I was sure it could be heard on the other side. I slowly and carefully placed the key inside the lock, trying not to make any noise. I steeled myself against the onslaught that I knew would greet me if someone was lurking in there.

The key turned and the tumbler of the lock clicked. I knew the noise of the tumbler opening signalled my arrival to whoever was inside. The sweat bubbled up on my forehead and soaked my hands too. Pulling the door open I braced myself.

Nothing, not a thing, greeted me.

Slowly, I cast my eyes around the storeroom. The light thrown in from the kitchen only lit up a small area of the room, hindering my view. My eyes pierced through the darkness, ever searching, as my hand slid along the inside wall searching for the elusive light switch. As my fingers found it, I held my breath as I turned on the lights.

Inside was the Filipino servant. She was lying naked, crying and scared on the floor. I had to get a grip and control myself.

Now rage took the place of the adrenaline which had surged through my veins: pure and simple rage. I held my breath in an effort to keep a lid on the feelings welling up inside me. I looked at the Military Attaché's son and wondered if he could see the disgust I felt etched on the features of my face.

"Your Excellency," I said, "May I be allowed to speak with this young woman on my own?"

"If you think you can find out who the person is that's trying to steal her away from me, then of course you can, you must."

"Thank you, Your Excellency," I said through gritted teeth. I wanted to rip his head off and spit down his throat but knew my career would end there and then if I did so. I wondered what I had got myself into. How come so many of these people were so fucked up in their heads?

Approaching the naked young woman, I took a sheet off a shelf in the store cupboard and placed it over her. I saw the pain this poor creature was experiencing. I didn't know what to say to her. After covering her, I asked her if we could talk.

"I need to understand what is going on here," I said. "Can you tell me your name?"

"My name is Perla, and I come from Dagupan City in the Philippines," she said, sobbing. "My master thinks I have a boyfriend here who is trying to take me away from him."

"Who is your master? Do you have a boyfriend here?" I asked her.

"No, I have no boyfriend and my master is the master of the house. He has sex with me when he wants and fears someone will take me away from him. He is sick and needs help," she said surprising me with her benevolence.

"He has sex with you against your wishes? Is that what you are telling me?"

"Yes, he likes to film us and his friend takes photographs of me when he does it to me. I am his sex slave. He does what he wants to me then I have to do whatever he wants me to do to him."

What a bastard, I thought. I wanted to hurt him badly. Instead, I took Perla out of the storeroom and sat her down on a sofa in the lounge.

"What are you doing?" the principal asked me.

"I'm making Perla comfortable. She has assured me that no one is trying to take her away; therefore, you have no need to worry. I want you to allow her to use one of the bedrooms to make herself comfortable. Is that all right with you?" If it wasn't, then tough, I would have to take matters into my own hands.

"All right, Perla can go to one of the bedrooms," he replied.

The bastard, I wanted to do him some serious harm. However, I knew that I couldn't do anything about the situation at all. If I did, then the Foreign Office would become involved and all hell would break loose. Nothing would happen to him because he would claim Diplomatic Immunity, and once he got Perla back to Saudi Arabia he would more than likely have her head lopped off.

This was the first sex slave I met. The principal was insecure and possessive. He was paranoid that someone else was having sex with Perla too. She was insistent that wasn't the case, but he did not believe her and so kept her locked up in the storeroom where he could keep her under his control. Although I had secured a little respite for Perla, I was sure that when I was out of the way he would imprison her again.

This guy was off his rocker. I must have checked the attic at least thirty times during the night as he said he kept hearing noises up there. The frustration built up in me hour by hour throughout the night. This guy wasn't just fucking Perla; he was fucking with my head, too. I was appalled at what I had seen and would report my findings to the office as soon as I could. I knew nothing would be done. It sickened me to see the abuse of the Diplomatic Immunity system.

In the morning, I reported directly to the office.

I was excessively vocal about my findings at the house the evening before, but was told, "Look, you know the score. If you don't like it or can't handle it, then do us all a favour and fuck off."

Therefore, that's what I did. I fucked off, spitting out as I left: "The Attaché's son is off his head, schizophrenic or something of the sort and needs treatment!"

After leaving the office, I got into my car. I felt my hands gripping the steering wheel as I cursed inwardly. I wished my hands were gripping the throat of that depraved, lascivious sick bastard.

During the drive home, the frustration welled up inside me, causing my blood to boil. These people, it seemed, were a law unto themselves. My hands, like any of the other guys on the jobs, were tied. I should have walked away from the business—but I didn't. That decision would cost me dearly in the future.

But for the moment, I would stay away from the Saudis. Or so I thought.

* * *

A few days later, I received a phone call from John, a colleague who'd come to England from Hungary some years previously claiming political asylum. He asked if I could cover one of his clients, a Sheikh from Qatar. John was a tough man and built like a brick house. He was a shrewd businessman.

The Sheikh was a member of the ruling family of Qatar. I had not had any contact with them before. I thought they couldn't be worse than the Saudis.

John rarely asked anyone to cover his clients; he was by nature a cautious person. We met and then went to meet Sheikh Abdullah Al Thani at the Royal Lancaster hotel in Lancaster Gate, London.

After introducing him and a couple of his aides, John left me to it. The Sheikh wore the traditional Arab *thobe* when we arrived. He went to change his clothes for the night out. I sat down and waited. I tried to chat with his aides but they spoke little English. With the amount of teeth they had, I wondered if they could talk at all. When they smiled, visions of the shark in the movie *Jaws* swam into my head. Finally, the Sheikh entered the room and I looked for the camera. I was sure this was 'Candid Camera' and someone was taking the piss. Maybe John had heard about my last job and was setting me up, I thought.

What was this world coming to? I asked myself. The Sheikh wore a pink suit with blue edging around the lapels, cuffs and pockets. Another Arab without dress sense—would they ever learn? I would be embarrassed while escorting this charge. At least by visiting an Arabic club he didn't look out of place. No doubt he thought he looked cool. After having my ears blasted by the ear-splitting noise they called music, the Sheikh decided to leave. The evening passed without incident and they enjoyed themselves!

It was five-thirty in the morning and the Sheikh had consumed a vast amount of Black Label whiskey. This was the whiskey of choice for those Arabs who pretended to fervently shun drinking alcohol.

On the way back to the hotel, I sat next to the Sheikh in the car. We sat in the back with one of his aides, so it was cramped. His other aide sat in the front next to the driver. That was where I should have been sitting, but the Sheikh had insisted I sit with him. Breaking with the usual protocol made me feel ill at ease. However, when the Sheikh placed his hand on my knee, I felt a little more than just uneasy. Maybe it's nothing more than a friendly gesture, I said to myself. Then he started to caress my knee in a way that left me in no doubt that he fancied me. Fuck me; are all the Arab royals gay? I wondered, not that I had anything against gay people.

I wasn't so forgiving and heard myself saying, "Not again, oh, no." The Sheikh wasn't happy with this, but he could stuff it as far as I was concerned. I called John from the hotel and pulled off the job. I had been down that road before, and I wasn't about to go down it again. Perhaps John didn't want to go down that road, either, so had sent me instead!

Back home, I had the choice of just relaxing and waiting for the next assignment or returning to the company for a refresher course. I decided my skills needed honing and so opted to go for the course. There were several modules to attend. Work commitments and laziness, if I'm honest, had ensured that I hadn't been able to put in the necessary training to keep the tools of my trade sharpened. "Controlled aggression is the key," I repeated over and again, as I trained. "There is only one-way to fight—to win," I kept telling myself.

Straight from the refresher I went to do some training at a local Karate club. My timing was well off, as well as my distancing. Another letdown was my footwork—I felt flat-footed. I spoke with the instructor and he arranged some interclub competitions for me. The thought of these coming up helped me concentrate my efforts.

I trained religiously for two hours each day, right until the first tournament. When I came out to fight, the butterflies churned in my stomach and the adrenaline raced in my veins. This was a feeling I had long missed.

I let rip with an *ushirogeri* (back kick) which caught my opponent in the solar plexus, lifting him from the floor. The momentum carried him over his teammates sitting just outside the competition area. The referee called the judges for a conference. I moved to my starting line, turned to face my teammates and knelt down, hanging my head low as I waited for the referee to decide my fate. I expected a disqualification for using excessive force. After a while, I faced my opponent, who by now had recovered.

The referee awarded me a full *ippon* (point). I had won the match. I was quite shocked as I thought I should have been disqualified.

Several fights later, I found myself back on form. I had missed the regular training, so this break had been welcome and I had enabled me to sharpen up. I knew, however, that it was only a matter of time before the next job would be in.

Chapter 7

1982

It was now late spring of 1982, and an interesting assignment was on the agenda. It would prove to be an eventful one, too.

Martin called me. He had his own investigation and surveillance company, and his old commanding officer from the Royal Military Police had asked him for help. Martin asked if I were free: I was and I liked the challenge he put to me. A patient wielding a club hammer had stormed into a doctor's surgery and assaulted a woman doctor in her office. Several items and a computer lay smashed on the floor after the attack. The doctor ran out into the reception area after suffering minor injuries. My job was to fix the problem. The sting in the tail was the patient was a six-foot tall transsexual with psychological problems. Martin told me that she was now on police bail. She was taking no notice of the bail conditions and was harassing the doctor and other patients at the surgery.

The first day, I met the staff and the doctors based at the practice. Both the doctors had equal standing in the practice. I discovered that the male doctor cheated on his wife and had a girlfriend who visited him daily. But my priority was to gather information about the offending patient. Everyone in the practice had a deep-rooted fear of the patient, as they expected violence from her as the norm. I sat quietly in the waiting room as if I were just another patient. I just melted into the background and waited. The staff panicked every time anyone resembling the patient came near the surgery. I expected no action at all and then for all hell to break loose.

The staff spoke openly of their fears and had been indiscreet enough to speak about them to the other patients. I needed to keep a lid on this pressure cooker. I reported daily to the office, and they backed the decisions I made. It made a welcome change.

Suddenly, on the third day I spent at the surgery there was an almighty bang on the plate glass window. The staff, scared witless, shouted out to me. Perhaps they thought I was deaf and the bang had not caught my attention.

They screamed, "She's got a hammer in her hand," as I walked briskly out of the surgery. I called out for the woman to stop. She did and spun on her heels to face me. She was aggressive—shouting and swearing—and swung the hammer high above her head. She asked, "What are you—the bodyguard or something?"

I asked her to stay still while I approached her. I held my hands up at chest height, palms facing toward her showing that I held nothing in my hands. I asked her name and she said, "Julie." I now knew what my target looked like. She had shoulder-length, dark brown hair and I could detect a trace of makeup as she glared at me. A heavy overcoat hid what she wore underneath. Her hands clenched the hammer tight and her stance was aggressive. She stood about six foot in height and looked formidable for a woman.

I said I would like to hear her views and that I didn't judge anyone without giving them the chance to speak first. Giving her the opportunity to speak gave me the chance to form a rough psychological profile of Julie.

She dropped her guard. I, on the other hand, kept mine up. I asked her to sit with me on a nearby bench. This took her legs out of play, controlling her movements to some degree. She began her story. As she told it, she cried, and I saw real pain in her eyes.

What had upset her most was the doctor had released her private and personal medical records to the police and some of the surgery patients; this had opened her up to ridicule from the locals. Julie had complained to the British Medical Council but was still waiting for their reply. There had been other issues and she complained about these too. The doctor had quickly struck Julie off the surgery's list of patients, which had only served to antagonise her further.

Julie told me her frustrations had the better of her and the police arrested her, bringing charges of assault and criminal damage. They released her on bail with conditions imposed. One condition was that she did not go within one hundred yards of the surgery. Julie had broken her bail conditions by making this latest approach. I felt Julie needed a little understanding but I said I would have to take action if she persisted in her behaviour. She understood, and I told her not lash out, but instead to catch my attention and I would leave the surgery and sit and talk with her.

Julie was happy with this, but she felt for her own peace of mind that she needed to put the fear of God into the doctor. I wasn't happy about this. But at least now I had set up a dialogue and had some control over events. I made it clear that if she overstepped the mark there would be trouble. I would achieve an end to hostilities.

Julie said she felt better as I had taken the time to listen to her. She also had an idea where she stood with me. There wasn't anything underhanded in my actions; they served a purpose. I had my doubts about the doctor and her own mental state.

The surgery was no longer under immediate threat so I had achieved my first aim. I was now working on my secondary aim. I contacted Martin and told him I had met Julie and that I was dealing with the problem. I also said a settlement agreeable to both parties should be forthcoming shortly.

In the meantime, I'd learned from the practice manager that all sorts of swindles were going on. The male doctor drove a new maroon TVR sports car, which the manager said he funded through the frauds he perpetrated. The surgery manager must have been unhappy with her position to reveal this information to me, I thought. And the more dealings I had with the female doctor, the more concerned I became. It was becoming clear to me the doctor was the one with the problems, not Julie.

At the end of surgery, I escorted the doctor to her car. Julie made sure she was seen, the doctor freaked out, and I had to calm her. She was in no personal danger. Julie was well aware of the doctor's psychological state. This was the weapon she chose to attack the doctor with, and it was proving to be more effective than the hammer she had used before.

Perhaps Julie had the better of me, too. In the shopping precinct away from the surgery, she set herself up with a billboard declaring her thoughts about the doctor. She announced to passers-by how the doctor had released confidential information about her; the doctor took exception to this and so I went to speak with Julie.

I paced out the distance between the surgery and Julie's location in the precinct and noted she was well beyond the distance set by her bail conditions. I also told Julie that the police were on their way.

When they arrived, Julie had decamped, although she stood nearby. There was a driver, a sergeant and a female constable in the van. The sergeant put his handcuffs on Julie. I asked why they had arrested her, because as far as I could tell she had not breached her bail conditions. The female officer told the sergeant that they might have a problem. He said they were arresting her anyway because he believed she had broken her bail conditions. I disagreed and he told me to mind my own business. This was a mistake on his part.

Later the police contacted me for a statement. I asked why they needed one and they told me they wanted me to be their witness. They were going to put Julie in front of the Magistrates and would seek her detention until trial.

I asked if Julie would be held in a woman's prison should they detain her. I was told she would go to a male prison. That thought horrified me; talk about kicking someone when they are down. I stalled on making a statement for a couple of days and contacted Martin at the office while I thought about what to do for the best. Speaking about my concerns, I said it appeared that while initially Julie had clearly been in the wrong, it had become obvious to me that the doctor was the one with the bigger problem. I also said that it would not take much for me to fix the problem. Martin said he was happy with whatever action I decided to take.

The next day Julie's solicitor called me at the surgery. He asked if I would be making a statement for the police. I said no, for the following reasons: one, Julie had not broken her bail conditions on the day the police were called as they had charged and two, it would not be right for Julie to go to a male prison.

I asked for an assurance from Julie that if I did not make a statement, she would in turn stop harassing the doctor. In addition, she must follow the proper procedures with her complaints to the British Medical Council. I asked her solicitor to relay my conditions to Julie, and if they were acceptable, to assure her that I would not make a statement against her. Julie agreed to my conditions. Her solicitor telephoned to thank me for my help, and said Julie considered me a good person. She asked if I would meet her for a drink. I declined with an apology.

I reported to the office and they said they were happy with this outcome. I explained the position to the doctors and assured them that no further action was necessary. However, the female doctor wanted Julie imprisoned.

I told them I was leaving and they said that if the problem flared up again they would like me back. Fortunately for everyone, though, there was no repeat performance.

* * *

"The King is dead," the newsreader reported as I turned up the volume of my car radio. It was the 13th June 1982 and King Khalid of Saudi Arabia had died of a heart attack. Noticing a telephone box, I pulled over and called Bill at the office. He said Crown Prince Fahd was now King Fahd. As a result, Martini was now the King's private representative in Europe, becoming even more important and powerful than before—so Bill expected more work.

I had served my apprenticeship with Princess Rima and now worked constantly for the upper echelons of the royal family. I had an understanding of the Arab mentality, but even so, there was always something new to learn each day.

A few days later, I heard from John, my Hungarian colleague. He had a job for me in Spain. After the crap jobs I had been subjected to in England, I thought a change of scenery would do me the world of good. The day of departure arrived and with some apprehension, I set off. My family were not happy I was on the move again, but supported me as always.

* * *

I met John at Heathrow Airport and checked in. We passed through passport and customs control and after strolling through the metal detector we completed the formalities. Next stop was a coffee shop where we got a cappuccino each, and sat chatting. Plans had changed as we now had to pick up a couple of cars in Paris and drive them down to Marbella in Spain.

After arriving at Charles De Gaulle airport, we got our gear together and set off for the hotel, the Prince de Galles, in the Avenue George V. After dumping our gear we went on a short tour of the city.

The following morning we were up early and checked out. We walked to a side street, the Rue Quentin, where we found the cars. They were not impressive. One was a BMW 735i and the other a Mercedes 280s. Both cars looked to be in good order, but the equipment on the Mercedes was bad; it had a manual gearbox, manual windows, and no air-conditioning.

I wanted to take the BMW, but John said he was driving it. As he was running the show, I had to concede. It was early July and hot. This would be an uncomfortable trip for me. We drove down the Avenue George V towards the Pont De L'Alma, which means "Bridge of the Soul," and is where Princess Diana lost her life.

We passed the Place De L'Ecole Militaire, turned into the Avenue Du Maine and stopped at a petrol station. We filled up and checked the water, oil and tyre pressures. I was sweating profusely and reached over to adjust the air-conditioning in my car by lowering the windows. I couldn't open the bonnet on the Mercedes and had to get help.

We dove to the Peripherique and on towards Lyon at which point John decided he had a date with the devil and drove like a lunatic.

About three and a half hours later, we passed Lyon with John still driving like a maniac. Both our speeding projectiles headed towards the border with Spain.

I turned on the radio and laughed as Meatloaf came on blaring out a "Bat Out Of Hell" as I shot off down the motorway. My foot was permanently glued to the floor with the accelerator pedal beneath it. I kept a towel on the seat next to me. This came in handy as it seemed every minute or so I needed to wipe my brow as the sweat poured down my face and into my eyes, obscuring my view. The drive was never-ending; the fun of it had long since evaporated.

Nonetheless, boredom soon set in as the scenery never changed and all motorways look the same the world over. Hours later we hit the border. Crossing the divide proved no problem and standing in Spain I felt a little exhilarated—at least until I got back into the Mercedes and set about the second leg of our journey. It had seemed like I'd been driving for an eternity, but we were only halfway to Marbella. I felt like dozing off for a few hours, but John had other ideas. I knew he had taken some amphetamine that morning. This brought a smile to my face, as it was ironic that he was on speed.

The heat was intense and I wondered how much more my body could leak before it ran out of fluid.

My thoughts centred on an old friend now, Steve Ives. A couple of years before our trip, he was killed in Barcelona when he was a member of a Karate team brought out by 'Ticky' Donovan. During an evening out, they found themselves in some difficulty. The outcome was that Steve Ives was shot and killed and another member, Alfie Borg, was wounded. I had become friendly with Steve and had mourned his death.

We made an unscheduled stop in Barcelona: I spent the evening thinking about Steve and the events surrounding his death. This wasn't the introduction to Spain that I'd envisaged. It was relief that greeted me as we left the outskirts of the city the following morning. John sped off towards the motorway and, for once, I was happy to speed along behind him.

Tarragona seemed a million miles away from the emotional roller coaster of Barcelona and I enjoyed every minute of it as I surveyed it first through the windscreen and then through the rear-view mirror as we zoomed by. The next exotic sounding destination on our itinerary was the Castello de la Plana, which drew about as much attention as Tarragona had before it. The only redeeming feature of Barcelona had been the welcome opportunity to shower, change, and catch a little shut-eye.

I was looking forward to reaching Marbella and getting out of this tin box—ever more so as the roads became more dangerous. I had designs on reaching Marbella in a tin box and not a wooden one! If John had an appointment with the grim reaper, then he could attend it by himself, I thought. The road curved this way and that, left and right, then it would rise and dip. Because of these features, this was perhaps the most dangerous part of the drive.

Before my eyes, an arch appeared and at that precise moment it felt like the gateway to heaven as I read the large word carved within it—Marbella!

We approached a junction governed by traffic lights and took a right fork off them. Looking to my left, I saw a large hotel set down by the beach declaring it to be the 'Gran Melia Don Pepe'. I noticed a nightclub close by that was owned by James Hunt, the former 1976 World Formula 1 Motor Racing Champion. His club was called 'Oscars' and it would not be long before I became embroiled in an incident there. But I didn't know that yet, and we meandered up the narrow road that would lead us to the villa that Prince Faisal Bin Yazid and his friend would be renting.

Pulling into the driveway, an exquisite villa came into view. Within minutes, I was in the bath scrubbing away the encrusted sweat. Shortly after bathing, in the privacy of my room, I lifted the telephone receiver and called Sue.

"Hello sweetheart," I said as she answered. "How are you and the boys? Are you all right?"

"We're fine, but we miss you so much."

"I miss you too. We've arrived safely and are at the villa now. Get a pen and paper and take down this number. That way you'll be able to contact me if you need to."

"Your mother has been taken ill again," Sue said.

"Is it bad, or is it the usual?" I replied, knowing that because she was alcoholic she was prone to bouts of illness.

"She's not too bad and there's nothing to worry about, I just thought you should know."

After chatting for a while, I hung up the phone and then went to sleep.

Chapter 8

Summer 1982

Paradise. When I awoke, I found myself in paradise. I showered and dressed. Wandering around the villa and out into the garden through the large opened sliding glass doors, I marvelled at the beautiful dark green lush, thick-bladed grass as it cushioned my steps, and I surveyed the scene before me. To my right were tall, regal palm trees and a kidney-shaped swimming pool, and bright blue skies and brilliant sunshine greeted me as I looked down the hillside beyond the Don Pepe hotel and out to sea. Something as simple as the grass made such an impression on me—so much so, that I felt I could very quickly become accustomed to working in this environment.

The villa had two master suites, both magnificently equipped. It also had several other bedrooms, furnished in a more modest manner. The floors were laid with imported Italian marble and all the walls were white and adorned with tasteful paintings.

One of the suites was located on the lower floor while the other occupied the entire upper floor. This particular suite was my favourite with its light and airy open-plan design. It had a large sunken bath, which was covered in the same Italian marble that adorned the floors. Louvered shutters shielded the room from the intense sunlight. With the shutters open, the views out across the Mediterranean Sea were to die for. The lounge area held a large, fully stocked bar that would take a hammering every evening the princes and their entourage were in-house.

After I had retired the previous evening, John had ventured out, been down to Puerto Banus, and arrived back in the early hours. When he emerged from his room, he told me we already had a member of Prince Faisal's entourage in situ. This guy was out partying the evening before and had met John in the port.

Taking the Mercedes, I decided to familiarise myself with the area. I checked out the local medical facilities, restaurants, designer shops and hotels; in fact, anywhere that may be of use to me over the coming weeks. I discovered that the principals spent much of their time in Puerto Banus, so I decided to check it out too. Driving there, I happened upon a beautiful building, which was set on a sloping site just above the N-340 road.

Intrigued, I made a detour and stopped in the car park of the Mosque. La Mezquita Del Rey Abdul Aziz was named after the first King of Saudi Arabia. It was built on the initiative of Prince Salman Bin Abdul Aziz. A member of staff there told me that the mosque could hold over eight hundred worshippers and housed a magnificent library. He also told me there were rooms reserved especially for the women to worship. The mosque had a large dome and a few stained-glass windows were set within its walls. Once back in the car, I jotted down the names and whereabouts of all the places I visited that day in the notebook I'd brought specifically for the purpose. It would prove to be invaluable some time later.

Making my way back to the villa, I idly wished that I could buy it, but that was just an impossible dream. On my excursion, I had seen a plethora of rich men's toys that included yachts, villas, helicopters, and expensive cars. I was convinced that Marbella spelt in English was "MONEY"!

Wandering through what I now considered a modest little villa, I found both John and our Arab houseguest, Khalid. John introduced us and as he stood, I shook his hand. We then sat down together for a while by the poolside. Khalid seemed to be a pleasant, mild-mannered person with a soft nature. How wrong I was.

Late afternoon saw us all venturing down to Puerto Banus for something to eat. I was surprised that several people went out of their way to come and say hello to John as they passed by. He was obviously a well-known figure in these parts. John stood as a well-dressed Spaniard approached our table and, reaching out his hand, greeted him warmly. This man, Jose, supplied the villa to the princes for their vacation. He was self-assured and confident, and seemed to have a close friendship with John. Sitting with us Jose told us the princes were due to arrive in two days, but that the princess would not arrive until the following week.

Jose also said that the princess would be staying in another villa away from the men, as was usual.

I thought I had a while to wait before being called on, in this case—but John had other plans for me. A little while later, Khalid took his leave and left the three of us together. John and Jose made plans to go on to a nightclub, but I decided to bow out and return to the villa. A little solitude and a swim were in order at the end of my first day in paradise.

Lying on a sofa with a cushion beneath my head, I looked at the gardens, trees and swimming pool, as the outside lights illuminated them. The only sounds were those of the cicadas in the background as I watched a gecko dart across the marbled tile patio. My thoughts were with the peace, which prevailed in this part of the world, but it was to be a peace that would soon be shattered.

* * *

At midnight, I retired to bed, and as I lay relaxing, I felt at ease with the world. I wondered what Prince Faisal Bin Yazid would be like. There were many Prince Faisal's in the Saudi royal family, and this was not the Prince Faisal I'd worked with in London. In fact, I hoped he was nothing like the Prince Faisal I'd worked with in England! I had not heard of this Prince Faisal before the job was offered to me, and with this thought in mind, I drifted off into a dream-like state as the warm Mediterranean Sea air enveloped me.

I did not hear the engine of the BMW, nor did I hear John enter the villa. I hadn't heard Khalid and the young woman exiting from their taxi when they'd arrived, either. What I did hear, though, was the scream that ripped through the villa, scything through the air. Leaping from my bed, I flew out into the lounge and found Khalid trying to rape the woman he had brought back. She was trying to fight him off and was crying, sobbing and screaming. Khalid was drunk and ripping at the woman's clothes. She in turn was lashing out at him and among it all, Khalid shouted, "*Sharmoota, sharmoota!*" which is Arabic for prostitute.

Pulling Khalid away from the woman, I restrained him. As I tried to make some sense out of the commotion, John arrived on the scene. Khalid was blatantly drunk and fell about. John seemed more than a little drunk too. Now I saw a different Khalid, as he became more abusive and vicious as a result of the alcohol he had consumed.

John took Khalid to one side, dealing with him away from us, while I tried to calm the unfortunate woman.

As events settled, John took Khalid to his room and told him to stay there. John apologised for Khalid's behaviour and I returned to my room. I wondered what I should do about the attempted rape. If the woman decided to call the police, I would have supported her and her decision.

It wasn't long before I heard another disturbance and went to investigate. I was amazed to find that John was now trying it on with the woman! He was trying to be subtler in his approach but he was nonetheless trying to force her down a path she did not want to take. Stepping between them, I guided John back to his room with some difficulty.

I wanted to drive the woman home, but knew the Mercedes was already running on the fuel gauge warning light so decided not to chance it. I did not have a number for the local taxi station either—something I'd put right the next day. It was almost 4am. I calmly spoke to the woman and offered her my bed, saying I would sleep on the floor by the door to prevent anyone from entering. She was grateful but said she would be happy to sleep on the floor. I couldn't allow that, though, and asked her to please use the bed. I left her alone to sort herself out, while I stood guard outside the door.

As soon as she called to say she was settled, I went in and lay on the floor, placing my head against the door to alert me if anyone tried to enter. Somehow, Marbella did not seem like paradise to me any longer—it was more like paradise lost. Reality had set in and smacked me in the mouth just as Khalid had smacked the woman. Spending a restless night, I wondered where it had all gone wrong.

Morning did not arrive soon enough; all I wanted to do was get the woman out of there. When she was ready to leave she opted to walk down the hill and catch a bus. Khalid and John were let off the hook, too, for she never reported the event to the police.

Later that day it was all hands on deck as we set about making the place fit for a prince, or in this case, princes. It would be interesting to see how people conducted themselves once they were on-site. What I knew for sure was that John and I would soon be sharing a room. I hoped their entourage would behave.

I felt, by helping the woman, I had put my neck on the line and wondered if both Khalid and John would somehow have it in for me. Neither of them referred to the matter again. I wondered if maybe they couldn't remember anything because of their intoxication.

While both Khalid and John were to attend the arrival of the princes at Malaga airport, I'd be left housesitting, which suited me just fine. I wanted to fade into the background and kept myself well out of the way. However, events did not pan out the way I imagined.

On their arrival, the princes walked into the villa and straight past me, their entourage following closely behind them. John called me and asked for a hand bringing in the luggage. Now I knew the Saudi's had arrived, because when it came to work they usually got a Filipino to do it, and if none were about then we would be commandeered to do it. Once the luggage was inside, John introduced me to both of the princes. The first was Prince Faisal Bin Yazid, and the second was Prince Mishari Bin Saud. The princess I was to work with was Prince Faisal's mother. The princes sat talking and smoking while a couple of their entourage busied themselves unpacking the luggage and preparing their suites for them. Prince Faisal took the lower floor while Prince Mishari took the upper.

John told me to make myself busy by emptying the ashtrays! He then suggested I ask the princes if there was anything I could do for them. This annoyed me—had I been relegated to a skivvy now? John assured me it was part of his 'game plan'. This aroused my suspicions, as I wondered why he would need a 'game plan' and felt decidedly uncomfortable with the idea. Bowing to his wishes, though, I ingratiatingly got on with it, emptied the ashtrays, and then asked the princes if they'd like anything. They immediately sent me to the bar to make up some drinks. While fetching drinks and emptying ashtrays were not bad in themselves, they were not tasks I was employed to do. It made me think that while, officially, slavery was abolished in 1963 in Saudi Arabia, it seemed from my observations that it continued in practice, especially as the princes expected anyone and everyone in their service to do whatever they asked. The conditions imposed on foreign workers in particular are appalling, too: I witnessed mental, physical and financial atrocities being meted out.

Over the next few days, I busied myself cleaning, tidying, skivvying, and housesitting as the princes got on with their vacation. I became happy to do these chores. It killed the boredom and boredom was a killer. I wondered if it was all a game plan by the Saudis. Whereas I had been miffed about doing the menial tasks to start with, I now relished them. In fact, I even thought about redecorating while they were out; I joke. It was uncanny how they managed to get in to your psyche. It was dangerous how you could be manipulated and directed without seemingly realising it. All you wanted to do was keep them happy. Your own happiness and well-being became secondary to their wants and needs. They had a knack for grinding people down, so much so that years later in 2010, a Saudi Prince would be convicted of murder in England when he killed his aide who appeared to give no resistance whatsoever as he was beaten to death.

Each evening on their return, I waited on them to make myself indispensable—indispensable as John saw it, that is. I played the game knowing that no one was indispensable in life and especially not to the Saudis. I thought then that I was capable of winning their game, but time would tell! They used people like paper tissues, quickly screwing them up and then throwing them away.

During the early hours of the sixth day, I heard the princes returning from their nightly jaunt. This time however, some people they'd befriended accompanied them. Sitting in a group, they chatted, smoked and drank while I waited on them like a butler. My ears pricked up when I heard mention of Karate. I listened intently as Prince Faisal claimed he held a black belt and watched as he sent Saleh, one of his servants off to his suite with a command and a wave of his hand.

Shortly, Saleh returned, ceremoniously holding this black belt across both hands as though he was serving it up to the prince. I stifled a laugh as I surveyed this pathetic scene but continued my eavesdropping. Prince Faisal continued his grandiose description of how he had achieved it and what holding a black belt in Karate entailed.

What a load of bollocks, I thought.

Listening to Prince Faisal waffling on I found it difficult to believe that he would have put in the hard work necessary to earn a black belt. Had he said a Filipino had been sent on his behalf to take his lessons for him I would have found him more believable! He then invited everyone to a demonstration the following day. Seizing the opportunity, I said to Prince Faisal that I had done a little Karate before and would be honoured to help him in his display. Asking the prince what time he wanted me available I then took my leave and left John to take care of the skivvying.

* * *

I awoke early the next day, and after showering began to stretch and limber up in private. After listening to the previous evening's bullshit, I still did not want to underestimate the prince. I did the splits to both left and right; while bending my body and touching my forehead to my knee, I held the position ever longer.

Making my way out to the garden area, I found the prince and his guests already assembled. Prince Mishari was noticeable by his absence. Prince Faisal had his legs stretched apart and was bending forward trying to place his forearm on the floor in front of himself. On seeing this I knew immediately that he was much too tight and not limber enough to be much good. Saying good morning to everyone, I moved up towards the prince and as he exercised, I lifted my left leg and threw half a dozen kicks to various target areas in front of him. His jaw hit his chest in surprise as I performed.

Prince Faisal asked me to attack him slowly with various techniques as he showed off defences against them. The demonstration continued for a while, and he took questions and gave answers as I continued to be his patsy.

As the session wound up, I took the initiative and suggested we give a demonstration of sparring. Prince Faisal agreed. I let loose and the prince did not know what was happening as he backed away, and tried unsuccessfully to defend himself. After the session, I sauntered off back to my room to shower and change. I wondered if I'd put my neck on the line once again. But in truth didn't care. Karate was a subject close to my heart, and I wanted to put on a good show.

Later that day, Prince Mishari asked if I would like to escort him that evening. I had become fed up with being stuck in the villa and jumped at the chance. He asked me how long I had trained in Karate saying he had watched our performance through the slats of the shutters that covered his windows.

*   *   *

I wore a white Pierre Cardin shirt and a maroon tie, while gold Pierre Cardin cuff links showed below the cuffs of my sharply cut black lightweight Pierre Cardin suit. Black polished shoes completed the outfit as I stood waiting for Prince Mishari just outside the front door of the villa. In front of me was the Ford Granada 2.8i Ghia the prince was using during his vacation. It was a normal family type saloon but at least it had the necessary bells and whistles including air-conditioning, an automatic gearbox, electric windows, and electric sunroof. Compared with the Mercedes I had driven down from Paris, it was a dream car.

Prince Mishari walked out through the door dressed in a silk shirt and razor-sharp creased lightweight trousers. Telling me he was going to drive, he jumped into the driver's seat and left me to walk round to the other side of the car. It would be a pleasant change—a prince chauffeuring me. Puerto Banus was one of the prince's haunts, and we made our way there.

We pulled up at the sentry post by the entrance to the port and the prince lowered the window to speak with the guard. The barrier was lifted and we drove through, parking on the left-hand side near the quayside. I noticed a light green Aston Martin Lagonda parked nearby. It belonged to one of the prince's brothers. We wandered down the quayside in front of the bars and restaurants.

We soon came across Prince Mansour Bin Saud, the owner of the Aston Martin. Walking a step or two behind him was a bodyguard called Patrick. After the princes greeted each other, I fell in behind them and walked alongside Patrick as we walked on again. I shook Patrick's hand and introduced myself. He was French, but spoke English well. Getting on with the job, we were unable to speak more.

Prince Mansour's villa, Saudade, was near the mosque. He was obviously wealthy, and by his age held a position of prominence in the ranks of the late King Saud's children. However, he did not have the looks of some of his brothers. Standing about five feet eight inches tall, he had a fat face with large cheeks and protruding teeth, reminding me of a chipmunk, and an ugly one at that. His hair was thinning badly, and he sprayed the bald patch with a black substance in a futile attempt to hide it. Walking behind Prince Mansour, I wanted to laugh as the lights reflected off his painted balding head. I found him an obnoxious character. He was spiteful and cruel to his staff, and because he was the oldest brother in Marbella, he had all his siblings dancing to his tune.

As we walked alongside the yachts berthed in the marina, other Saudis wandered over and exchanged kisses on both cheeks with the princes, or a kiss on the shoulder or bridge of the nose. Neither prince knew that I had close connections with their brother Prince Walid. I had seen Prince Mansour on several occasions at his mother's house in Farnham Common where I had spent many hours. But as I had kept myself out of the way on his visits, he did not recognise me now.

Reaching the end of Puerto Banus by the restaurant Silks, we turned round and made our way back towards the lighthouse. On meeting more Saudis, the same kissing rituals took place. Men kissed other men; they never kissed the women.

Berthed by the lighthouse was Prince Salman's yacht, the SHAF. I had worked for him too. He had six or seven villas in a large compound behind the mosque and near the villa of Prince Mansour. Prince Salman had a bridge built that spanned the main road for everyone to use. It was erected because the road was too dangerous to cross and the prince did not want either himself or his family killed in a road traffic accident.

Prince Salman is one of the 'Sudeiri Seven'. These were seven full brothers by Hussa Sudeiri, the favourite wife of King Abdul Aziz. Prince Salman is the Governor of Riyadh, the capital city of Saudi Arabia, and is extremely powerful. The yacht before us was huge and reputedly cost $20 million in the late 1970's.

Spinning on my heels, I faced back the way I had just come and once again, we wandered down the marina towards Silks restaurant. I cannot imagine how many times over the years that I've walked back and forth along the marina in Puerto Banus. It was the Saudi catwalk where all the royals came to parade in front of their peers. They often strutted along like peacocks with their tail feathers extended. Finally sitting at a bar, I managed to rest my feet as the princes eyed up the talent walking by. Soon two more of their brothers joined us. One was named Sattam, and the other Muatassim. They both had pronounced effeminate mannerisms, but each was married. Muatassim had a soft and caring nature with a mild manner. Sattam on the other hand was bitchy and thought the world revolved around him. Both of them had small villas and I guessed they did not hold much wealth—at least not comparatively speaking.

Patrick and I sat at the table with the princes, but kept our mouths shut. We knew our place and knew we had to stay in it. Anyhow, it gave me a chance to see what little snippets of information I could pick up. Soon other brothers arrived as if they were coming out of the woodwork. One, Talal, was the head of the Basketball Association in Saudi Arabia. He was fat and heavily built, with large dark eyebrows and a large thick black moustache. Over the years, I came to like him and he always gave me good advice.

Chapter 9

Oscar's

Prince Mansour, as the eldest, was the first to leave, saying he was making his way to Oscar's nightclub. The other princes sat a while longer before making their way to the main entrance of the port.

A sheepish Prince Mansour stood by his Aston Martin, which wouldn't start. Several people sniggered as they passed by. A driver had arrived with the Mercedes I had driven down from Paris. I smiled, noticing no one was able to open the bonnet of the German car. Prince Mishari wandered over to ask what the problem was and as he did so, I popped the bonnet of the Mercedes with ease. For a short moment, this act made me the focus of attention. How could they know that I had suffered the same embarrassment only a few days before? With battery leads attached, the Aston Martin roared into life and Prince Mansour was soon on his way.

Walking to our Ford, Prince Mishari asked me to drive as his brothers Sattam and Muatassim were coming with us. It came as no surprise that we too were going to Oscar's. Perhaps this was necessary so we could jump-start Prince Mansour's car should it die on him again. I noticed none of the princes paid the entry fee. The management turned a blind eye and allowed us through to the dance floor. I checked out the whereabouts of the exits and the toilets, knowing I would need one or the other of them during the evening. The princes sat at one table while Patrick and I sat directly behind them. Within seconds, waiters descended on our tables like vultures. I drank a Coca-Cola with ice and lemon, as did Patrick. The princes went for Johnny Walker Black Label whiskey with ice. None of the princes danced, but Prince Mansour became louder and more aggressive as he consumed more alcohol.

Patrick became edgy, knowing his charge would upset someone. I watched as it kicked off. Insults were flying between Prince Mansour and some guy in the club, which resulted in the prince lashing out and slapping him. Patrick jumped between them and calmed them down. The prince started shouting at Patrick while his brothers and I watched. Sensing it was time to go, Prince Mishari signalled to me to make a move. With this, all the princes rose and made their way to the exit.

The Aston Martin started without problem and Prince Mansour's younger brothers bade him goodnight. I jumped into our Ford and Prince Mishari told me to drive the other princes home first. Much animated conversation over the events at Oscar's took place in Arabic. I kept my mouth shut.

We dropped off Prince Sattam and Prince Muatassim and then made our way back to our peaceful and serene villa. Prince Mishari never spoke of the incident, and I never brought up the subject either.

The following day, Prince Mansour called me through to see him when we visited. All the brothers met and spent their afternoon's playing cards. The previous evening's events were the topic of conversation as I walked out to the rear garden where they sat on the grass. I was asked about how Patrick had conducted himself. I found myself in an uncomfortable position—should I placate the prince or call it as I saw it? Deciding on the latter, I said that Patrick conducted himself correctly. I explained the argument had come about by drinking too much alcohol that Prince Mansour was the physical aggressor, and that Patrick had stepped in to protect the prince from any physical attack from the guy he had slapped. It wasn't Patrick's job to step in and continue the assault. His job was to protect the prince and he had done so. This wasn't what Prince Mansour wanted to hear and he dismissed me with a nonchalant wave of his hand. What was noticeable was the silence from his brothers as I spoke. I expected some fallout from my comments, yet heard nothing more about the subject. I wondered if I had alienated Prince Mishari from me, but if anything, it seemed I had gained his respect by speaking my mind. From then on, Prince Mishari began asking me my thoughts about all manner of subjects. It appeared he became more interested in me as a person rather that just a hired hand.

* * *

Jose, the estate agent, came by often to see Prince Mishari and brought with him brochures of property for sale in the Marbella area. We never went to see any of them so it was obvious nothing he had found impressed the prince to any degree. In the evenings, I continued my waiting duties, serving drinks, tidying up, and making myself useful.

I was painfully aware the princess was due in and that then my time with Prince Mishari would end. I had come to get on with him well, so would have preferred to stay with him. However, that was out of my control and I resigned myself to moving over to Prince Faisal's mother when she arrived. I wondered what Prince Mishari's thoughts might be on the subject. When John told me the princess would be arriving in a day or so, my honeymoon period with the prince looked ready to come to an abrupt end, or so I thought.

That evening, Prince Mishari asked if I would continue working with him. I said he would have to clear it with Prince Faisal. He went to see him and on his return, he said it was a surprise to Prince Faisal that I was to work for his mother, and that Prince Mishari could keep me, passing me about as though I were some plaything.

I said it was my understanding from John that I was in Marbella specifically to work for the princess. When John arrived, I asked him exactly what my position was after telling him that Prince Mishari had asked for me. John said he was hoping to push me into a position with the princess once she arrived. Not happy to discover that he was trying to foist me on to someone, I wanted to tell him to go and fuck himself, but I kept my temper.

After the princess arrived, many changes took place. Prince Faisal and his people moved into another villa, while Prince Mishari moved into a local hotel with his wife and young son who had also turned up. As a result, I stayed at the villa on my own, and was happy to do so. A day or two later, there was a knock on the door of the villa. I jumped out of bed naked and wrapped a towel round myself. I rushed down to open the door to find three princesses standing there.

They announced they had come to use the swimming pool, so I showed them through to the garden.

I went up to the suite I had commandeered since the princes had left. Looking through the shutters, my eyes met the sight of a beautiful woman with a good figure. Somehow, I did not think Prince Mishari would be too happy if he knew that I was looking at his wife. The princesses were not naive enough to think I would not be looking at them. Princess al-Anud was intellectually sharp, had great dress sense, looked great in a swimsuit, and was nobody's fool.

Each evening in Puerto Banus, we attended the Middle Eastern fashion show, as I liked to call it. The princesses, all dressed in their finery and Paris fashions, would strut back and forth through the port. This was in sharp contrast to how they dressed in Saudi Arabia. There they cloaked themselves from head to foot in their black *abaya* and couldn't mix freely with any men. In Marbella, however, they were openly on show and often Princess al-Anud would wear low-cut dresses which showed off her ample bosom.

Jose finally found a villa that caught Prince Mishari's attention. The following day the prince, the princess and I went to view it. The villa sat between the Marbella Club and Puente Romano hotel, but on the opposite side of the road. This was the middle of the Golden Mile and the real estate there is expensive. The mosque lay about five hundred metres to the west on the same side of the road—although the only time the princes went to the mosque was when Prince Salman, the Governor of Riyadh, was in town.

It would have been easy to miss the little side road as we approached it. We passed the Marbella Club on our left and slowed on noticing the El Vicario sign; we turned right and drove up the small hill. About two hundred metres on the right-hand side we noticed the open front gates of the villa and Jose's car parked in the driveway.

The prince and princess stepped from the car and Jose greeted them. I walked away, leaving them to get on with their viewing in private. The villa was large and impressive and looked out to the sea. A large quarter circle white Italian marble tiled entranceway led to big wooden double doors. To the left of them was an anteroom, entered via a glass sliding door. Directly behind this room were the housekeeper's quarters. To the right of the main entrance was a huge white Italian marble patio area with imposing columns that supported the balcony attached to the main bedrooms. The lower floor lounge had large glass sliding doors leading to the patio area. To the left of the patio looking towards the sea was a stairway leading down to the lower level garden area.

Inside the villa, there was a large open-plan lounge area with a central fireplace. Away from it were more visitor bedrooms with en suite bathrooms. There was a large dining room, and crystal chandeliers hung from all the ceilings. The villa was exquisite, and the prince asked me my thoughts on it. Of course, I was impressed; anyone would have been and I told him so. He then told me the asking price—it was on the market at $4.5 million. I gulped in a breath of air as he asked me if I thought the price was fair. I had no idea, and told him so: he was talking telephone numbers now as far as I could tell. The money these people had was in another stratosphere.

Over the next few weeks, the family visited the villa several times. They wanted to buy it and so Jose arranged appointments at the Notaries office and with the manager at the local Arab Bank. Apart from tying up the legalities, the prince needed to arrange for funds to be released to cover the various building projects he had in mind for the villa. These included a swimming pool and fountain in the middle of the driveway, a large garage, a separate staff room, and a big ornamental stone balustrade on the steps leading down to the lower garden area.

The completion for the sale would fall towards the end of December and require another visit from Prince Mishari to close the deal.

As we drove back towards Marbella the prince asked me how long I had known John and whether I 'worked' for him. I was open and honest, telling him I had known John for some time but only as an acquaintance and that I did not 'work' for him at all. The prince told me that John had told him I worked for him and that he had taught me all I knew. I put him right on both points. Prince Mishari then asked me to work with him when he ventured outside Saudi Arabia and I said I would be happy to do so.

Their vacation over and their villa to be completed, I said farewell, as Prince Mishari and his family left Malaga airport back to Saudi Arabia. I caught a later flight to Heathrow. I knew Sue and the boys would be waiting for me at the airport. Clearing passport and customs control took forever but was worth the wait when I first caught sight of them.

"Daddy, Daddy," the boys shouted as they ran up to me. I lifted them up in my arms. Sue followed closely behind with tears welling up in her eyes.

"We saw some aeroplanes and we saw some funny people wearing some funny clothes," the boys continued.

I snuggled in closer to them all and whispered in Sue's ear, "I love you so much."

"I love you too. Now let's get you home where you belong," she said.

It was pure joy to be with the family; *my* family this time! I had worked all through the boy's summer vacation from school. While I was away, I thought about them constantly. Now I had the chance to spoil them rotten and did so. Even so, I felt there was nothing I could do to make up for the lost time.

Soon John called me up to see him.

"How did it go with Prince Mishari?" he asked. "Did you bring the twenty per cent you owe me?"

He was speaking of the twenty per cent he wanted from my earnings for working with Prince Faisal's mother. I handed it over.

"I want twenty per cent of any future earnings you receive from working with Prince Mishari."

"No way, I gave you this twenty per cent because we had agreed on it. As it was, I never got to work for Prince Faisal's mother, but I'm happy to give it, as it was you who took me out to Marbella. However, that's it. Prince Mishari approached me of his own choosing and not because of anything you may have said or done. So that's it," I said as I stood to leave. John wasn't happy with my outburst as he showed me out.

90

"I'll call you in a couple of days," he called behind me.

Had he wanted ten per cent I would have probably agreed to it. However, as I felt he'd been greedy, I had gone the other way. Because of his greed, he was the loser.

Chapter 10

Late 1982

Two weeks later, I called Martin, the colleague who'd given me the job looking after the doctor.

"Hi Martin, how's it going?" I said.

"Great, just the man, I've a surveillance job in Kent for you," he replied.

"Yes, Martin, I'm fine, how are you?"

"Sorry," he said, "I'm snowed under and could do with some help. Are you up for it?"

"Sure, I could do with a change of scenery. Give me the details and we'll take it from there."

On the Wednesday, I drove down to Faversham in Kent to carry out a photographic and video surveillance. A carpenter had allegedly injured himself and had made a large insurance claim. I had to check if he was working, and find out what dexterity he had in his injured hand. Easy job, I thought.

The next morning, I was in position. At 7.50am, the target left his house. I noticed a small bandage on his right hand. He approached a white van, unlocked it using this hand and drove off. I followed at a safe distance. The van made off in the opposite direction to that of the carpentry business.

We left town and then, about two miles down a long straight road, he pulled over. I drove on by. The van remained stationary. When I was out of sight I too pulled over. Crossing the road, I walked back towards the area where the van had stopped and was surprised to see it doing a three-point turn in the road. I dashed back to my car, turned around myself and set off in pursuit of the target. Staying well back and behind several cars, I kept watch.

Back in town, he started driving up and down a few backstreets. He was obviously surveillance aware. I dropped off from following him and made my way to the carpentry business. I waited some distance away. Sure enough, a few minutes later the van pulled round and stopped outside the carpenters. The target got out and furtively looked around. Reaching for his keys, he locked the van—again, using his bandaged right hand. This time I recorded it. He went inside and I waited. About 10am, he came out carrying a mug of tea in his right hand. Two other men also carried mugs of tea. I assumed this was their tea break and that they were going to sit in the park opposite the business. Cautiously, I positioned myself and as they laughed and joked, I recorded them. The target showed good dexterity in his hand movements. After their tea break, they made their way back. Again, I waited. Lunchtime approached, and out they came. This appeared routine. As the target ate his lunch I recorded him. He showed good dexterity, I thought, but reminded myself that was for others to decide. Then in they went and I waited once more.

At 5.30pm, the target came out once more. He got into his van and set off, and I followed him—directly back to his house. For the next few days, I played cat and mouse with him. Then, on the Thursday of the following week, as I arrived at the target's house, I found that a professional sign writer had been at work on the van: emblazoned across it for the entire world to see was the carpenter's business address and telephone numbers. I called the office and gave them the news. I was told to hold fire while they contacted the insurers to see if this would be enough for their investigation. Minutes later, Martin called back.

"Mark, come on in. That's a job well done. The insurers are happy with that."

"I will be in the office in a couple of hours and we can go through the surveillance tape and photographs then," I said, and hung up the phone. Then I went to a one-hour photograph developing shop.

Christmas rushed up and I looked forward to a family get together.

However, I had not accounted for my old charge, Prince Mishari and his plans. He wanted me back with him. We were to meet up in Marbella on 19th December 1982. With sorrow, I told Sue that Christmas had been cancelled for us. Although not at all happy, she supported me and waved me off from Heathrow Airport when I left. Watching her and the boys waving as I walked through passport control broke my heart.

At Malaga Airport, I met up with Jose and then waited for Mishari. Jose said the reason for his visit was so they could tie up the loose ends of the property sale.

Looking through the windows of the airport, we saw Mishari and his companion get off the jetliner. Neither Jose nor I had seen his companion before. Shortly afterwards, the prince wandered through customs control and into the arrivals hall.

He walked straight ahead, looking to neither left nor right. He knew we would find him so he wasn't about to concern himself with looking for us. I greeted the prince with a shake of his hand and took his briefcase. Jose welcomed him and also shook his hand. The prince then introduced his short, stocky, fair-skinned companion. His name was Khairy, and he originated from Syria. I could tell he was loud and brash, which did not bode well for me. Instinct told me that we would clash, and I wasn't wrong.

The drive into Marbella was uneventful but noisy. Khairy was like a terrier dog—yelping and snapping at everyone's heels trying to get some attention.

Over the next few days, discussions took place about the plans Mishari had in mind for the villa. By Christmas day, the prince owned the villa and possessed all the documentation to prove it.

Mishari introduced me to his bank manager at this time. During the few days of this visit, I befriended the bank's security guard, Pepe. He helped me over the coming years with advice and introduced me to numerous contacts.

On Christmas day, I wondered what my family were doing. Later that night I rang home. Sue was missing me and said both the boys had cried when I had gone through passport control. Feeling down, I said I missed them all, too. I told Sue that Jose had been gracious enough to invite the Prince, Khairy, and me to Christmas dinner.

Jose was an excellent host and even had presents for each of us—I got a black lizard skin belt. Khairy, in contrast, gave me a hard time. He chided me repeatedly, asking me if I missed my family, what they would be doing without me, and a few other choice comments thrown in for good measure. The tormenting was relentless, and I became more and more upset with him. Being tormented about Christmas itself had no impact on me, but bringing my family into the equation did. Even so, I kept my cool; but I felt unhappy that the prince allowed the chiding to continue.

Even though he was more used to some Arabs' intolerance of other religions than I was, Jose too was uncomfortable with Khairy's comments, not just the ones about Christmas, but also those made about my family. I didn't appreciate them, nor would I forget them: Khairy and Mishari in his complicity would pay a heavy price, but that would come later.

On 30th December 1982, we drove to the Prince's villa. Stopping by the open gates, Prince Mishari stepped from the car to admire the newly erected nameplate for his latest possession. It read Casa Tam—the first letter was of his son's name, Turki, the second of his wife, al-Anud, and the third of his name, Mishari, hence, (Casa) TAM.

The following day I saw the prince and Khairy off from Malaga Airport and caught a later flight home to welcome in the New Year. From Prince Mishari's point of view the trip had gone well, but that was not so for me: I hated being separated from my family. Sue never complained. With the Saudis there was no place for Christmas in their employees' lives. Everything revolved around what they wanted and we fell into the trap by giving them just that. It was not just a job it became a vocation. Even so called respected politicians found themselves supplying prostitutes for the princes. Me and mine, we had just given up our Christmas for them.

* * *

Jan 1983

The call came a week later. Bill asked me to join a team looking after the King's eldest son who was due in the next day. I accepted. Bill was partners with Martini at the Saudi Arabian Embassy. After getting off the phone, I called out to Sue.

"They've called me in for an assignment. It starts tomorrow. Is that all right?"

"Of course it is," Sue replied. I then polished my shoes. This was something I did whenever I received a call to start a new job. I never knew why, but it caused Sue much merriment.

The upshot of the job offer I received in that phone call was that I would work for both the King and his immediate family for many years.

Prince Faisal Bin Fahd was not just the King's eldest son; he was also another hypocrite. He was yet another alcoholic and drug addict, and a homosexual who engaged in many sexual liaisons with both male and female prostitutes. It was deeply ironic that he became the President of the National Committee for the Fight Against Drugs in Saudi Arabia. Indeed, Prince Faisal received many honours during his lifetime, which amused me no end—having witnessed his drunkenness and sexual jaunts, and having even saved his life when he overdosed on cocaine, heroin and whiskey. This was the man who was also President General of Youth Welfare in Saudi Arabia. What an example to the up-and-coming generation! No wonder the country is in such turmoil today.

On the prince's arrival at noon on the Monday, an entourage followed. There was his secretary, Eduardo; a chef, Saleh; a valet, Ahmed al Sheikh; Saudi Royal Guards and more besides. We had eight drivers, six cleaners, and twelve security personnel on-site too: there were people all over the place. Martini's driver, Martin, was assigned to the prince—and was a spy in the camp who reported back daily to his boss.

The prince's luggage arrived: there were over a hundred big trunks. The mind boggled, as the luggage of the entourage had yet to arrive! The housekeeper, Kamal, told us to take the luggage in and up to their rooms. I thought he was joking, but he wasn't. Kamal was Egyptian and he told us, "Mr Martini says if any security man refuses he can go home."

One problem Saudi Arabia faces today is there is an underlying policy in their culture that a Saudi national does not do manual labour. This deeply embedded belief causes all sorts of problems for the Saudi government: they try to get their subjects to work, but they resist and often turn to crime instead. The government therefore have a situation where their unemployment rates soar along with the crime rates. Saudi Arabia only a few years ago could boast at being an almost crime free country—not so now.

The entrance to the house in Prince's Gate, Knightsbridge was large. It had a double sized entrance door, which was very wide, and yet when the prince went to walk through it, he nearly walked into the wall!

It was obvious something was seriously wrong. Immediately, I suspected that more drugs and alcohol coursed through Prince Faisal's veins than blood.

As the prince entered the house, I noted a couple of officious looking chaps with him. When we were introduced, it became clear they were Special Branch police officers. The King had expressed concerns to the British Government about the well-being of his son. They had in their wisdom supplied Special Branch officers to watch over him. My intuition warned me right then that there would be problems—and there were! Just for instance, it was the Special Branch officers who insisted we conduct body searches of all staff and any visitors—that is, absolutely everyone who came to the house. Often these searches caused offence, but they insisted nonetheless.

The following day as I walked through the lower ground floor of the house, I heard an almighty commotion in the kitchen. Peter, a fellow bodyguard, dashed down the corridor ahead of me to check it out. On entering the room, a carving knife flew past his head and stuck into the doorframe. A fight had erupted between the chef, Saleh, and one of the kitchen helpers. Peter calmed them down, although it took a while. Saleh, we thought, had some mental problems, and we 'marked his card' for future reference.

Early evening found Peter and me standing guard outside the door of the swimming pool. We watched over Prince Faisal while he swam with some topless party girls. One of the waiters, Soapeh, served alcoholic drinks, and everyone was merry and having a good time. I kept a close eye on the prince. Other than some fondling, kissing, laughing, drinking and drug taking, nothing much else happened although I was called into the pool area when a couple of the girls became a little rowdy. Prince Faisal was out of the pool, sitting with Cleo, his favourite girl. Eduardo sat with them and they spoke in English. They talked about a woman called Janan Harb. I thought she was a hooker but I couldn't place her in my mind.

Prince Faisal told Cleo the King still kept in contact with Janan. I realised this Janan character was involved not with Prince Faisal but with the King. The prince became more and more agitated. Finally, he lost his temper, shouting that his father had moved $20 million into a company called Saudi Oger for her. When Prince Faisal was fit to burst, Eduardo ran out of the pool area with Prince Faisal not far behind him. We followed. The prince went to his suite; minutes later, Martini arrived and went to see him. Shortly after that, Martini ran down the stairs with Prince Faisal screaming at him from the top flight. This behaviour was normal for the prince who was known to be hot headed, unpredictable and dangerous. He had no regard for life—his or anyone else's, unfortunately. Additionally, his temper was ferocious: after becoming upset with one of his male lovers, he murdered him! In my opinion, Prince Faisal was a waste of space and lost his father's attention for indulging in drink, drugs, murder, and homosexuality. It was fortunate for him that it was just his father's attention that he lost!

Over the next few days, I became friends with one of the SB officers. His name was Mike and he read a lot, as, like us, he had a lot of time to kill. I showed an interest in a book he was reading, an Executive Protection Manual. He recommended the distributors to me so I could buy a copy, as it wasn't on general release.

No doubt, the SB supplied the security services with intelligence on Prince Faisal and his indiscretions, as well as looking after his "well-being" and hanging out with me and the staff.

The prince rarely went out. Eduardo would arrive each evening with various women of different nationalities, all beautiful. They were prostitutes and our suspicions were that he had tried them out himself. Occasionally, a guy accompanied them. Cleo visited often: she was pretty, had large boobs, long hair, and a bubbly personality. She took a shine to me, and would make a beeline for me, so that I could search her. She had detected that I was uncomfortable searching the girls and teased me for it. The truth was we could only conduct cursory searches, anyway, as Eduardo had countermanded the orders of the Special Branch officers.

Chapter 11

Overdose

Earlier than usual on the seventh night of the prince's visit, a knock came on the front door and there stood Eduardo with Cleo and a Hawaiian woman in a tight-fitting red dress. The Hawaiian was stunning. She had long, dark, flowing hair and long legs accentuated by red high-heeled shoes. Gold earrings gleamed against her dusky cheeks. Her large, dark, piercing eyes met mine and the lipstick she wore glistened from the light cast by the expensive French crystal chandelier above us. Her nipples protruded invitingly through the flimsy red material of her dress. After the cursory search, I escorted them through to the lobby area. Eduardo asked me to sit with them while he went up to see Prince Faisal.

We sat and chatted. Cleo was in a buoyant mood. By now, I had got to know Cleo fairly well. She teased me about the searches and joked about life in general. As I had developed this 'friendship', I chanced my arm and asked about the upset on the second day of the visit. She told me that Prince Faisal resented Janan who had married his father in 1968. Prince Faisal's uncle, Prince Turki, had thrown Janan out of Saudi Arabia a couple of years later (which is ironic as the disgraced Prince Turki now lives in exile himself, in Cairo). The King kept a relationship going with Janan Harb when he travelled outside Saudi Arabia. He had a soft spot for Janan and had, he thought, secretly provided for her through his company Saudi Oger. But somehow Prince Faisal heard about the $20 million investment, and he was livid about it. What annoyed him more was that he could in no way question or talk of it with his father.

Soon, though, the subject of sex came up, and Cleo was back to teasing me once again: she told me that Prince Faisal liked to watch her performing with other women! She said that this evening she was going to perform with the Hawaiian woman while the prince masturbated. The previous night, a guy and two women had performed while again the prince had masturbated—she said the guy involved had a fourteen-inch penis with a thick girth. Yeah right, I thought, but they said the women loved it! The prince himself couldn't keep his hands off it, she said, and had engaged in homosexual sex.

After a long night, Cleo emerged from the elevator. The Hawaiian girl had long since gone. As Cleo approached me, I detected that she was more than agitated about something.

"Mark, can I speak to you outside? It's important and I don't want anyone else to hear what I have to say."

I called one of my colleagues over and told them I would be outside for a moment.

As we walked down the steps to the pavement outside, I said, "What's the problem, Cleo?"

"Mark, I'm petrified; I don't know what to do. You must not tell anyone that you got this information from me."

"Cleo, calm down. Now tell me what's causing you such distress?"

"Faisal's dying! He has overdosed on heroin and cocaine, he's drunk several whiskeys and he is on the bed with his eyes rolling in the back of their sockets! I don't think he'll survive it," she said, gasping for breath.

"Cleo, just go, quickly. I will deal with it."

My heart pounded as the adrenalin coursed through my veins. I ran up the stairs and back into the house. I dashed down to the basement to find the team leader whose name was Mick.

"Mick, we have a crisis on our hands. Prince Faisal has overdosed on whiskey, heroin, and cocaine. It looks like he's dying."

"Who told you this, how do you know?" he replied.

"Mick, we don't have time for this now. We need to help the Prince."

"Forget it, if it proves to be untrue we could find ourselves in a whole world of shit. Anyway, we're about to change shifts, so let the others have the problem," he replied.

"All right Mick, can I leave now?"

"Yes, I'll see you tonight," he said.

I dashed out of the house and jumped into my car. I rushed to the nearest telephone box and called Martini. I couldn't call the emergency services for diplomatic reasons—and even if I had, the guys on the next shift wouldn't have let them in unless they were sure there was a problem.

As Martini awoke, he mumbled, "Yes, what is it?"

"Sir, its Mark from Prince's Gate, we have a problem."

"What problem?"

"Prince Faisal has overdosed on heroin and cocaine, he's drunk and he is on his bed gasping for breath with his eyes rolling in their sockets."

"Are you sure?"

Taking a huge gamble I replied, "Yes, sir."

"I will deal with it," he said, and hung up the phone.

There wasn't anything else I could do. As I drove home, I tried to calm myself. My adrenalin level had shot through the roof and I needed to relax.

* * *

I heard nothing all the next day. But when I arrived at the house in the evening, I found out that the prince had been admitted to a private clinic. He had been taken there shortly after I'd called Martini, who, fortunately, had acted quickly on my revelations and took the necessary steps to attend to the prince. I was told the prince would have died if he had been left for another couple of hours!

And that was when the fun started. I was called to speak with the SB police officers. They wanted the details of the previous night's events. Given they were official police bodyguards, supplied through the government at the request of the King, one could say they had fucked up! As they knew Prince Faisal wasn't going out in the evenings, they decided not to have night time cover: it saved on overtime payments. Anyway, I filled in the details for them, painting the picture graphically, but there was a problem—they wanted Cleo's details.

I would not give them the information, and it started to go a bit pear-shaped for me. I said I would contact Cleo to see if she'd agree to a meeting with an SB officer of my choosing. Luckily, Cleo agreed to it. God knows what I would have done had she refused, but I would not have revealed Cleo's name or details without her permission.

There were obviously some serious issues that needed to be resolved, the most important being from where and from whom the prince had got the drugs. This was a major concern to the police, and Cleo had assumed they would view her as the prime suspect.

After she had spoken with the SB, I contacted her to find out if she was all right. Cleo said she was fine and we became friendlier because of the incident, and kept in touch for some years afterwards.

Prince Faisal's condition was serious. We did not know if he would survive. He was undergoing detoxification in the clinic, which would take a while. The King's personal doctor, Dr Kharter, arrived to oversee matters and sent daily reports of the prince's progress back to the King. A security team with Special Branch officers was deployed at the hospital, while I stayed at the house and took care of security there.

The house was large—it had six floors and overlooked Hyde Park. It was also a couple of doors away from the Iranian Embassy, which had been besieged three years previously, in 1980. The house furnishings were ostentatious—the whole house had French antiques throughout. In the basement, apart from the swimming pool, there was a bar and a bedroom. Plenty of sexual exploits took place in this bedroom whenever the prince became aroused to any degree in the swimming pool with the topless and often naked and nubile young women. Sometimes a male friend would join them, too.

There was a lift to all floors and the prince's suite took up an entire floor of its own. The outer windows of the house were all armour-plated, and from the pavement there were stairs leading down to the reinforced and alarmed basement door. Closed-circuit television cameras oversaw the property twenty-four hours a day.

The prince stayed in the clinic for four months, and after leaving it, within a few days, his father called him home. When the prince then arrived back at the house, he was a different person. He was clean of the drink and drugs and looked well, considering. He even managed to walk through the main door without a problem.

No praise came my way, though, and it seemed as though the incident had conveniently disappeared from the royal family's memory. Also, Martini doubtless thought it best he take the credit. It was comedic to see in the years that followed what so many of the family got up to. Many of them were in a constant search for the next thrill: drugs, drink, girls, twosomes and threesomes, boys— they experienced all this and more. In my view, many of them behaved this way because they were deeply unhappy; certainly a few showed signs of deep depression.

So, Prince Faisal was temporarily clean of both drink and drugs on his departure from the clinic. But at the same time, I noticed a few boxes of Johnny Walker Black Label whiskey packed up by his staff and sent back to Saudi Arabia on his behalf—in a diplomatic bag, of course! Those diplomatic bags have a lot to answer for.

Apart from the whiskey, Prince Faisal decided he wanted his black Stutz motorcar sent to Saudi Arabia, too. It looked like a classic pimp's car and had cost a cool quarter of a million dollars. Before shipping it back, the bar would have to come out because of Saudi laws against consuming alcohol. But from what I saw, there was probably more alcohol in Saudi Arabia than oil.

Many Saudi princes carried a firearm, and given that many of them also drank too much or were high on drugs of some sort, this was of real concern. The Saudi guards also carried firearms and although the Special Branch police were aware of this, they ignored it. So much for the safety of the British public, I thought: the British Government and police force, like so many others, are happy to flout the law of the land when it suits them.

Part of the prince's protection was a Rolls Royce which would have done James Bond proud. Included in the specification, apart from the armour-plating and 2-inch thick bullet-proof glass was a loud hailer to ward off intruders. It sported twin blue flashing lights hidden behind the grille for emergencies. The boot supported an oxygen tank to afford a safe environment for the occupants in case of gas attack. It also had a remote control starting remote and special run-flat tyres, so the car could stay mobile in case they suffered a puncture by fair means or foul. Many more 'extras' adorned the car in case of ambush—it would have been the safest place to be unless one of the Saudi Royal Guards was inside. They would probably shoot at anything that moved, and in that case, with them loosing off a few rounds, I think I'd rather take my chances outside the car! But with all this protection, there was one weak link—and that was the prince himself.

Prince Faisal was extremely rich, but the way he amassed his wealth harmed his people. For instance, he had $200 million siphoned off from the oil revenue he controlled paid into an associate's Swiss bank account. He also had an annual budget of $20 billion for his government department and took a hefty thirty percent of that as his 'commission'. In doing so, he was effectively denying his people the benefit of that revenue. As if that were not bad enough, he would take a further commission from the earnings of the facilities his department had built. At one time he had taken $40 million commission from a company employed to update his country's telephone systems. However, one of the most despicable acts he performed was to confiscate lands belonging to the poor people. Those embezzlements earned him much more than the commissions through his government department.

So, it was a relief to me that within a few days of the prince getting out of the clinic, I bade farewell to him and his sizeable entourage. I was at last looking for a little relaxation. My assignment to Prince Faisal had lasted four straight months, working twelve hours a day, seven days a week. The job had also entailed a sizeable amount of stress and thus I felt drained: it was good to get away from it.

* * *

Prince Faisal died on 21 August 1999.
He was 54 years old. One of his closest aides told me that he'd overdosed on Johnny Walker Heroin and Cocaine, just as before. He never became free from them during his lifetime.

Chapter 12

April 1983

John called again and asked me to cover another of his charges. The timing was perfect as I was running short of cash. John went with me to the Heathrow airport VIP lounge where we met an aide of Prince Khalid Bin Fahd Bin Mohammed, who had himself flown in from Geneva only two hours earlier.

When the prince arrived, John formally introduced me to him. He seemed familiar to me, although I couldn't place him. I'm sure he felt the same. As we drove out from the suite, he said he wanted to go to the terminal exit point to meet his girlfriend. It seemed they had flown into Heathrow aboard the same aircraft but had exited by different routes, which confused me.

We waited in the car, which I'd parked out of the way and in the shadows. When she appeared, I noticed she was wearing a Saudia airlines flight attendant's uniform. This intrigued me.

Prince Khalid got his aide to fetch her, and as she spun around, I saw her face. I knew her and I must have looked surprised. This girl, I knew, was the girlfriend of Prince Faisal Bin Yazid.

As she neared the Jaguar, Prince Khalid got out and they hugged and kissed. As she looked over his shoulder and saw me, an expression of shock and surprise crossed her face. She was just as surprised to see me as I had been to see her moments earlier.

We put her luggage in the boot, got into the car, and made our way to the Royal Lancaster Hotel. The prince asked the woman to wait in the car with me while he and the others went into the hotel. Something wasn't right about this, but I wasn't aware of its full significance until a little later.

She asked me if I was going to say anything to the prince about her and I replied that it was none of my business. She said they had met recently, when she had been an attendant on a flight he had taken. Obviously, seeing me disturbed her. The twists and turns were coming thick and fast and all the warning signs of trouble to come were there.

After ten minutes, John came out to get us. As we entered the lift, he took hold of my arm and whispered to me.

"Mark, Prince Khalid bugged the car, he knows what you were talking about."

"Shit, that's all I need," I replied. "What happens now?"

"I don't know, we'll have to play it by ear," John replied.

His comment unsettled me. I'd never thought there might be an electronic bug in the car. But now it became clear that the prince had left us there for a reason.

We entered the suite and Prince Khalid acted normally. At least John had forewarned me. I carried on in my usual manner although I wanted to tell the prince to get stuffed. I had given John my word that I would cover him, and so I had committed myself to the job.

It wasn't long before Prince Khalid broached the subject of the woman, saying he had noticed my reaction to her at the airport. Did I know the woman? Had I met her before? Had I seen her with anyone else before? The questioning was relentless. Perhaps he thought he was a good interrogator, but I found him about as discreet as a fox inviting himself to dinner in a chicken run. Nonetheless, I played the game and fended off his questions.

Towards the end of his visit, he started in with the questions again. He did like to piss me off, but I kept my cool. Firmly, I told him that if he wanted to know about the woman then I'd tell him, but was sure he wouldn't want to hear what I had to say. He backed down.

John told me the Princes always propositioned the attractive flight attendants who worked the first-class cabins on Saudia airlines. Later, I would witness this myself and see the women prostitute themselves at parties held in the royal princes' homes. The princes even visited brothels in Saudi Arabia. The Saudi royals are forever boasting about how they are the custodians of the two most holy places in the world, Mecca and Medina, and how they strictly follow Wahhabi Islam: puritanical, Wahhabi Islam regards all other sects as heretical, and remains the official religion and ruling ideology of the Saudi Arabian Kingdom.

All I can say is that I found many members of the Saudi royal family to be among the biggest hypocrites I've ever come across. I found it laughable that Prince Fawaz, an alcoholic, was governor of Mecca for a while. Then there was the drug addicted Prince Faisal Bin Fahd, son of the King, who was the President of the National Committee for the Fight Against Drugs.

As the assignment drew to a close, John advised me what to charge for my services. I thought the figure he proposed was excessively high, but he said it was his normal rate. I gave the Prince the bill and he paid it without flinching. This was a surprise, but it came back to haunt me when John took a large commission. I looked after the Prince and kept him safe only for John to come along and rob us both! The whole assignment turned into a nightmare. Having been bitten by John before, I should have expected to get bitten again. I decided I had no one else to blame but myself.

I called Martin and let him know that I was free and soon found myself on surveillance, homing in on a target once more. However, this time there was a difference. I used to enjoy surveillance work but now found myself questioning the ethics of it. Catching the 'bad' guy was a good thing, I reasoned. Yet, many times the surveillance I carried out was on, in essence, totally innocent parties. What right did anyone have in prying into the private lives of ordinary people, I questioned. Yes, I had caught out the carpenter and that felt good but after being on the receiving end of a surveillance sting, I didn't like it. For sure we were becoming a surveillance society. Even people such as Princess Diana found themselves on the receiving end of it. More thought was in order. A hypocrite was not something I wanted to be.

* * *

May 1983

I found myself doing more work for Martin. Apart from surveillance, he kept me busy process serving, which involved serving legal papers on people at their home or place of work. Although there wasn't much money to be earned, it kept the wolf from the door. Other times, I found myself on someone's doorstep asking for their credit cards. I cut them up so they could not and would not use them again. I also worked with other companies—some not so reputable, but I had to make a living and was grateful for any work I could get. I had a good reputation so my integrity was never in doubt.

Then, in early March, I went to work with the ruling family of Abu Dhabi. I thought this would be a pleasant departure from working with the Saudis.

The Sheikhs and Sheikha's I would be working with were from the top-flight of their royal family: my very first job was for the Crown Prince of Abu Dhabi. His London mansion was just outside Ham Gate, adjoining Richmond Park. The mansion stood in large grounds. I was chosen to guard the Sheikh.

It was no surprise to find Sheikh Khalifa had a severe alcohol problem and when the Sheikh slept, I had to sit outside his bedroom door—maybe I was there to ward off his demons? The mansion had thick carpets and after walking on them for a while my ankles would ache severely. It amused me watching another charge wobbling along in a drunken stupor.

I was, though, surprised to discover that Sheikh Khalifa had a gold-plated air rifle and enjoyed shooting at the guards as they patrolled the grounds. The guards were not too happy about this, and complained to the boss. The guards were told to hide in the grounds or behind the trees whenever they saw the Sheikh. As the Sheikh was always drunk, I doubt if he would have hit anything he aimed at anyway, unless it was by accident. In effect we were told to give the Sheikh carte blanche to carry on shooting at us. What was inexplicable was that we agreed to duck and dive in order to avoid the pellets as they whizzed about. Our self worth and self-respect just went out of the window and it was us who had thrown it.

At one point, when I was taking a break with Peter, we heard an almighty crash. It was a thunderous bang, and sounded like an explosion of some kind.

I shouted to the relief bodyguard outside the Sheikh's room to stay put. The other members of the team held position, too, while Peter and I went to investigate. This is where discipline is essential: for all we knew, this crash could be a diversionary tactic to draw us away from protecting our charge.

Peter and I made our way toward the garage block, which adjoined the street. At night, the street was a cul-de-sac; a dead-end with the gates to Richmond Park closed. We saw that a car had driven at speed straight into the side of the garage block, smashing a cast iron drainpipe and causing the loud crash. Two men were in the front seats. They reversed spinning the wheels as they tried to get away. His control of the car was so bad, I assumed the driver was drunk. Perhaps he was related to the Sheikh, I thought?

I tried to open the passenger door, but it was locked. We shouted at them to stop, but they went to flee. Uncharacteristically, Peter lost his self-control.

He kicked at the driver's side window—but, not realising the driver's window was fully open, his leg shot through into the car all the way up to his right hip. The car sped forward, but luckily for Peter, the momentum and direction combined to spin him round and propelled his leg back out through the window. As the car screeched away, we took note of its registration number and called the police. The car was stopped and the driver breathalysed. He failed the test and was arrested. Apart from having to pay for the damages to our building, he had to pay the price for drink-driving too. Peter, on the other hand, was lucky. He did not have to pay the price for his stupidity.

Sheikh Khalifa only stayed for a week, but as soon as he left, we started work with his son Sheikh Sultan, at his apartment in Hans Crescent, Knightsbridge. Sheikh Sultan was twenty years old and we were told he loved horses and horse racing, and his other passion was cars. I soon found out that the people from the UAE (United Arab Emirates) were much more civil and caring than the Saudis; when they weren't shooting at you, that is!

Sheikh Sultan was in England for an officer-training course at the Royal Military Academy in Sandhurst. When his course started the farce began as he would pay some of the guys fifty pounds each to polish his boots each night. He proved to be physically unfit and couldn't run any distance. The leniency he received was exceptional, no doubt for diplomatic reasons. Because of this, he managed to get through the induction. This was no surprise to us: whether they like to admit it or not, many foreign students, usually 'Royal' ones, do not meet the necessary standards to pass. Nonetheless, they do. I imagined that in a year or two he would doubtless be a Colonel or General or some other exalted rank.

When Sultan got his first break from the Academy he went back to Hans Crescent. Static guards were placed outside the apartment doors and I took the opportunity to get some fresh air. On the steps outside, I watched an Aston Martin Lagonda drive up and noticed the bodyguard in the passenger seat. He noticed me. We knew each other; he was ex-Special Boat Service and worked for 'Saladin'—a company that supplied personnel for British government deniable operations with Keeni-Meeni Services, Defence Systems Ltd., and others. I had clocked his charge, the Oil Minister of the UAE, Sheikh Mana Al Otaiba. After the minister entered the property I chatted with his bodyguard, Terry. It wasn't long before the minister emerged and he and Terry left so it was back to work.

After Sheikh Sultan completed his course we got ready for his departure. Two days after he left, a bomb exploded outside Harrods. The blast caused damage to his apartment, and debris lay where I had stood not much earlier. A few days later, I went in to London and went shopping in Harrods. As I emerged into the street, I came across an argument going on in the street. A Lamborghini Countach caught my attention; it was parked on yellow lines and the police were trying forcibly to move it. They had broken the door locks, but still couldn't open them. I recognised Prince Turki, one of Prince Walid's brothers, arguing with them. I went over to help and noted the car had diplomatic plates. Prince Turki asked me to go to the Saudi Embassy. An Embassy official hastened to the scene and a compromise was reached. I told the prince there was a Lamborghini dealership close to my home and suggested the car be taken there for repairs. He gave me the keys and told me to take the car. I loved driving the Lamborghini. The police had caused the damage to the door locks because they had yanked at them to open them outwardly. What they did not know was the doors on a Lamborghini open upwardly, directly above the car. A while later a letter of apology and a cheque for the damage to the prince's car arrived from the police.

Chapter 13

June 1983

Summer was approaching when Prince Mishari telephoned. I had been free to work with other members of the royal family during the time I spent away from him.

The prince asked me to book my ticket to Malaga for the following Friday so I would arrive the day before his family. Leaving the booking for a couple of days would not hurt, I thought. Two days later the prince was on the telephone again, asking if I had made my booking yet. Admitting I had not, he said that was good, as he now needed me to go to Paris instead. He explained that two cars had gone astray, arriving there from Saudi Arabia when they should have gone to Malaga.

Prince Mishari told me Jose's brother Juan, would meet me at the Prince de Galles hotel in the Avenue George V. From there, he would drive one of the cars back to Marbella while I drove the other.

I booked a flight to Charles De Gaulle airport near the village of Roissy-en-France, 23 kilometres northeast of Paris. I telephoned Bill at the office to let him know I would be off the circuit for the summer period and told him I had to pick up a couple of cars from the airport in Paris. He told me that he had a friend who worked in the freight department there and if I asked for her, she would help me through the formalities necessary to release the cars.

Within hours of leaving home, I stood in the plush hotel lobby registering with the concierge. Jose's brother, Juan, tapped me on the shoulder and said he already had the room key.

At the bar, Juan said Jose had sent enough funds to cover the cost of the hotel and any other expenses we may incur. I told Juan we should split the funds in case we got separated. He disagreed, and for some reason would not give me any of the money. I wasn't about to get into an argument over it, even though I knew somewhere along the line he would surely cause me trouble—another prat who did not know what he was doing.

We picked up the cars at the airport. One was a black and gold Chevrolet Camaro Z28 and the other an Audi 200 Turbo. Juan nearly wet himself—he was like a little kid in a sweetie shop. He said he would drive the Camaro. I had been in this position before, though, so insisted that I'd drive the Camaro, as it was the Prince's car. He was lucky either way, as both cars had all the bells and whistles, including air-conditioning. What did piss me off was when Juan then asked me how to drive an automatic, as he'd never driven one before. Now I knew I had been right not to let him anywhere the Prince's car!

The last journey down to Marbella had proved uneventful; however, this time I would have no such luck.

Juan was going to lead the way in the Audi after I showed him how to drive it. I told Juan that should I get into any difficulty, I would flash my lights constantly to get his attention.

We left Paris and we travelled at speed along the motorway. Suddenly, a loud grinding noise erupted from the rear of the Camaro. Flashing my lights, I signalled that I needed to pull over. Leaving it as long as I could, I pulled off the motorway at the next service station as I watched Juan disappear into the sunset.

I waited for over an hour for him to return. He never showed up. Finally, I called a local garage for help. The mechanic was quick to point out that he thought the rear differential had failed. He said he would send a tow truck in the morning and get the car back to his workshops. It would be necessary to leave it there while he tried to find a new differential, he had said. Bollocks to that, I had thought.

I contacted the prince in Saudi Arabia and explained my predicament. He wasn't happy about, it especially when I told him that Juan had driven off with all the money. I said I thought the problem with the car wasn't serious and that I could get it fixed but that I needed funds transferred to me so I could get the car down to Marbella. I only hoped that I was right.

He took my number and said he would call me back. Within minutes he called and said if I got back to Paris I could collect some money from his brother Prince Mishall Bin Saud at his Avenue Foch apartment.

By this time, it was dark. I went to sleep in the car. Waking in the early hours, I thought I would take the car for a slow drive around the car park to see how bad the noise was from the rear. With the windows down, I drove along listening intently. There was no sound at all apart from the burbling of the five-litre V8 engine. Inspecting the car more closely as the sun came up; I decided the brakes had been binding.

Before the tow truck arrived, I made off for the Avenue Foch. After waiting until a more sociable hour, I pushed the intercom button and waited for a reply. I was let in and made my way to the apartment, where I rang the doorbell. A tall, stunning woman with long, flowing dark hair opened the door. She stood serenely, dressed in what I thought was a man's white *thobe*. I had never seen a woman wearing a *thobe* before, nor have I since. She said hello, invited me in, and asked me to sit in a large, ornate armchair. She left only to reappear shortly afterwards with the money from Prince Mishall. Thanking her, I resisted flirting and bade her farewell. This was the first time I met Princess Lamia Bint Mishall, later to become the wife of Prince Ahmed Bin Salman.

I telephoned Jose and told him that Juan and I had become separated and that I had returned to Paris. He was already aware of it and was angry that Juan and I had not split the funds he'd sent. I told him to speak to his brother about that. Jose told me where Juan was waiting for me and later that day we met up and set off again.

Making good time, we flew along and were soon on the motorway in Spain. Dropping my guard was a big mistake, however. Shock and horror hit me as I saw the reversing lights of the Audi suddenly come on. Its wheels locked up, black smoke billowed into the air as the tyres belched smoke and the car screeched to a halt. I hit my brakes instinctively and sent plumes of smoke belching from my own tyres.

How I managed not to hit the Audi, I will never know. After both cars were off the motorway, I got out of the Camaro and went over to inspect the Audi. I couldn't see any visible damage or any fluid leakage from it. I asked Juan what had happened and the idiot said he enjoyed driving the automatic gearbox through its gears and had been pushing in the safety switch on the gear lever. This switch would prevent the selector from engaging reverse gear by accident. He had not listened to my instructions about how to drive the car. A motorcycle police officer pulled alongside us but luckily all he did was wave us into our cars and to tell us to move on.

In all the time I worked for the prince and his family, neither the Audi nor the Camaro ever suffered any further mechanical defects.

I couldn't wait to arrive in Marbella where I could unload the cars—and Jose's brother, for that matter!

* * *

Back in the familiar surroundings of Malaga airport, I waited for the arrival of Prince Mishari and his family. Jose and two national police officers waited too. They had arrived of their own volition, and I was sure the prince would not appreciate the welcoming committee.

The family emerged into the arrivals hall and Jose and the police officers descended on them like vultures. I stood back, waiting for the melee to die down. The prince looked over Jose's shoulder and nodded to me; I in turn, responded. Stepping forward, the prince handed me his briefcase, which contained traveller's cheques, cash, jewellery, and his .38 Smith and Wesson snub nose revolver. With my other arm, I picked up the young Prince Turki and walked behind the prince and princess to the waiting cars. Walking closely behind me was Elena, the boys' Filipino nanny who no doubt kept a close eye on both the boy and me too.

I sat in the driving seat of the Audi Turbo and the prince sat next to me in the front. The princess, Turki, and Elena sat in the back seats. I insisted they put on their seat belts and made sure they were all belted up before I drove off. They knew I would refuse to drive until they were safely buckled in.

Jose was left to sort out the luggage and planned to meet with us later at the villa. The two police officers got into their car behind us. A small blue Fiat Panda 1.2 litre hatchback was their backup car. What a joke! If I accelerated briskly, our exhaust gases would blow their car over, I thought. I set off at a slow pace so I would not lose them. Before going to the airport, I had refuelled and checked all the levels on the Audi. I wanted a clear, non-stop journey. Some time later, I watched in my rear-view mirror as the police officers disappeared into a petrol station to refuel. No way was I going to stop and wait for them, so I carried on, driving at a normal pace.

We arrived at the villa, the gates were open and the housekeepers were waiting. Prince Mishari asked what had happened to the backup car, so I told him. He took his briefcase from me as he shrugged his shoulders. Turki went to play on the front lawn with little Diego, one of the housekeeper's children. Elena walked over to keep an eye on him as the prince and princess entered the villa through the main double doors. I walked over to my room near the housekeeper's quarters. I entered through one of the large glass sliding doors and pushed the heavy drawn curtains to one side letting the air-conditioning waft over me. My quarters were small but clean. There was a sofa bed, a wardrobe, a fridge and a couple of pictures hung on the whitewashed walls.

In the centre of the driveway was a white circular fountain. To the right of my room was a rectangular stone fountain, which had water cascading from the top level. At night, coloured lights lit up the water and the fountain gave off a wonderful glow.

I watched as the police officers arrived in their backup car. Right behind them was the luggage van, so at least they had protected something, I thought. As I lifted the baggage from the van, the officers came over to give me a hand. The prince called Jose in and told him not to bring the police to the airport again. Jose had acted with the best of intentions, however—the officers had let themselves down.

The family brought more staff with them on this visit. There was Elena, the nanny, and Zeinob, the maid. Additionally, there was Joha, who looked after Turki and did the household shopping. This wasn't good. I knew Joha was an odd job guy for them back home. For some reason, they thought he would also be of use looking after their son. His heart was in the right place but he had no idea about personal security. I could only advise on security measures and should they choose to ignore my advice then that was up to them.

Often, this would cause me real frustration—but every bodyguard the world over has felt that same frustration at one time or another.

Prince Mishari was mild-mannered and many people inside the royal family liked him a great deal. Later, though, I would see another side to him.

Both he and the princess manipulated people around them. The prince came from the Al Saud branch of the family and his father had been king. The princess, on the other hand, had an inferiority complex, which I felt stemmed from her origins, which were from the lesser side of the royal family, the Abdul Rahman branch.

She was attractive and dressed well to complete the package, but she couldn't get over her inferior background—inferior to the Al Saud, that is. The main way the princess boosted her self-esteem was by strutting back and forth along Puerto Banus in Marbella, the Champs Elysee in Paris, or the Croisette in Cannes—showing herself off whenever she had the chance.

Having dealings with many of the royal family over the years, gave me a broader insight into their real characteristics. I observed that the family members were so jealous of each other that if one bought a yacht, his brother had to buy a bigger one. If one bought an aeroplane, another had to buy a bigger one and so it went on. For this reason, it wasn't unheard-of for a prince to buy a Boeing 747 Jumbo jet even when he had other jetliners for his personal use. Minor princes had bank balances running only into the millions; major princes, on the other hand, had accounts running into the billions. Each one of them may have now and again passed out a minor bauble as a gift, but they never really took care of the people around them.

As I thought about this and the family settled in, I went to check out the grounds and the perimeter. The static security was the domain of the Spanish national police, yet I still felt compelled to run my own checks. I even checked the flat roof of the garage, as it wasn't visible from any vantage point on the property.

I was aware some of Prince Mishari's brothers and sisters were in Marbella. Nonetheless, I ordered the police officers not to allow entry to anyone they did not recognise. I would accept all responsibility for their actions. The following day the officers faced their first test when they stopped the prince's older brother, Prince Mansour, from entering. They held their ground when Patrick, Prince Mansour's bodyguard, tooted his horn several times and then again when the prince argued with them to let him in. Only after I identified the occupants of the car, did they allow them entry.

Had Prince Mansour notified us he was on his way, I would have taken the necessary measures to prevent him suffering any embarrassment.

I walked over to the prince's door and opened it for him. His face looked like thunder as I apologised to him for the hold up. I explained that the police officers were following my orders and was sure he would expect the same from his security. Although he agreed with me, his facial expression did not change and I knew this would not be the last I heard about this matter.

Shortly after Prince Mansour left, I stood in front of Prince Mishari explaining my actions to him. Knowing I had been acting in his best interests, he accepted my explanation and dismissed me. I went over to the police officers and congratulated them on a job well done. I reassured them that no repercussions would be forthcoming. I knew that Prince Mishari was happy that his brother had felt belittled. It was all a game of one-upmanship.

It did not take the family long to settle into their vacation and it wasn't long before I took the prince to meet a hooker at the Andalucia Plaza hotel. He had sex with her while I waited for him nearby. He often had these liaisons, and clearly the suspicions of the princess were roused as she asked me if her husband ever went with hookers. The only response I could give was that I had never personally seen him with a hooker. I justified my answer in my head by thinking that I had not seen him in the act of having sex with them, but I knew it was a lie and so did she.

A few days later Prince Mishari met with another hooker at the Incosol hotel a few kilometres outside Marbella. This time, he booked a room for the night, although I knew he had no intention of staying. At the concierge, he produced his passport and signed in, booking the room for two people. This was lax security on his part: I should have booked the room in my name. The form with his details and signature was left lying on the counter for all to see. Pointing out the form to the concierge, I asked him to please put it somewhere out of sight. He ignored my request. The prince and I made our way upstairs and he entered the room alone. I sat on a sofa a little way down the hall, keeping watch on the room. It wasn't long before a young woman arrived and knocked on the door. The prince showed her in as his eyes searched the corridor to see if anyone was about.

Once they had finished and the woman had left, the prince called me in to the room. He asked me to tidy up and make up the bed while he took a shower. Cleaning the room meticulously, I removed a towel from the bed that they had clearly laid on. Puffing up the pillows, I rearranged the covers and made the bed. I removed other remnants of his visit, including some discarded tissues in the rubbish bin. Just before we left, I double-checked that I had left the room sterile.

Making our way through the lobby, the prince stopped at the concierge to check out and pay the bill. Looking on the counter, I noticed the prince's check-in form still lying in the same place. As Prince Mishari dealt with the concierge, I lifted the form and placed it in my pocket. As the prince drove along the winding exit road, I took the form from my pocket and showed it to him. I told him there would now be no record, at least not on paper, of him booking a room there. I said that sometimes my job did not just entail looking after them physically, and he laughed as I tore the form into tiny pieces.

Prince Mishari was forever on the lookout for young women and did his utmost to impress them. He wasn't the only prince who used hookers and slept around: almost all the ones I met did the same thing.

* * *

A few days later, the princess asked me if I would give her driving lessons. I said I'd be happy to, but she'd have to clear it with the prince first. I never expected for one minute that he would agree to it, but he did. It was with some anxiety that I set off with the princess to a traffic-free area so she could take the wheel. I felt uncomfortable being in the car on my own with the princess. If one of the prince's brothers saw us, all hell would break loose. These lessons continued for just over a week and then suddenly stopped. Perhaps we had been spotted and a cautionary word said to the prince. Either way, that was it for the princess. She would just have to make do with her daily fashion flaunting. Therefore, as usual, every evening we would venture down to Puerto Banus and I watched as the princesses took to their catwalk. We often stopped every few yards or so as we came across someone they knew. It was during one of these walks that we were accompanied by Prince Mishari. As we sauntered along the prince told me he and his brothers had decided to dine alone at Tony Dalli's Italian restaurant the following night. He said I should accompany him. This would make a welcome change for me, as I thought I could do with a good Italian meal.

The following evening, I drove Prince Mishari to his brother, Prince Sattam's villa. On arriving, I saw a child about eight or nine years old holding a lit firework in his hand. As the prince wandered into the villa, I took the firework away from the boy and threw it away. I explained how dangerous it was to him. As I waited for the princes to emerge, I admired a nearby palm tree. When the princes emerged from the villa, I spoke to them about the incident and explained diplomatically the dangers of fireworks. They weren't stupid they knew very well but I felt better voicing my opinion to them in the hope that they would stop the child playing with the fireworks again.

Prince Mishari barely even acknowledged my concerns as he and Prince Sattam walked over to a metallic green Mercedes 380 SEC. He told me to follow them in the Camaro to the restaurant. Pulling on to the forecourt of Tony Dalli's, we found many of the parking spaces taken up by the other brother's cars. Once we had parked up, Prince Mishari told me to wait outside with the other security and drivers. Security, I wanted to laugh. What a joke, I thought. This was just one example of behaviour which sometimes made it impossible to provide proper security as they did whatever they liked whenever they liked.

Six security guys and six drivers stood outside the restaurant waiting. We were all expert at it by now. Lights lit up the front of the restaurant and illuminated the main road outside.

Chapter 14

Crash

Suddenly, we heard an almighty crash a little way down the road. Looking from the car park area, I could see bodies strewn across the road. A beach buggy motor car was on its side and its engine had been ripped out and lay about fifty metres away. Another car had spun round several times, judging by the tyre marks on the road. Fluids of different sorts washed over the road and broken glass shimmered underneath the street lights.

I shouted to Patrick, Prince Mansour's bodyguard, and asked him to keep an eye on Prince Mishari for me while I went to see if I could help the injured. "No problem" he called after me as I rushed over to help. Blood and guts spilled out on to the ground, and I went to work trying my best to make the injured comfortable. Minutes passed slowly as I waited for the ambulance and police to arrive. I could have done with some help from my colleagues but none was forthcoming. Looking up the road, I saw the flashing lights from the ambulances and they were soon joined by the Guardia Civil. I tried explaining to the medics as best I could what the Americans were trying to say to them as they lay on the road. Three men and two women had flown out of the beach buggy as a result of the impact.

The Guardia Civil and the medics took control of events as I headed back to the restaurant. I knew that in my role as a bodyguard I really should not have left my charge, but reasoned that I had been the one left by my charge when he entered the restaurant. And, rightly or wrongly, I felt morally obliged to help. But once the princes heard of my escapades, I was in the shit again.

Comments they made to me ranged from "Oh, you are the one who saves lives, aren't you?" to "What kind of bodyguard are you, leaving His Highness alone?" Considering Prince Mishari was with six of his brothers and there were five bodyguards and six drivers outside waiting for them, could it be considered that he was on his own?

Prince Mishari's brothers gave him hell over it and he wasn't happy with me. Once again I found myself standing in front of him explaining my actions. What I had in my favour was that his brothers were jealous of him having me working for him. The prince had disclosed this snippet of information to me some time previously and I always kept it in mind. The truth was that I was just a possession that his brothers wanted. I was valuable, an asset to him as he had something his brothers didn't possess. Sure they had their own security and drivers but they didn't have me! What they found so special about me, I'll never know, but for the time being it worked in my favour as the prince listened to me, occasionally. Mind you, I could have been a brass monkey and if his brothers liked the look of it they would be jealous because they couldn't have that either.

* * *

Two days later, Turki, Elena, and I sat watching a video in the ante-room as the prince and princess entered. I jumped to my feet. They sat and invited me to sit too, as they chatted with Turki. Both principals often spoke freely and openly with me on all types of subjects. When the subject of the television movie *Death of a Princess* came up they surprised me with their candour and said everything shown in the programme was true. This wasn't news to me as Princess Rima had discussed it with me before, when I worked for her. The truth came to me by the mouths of the Saudi royal family, so there you have it!

The following lunchtime, Prince Mishari and I went over to Prince Sattam's for their daily card games. As we got out of the Camaro, I noticed the boy I had taken the firework from standing nearby. His arm was covered from the tips of his fingers to his elbow in bandages. I asked what had happened and was horrified to hear that he had been burnt by a firework. I was annoyed no one had taken notice of the advice I had given them. Prince Sattam always knew better and most of the time, when I spoke with the 'royals', I felt as if I was talking to brick walls.

As I walked near the villa, I caught sight of a huge two-door black Lincoln motorcar. The car was a monstrosity and personified the garish taste often displayed by members of the royal family. As the princes sat on the tiled marbled floor playing their game, I sat on a sofa watching them. It wasn't long before Prince Mishari got up and went to the bathroom and as he did so, he called me out. He spoke softly, saying Prince Mansour had complained about my sitting on the sofa. He said it was bad etiquette to have my head higher than theirs, so I should sit on the floor when I went back into the room. Tail between my legs, I wandered back into the lounge while Prince Mishari disappeared off to the bathroom. I sat on the floor and then Prince Mansour said that it is all right for me to sit on the sofa. Fuck me, I thought, I wish he would make up his mind. Because I stood taller than they did, I also wondered, should I cut my legs off at the knee? Maybe my previous advice on the fireworks had upset them and they were now just putting me in my place.

I wasn't having a good day. Could it get any worse? I would soon find out.

The next afternoon, the prince sent me out with two of his sisters. Princess Zahwa was heavily built but had a pleasant enough personality. The other sister, Princess Shaha, was more attractive and bubblier. Secretively, they asked me to take them to a secluded beach area. Once there, they said I could go and come back at five in the afternoon. Returning before five, I sat waiting for them. At six o'clock, I was pissed off enough to look for them. They were sunbathing in their bikinis and I asked them if they realised what time it was. Startled, they jumped up and covered themselves with their towels. They sent me to the car saying they would follow in a minute.

Driving through the villa gates sent them into a blind panic as they noticed their brothers sitting on the marbled patio area playing cards. I settled the princesses and said I would move up close to my room. From there, they could slip down the passageway that led to the back of the house. Still in their bikinis with their towels wrapped around them, they slipped out of the car. Should their brothers see them, heads would roll—mine included.

123

Panicking as they exited the car, they left some possessions behind. Retrieving them, I made my way to their rooms. Walking up to Princess Shaha's room, I went to knock the door. Turning to my right I found the door open and the princess standing in her room with just her bikini bottoms on. I apologised as she jumped, covering her breasts with her hands. Without thinking, I said, "Too late and nice they are, too." I put their belongings down and made good my escape. I couldn't imagine why I had made such a stupid comment. Perhaps it was because I had also been caught off guard.

I kept my mouth shut about the incident and when the princesses left, they deposited 30,000 pesetas into my shirt pocket and thanked me for my discretion.

Days came and went with regular monotony. I had settled into the job and that was my next mistake.

'Saudade', Prince Mansour's villa, was the setting and the princes once again sat playing cards. Often waiting for them drove me nuts, but it was part of the job, so I got on with it. Sitting in an alcove, I chatted with some staff as I drank a Coca-Cola. Patrick was called over to the princes and returned saying that he had to make a telephone call. Abdullah, the telephone operator at Prince Mansour's house, came storming out and a commotion broke out. Abdullah shouted and swore at Patrick and swung his arms around in a menacing fashion as the argument became more heated. Looking on in amusement, I waited for blows to be struck and wondered who it was who would strike first blood: I said nothing, but enjoyed the spectacle unfolding before us.

Patrick had not asked Abdullah for permission to use the telephone. He had taken it as a personal insult and therefore had flown out to confront Patrick. What a load of bollocks.

This became my catchphrase as it described my working life with the Saudis perfectly.

Once the fracas died down, Tony, who was Prince Mansour's secretary, came over to ask me what I had seen and what my thoughts were on the episode. I said it was none of my business and that he should ask the others. He asked me again. I said I would only discuss the issue if he was asking formally. I had been caught out like this before.

He said, "I am formally asking you for your opinion, now will you tell me what happened?" I told him what had happened. He asked me my thoughts on Abdullah's conduct. I replied that if Abdullah carried on like that towards me, I would run him down. Not the smartest remark I've made and the grief it caused me was soon in coming: Abdullah overheard me and went off moaning about it to Prince Mishari.

Prince Mishari approached me a little later and gave me a severe dressing down in front of everyone, finishing by telling me that it was none of my business. He went back to playing cards and I went back to sit down, seething inside. Getting angrier by the minute, I set off to find Tony. Getting hold of him, I wanted to know how the prince had heard about our conversation. He said Abdullah had overheard us. For the rest of the afternoon I sat brooding. I told Tony had better explain to Prince Mishari that I had only become involved after he made a formal request for me to do so. He said he would but I didn't believe him. They were all afraid of the princes, whereas I always called it as I saw it. Whether that was a good thing or not, I don't know.

The afternoon drew to a close, as did the princes' card game. I watched the princes making their way to the cars parked in the driveway. Prince Mansour said "Good afternoon" as he got near to me. I moved forward to greet him as Prince Mishari said "Say good afternoon to His Highness." I cut him a filthy look and ignored him. Then I extended my hand to Prince Mansour, shook his hand, and bid him a good afternoon.

Prince Mishari said he would drive. During the drive back to Casa Tam, neither of us said a word. The police officers opened the gates and we drove through. The prince stopped the car.

"Are you angry with me?" he asked.

"Yes, I am."

"Is it because of what I said to you at Prince Mansour's villa?"

"Yes it is. Correct me if I'm wrong, but doesn't it say in the Koran—your holy book—that before a person judges an issue he should first hear both sides?"

Surprised, the prince said, "You're right."

"I made no comment until Tony formally asked me. In fact, when first asked, I said it was none of my business. I'm also angry that you bawled me out in front of everyone."

Prince Mishari leant across the car and kissed me on the cheek. He said, "You are right, and I was wrong." I decided to read more of the Koran, especially if it helped get me out of trouble in the future.

Darkness set in, as the principals readied themselves for the party at Prince Sattam's villa. I showered and changed, too. Hearing a knock at my window, I looked out and was told by one of the police officers that the principals were exiting the main house. I went to the car and fired it up. As Prince Mishari approached, he said he would drive. I clambered into the back of the car.

The parking area at Prince Sattam's villa was choc-a-bloc with cars. Nonetheless, the prince drove right down to the doorway and got out with the princess, leaving me to sort out the car. None of the security guys or drivers was allowed into the villa. Later that evening, I wandered up the driveway and saw someone sitting in the driving seat of Prince Mansour's Aston Martin. I could hear him revving the engine and noticed Patrick was nowhere in sight. Walking behind me were Abdul Rahman's wife and child; they were friends of the family.

Instinctively, I grabbed both of them and pulled them out of the way just as the Aston Martin shot forward. It flashed passed us and flew down the drive after which there was a loud crash. I chased after it and was confronted with the scene of a crumpled car. Luckily, no one had been injured in the accident. The engine screamed and fluid poured out on to the driveway. I leant across the driver and turned off the ignition as he sat bolt upright in shock. Substantial damage had occurred to the Aston—its bonnet bent upwards in the shape of a pyramid. The A-pillar, which joined the roof to the main body, was split right through. Broken glass littered the drive. Security men and drivers looked on at the mangled wreck. Patrick was the only one allowed to drive the Aston so why was this person in it? I wondered.

Taking my life in my hands, I walked into the villa only to be confronted by Prince Sattam. He waved his arms trying to shoo me out, but I told him to walk out with me. When he saw the Aston Martin, he held his head in his hands. Turning round, he set off to find Prince Mansour and as he did so, Prince Mishari walked out. His first reaction was *"Ya Allah!"* This means "My God" in Arabic. Turning to me, he said, "Did you see it?"

"Yes," I said.

His response was, "You saw nothing, remember that." Prince Mansour came out and raged at me as I was nearest to him.

"What happened, did you see it?" He demanded.

"I did not see anything," I replied.

Prince Mansour screamed at the unauthorised driver and lashed out, hitting him several times about the head. He threatened him with death and shouted how he would be sent back to Saudi Arabia to be dealt with there.

An engineer from Aston Martin was flown down to inspect the car. He said it would have to go back to Aston Martin and estimated the cost of repairs at $100,000.

On the way back, Prince Mishari asked how I'd saved the lives of Abdul Rahman's wife and child. I said I wasn't aware that I had.

"Abdul Rahman's wife told everyone how you saved their lives. I want to hear about it."

This was all I needed, I thought, more shit to follow from his brothers who now saw me as a regular hero. I just saw me as in the shit again. I told him everything.

"What are your thoughts on the evening's events then?"

I said, "Allah must have looked down and decided to punish Prince Mansour for the derogatory remarks he made about me when I had helped the victims of the beach buggy crash." I went on, "Allah must have decided to hit him where it hurts, in his pocket, by smashing one of his prized possessions—his Aston Martin."

Neither principal said anything. The Saudis are fond of beheading in their country, and I had placed my neck on the chopping block only to have it spared once again.

* * *

Shortly we would move on to Paris and by now I had become the family's Mr Fix It. My duties ranged from the simple, like tying knots in the prince's ties, to the most difficult such as getting members of the entourage into foreign countries when they had no visa's or indeed had lost their passports. They found I had an aptitude for getting things done and so there was little I did not do for them. Some of the menial tasks I performed were amusing, such as collecting Prince Mishari's dirty money—usually winnings from his gambling in the casino at the Andalucia Plaza hotel. After he finished gambling and drinking, I would cash in his chips. He ordered me to keep the dirty money separate from the regular cash I carried. He was insistent that I not use this money to benefit the family. If it made him feel better to think that, then who was I to point out that all money I spent benefited the family in one way or another? Even though the prince called it dirty money, I noticed he never gave it away and that was because he knew it benefited him. He wasn't the only prince to gamble in Marbella; several of his brothers did, too. Gambling was also against their strict Wahhabi Islam religion. The Saudi Royal family were the greatest practitioners of DO AS I SAY, NOT AS I DO.

It was obvious to me that the Saudi royals buried their heads in the sand (and there is plenty of it in Saudi Arabia) when they did not want to see or hear anything they construed as 'unpleasant'—including gambling, and financial gains from it. They would do anything to save face.

* * *

On our arrival in Paris in mid-October, I collected all the passports together, ready for the immigration officers. While these formalities took place, I darted off to the luggage carousel and grabbed a few porters and trolleys to get the baggage sorted. In Marbella, I had tied a pink ribbon round every handle. This simple act saved me a lot of time and trouble when collecting the baggage as they became readily recognisable. After sorting the luggage, I darted back to the family and guided them through the arrivals hall like a shepherd tending his sheep.

Constantly I searched the crowds for any signs of compromise to the family; I also kept an eye out for the drivers and suchlike that would meet us. Security, as ever, was a joke, but I went through the motions anyway. On arrival at the George V hotel, I knew I had a few more balls to juggle. As the principals debussed, I searched the vicinity. Noticing a person standing with his back towards me looking at a white Cadillac Fleetwood motor car, I smiled. I had not got through the door of the hotel and already recognised someone I knew. Peter was a colleague and the car was Princess Um Mansour's. Calling out to him, he spun around to face me in the noonday sun, and a grin stretched from ear to ear on his face as he recognised me.

"What are you doing here?" I asked

He replied, "I'm in the shit! I was bringing this car back from Morocco for the princess and the brakes packed up." He went on, "I can't get any help—as soon as they hear it's a Cadillac, they don't want to know."

He had tried everywhere including the national breakdown service. But after making just one telephone call, I had the problem all but fixed. The only snag was the car could only be attended to the following morning. Peter had nowhere to stay that night and precious little money either. I told Peter to wait by the Cadillac and went over to speak with Prince Mishari. After explaining Peter's predicament, I asked if it would be all right for him to stay overnight in my room.

"Can you trust him?" the prince asked.

"If I were at all unsure, I would not ask."

"One night will be all right." I bounded over to Peter to give him the good news. Patrick, Prince Mansour's bodyguard, had his own chauffeur company and employed his own mechanic. Patrick was happy to let me use his mechanic. The next day Peter and the Cadillac left for England and we left for the zoo.

Later, we stopped for lunch on top of the Montmarte hill and admired the large white Sacre-Coeur Catholic basilica. In the evenings, I escorted Princess al-Anud, as she liked to drive by the hookers soliciting for work in the Bois de Boulogne. After this three-month tour, they finally flew back to Saudi Arabia, but I'd soon be back with them again.

Chapter 15

October 1983

My next job saw me working with Saudi Arabian Defence Minister Prince Sultan Bin Abdul Aziz's daughter, Princess Munira Bint Sultan. She was the wife of Prince Faisal Bin Fahd, the drug addicted, alcoholic murdering son of King Fahd whom I'd worked for earlier in the year. The princess was due to stay for three weeks at their house in Prince's Gate, Knightsbridge. Money was no object on this visit. Martini was in for a bumper payday and he knew it. Not only could he pocket the bonuses paid out, but the Halal shops he had an interest in would supply the household with their foodstuff.

I was team leader even though the princess had several Royal Guards who came with her. They were a law unto themselves, answering only to the princess. Our group of security consisted of half a dozen bodyguards and three static men. Several drivers and the usual cleaners completed the package. All of us worked through Martini in one way or another, and he took a percentage of our wages. He often took a percentage, if not all of any bonus the principals left for us at the end of the job, too.

Our friend the chef, whose card we had marked for the knife-throwing incident during a previous visit, was in charge of the catering. A couple of assistants and waiters also worked in the kitchen.

There were no Special Branch police officers on this visit. The ocean blue armoured Rolls Royce arrived with Anil in the driving seat. Two other Rolls Royce's were also on site. The entourage accompanying the princess was vast and would cause no end of problems, as usual.

Both main front doors were manned. One door was for person entry; the other was for the suitcases, trunks and suchlike. When the furniture trucks arrived with the luggage, our jaws dropped. We unloaded and brought in the cases. Some of these were going up to the fifth floor! People became severely pissed off, and rightly so, as no one received any extra payment for this work. After bringing in the luggage, Yasser, the house manager, dismissed the guard on the second door. I was unhappy about it and made clear he had to accept the responsibility for his decision.

I placed the guards and assigned the bodyguards their charges. When Martini arrived, he went for a look round. Shortly after he left, I received a call from Bill at the office, and he went ballistic. He said if you're not up to the job, then I'll get someone who is. When he calmed himself, I asked what the problem was. He said Martini phoned and complained that there was no guard on the second door. I explained why and called Yasser to the phone to confirm that he had revoked the order.

When Martini next visited, I made a beeline for him. I explained what had happened and asked him to speak with Yasser, who would confirm it. For good measure, I said that if in the future he had any criticisms to make, then he should make them to me. To his credit, he apologised.

Within a few days, there was trouble brewing in the ranks of the security guys. One of the guards, an ex police officer, had a drink problem and yet another tried to undermine my authority at every turn. Petty problems would flare up but that wasn't unusual and on one occasion a driver ignored his call three times and a parking ticket landed on his windscreen. When he emerged, he launched into a diatribe against the guard on the main door and the argument almost erupted into a fistfight. Stress caused tempers to flare among the staff because of the working conditions. The food went upstairs to the principals and when the leftovers came down, the waiters dished it out to the security staff. This in itself wasn't a problem as it is the usual practice in the Saudi royal households, so we accepted it. However, when the security staff found out that the Arab household staff and cleaners got their food at the same time as the principals, the shit hit the fan.

This situation brought about a 'them and us' way of thinking and when jobs lasted as long as four months or more, the tension and stress became unbearable. Part of my brief was to keep a lid on this pressure cooker. And whilst I juggled with those troubles, I noted the guy with the drink problem had disappeared. I looked for him in the nearest pub and surprise surprise there he was propped up against the bar. I bollocked him—and he never stepped out of line again. I told the guys if they had a problem, they should discuss it with me and I would cover them if I could: but if they kept me in the dark, I couldn't help them. So I was none too pleased when Yasser came storming up and asked why there was a guard sleeping in a car in front of the house.

I went out and confronted the guard. I said he was taking the piss. He told me the guys had got him drunk after work because it was his birthday. Another guard had then told him to sleep it off in the car, so I bollocked them both. Then one of the team asked for a couple of days off the following week, for personal reasons. This was a guy who had challenged my authority on numerous occasions previously, so I said he could have both days off and told him that I did not want him back: I told him to phone me and say that for personal reasons he would be unable to return to the job. This would save him embarrassment and avoided compromising his future employment on the circuit. I suggested he use his time wisely to think over recent events. All the guys could do with a couple of days off for personal reasons, I thought. Personally, I ached for time off but that sacrifice pretty much goes with the job.

I had to manage the staff as best I could so I made no excuses for what I had done. And from that moment on, I had no problems with our guys. I set about dealing with the "them and us" situation through discussions with Yasser. At last, improvements came about within the household. All the staff got fed at the same time and coffee and tea was regularly served with regular breaks factored into the shifts.

I also gained the respect of the princess' secretary, Eduardo, whom I'd met and had some dealings with previously. These had taken place when Prince Faisal had survived his drug overdose. No doubt because of Prince Faisal's drug, alcohol and other addictions, Eduardo's bank balance had swelled: as he was responsible for all payments made to retailers, hotels, casinos drug dealers, hookers and suchlike he made up his own figures. The prince never questioned the outgoings as he wasn't even on this planet.

After dinner, Princess Munira came down for her nightly walk round the block. A woman friend accompanied her. I escorted the princess with a Saudi Guard. It was a pleasant summer's evening. We set off at a fair pace. If these after dinner strolls were to keep her weight down, they had not been too successful, I thought. As we neared Kensington Road, I walked closer to the princess. I had a gut instinct something was going to happen. I do not know why I felt this; I just had an uncomfortable feeling.

As we rounded the corner from Prince's Gate on to the Kensington Road, the Royal Guard reached out for my arm and signalled that I should back off. I was uncomfortable with this but our orders were to obey the Royal Guards, so I retreated. Not ten paces further, I noticed a black taxi coming toward us and saw the rear window slide down.

I knew I had to move forward—this was what my gut had been telling me. But the distance was just too much to cover. An open can of beer flew out from the taxi window at the princess. Shit, I thought as it flew past her and hit the ground, spurting its contents all over the pavement. The can was almost full. As I had followed the Royal Guard's orders, we were now in a right fuck up. The Royal Guard looked at me and his expression spoke a thousand words. I'd known something would happen; my gut instinct never let me down before, and it had not let me down now—but a Royal Guard had. The princess looked at us and I wanted to melt away. The princess often looked over to see if we were paying attention to our work. I think it was a little game for her; maybe it helped to break up some of the monotony in her life. It proved to be a bind sometimes, though, having a Royal Guard with us each day, as some of them hardly spoke English and their sense of humour was non-existent.

Two days after the security guy left, I received his phone call; on cue, he said he was unable to return. Although he kept a clean record on the circuit, I never saw him again. Many guys made trouble on these jobs. It was a competitive business.

The guys I found most reliable on static duties were the ex-squaddies. They were so used to doing static duties in the forces that if you asked them to stand on a door for twelve hours and not let anyone through, that's exactly what they would do. This was a valuable asset.

The Special Forces guys were good news for me. I always tried to surround myself with them and would pick their brains as much as they allowed me to. I made several friends from within their ranks, and I think they appreciated that I was willing to listen to their experience.

Other guys on the circuit I found interesting were the ex-French Foreign Legionaires. I found it strange that some of the other guys had a problem working with them. I put it down to inferiority complexes and their overblown egos.

After the guy who'd wanted time off left, and after my experience with the Royal Guard, I decided to move the team around. I spoke to the office and asked for Bruce to partner me. He was ex-SAS and had served nine years in D Squadron. He was one person I knew for sure would watch my back—and he, in turn, was sure that I'd watch his.

On the day that Bruce started, the princess and I went shopping and on our return trip we passed through Swiss Cottage in North London. The princess noticed the Japanese restaurant, Benihana. Anil was asked to stop. We now had to suffer a Japanese meal. My, how I suffered, and I suffered until I couldn't suffer any more. The Japanese chefs cooked the food in front of you, and they were masters with their knives. They threw them about all over the place, and so long as they did not throw them my way, I was happy. Even when eating in a good restaurant, it's important to keep your wits about you. You should never lose track of what you are there for.

That said, one evening, I wandered upstairs to relieve the guard on the main door. He'd left his book on the windowsill by the side of his chair, so I decided to have a read: the book was *Hitler—My Part in His Downfall*, by Spike Milligan. As I read, I began to laugh, and after a while, I was laughing so hard the chair I was sitting on began to rock. Milligan's humour hit my chuckle muscles and it wasn't long before the Royal Guards came out of their ante-room to see what all the fuss was about. I put the book down before I disturbed anyone else. I make a bad static guard, I thought, still laughing—but to myself, this time.

The three weeks flew by and departure time arrived. The 'departure nightmare' started. The luggage trucks turned up and Yasser asked us to help shift the cases out to them. We wanted to tell them to piss off but our hands were tied. Had we refused, Martini would have heard about it and word would go out not to employ us again. This ate at your self-respect. I wasn't happy to shift the luggage, but instead of looking at it negatively, I put a positive slant on it by using it as an exercise regimen.

There was a private Boeing 707 waiting at Heathrow airport for the princess; perhaps it was one of the royal flight aircraft. At least she wouldn't have to pay any extra baggage costs, I thought. It pays to keep a sense of humour sometimes. I would now get a rest, which I sorely needed as this job had been draining. Trying to keep the peace within the various factions at the house had been nearly impossible. The bosses thought the job had gone well and sent me a note praising my work: this was unheard of before, so they earmarked me for more team leader positions.

This proved to be a double edged sword. I felt really good having completed such a gruelling task with distinction. However, was it all worth it, I wondered, as the responsibility had weighed very heavily on me.

Chapter 16

Start of 1984

Prince Mishari telephoned to tell me he was coming to London with a male companion. He was now the Under Secretary of the National Guard in the Eastern Province. The Prince asked me to liaise with the Saudi Arabian National Guard (SANG) office in London. He wasn't happy with the office as they were unable to secure him any accommodation in a Park Lane hotel. He wanted me to show them up. I placed a call to the Intercontinental Hotel, Park Lane, as I had many dealings with them in the past and knew some of the key personnel well. Of course after Princess Munira's recent visit and the constant sounding of the fire alarms, how could they forget me! Within minutes, I managed to book the necessary rooms and called the prince in Saudi Arabia. I then called the SANG office in London and arranged to meet their manager on the day of the prince's arrival. I told them I had booked rooms for him at the Intercontinental Hotel. They were not impressed with me and were rude—but I was a big boy with wide shoulders, so I could take it.

Two days later, at four in the morning, I arrived at the office and was invited in. A brusque man, the manager, showed me through to a waiting room. I picked up a newspaper. The green and white Al-Sharq Al-Awsat newspaper was a familiar daily paper I'd often seen. On the front page, I noticed a picture of King Fahd—and that someone had gouged out his eyes.

Embarrassing the office further, I pointed out the picture and said it surprised me that visitors to the office could view a newspaper in that condition. The manager grabbed the paper and ripped it up. Before we got to the car, he asked, "What is the prince like?"

Seizing the opportunity, I said, "He is strict and does not suffer fools gladly." I added for good measure, "He's also upset the office did not secure the hotel for him."

136

Silence reigned during the journey to Heathrow. Due to the prince's new position, we found ourselves being escorted to the door of the aircraft to greet him. As he walked through to meet us, the prince leant forward, signalling for me to kiss him on both cheeks.

This was the only time he did this and I knew he was making a statement to the SANG manager. He then passed me his briefcase and only then did he respond to the manager. Feeling uneasy, I made my way through the airport with the prince. I knew his .38 snub-nose Smith and Wesson revolver was in his briefcase. This was illegal and yet should he be arrested in possession of a firearm, he would simply claim diplomatic immunity and walk free. Now it was in my possession, should I be arrested, I would be looking at a long jail sentence. I was really uncomfortable being placed in this position. As much as I wanted to hand him back his briefcase, I couldn't, as it would cause him offence and embarrassment in front of the SANG manager. I would just plead ignorance and hope for the best as I always did when placed in this type of situation.

Once he settled at the hotel he asked me to call Sue, my wife. He said he planned to visit her in a couple of days and asked that she bake a cake. This was a surprise to me and no doubt to her too. Sue was put out by his assumption that she would bake a cake for him. In fact, I had a hell of a job persuading her to allow him just to visit. She had her sister bake a cake and bitterly resented the intrusion of the prince coming to call. She felt the Saudis intruded on our family life too much already without them coming into our home as well. There was only one reason she met him and that was for me.

The following morning, we wandered down to the lobby to visit the Cartier shop. Prince Mishari told me he was going to visit his aunt in the afternoon and wanted to choose a watch for her. I knew what he was up to, and, knowing which colour Sue would prefer, I made the choice. The afternoon visit to his aunt never happened, but the next day the prince, his driver and I set off to my home. Once we arrived, I invited them both inside but the prince sent the driver off to refuel the car. As I introduced Prince Mishari to Sue, I could see him eyeing her up. Was no one off limit, I wondered? The prince was soon presented with a cup of tea and a big slice of the cake he'd requested. Complimenting my wife on the cake, she said her sister had baked it for her. The prince said he was disappointed, but gave her the Cartier watch he'd bought the previous day. Prince Mishari laid on the charm and gently flirted with her; even I had to admit he was a charmer and knew how to play the game.

As we walked down Bond Street the next day the prince decided to play the game once more. Looking through a shoe shop window, he noticed a pretty young woman. He told me to wait outside while he disappeared inside to charm her. Half an hour later, he emerged with a £500 pair of handmade shoes and nothing else. Prince Mishari was forever chasing after the girls and I lost count of how many he had sex with. He preferred not to pay for sex, but if that were the only option, he would do so.

In the evening, as we prepared to go out, the prince asked me to knot his tie for him. Then I made a prat of myself as he asked me to scrape the bottoms of his new shoes so he would not slip when wearing them. Scraping away at one of the soles I tried to take away the shine. Horrified, he asked what I was doing and I said, "Scraping the soles of your shoes as you asked."

He picked up the other shoe and said, "Not like that, like this."

I watched what he did and said "That's scoring the bottoms, not scraping them." I did not have the heart to look at his shoes that evening and never knew if he ever wore them.

A week or so later, departure day arrived and we set off to the airport. The SANG manager officially bid farewell to the prince. As he left, he said he would see me soon; I inwardly admitted that I was sorry to see him go.

* * *

Marbella, Spain: Midsummer 1984

Casting my eyes round Malaga Airport, I thought, 'it's déjà vu. Looking at the flight arrivals monitor, I saw they were clearing customs. Minutes later, Princess al-Anud and her children (now two of them—a boy and a girl) would walk into the arrivals hall, but Prince Mishari's duties held him up in Saudi Arabia.

Time had flown by since I'd last seen the family. During that time, I had spoken several times with the prince, and he often asked me to send some item or other over to him. Not being on a retainer for the family, though, I worked as usual with other members of the royal family to supplement my income.

As I waited, I recalled how the prince had asked me to get a prescription from my doctor for Zovirax. At the appointment, I'd asked for a prescription for the medicine.

"Mark, I wasn't aware you suffered from herpes," the doctor said, and I had to admit neither was I. I found myself explaining the telephone conversation with Prince Mishari the previous day. The doctor would not give me a national health prescription but he was happy to give me a private prescription, which meant the prince would have to pay for the medicine.

I called the prince and told him, "I'm not too happy, as I was almost diagnosed with herpes." This did not concern him in the slightest. However, when I said, "I have to pay privately for the medicine," that concerned him. I believe the prince felt I was cheating him of the money for the Zovirax!

As I watched the family enter the arrivals hall, I noticed that Turki had grown and was more unruly than before—while Princess al-Anud, as ever, looked like a fashion model. The staff wandered along behind her. Elena and Joha had their hands full as they took care of Turki. Porters brought up the rear with several trolleys piled high with Luis Vuitton luggage. Looking over to the driver of the luggage truck, I signalled him to take care of the baggage, relieving me of one less hassle, and allowing me to concentrate fully on the family.

I had the family's new maroon Mercedes waiting, as well as the Audi 200 Turbo in which the staff would travel, with a driver hired for the purpose. The staff sorted themselves out behind us, but as soon as I had the principals on board the Mercedes, I was away.

Once back at Casa Tam, the family entered the villa and prepared to settle in. The children never took much notice of where they were; they just got on with the business of playing and doing the things that children do.

Within hours, I noticed the princess was keeping a tight rein on the finances—something that ended up giving me trouble throughout the visit.

A couple of days later, Prince Mishari arrived. I picked him up and instead of going to see his family, he told me to go to Puerto Banus. I dropped him at the main gate and parked in the new car park. After an hour, the prince asked me to fetch the car. As I approached the barrier, I opened my bag to find I didn't have enough money to get out. I had to go back to the prince and ask for money to pay the car park fee. He wasn't amused and laid the blame squarely at my feet. I explained that the princess wouldn't give me money to pay the bills but he just shrugged it off.

Over the next few weeks, I would repeatedly be embarrassed as I asked for money to pay even the smallest of bills, such as the dry cleaning. The cars hit the red lights on their fuel gauges before she'd provide the money to refuel them. Even the chef at the villa left because he said he couldn't prepare meals on the allowance they gave him. Prince Mishari asked me to drop my salary and like a fool I agreed, dropping it 30%. Two years later I asked for a salary increase. He said no, as he was going through a rough patch financially. The staff told me he was having a new palace built in Saudi Arabia, so I suppose he was suffering to some extent! I was dumbfounded at the way they took the piss, though. After taking up his position in the National Guard the prince's income increased dramatically. I felt sorry for him as he vacationed in his multi-million dollar villa and drove around in his Ferrari crying poverty. What a load of bollocks.

Shortly after the chef left, Turki's swimming instructor left too. He couldn't put up with Turki ignoring his instructions, nor the boy's continual crying and playing up. Elena had tried her best to soothe Turki, but it became too much for the instructor who called him a brat as he waved goodbye and drove off into the sunset. The trip, I thought, had the makings of a disaster written all over it.

The Spanish National Police, who provided the static security, complained about various issues, too—something unheard-of previously. Then one afternoon as I waited at the villa, a call came in from Elena. I lifted the telephone receiver and she asked me, "Is Turki there with you?"

"No."

"We've lost him, but don't tell Princess al-Anud," she said.

I replaced the receiver, my head spinning as I made my way to the princess. I had to tell her. Climbing the marble stairs, I composed myself ready to break the news. I found her lying on a sofa, and as I announced my arrival, she sat bolt upright. I knew I had broken the rules by going into her suite, but the severity of the situation overtook etiquette for the moment.

Kneeling on the floor beside her, I broke the news as softly as I could: "Your Highness, Elena called and said they've mislaid Turki."

Mislaid? I heard myself saying, mislaid? They had lost him, he was missing—mislaid didn't sound right somehow. I told her I would leave immediately and said, "Don't worry, I'll bring him back." Whether I would, I didn't know—but it was the best I could offer her at that moment. Princess al-Anud was having none of it and told me to prepare the car, as she would be going with me.

We set off briskly towards the main road from the villa. Just as we reached the junction, the Audi turned into El Vicario. Joha sat in the driver's seat and smiled at us. They had found Turki—and a whole lot of trouble too, though, which would shortly be bestowed on them by the princess.

My duties changed that day. I now became responsible for the safety and security of the children, too. A few days later, Princess al-Anud asked me, "Mark, how much money does Turki spend in the afternoon at the arcade?"

"Including the machines, drinks and ice creams that he the nannies and Hala consume, it's around five thousand pesetas," I said. This worked out to around $40, and it horrified her.

I said, "The machines use money quickly and once Turki gets on them, you can never get him away from them," thinking of the times we'd spent close to four hours at the arcade and it drove me nuts.

Princess al-Anud took 2000 pesetas off his afternoon allowance and told Turki he could only spend 3000 pesetas a day—and that when it was gone, he had to come home.

* * *

I'd hoped to spend more time with Prince Mishari during this job, but it wasn't to be. My duties now included working with the children, so I was always busy. I never accompanied the prince to visit his brothers any more, and it became obvious that my working relationship with the prince was doomed.

In the mornings, I conducted any business the prince had set me. About three in the afternoon, Turki, Hala, Elena, Hudda and I would go off to the town centre amusement arcades. Princess al-Anud usually then caught up with us there at five to five-thirty, and by six to seven in the evening we'd be back at Casa Tam. From about nine in the evening we went to Puerto Banus where the family, minus Hala, would have dinner. Often Turki fell asleep at the table and I would have to take him home. Hala would stay with her nanny, Hudda, and a Nubian woman called Zeinob. After dropping Turki off, I usually had to drive back to Puerto Banus to meet the prince and princess. As a result, I rushed everywhere trying to keep the whole show together.

Then one day, one of Prince Mishari's sisters arrived. Her name was Princess Sita and she booked herself into the Puente Romano hotel just across the street from Casa Tam. Her suite was close to 'Regine's'—the discotheque where the prince and princess spent many late nights. Prince Mishari had often entertained several young women there and was nearly caught doing so a few times. Even so, it seemed I was the one who always got in trouble, while the prince came up smelling of roses. The following evening would see me in trouble once again—and in a highly dangerous situation, too.

Prince Mishari called me to the main doors of Casa Tam and said, "Princess al-Anud is waiting at Princess Sita's suite. Go to her and say I sent you, wait with them there and I'll follow you shortly."

I knocked on the suite door, and a Filipino maid slowly opened it. Princess Sita was standing behind her. She motioned me in and said, "You can sit down and wait in here."

Accepting her gracious offer, I entered and sat on a sofa in the lounge. Princess Sita asked, "Would you like a drink?"

"Yes, please, Your Highness. A Coke would be fine." Her maid went to the fridge and brought me a can and I thanked her. I listened to Princess Sita and Princess al-Anud as they chatted. Then, hearing a knock on the door, I went over to open it. Prince Mishari stood just outside the door—and when he saw me, his facial expression changed. "What are you doing in here?" he asked.

"Waiting for you as you asked me to."

"Wait in the car," he said.

I hotfooted it away and as the suite door closed behind him, I could hear him shouting at the princesses. He was telling them off for letting me into the suite. I laughed, acknowledging the double standards Prince Mishari used, just like all the Saudi royals, females included.

Ten minutes or so later Prince Mishari, Princess Sita, and Princess al-Anud emerged from the suite. Each one of them smiled, obviously disguising the earlier upset. Setting off for Puerto Banus, I was in a jovial mood, as for once I knew that they were all pissed off and I wasn't. After parking the car, I escorted the principals to the restaurant where they were meeting with other family members. After that we made our way over to Ra-Ra's nightclub where we stayed until one in the morning. After leaving the nightclub, I took both princesses and Prince Mishari back to the villa in El Vicario. As the principals debussed, I thought that I was finished for the night, but I was soon proved wrong.

Before entering the main doors of the villa, Prince Mishari turned to me and said, "When Princess Sita comes out, I want you to escort her back to the hotel." I acknowledged his command with a nod of my head as inwardly I cussed to myself, pissed off that I had to suffer yet another late night.

I went to my room and called over one of the police officers who was on a static duty.

"Pablo, when Princess Sita comes out will you let me know?" I said.

"Yes, no problem," he said, in English.

I entered my room, took off my shoes, and then lay down on my bed. It only seemed a moment before the dreaded knock came on the door. Glancing at my watch, I saw it had not been half an hour since we got back. I walked over to the car and smiled at Princess Sita as I opened the door for her. Once she settled herself inside, I closed the door.

Would I survive the long drive back to her hotel? I wondered. After all, it was at most two hundred yards from door-to-door. Two minutes later, I rung the doorbell to her suite and waited for an answer from her maid. As the door opened, Princess Sita stepped inside and said to me, "Please come in; I want to talk to you." Following her, I wondered what her dear brother would make of this.

"Would you like a drink?"

This was déjà vu, I thought, as I said, "A Coke would be fine." The Filipino maid brought me a Coke and delivered a smile with it, too.

I took a sip from the glass and Princess Sita said, "I will just be a moment," and went off to her bedroom. Reading the Filipino maid's expression, I knew I had entered the lioness's den, and was soon proved right. Princess Sita returned dressed in a fine white lace negligee. Looking at both Princess Sita and her maid, I wondered if this were a common event—would I be their latest victim?

I felt as though I was being drawn into the spider's web. Nonetheless, I was enjoying the newfound attention I was receiving. I had flirted with many Saudi princesses. This time, I was left in no doubt where Princess Sita was heading: she was heading for her bedroom and she intended taking me with her. When she sent her maid to the room they rented next door, my suspicions were confirmed.

"Does it bother you being here alone with me after Prince Mishari's outburst earlier?"

"No, should it?" I replied.

"Aren't you worried at all about what they would do to you if they found you here alone with me?"

The princess was obviously more knowledgeable about these things than I was at that time. I naively replied, "I'm a big boy now and can look after myself."

"Do you like my negligee? I don't suppose you have seen a princess in a negligee before have you?" She said laughing.

"No, I have to say it is a first for me but I've seen a number of princesses in bathing suits before. Some of them looked pretty good, too, from what I could see," I said, smiling at her.

The next half hour or so was spent flirting as I pondered what my options were. Before I had the chance to contemplate any further, I was stunned as the princess asked, "Would you like to stay the night with me?"

I knew right then that I needed to take my leave. Thanking her for her hospitality, I stood up, and dumbfounded, she stood too. I leant forward and placed a soft and gentle kiss on her cheek. I opened the door and bid her goodnight, pulling the door closed behind me as I left. Stealthily, I made my way back to the car, making my escape from this highly charged temptress. My mind-set was to do the 'right thing' by both my wife and the royal family, which in this case was to run away. Princess Sita never spoke to me again. Driving back to the villa, I laughed aloud at the absurdity of the night's events. Looking back now, I think perhaps I should have fucked her in return for all the times the Saudi royal family fucked me!

* * *

The following evening, I stood next to Prince Mishari in Regine's discotheque after we'd gate crashed a private party. The prince spoke to Philippe Junot (the ex-husband of Princess Caroline of Monaco) as I noticed a deeply tanned, scrawny man to my right. He looked vaguely familiar, and was surrounded by a bevy of beautiful girls. He opened his mouth and smiled, whereupon I was nearly blinded, as his bright white teeth appeared to illuminate the dance floor. Now I recognised him as the singer Julio Iglesias, whose party it was. A little later, I chatted to one of his companions who told me the girls surrounding the Spanish crooner had been supplied by a local modelling agency at a cost, to make him look good. After the night's entertainment, I escorted Prince Mishari towards the exit of the nightclub. Passing by the club manager, I slipped him the 5000 pesetas I always gave him as we left. At the door, I passed across 1000 pesetas each to the doormen, a tip for allowing us entry. This time Prince Mishari noticed me giving it to them and said, "Why are you giving them money?"

"I always tip them because we never pay entry fees or queue up outside. Also, when there are private parties they always let us in".

"In the future, you don't give anyone any money unless I tell you to, do you understand?"

"Yes, I understand you clearly," I said, thinking to myself, you tight bastard!

Over the next two visits to Regine's, I paid nothing out and on the third visit, we were denied entry with the excuse that a private party was being held. As we turned away the prince felt belittled by the snub and said, "What is wrong with them? You must have upset them, what have you done?"

"It's because you stopped me from tipping them," I said.

"No it's not, it's because you've upset them." No way would the Prince accept responsibility for his actions. You just couldn't win with this lot, I thought, as I took the dressing down he meted out.

As soon as I arrived back at the villa I learned that Jose, the house manager, had been sacked. This had come as no surprise to me as Aurora the housekeeper and her husband Diego kept sniping about him to the principals. They had been told Jose had been taking commissions on the cash he had been given to pay various bills, and from then on, it had only been a matter of time before he got the chop. The Saudi royals creamed off huge commissions but if anyone around them did so, they were dead meat. I wondered if I were next on the list as their vacation drew to a close. It was the last week of September as I bid them farewell at Malaga airport.

Before leaving, Prince Mishari asked if I would like to visit them in Saudi Arabia in January. "I would like that," I said. "Good, then I will arrange it and call you."

Chapter 17

The McCartney's: November 1984

After Prince Mishari left, I received a call from Cameron, a colleague who had served in the Special Investigations Branch of the Royal Military Police. He was on assignment with a singer named Paul Young who he said wanted to learn Karate.

Cameron asked if I could teach Paul Young while he stayed on Jersey in the Channel Islands. I passed on the offer but as a favour to Cameron, I checked out the instructors on the island. I suggested Peter Dennis, an excellent *Ishinryu* instructor of the style developed by 'Ticky' Donovan. I had been loath to work with any celebrity before, as I heard too many stories about their egos and temperaments. In truth, I also felt working with them would lower my status in the business. In retrospect, I should have been examining my own ego because of my prejudice against working with celebrities.

Therefore, it was out of character for me when I accepted a job with Sir Paul McCartney and his wife Linda on the 20th November 1984. This assignment, however, could be exciting and potentially dangerous: a kidnap threat had been made against Linda McCartney, and the family took it seriously. Their security was upgraded and the security guys were also given the use of a nearby hotel.

I arrived at their farm and parked across the lane leading to the farmhouse, effectively blocking any access to the property. I didn't expect anyone to come out, with a high status alert in place. However, as one of the guys, briefed me, a tatty-looking beige mini estate car drove up from the farmhouse. The driver tooted his horn and I looked at him—it was Paul McCartney, and his wife, Linda. Two of their children sat in the back seats. I moved my car. I was told they took the kids to school every morning. It would have been handy if I'd known that fact a little bit earlier, I thought.

Something seemed awry to me. This wasn't the behaviour I expected from the principals. They were too comfortable, too relaxed for my liking. I felt something wasn't right about this assignment. Even so, I erased those thoughts from my mind and concentrated on doing the job particularly as the threat was by now leaked to the press. Within hours we found the newspaper reporters circling the farmhouse. It appeared to me that they weren't interested in how the threat would pan out so long as they got a story—any story.

Call me cynical, but the thoughts of a stunt re-appeared as it appeared convenient that the threat lead to heightened publicity just as the English premiere of Paul McCartney's movie, *Give My Regards To Broad Street* was about to be screened. Five days after starting the assignment we found ourselves preparing for these showings. They would take place on successive evenings, first in Liverpool (Paul's home town), and then in Leicester Square, London. On Wednesday 28th November 1984 we guarded Paul and Linda as he received the Freedom of the City honours at the Picton Library in Liverpool. Later that evening we watched over them as his movie was premiered in the city's Odeon Cinema.

Outside the Empire theatre in Leicester Square, London on 29th November 1984, I stood waiting for Paul and Linda's limousine to arrive and watched the fans standing behind the crash barriers. There was a large police presence around the square, too. Their Mercedes with the registration number MPL 500 pulled into the square. I walked by the door nearest me and secured it.

As I escorted Paul into the theatre, he chatted with me. He relished the scene, yet was concerned his guests would not enjoy themselves. During the screening, I stood close to the principals. The movie was well made but none of us guys could understand what it was about. We dismissed it as a vanity project.

After the premiere, on that cold Thursday night, we escorted Paul and Linda to a buffet arranged at a hotel afterwards. They had also arranged for their local community members to attend the premiere and the buffet in London, too, if they so wished. At the buffet we were given badges, brochures, programmes of the film and other paraphernalia. I gave them to my kids. All they said was, "Who's Paul McCartney?"

The next morning we were back at the farm and life carried on as usual as Paul went for his morning run along the country lanes alone. I again had serious doubts about the whole affair. The locals saw Paul and his family in the community regularly and were respectful of their privacy. What's more, should anyone outside the community ask questions about the McCartney's, word would soon get back to them. The whole kidnap threat quickly quietened down after the premieres, which once again raised my suspicions. Perhaps it was a publicity stunt—it all seemed a little too convenient for my liking. After the premieres, the kidnap threat disappeared into thin air along with the movie as it flopped on the big screen. However, there was an upside to the whole affair as the soundtrack to the movie sold really well!

As a member of the team on duty at that time, I can categorically state that we were told the kidnap threat was in force at the time of the movie's release, and when the story was published by the English newspapers. However, two reports give different years for the plot: *Blackbird: The Unauthorised Biography Of Paul McCartney*, written by Geoffrey Giuliano and Dennis Laine reports that:

> Life in the passing lane has not always been easy, and in 1983 this unhappy truth was brought all too close to home with the uncovering of a deadly serious plot to kidnap Linda from the McCartney's' Sussex home and hold her for $12.5 million ransom. It was masterminded by former Brit soldier ***** ******, who, along with two additional unnamed co-conspirators, planned to snatch Paul's unsuspecting missus in a Rambo-style military raid on the McCartney compound. Said to have spent the better part of a week stalking the famous pair, ****** had intended, after the abduction, to hold Linda at a remote farmhouse until the always tricky transfer of funds could be accomplished. "I could have done it easily," he later bragged to London's Sun, "despite McCartney's state-of-the-art security measures." Fortunately, the would-be kidnappers never got the chance, foiled by local

149

cops before they could make their big move. A McCartney spokesman would say only that too much was being made of the affair, noting that by the time the story reached the attention of the media, the incident was already more than a year old. (p. 266; NB: I've removed the alleged suspect's name from this excerpt, as there is no evidence to support the authors' claim of that person's involvement in the plan.)

In contrast, this is the entry under the title "Paul McCartney Job, The" by Bill Harry in *The Paul McCartney Encyclopedia*:

The name by which the Newhaven CID referred to the 1984 plot to kidnap Linda McCartney. Detectives said that they had uncovered a kidnap plot in which Linda was to be snatched in a military-style operation on a country lane near the Sussex farm. The kidnappers intended to hold her hostage in a woodland lair and demand $12.5million ransom. Paul was reluctant to discuss the matter, commenting; "Any talk of a kidnap plot is bound to give ideas to all sorts of nutters." (p. 28)

I had to put my hand on my heart and admit to myself that I had enjoyed my outing with these particular celebrities. True I had found Paul to be both vain and egotistical, but then I suppose he had every right to be that way. The only episode which caused me a short pang of anxiety during the course of the job, was when Paul and Linda decided to have a blazing row. As I and one other guy stood by the entrance to the property, loud screams and shouts echoed up the driveway from the direction of the farmhouse. Concerned that an intruder may have gained entry, I went to make my way to the house. I had felt a tug on my arm as my colleague held me back and laughed. He told me to settle down as this was a regular occurrence. Paul and Linda, it was said, had a very volatile and vociferous relationship. Nonetheless, I had been pleasantly surprised working for them. I would have liked to continue working with the agency that had supplied us but very soon afterwards and for no explicable reason it closed down. Unfortunately, for the time being that sent me right back into the hands of the Saudis once again.

* * *

December 1984

On a Saturday evening in mid December 1984, I arrived at 2 Bolney Gate, Knightsbridge and the house manager, greeted me. I had worked with the staff at this house often and they knew me well and so this lent itself to a comfortable working environment. King Fahd's second son, Prince Mohammed Bin Fahd, (Assistant Minister of the Interior but soon to become the Governor of the Eastern Province) and Prince Saud Bin Naïf, (son of the Interior Minister, Prince Naïf Bin Abdul Aziz), were expected within the hour. This was just another one of their many stopovers to the UK. I worked for them many times, and was once again called in by the office.

As I sorted myself out in the lobby area, I recalled how I had noticed in 1982 a copy of a House of Commons Question Time paper from Jonathan Aitken, Member of Parliament, left lying on a coffee table. I had picked it up and looked at several questions marked with a highlighter pen. It became clear from the paper that Aitken had asked those questions in the House of Commons on King Fahd's behalf. Clearly, the King had put forward a Peace Plan for the Palestinian problem in the Middle East, and the questions put forward related to that Peace Plan. Aitken had left the paper for the prince to peruse after his arrival. It had not come as any surprise to me as it was well known that Aitken had become King Fahd's spokesperson in our House of Commons then.

In 1982 King Fahd had made a proactive move towards an Arab-Israeli solution by proposing a peace plan which for the first time recognised Israel's right to exist provided certain conditions were met. Sir John Wilton's report on the Fahd Plan to the House of Commons on 31 March 1982 proves that the UK government was well aware of Saudi Arabia's economic power and how its loyalties could change in volatile times. The Wilton report described Saudi Arabia as a stabilising force, which to a large extent it was, but also warned against complacency: at the moment the Saudis were anti-Communist, yet, like the Syrians, they might be pushed into revising their policies and turning to the Soviet Union if neither the UK nor the US put effective pressure on Israel. Supplying Saudi Arabia with weapons would show the UK's support of an Arab state which was publicly and financially committed to the Palestinian cause, and therefore indirectly of the Palestinians. This support would be a guarantee of oil.

(Source: Campaign Against Arms Trade, **http://www.caat.org.uk**)

Shortly after my arrival, I heard the sounds of the motorcade pulling up outside. I opened the door wide and stepped out to greet the princes. With their usual aloofness they just brushed on by, but as he passed, I recalled that various princesses had commented to me that they found Prince Mohammed attractive. He was tall, about six feet three inches, had coiffed brushed back black hair, and was well-built, but not fat, and he exuded class. In the house, he always wore his *thobe,* but outside he was always immaculately dressed.

Prince Saud Bin Naïf entered the house close behind Prince Mohammed. I was well aware that the princes were business partners and had a trading company with offices throughout the world. The managing director of their London office, Al Bilad (UK) was Jonathan Aitken, MP. Prince Saud also had another company setup called SNAS—the initials stood for Saud Naïf Al Saud, his name.

These two princes were close to the top, if not at the top, of the list of the greediest and most corrupt people in Saudi Arabia. They involved themselves in crooked deals the world over. In Britain, they had illegally bought a major shareholding in TV AM and then put Jonathan Aitken, in as their front man. When the Saudi involvement became known, they had to sell their shares in the television station. Prince Mohammed, Fahd Al Athel, Said Ayas and some other of his companions had then bought Inglewood health farm near Newbury in Berkshire, and Jonathan Aitken became ensconced as a director there too.

As I worked for this lot I kept my eyes and ears wide open, I enjoyed the intrigue and all the dodgy dealings they got up to; it gave me something to think about as I whiled away the hours waiting at one of the various houses they owned.

While the princes settled in, I caught up on the gossip with the prince's drivers and aides, Jeff and Gerry. It appeared from what they said that Prince Mohammed had upset the Americans over a contract he had just secured. The prince had, according to the Americans, 'stolen' the contract to supply the telephone communications system throughout Saudi Arabia. The contract's value in December 1984 was an unbelievable $10 billion! Gerry had laughed as he told me America had sent a special envoy to meet the King with the intent of securing the contract. Somehow, Prince Mohammed had heard the envoy was on his way and had used his position to have the Minister responsible for the contract woken up. He got the Minister to sign the contract in Prince Mohammed's favour, which meant when the special envoy arrived, it was too late. The contract was lost and the King was saved from an embarrassing political situation. Coincidentally, of course, neither the King nor the Crown Prince was available to receive the American Ambassador, William Porter. Even though Prince Mohammed had secured the telephone contract, other parties had put in lower tenders. Whenever these parties then tried to lodge a complaint with the prince, he was never available. The commission taken by Prince Mohammed on this deal alone was around $1.3 billion. There was also a considerable additional commission on the continuing maintenance contracts.

Jeff and Gerry then went on to speak about a sting that Prince Mohammed had set up. It involved a 'Japanese' company called Petromonde. The company bought oil from Aramco and sold it on at a profit. The twist in this deal was there was no buyer—the so-called Japanese company was part of Prince Mohammed's group, Al Bilad. This sting alone brought the prince in around $11 million a month for more than a year.

153

It was at this point that there was a knock on the front door. I stepped forward and peered through the spy hole in the door. I was greeted by the face of Jonathan Aitken. I opened the door and welcomed him. After a casual acknowledgment he brushed pass me in the same way as the princes had done, some forty-five minutes or so before. I smile as I recall how every time I saw Jonathan Aitken near the prince, he seemed so subservient—he seemed like just another puppet whose strings the prince pulled at will. At least this small thought made me feel better. However, it was widely known that Aitken's position with the prince and the British government would prove invaluable to them both.

I sat down with Jeff and Gerry again and we started to talk about the time at 'Cleve Lodge', Prince Saud Bin Naïf's house, when Jonathan Aitken had told us guys to buy shares in a company called BMARC. As we chatted Cliff Garlick's name cropped up. Cliff had been Aitken's driver at the time and had once shown us the deeds of an apartment, which Aitken had told him to give to a former TV AM presenter. We knew that Aitken had been having an affair with her, and it had run its course. This apartment was allegedly a pay off. Aitken's arrival had seen a shift in our conversation and I mentioned about the first time Aitken had come to my attention when I worked with Prince Talal Bin Abdul Aziz, a friend of Adnan Khashoggi, the arms dealer. Aitken had an affair with Khashoggi's wife, Soraya, and their liaisons had not gone unnoticed. Aitken had a reputation as a lady-killer: he stood about six feet two inches in height, had dark hair, and was athletic in build. After his arrival all we had to do was wait and see what developed.

Chapter 18

Gun Incident

A couple of hours or so after the princes' arrival, word came down that Jeff and Gerry could go as the princes were going to stay home. Another hour or so after business discussions, Jonathan Aitken, Fahd Al Athel, Said Ayas, Jamal Izzat, Peter Custer and Roger Kraillion left. I closed the door behind them and turned around. Directly in front of me was the lift door, and a large mirror covered it. I smiled, seeing in my mind's eye Prince Saud checking himself out in the mirror—he was vain, too. Oh well, I thought, and followed Prince Saud's lead and checked myself out.

If this mirror could speak, I thought... and recalled watching in disbelief as a Special Branch police officer practised drawing and holstering his weapon in front of it one time.

As if that wasn't bad enough, I'd opened the door one morning to the paperboy, who suddenly looked pale and frozen. I caught sight of a revolver over my right shoulder: the Special Branch officer was pointing his gun at the boy! No wonder the kid looked shocked—I was shocked too. I complained about this, and got an apology.

The officer's nickname was Mad Mick. He was the only officer who volunteered for duty in Northern Ireland. Why the authorities still kept such a liability on the force, I'll never know. I never heard if Mad Mick or the force apologised to the poor unfortunate paperboy.

The following morning, Sunday 16th December, 1984, there was a knock at the door. I opened it to Jeff, who had brought Mike Le Havre with him—a car dealer who specialised in rare cars. Many of the princes knew Mike, and many bought cars from him over the years. Prince Mohammed was a particularly avid car collector. His collection numbered over one hundred cars, kept in an underground car park at one of his estates in the south of France.

I looked at the cars Mike had brought. One was an original AC Cobra, the other was a 1966 Corvette Stingray Coupé. The prince was going to try them out, but I knew there was no chance of him buying me one. The prince came down from the lounge, and I followed him outside. He walked around the two cars, examining them meticulously. Then he jumped into the Corvette and sped off. Scorched rubber lined the road and the car snaked from side to side as he accelerated away.

He tried both cars, got out and walked back into the house. Mike asked Jeff what the prince thought of the cars; Jeff said the prince would call him shortly. He bought the Corvette. He couldn't get on with the Cobra, as he wasn't able to change gear in it. Prince Mohammed had only just had a Mercedes 450 SEL 6.9 stripped down and sent out to his collection in large crates. I recalled admiring an unusual car, bought as a present for the prince by one of his friends. It was a Panther Rio, and although I was familiar with the Panther marque, it wasn't a model I'd seen before. It looked like a miniature Rolls Royce Silver Shadow.

A little later that day Jamal Izzat, a strange fellow of Syrian extraction, arrived at the house. He always dressed like an English gentleman, and had the habit of calling me by my surname.

His hair was thin on top, but long and straggly at the back and sides. He wore gold-rimmed glasses and a gold pocket watch with the chain running from one pocket to the other on his waistcoat. He knew many people, and this had endeared him to the prince and his circle. He was a Mr. Fix–It, and had sorted out a variety of problems for the prince. He was friendly with Bill, at the office, who had introduced him to Freemasonry.

That evening the princes went out for dinner and then paid a visit to the Knightsbridge casino. They visited various casinos—the Ritz, Aspinalls, the Playboy and the Victoria Sporting club among them. The princes were 'fair-weather Muslims': I met many of them over the years, and only ever found four whom I considered good Muslims. Most of the royal family moved the goalposts when it suited them.

At the Knightsbridge casino, Prince Mohammed went to the toilet, screamed, ran out of the casino, and jumped into his car. As he ran past Prince Saud, he'd shouted at him to call a doctor.

Bolney Gate was less than two minutes from the casino. Prince Mohammed leapt from his Rolls Royce, screeched into the house and ran upstairs, shouting at me to get a doctor NOW!

A second or two later, Prince Saud and the panic-stricken entourage followed.

One of the drivers had called the police and asked for the telephone number of a local doctor. Of course, once he gave our address, it was red flagged as belonging to King Fahd. Within minutes, we had not two, but *three* doctors on scene. Two of them were upset at being disturbed for what they saw as nothing, but they became a lot happier once they were paid off.

As I stood near the open front door with Jeff and Gerry, there was one hell of a commotion going on upstairs. Two police cars arrived with sirens and blue lights flashing. The cavalry arrived and a Chief Inspector made his way to the door. He said it was normal practice for them to attend the scene after a doctor was called through them. I assured the officer that everything was fine. Nonetheless, he asked to enter the house so he could speak with the prince.

I denied him access. A discussion followed. They left, as did the doctor shortly thereafter. What all the fuss had been about, I wondered.

It turned out that when Prince Mohammed went to the toilet, he'd peed blood and panicked. The doctor diagnosed a sexually transmitted disease and injected him with antibiotics. The prince lived to see another day, although it wasn't about to teach him a lesson.

* * *

Prince Mohammed, Prince Saud and their entourage only stayed a short time on this occasion, and then set off for Santa Barbara, in America. They would be in the states for a week or so and then return to the United Kingdom. I therefore had a break and used the time off to chill out before their return.

157

On Saturday 29th December 1984, Prince Mohammed and Prince Saud flew back into London. After the princes passed by, their aides followed, and I noted how each of them were worth a fortune in their own right. It was quite surreal as despite their wealth they were just members of the prince's staff. One was more than friendly with Jonathan Aitken. His name was (Mohammed) Said Ayas, whom we nicknamed Midas, as everything he touched turned to gold. He was Prince Mohammed's secretary, a Mr Fix-It.

Each evening, the princes would go to the Al Bilad office, which was in South Audley Street, Mayfair. Invariably, Aitken was there too. He used the office and the facilities as his own, and there were many other benefits for him as a director of Al Bilad. Equally, he was a valuable asset for the princes, and they made sure they got their money's worth out of him.

From the office, we went to dinner at Le Gavroche in Upper Brook Street, Mayfair. Then we went on to the Ritz Casino in Piccadilly. I wasn't a gambler, but I enjoyed the atmosphere. While they gambled, I wondered what Prince Mohammed would say if he knew that I'd been the person who had been instrumental in saving the life of his older brother, Prince Faisal. Thinking about it, I don't suppose he would care one way or the other!

I knew, however, that he would never find out. I wasn't about to tell him, and I was sure Martini wouldn't tell him either. When Prince Faisal had overdosed my actions were simply taking care of business. If it becomes necessary to protect the principals—even from themselves—then I feel it my duty to do so.

Both princes enjoyed their gambling, even though it was against their religion. Then again, almost everything they did was against Islam. Islam is a complete way of life, not a Sunday religion, only they forgot to tell the Saudi royals that. One of the group, Sheikh Enany, dropped $11 million trying to break the bank in Monte Carlo. Some years later authorities in Germany would investigate claims by a businessman that he was approached by Sheik Enany, seeking to procure missiles and potentially dangerous substances for associates of Osama bin Laden.

On the 3rd January 1985, Prince Mohammed and Prince Saud left for Geneva. They were trying to tie up another arms deal. On the

Sunday, the 6th January, they returned from their jaunt. This time, instead of staying at Bolney Gate, they set up in Prince Mohammed's house in Winnington Road. This place backed on to his father, King Fahd's house, Kenstead Hall in Bishops Avenue, Hampstead. As the princes were in a party mood, I thought they must have secured their deal. Either way, it was party time. Jonathan Aitken arrived with some hookers; then, shortly afterwards, another young woman turned up with her friend. I sensed there was something distinctly different about these two. While they waited, they sat talking with me. The first girl said she had slept with Arabs for money before; the second young woman had not. In fact, she had not slept with anyone for money before. She had just split up with her boyfriend and was on the rebound. She had only come with her friend because she told her that a party would cheer her up.

Her problems started when one of the Arabs, Prince Saud, fancied her. She changed her mind and wanted to leave, but her friend tried to pressure her into having sex with him. She was insistent, she did not want to. Her so-called friend applied more pressure.

Of course, it was all just emotional blackmail; she bombarded the poor girl and she did not know what to do. She asked for my advice even though it was none of my business.

But I had to do it: I opened my big mouth. My advice was for her to let me call a taxi and get well away from the house. I tried to help her because she was vulnerable: being on the rebound, she didn't need this to deal with.

Meanwhile, her friend continued—"Think of the money; think that you would have slept with a prince; think how you would get your own back on your boyfriend"— and on and on it went: "I'm your friend—it will look bad for me, just do it for me."

What a sorry state of affairs it was becoming. The poor woman was worn down over time, and finally succumbed to the prince. This made him happy—he knew she wasn't a prostitute and it made the whole affair sweeter. When she emerged, she sat next to me and cried. She was distraught; she was asking how she could live with herself after what she had just done. There was nothing I could do or say—it's at times like these that these people piss you off. She had

159

enough to cope with before, and now she sat and sobbed her heart out while she waited for her 'friend'. I thought the evening couldn't get any worse. But I was wrong.

I passed by the lounge door and could see the princes smoking dope, laughing and joking as they drank alcohol and played cards. They were happy; more than I could say for some people that evening. I looked further round the house and saw some servants cleaning and polishing.

Eventually, all became quiet and the princes retired. Aitken had left a lot earlier. The servants were now smoking dope, drinking Black Label whiskey and played cards. I watched them from a distance. I was the only security guy in the house. Occasionally, I would check the CCTV monitors. I had made quite sure the house was secure and did not expect any incidents.

The thought of that young woman forced into having sex kept coming to mind. I wished she had taken my advice and left. Unfortunately, the princes were experts at corrupting people. Nonetheless, I felt bad for her—after all, here was another person fucked up by the Arabs—and fucked over by her own friend, too, of course.

Suddenly, an almighty shouting match broke out on the first landing. I thought the din would wake the princes and all hell would then break loose. I dashed upstairs and saw that all hell was already on us. One servant screamed at another and chased him around the landing with a .38 snub nose revolver.

I just reacted. The servant causing most commotion held the handgun. They were out of control and if not stopped quickly, someone would be shot. Knowing my luck, it would be me. I remembered Steve, my friend shot and killed in Barcelona, and I did not want to join him.

I moved on the servant with the gun and disarmed him. I was fucking fuming, both with them and with me. They stood in silence looking at me so I pushed them away towards their rooms. As my adrenaline rush subsided and matters quietened down, I descended the stairs and sat in a chair. The shock started and beads of sweat broke out on my forehead. My stomach churned, and I felt sick as the palms of my hands sweated. I bent forward with my head between my legs trying to make the nausea subside. I got angry, as I wondered what the hell I was doing. If a couple of servants wanted to kill each other, what the hell did that have to do with me? I was there to protect the princes, not for them.

I telephoned Bill at the office and ranted at him. It was after two in the morning, and I don't suppose he appreciated the call. After what I had been through that evening, though, I didn't give a shit.

In the morning, the servant asked for his gun back and I told him to get fucked. I gave it to Said Ayas, the prince's secretary. When I gave him the weapon and told him about the incident, all he said was thank you, and that was it. I should have called in the police and let them deal with it. Mind you, for diplomatic reasons they would have looked the other way. I knew from experience they were good at doing that. I wondered what a servant was doing with a gun, anyway, and how had he brought it in through Customs?

On the Wednesday, the 9th January, two or three nights after their last sexual exploits, I was told to expect a young woman. I knew immediately what this meant—a prostitute. Obviously their escapades on the Sunday some three nights before hadn't satisfied them.

When she arrived, I invited her in and sat her down. I let them know that she was there. While she waited, we talked. As was the custom, Jameel came in and introduced himself. His job was to eye the woman up for the prince. If she spoke well and met with the requirements, Jameel would ask her to wait a moment while he reported to the prince. It was a well-rehearsed routine, and I saw it many times. If approved, the woman would be invited in to the lounge where all the men sat. This was the first stage. Prince Mohammed would then decide if she were to his liking. If not then he would just pass her on to one of the others as a gift.

On this occasion, he was satisfied and Jameel took her to the prince's bedroom. When it was over Jameel returned her to the lobby area and asked her to wait, probably for her money. As I looked at the girl, I could see bruises and scratches on her face, arms and legs, and also that her knees were red. She looked distressed. I felt uncomfortable and asked her if she were okay? Did you want to speak to me, to tell me about it, I asked.

161

With a sigh she began, they 'welcomed' her she said, as she entered the lounge, and asked her to sit while the men continued playing cards. Jameel stood up, brought her a drink, then sat down and talked to her. The prince was taking more notice of her than she realised. Jameel was told to take the young woman upstairs and prepare her. The prince wasn't aware she knew who he was. She was told to take off her clothes and bathe. Afterwards, she was to get on to the bed on her hands and knees with the lights turned off, and she had to wait like that. This is what she did, and after a good while, the door opened and in walked the prince. She looked around briefly and saw him under the hall light. He had told her to look away: he obviously did not want her to see him and if he had realised that she had already, then he would have ended the farce immediately.

He took off his *thobe,* got on to the bed, and took her from behind. He never once spoke to her; he never kissed or cuddled her, or performed any foreplay: he just entered her, had sex and 'roughed her up'—her words, not mine. When he finished, he left the room. Jameel came back in and told her to dress. She was brought back down to the lobby and waited there for Jameel to pay her.

She said if she had not turned around just for that split-second, she would not have known which of the men had been with her. She was angry, fuming in fact at being 'roughed up', too. The girl asked what time I finished my shift and if I could meet her at a coffee shop nearby a little later. She gave me the address and I said I would try. However, I was not about to get involved in any way and never went to meet up with her.

Shortly after this, the *News of the World* newspaper published a story about Prince Mohammed from Saudi Arabia roughing up a girl who had been with him. When the story hit the streets, he made his escape back to America. Other claims of his sexual misdeeds were to follow later.

After Prince Mohammed became the Governor of the Eastern Province, a statement from the 'first independent human rights organization' in Saudi Arabia appeared which read as follows:

The Committee for the Defence of Legitimate Rights in Saudi Arabia based in London through their Saudi dissident leader Mr Masari stated:

"Prince Mohammed bin Fahd, Governor of the Eastern Province has been accused by the Al Saud newsletter of condoning sex slavery within his administered area. We have been told Governor Prince Mohammed is an active participant in the child sex rings of the Eastern Province. We have been told he has parties for his friends with child sex as the main entertainment. Governor Prince Mohammed likes Hollywood where there are many boys and girls from which to entice into becoming sex slaves in Saudi Arabia under the ruse of film and modelling contracts."

(Source: **http://www.sauduction.com/issues/13**)

Chapter 19

Saudi Arabia, 1985

On the evening of the 20th January 1985, Prince Mishari telephoned and said, "There's a ticket waiting for you at the Saudia desk at Heathrow Airport. You will need to go to the Saudi Embassy and get your visa; I will phone them and make the necessary arrangements for you?"

"Your Royal Highness, that's fine, I'll go to the embassy in the morning," I replied. Excitement bubbled up inside me as I thought about the visit. Would I become the next Lawrence of Arabia, I wondered? No chance came the answer. Why did Prince Mishari want me in Saudi Arabia? I would not know the answer until the end of the visit but still, I was curious.

The next morning I arrived at the embassy in Belgrave Square, London. I had expectations of a hassle-free visa application and of some preferential treatment, too, if I'm honest. It wasn't to be, as one of the Egyptian staff running the visa section dealt with me rudely. His and the entire staff's manner towards the visa applicants was one of contempt. I said aloud, "If this is the first contact most people have with Saudi Arabia, it is a wonder that anyone bothers going there." I felt like telling them all to get stuffed but kept that thought to myself. Several hours later, still without a visa, I returned home. I telephoned Prince Mishari's palace: "Have you got your visa?"

"No, Your Highness."

"Why not?"

I blurted out, "Frankly, I'm disgusted with the treatment I received today. If this is the first contact people have with Saudi Arabia it's a wonder anyone bothers going there."

The prince wasn't pleased with my comments, and was taken aback: "I want you here and you want to come, so go to the embassy tomorrow and ask for the manager. Tell him I've sent you back and tell him to call me from there."

"Yes, sir," I said, and with that, the conversation ended abruptly.

The following day saw me standing in the queue at the embassy yet again. I finally reached the officer at the desk.

"Yes?"

"I would like to see your manager, please."

"Why?"

"Because Prince Mishari Bin Saud Bin Abdul Aziz wants to speak with him, that's why."

With that, the officer scurried away. Within minutes, the manager came through to see me. Before I could say anything, he extended his hand to shake mine. "His Highness spoke with me this morning and told me to extend you every courtesy. If I could have your passport please, I will have the formalities completed immediately. Please sit down, I will be back shortly." I sat and waited, surprised at this turnaround in their attitude.

On Friday 25th January, I picked up my airline ticket at the Saudia airlines desk at Heathrow airport. These days, all I did was stand in queues at various desks waiting to be processed. I watched my suitcase disappear as it was carried along the luggage conveyor belt towards the aircraft. I cast my mind back to when I was a child watching Arabian-themed films on television. I fantasised that the aircraft that would carry me to Saudi Arabia was a magic carpet. What wonderful experiences would I soon be having? Would I find myself among the Sultans and Caliphs of Arabia, or in the company of Ali Baba and the forty thieves?

In the departure lounge, I cast my eyes over the other passengers waiting to board. Most of them were Arabs, but some Indians, Pakistanis and Filipinos also littered the crowd. Only half a dozen Europeans, including three women, waited. Each of them looked apprehensive. I wondered if they saw the same in me. I was certain no member of the royal family sat among us. They would be ensconced elsewhere in a VIP suite.

The late evening flight passed quickly as I shut my eyes and drifted off to sleep. On awakening, I engaged in conversation with an Englishwoman sitting next to me.

"I'm surprised to find an Englishwoman travelling to Saudi Arabia," I said, opening the conversation.

"It's my home," she replied enthusiastically, which surprised me. I didn't think Saudi Arabia would be to any Western woman's liking, given their strict laws and codes of conduct.

"Where in Saudi Arabia do you live?" I enquired.

"I live in the Aramco compound in Dhahran, which is different to the Saudi Arabia which exists outside its boundaries. It's like a Little America; it has its own golf course, swimming pools, schools, a theatre, a bowling alley and a library. The neighbourhoods are quiet and well-kept, and you get to know your neighbours well if you're living in the family housing, although I cannot speak for the bachelor housing," she said. "If you have children, the Aramco schools are wonderful, with excellent instructors and an advanced curriculum compared to public and private schools in America. If you're married, your wife will be able to drive within the compound, but not outside it, as women are not allowed to drive in the Kingdom. The scenery is beautiful and there are opportunities for scuba-diving."

"Are there any particular formalities we have to adhere to at the airport on arrival?" I asked.

"Once the plane stops, we walk down the steps and get on to the bus and it takes us to the terminal. From there, we'll join the massive queues waiting to be processed by passport control and then collect our baggage and go to the customs control."

"Much like anywhere else then," I chipped in.

"Oh no, they check every bag and suitcase thoroughly, it takes forever to get through." With that sobering thought, I decided to remain quiet as we prepared for landing.

The aircraft touched down and the engines almost immediately reversed their thrust, sending a sharp vibration through its fuselage. As we taxied towards our allotted parking spot, I imagined the wait in the long queues ahead. Just as the aircraft stopped, a call came across the tannoy speaker unit: "Would Mr Mark Young come to the forward cabin and identify himself to the flight crew, please."

"That's me," I said to the woman next to me. A look of utter surprise crept over her face, leading me to wonder if I had a date with the executioner's sword! With this thought in mind, I approached the flight deck. "Hello, I'm Mark Young; I was called over the tannoy speaker unit and asked to identify myself."

The stewardess pointed toward the open door of the aircraft and said, "There is a Captain Mansour waiting at the bottom of the steps for you, just identify yourself to him."

"Thanks so much," I replied, and then descended the steps a little apprehensively toward the Saudi Arabian National Guard Captain standing next to a Mercedes motorcar. "Hello, my name is Mark Young," I said.

Stretching out his hand to greet me, the Captain replied in good English, "Welcome to Saudi Arabia. Please get into the car and I will guide you through our formalities."

Two minutes later and we were walking through the terminal building's door. I looked aghast at the number of people queuing to show their passports at the immigration desk. There were hundreds and hundreds. Captain Mansour held out his hand and said, "May I have your passport, please?" As I handed it to him, he strode off purposefully to the front of the queue. I automatically followed him as he stopped in front of the immigration official. Speaking to the officer, the Captain motioned towards me. As I nodded my head, I saw the official stamp my passport. I could feel the eyes of the other passengers burning into my back, obviously wondering what was going on.

"Mark, can you come with me and identify your luggage, please?" Before I could reply, the Captain was on his way towards the Customs desks. Looking at the huge stacks of baggage piling up, I was pleased I'd taken my usual precaution of tying an identifying ribbon around my bag's handle. Only two minutes or so later, I had my suitcase on the desk in front of the customs official. He looked at me and opened the case. A second later he closed it, job done.

"That's it, all done. I have a car waiting to take us to Prince Mishari's palace. Please follow me," said the Captain. Walking across the white marble tiled floor toward some excessively large glass doors, I noticed a picture on the wall.

Looking down at me was the first King of Saudi Arabia, Abdul Aziz, and next to him were King Faisal, King Khalid and King Fahd. Prince Mishari's father King Saud was noticeable by his absence and I wondered why. I made a mental note to ask the prince about it.

On exiting the airport building, another Mercedes waited for us. The Captain motioned to the porter to deposit my baggage in the boot and then he opened the passenger door for me. The Captain, I noticed, had impeccable manners and was a credit to the prince. On the way to the palace we made small talk and exchanged pleasantries, just killing time on the journey.

The driver drew up by some steps and then stopped. Someone opened the door for me and I thanked him. Captain Mansour walked around the car and stretched out his hand once again. Shaking it, I thanked him for his help and hospitality. I noticed my suitcase was carried through a door into the house beside me. Then Sultan, one of Prince Mishari's uncles, greeted me and took me through into a large sitting room. Chairs lined the walls and a couple of coffee tables were placed in front of them. At one end stood a large television, a rug lay in the centre of the room, and the decoration was quite plain with ordinary light fittings. This wasn't quite what I was expecting and asked Sultan incredulously, "Is this Prince Mishari's palace?"

"For the moment, Prince Mishari is renting these houses. He is having a new palace built nearby." Now it made sense, as I had never before seen the princes in such unpretentious surroundings.

"Prince Mishari won't be long; he has been at dinner with Prince Mohammed," said Sultan—referring to Prince Mohammed Bin Fahd, whom I'd just finished working for a few weeks before. He had been the acting Governor of the Eastern Province in 1984 and was made the full Governor in 1985. Again, I found myself making small talk as we waited for the prince to arrive.

Some ten minutes later, Prince Mishari breezed into the room. We jumped to our feet in a show of respect, as usual. A smile beamed across the prince's face, and I knew then the executioner's sword would have to wait. "Hello Mark, welcome to Saudi Arabia and to my home. Have you been taken care of since arriving?" he questioned.

"Yes, Your Royal Highness, I thank you for your hospitality."

"I wanted to meet you personally at the airport, but I'm afraid dinner with Prince Mohammed took a little longer than I expected." I wondered if he was telling the truth.

"Well, Mark, I just wanted to greet you. I'll have someone show you to your rooms so you can unpack and settle in. They will bring you to my office in the morning." With that, he spun on his heels and made off through the door he had entered only a minute or so before. Sultan showed me to my rooms. He seemed happy to have me there and I wondered if I would become his best buddy during my visit.

The next morning, a member of the prince's staff called Mohammed came to escort me to the breakfast room. He wore the typical Arabian garb: *thobe*, headdress, etcetera. He stood about five feet eight inches tall and was portly with a large stomach protruding under his *thobe*. A dish of *Shakshuka* was placed in front of me and I tucked into it. I was familiar with this dish and loved it: it consisted of scrambled eggs, fresh tomatoes, garlic, salt, sweet paprika, and vegetable oil and tomato paste. I liked to pick up mouthfuls of the *Shakshuka* with a piece of pita bread and savour the taste for as long as possible.

After breakfast, Mohammed drove me to the prince's office at the National Guard Military City in Dammam. As we approached the main gates, the guards stationed there signalled us to stop. But after a quick word from Mohammed, the gates were opened and we set off towards a large rectangular building. As I stepped from the car, the heat hit me full on, and this was supposed to be the cooler part of the year. In complete contrast, as I walked through the main doors of the SANG (Saudi Arabian National Guard) Eastern Region building, I was bathed in the cool air emanating from the air-conditioning. The other air I noticed was one of efficiency as the guards went about their business. Within a minute or two, Captain Mansour came over to greet me once again. He escorted me up to the first floor of the building where the prince's office was located.

Entering a large room, I was immediately struck by how plush it was. Large leather seats were placed around the walls and smart, ornately designed coffee tables sat in front of them. Sparkling crystal chandeliers adorned the ceilings. At one end of the room sat a large desk with papers neatly placed on top of it. A high backed, deep-buttoned leather seat was behind it. This, I thought, was the prince's desk—but I was wrong. Captain Mansour introduced me to the office manager who asked me to sit down and then offered me tea or coffee. Tea was my preferred choice, and within a minute or two, a tray arrived with a pot of the sweet mint tea that I'd become very partial to. I picked up a glossy magazine from the coffee table, but soon put it down again. The heavy censorship had dissolved any interest I may have had in reading it: almost every page had been scribbled over with a black magic marker pen as though a young child had been let loose on it. I smiled and thought how pathetic it was. With their 'gender apartheid' and censorship, one wondered what part of the Stone Age they still lived in.

Instead, I put my mind to work analysing the various characters as they sauntered in and out of the office. Before long, I was shown into another, even larger office, which was plusher than the one I'd just left. An Arab sat opposite me. He nodded his head, and I smiled at him. He smiled back showing a near perfect set of gums with only a few teeth embedded in them. His skin was leathery and weather-beaten, yet his eyes were dark and piercing like those of the desert falcon and I doubted much escaped him. As we sat there facing each other, our worlds seemed so far apart and yet for one brief moment, they had come together.

I sat with my back towards the dark-green tinted windows that shielded the air-conditioned room from the sunlight. To my left were two excessively large, highly polished wood doors and I wondered what lay beyond them. Could it actually be the prince's office, or was it yet another anteroom? Suddenly, one of the doors opened wide and another Bedouin-looking character emerged through it. Looking at me, he grinned, and as I smiled back, I noticed he too had gums which glistened at me. My newfound friend stood up as he was beaconed by one of Prince Mishari's staff, who then ushered him through into the other room.

My mind wandered as I sat there alone, contemplating why I felt so uncomfortable in my western clothes. Wherever I went, I drew attention like a lighthouse beacon flashing brightly in the darkness of the night.

At last, the door swung open and my chum who I had named 'smiler' was ushered out. I then entered a grand office, which made me feel as though I was standing on the set of *Dallas*. Prince Mishari's office was luxurious and inviting; wealth, power, and position surrounded me and I now saw the prince in a different light. Before, I had seen him as just a playboy and a gambler; now I saw him in a quite different role.

Prince Mishari smiled and gestured me to sit in the leather chair opposite his desk. He sent an aide to fetch some more mint tea. I looked at the trophies packed into several glass-fronted cabinets on one side of the room and wondered what they'd been awarded for, but never got up to have a look. I knew they were not awarded to the prince for sporting achievements, as he was overweight, unfit, and like the other Saudi royals, averse to doing anything strenuous.

"Well, Mark, what do you think?" he said.

"Impressive," I replied as my eye caught sight of a portrait hanging on a wall. It depicted images of King Abdul Aziz, King Faisal, King Khalid, King Fahd and the Crown Prince Abdullah. "I would like to know why does your father not appear in any of the portraits of the past and present rulers of Saudi Arabia?"

Without showing surprise, the prince answered: "For many years my father was frowned on by other members of the royal family. There were many reasons for this. One was because of his excessive spending; another was because of his perceived lack of leadership. There were other reasons, but I do not wish to go into them. There has recently been a change in attitude towards my father, and more and more he will feature in the portraits you speak about."

Enough said, I thought. I knew a bit about King Saud's reputation anyway. It was reported the CIA supplied him with young boys and that he nearly bankrupted Saudi Arabia during his reign. He spent millions of dollars foolishly, once spending $10 million on a palace, only to have it knocked down and rebuilt in another style costing a further $30 million. He drank himself into a stupor daily. He had an insatiable appetite for young girls. It wasn't unheard-of for the servant girls to hitch up their clothing to their waists as they scrubbed the marble floors on their hands and knees when they knew King Saud was passing: they knew he would be unable to resist them and if they fell pregnant then they were made for life. No more cleaning, skivvying or struggling for them, as they took on the title of Princess Um (Princess the mother of) followed with the name of the child they had borne.

"I will have someone take you out, where you will wait for me. Then you will go with me to dinner. Tomorrow, Mohammed will take you to the *souk* (market) where they will provide you with a *thobe* and the clothing which will allow you to feel more comfortable." I wondered if he had read my mind as I had sat waiting in the anteroom.

"One other thing Mark. If the police or other officials stop you, you must tell them to contact me. I will sort out any misunderstandings, is that understood?"

"Yes, Sir, clearly understood," I replied as I got up from the luxurious, deeply upholstered and deep-buttoned leather chair of which I had grown rather attached to, in the few short minutes that I had spent sitting in it.

I was escorted back to the original anteroom and noticed Tony, the Lebanese secretary-cum-hairdresser and whatever else he may be to the princes, sitting there. I thought he worked with Prince Mansour but then again, Tony had a good rapport with many princes and was often called on to cut the hair of the Governor of Riyadh, Prince Salman Bin Abdul Aziz. It wasn't unknown for a helicopter to pick Tony up, just so he could cut a prince's hair. Tony was slim, with thick black hair, and a thick black moustache. His skin had an olive complexion and his eyes were dark brown. I also noted that he was dressed in his usual western style clothes, which consisted of a brightly coloured striped shirt with the top two buttons undone and beige coloured trousers. The thick gold chain he normally wore also hung around his neck and rested on the thick black hair that covered his chest. To keep his feet cool, he wore sandals.

"Hi Mark, how are you? I heard you were here, have you been here long? When did you arrive? What are your thoughts on Saudi Arabia so far?" He bombarded me with questions, but before I could answer him we were told Prince Mishari was about to leave.

Chapter 20

Lunch

Along with the office staff, Tony and I went out to wait on the large landing area at the top of the stairs, which led down to the lobby. Looking down the corridor, I could see large main doors, which led to the prince's office. Two National Guard soldiers guarded the entry. Both came to attention as Prince Mishari breezed out of his office and entered the corridor. Walking towards us, the prince exuded confidence and power. He stopped briefly and spoke with Tony before continuing down the stairs toward the lobby. Again, Prince Mishari stopped, this time to speak with Captain Mansour. Several National Guard soldiers stood to attention and saluted the prince as he passed them. Prince Mishari then walked out of the air-conditioned lobby towards the waiting Mercedes 560 SEL limousine. This car was a gift to him from the deputy Governor of the Eastern Province, Prince Fahd Bin Salman, one of the Governor of Riyadh's sons. I watched intently and realised for the first time just how important Prince Mishari's position really was.

Ahead of his Mercedes was a white American Chevrolet. On its front doors was a large National Guard symbol and a large blue stripe ran along the flanks of the car. Red and blue lights flashed on its roof. The vehicle reminded me of an American police car. As I walked towards it, Captain Mansour stopped me.

"Mark, His Highness wants you to travel with him in his car," he said and opened the rear passenger door. I'd been out with the prince many times, but this time was very different: Majid, his driver, moved off behind the lead car as several soldiers saluted the prince. As we neared the main gates, we found the soldiers had stopped the traffic on the dual carriageway to facilitate a quick, safe and easy exit. The soldiers saluted Prince Mishari as he drove by. I could see this was normal for them but for me it was a new experience. With lights flashing brightly on the roof of the lead car, we careered along the dual carriageway towards our lunch date. Just where we were going to, I had no idea, but judging by the sun's position, we were heading in a southerly direction.

Thirty minutes or so later, we arrived at a small village. Where I would normally jump out and open Prince Mishari's door, I found that role taken by Majid—while Captain Mansour opened my door. I thanked him, but found myself feeling a little uncomfortable with my newfound status. Not to worry though, it wouldn't last long, I thought.

Several people stood in line to greet the prince. I noticed a few of them glancing my way, no doubt wondering who this Western infidel was. Sultan, Prince Mishari's uncle, stood nearby and when I noticed him, I felt still more uncomfortable. Between Sultan, Majid and Mohammed, who had also turned up, I hoped I could lose myself among people I knew. No such luck. Captain Mansour came over and told me Prince Mishari wanted me to follow him into the *majlis* (a large sitting room) where the men had gathered. On the large sofas that lined the walls of a large room sat at least fifty men. As almost every seat was filled, I walked up to the sofa where Prince Mishari sat. As I went to sit, the prince said to me, "Mark, not here, find another seat quickly." Luckily, my backside had not yet hit the sofa and I leant forward towards him as though I wanted to speak with him. From that position, I stood upright and made my way to a seat near the door, hoping no one had noticed my blunder. If they had, they hid it well, perhaps out of respect for the prince.

I sat for a few minutes and then went outside to join Sultan and the others. They were enjoying a brew, the sweet amber nectar that was mint tea. I squashed myself between them and Sultan poured me a glass. I took a sip and let the sweetness wash over the taste buds of my tongue. Before I could take another, Captain Mansour was beside me, but this time he was laughing.

"Mark, Prince Mishari wants you to return to the *majlis* and Mark, just remember only the prince sits on a sofa by himself. It is protocol, Mark." Obviously, my cock-up had not gone unnoticed and I winced inwardly. I thought I had disentangled myself rather deftly from the situation, but clearly, I had not.

"I wish someone had told me that before; I feel a right prat now."

"What is a prat, Mark?" asked Captain Mansour.

"I'll tell you later, Captain, but for now I had better get back before I make another mistake."

"You already have Mark; you left the room before the prince without asking permission. That could be taken as an insult."

"Oh shit, out of the frying pan and into the fire," I said knowing the Captain had no idea what I was talking about.

As I re-entered the *majlis* I placed my right hand on my heart and nodded my head in some gesture of an apology. All eyes focused on me as I sat down on the sofa and tried to melt into the seat beneath me.

Nearly an hour later, Prince Mishari stood and we jumped up. The prince led the way through to a large room where masses of food was placed on an ornately embroidered Arabian carpet. I watched as Prince Mishari sat cross-legged on the floor. All the other men followed him into the room. I sat next to Sultan and found myself sitting almost directly opposite the prince. In the centre of the carpet was a large silver salver covered in a bed of mutton *Al-kabsa*, which is a classic Saudi Arabian dish of meat mixed with rice. On top of the rice was a whole cooked sheep. Baskets of *khubz* (Arabic bread) and dishes of *hummus* (puree of chickpeas), *falafel* (deep-fried patties of ground chickpeas), *kibbeh* (oval shaped nuggets of ground lamb), *kofta* (balls of minced meat and spices), *Shawerma* (pressed lamb) and salad looked inviting.

Prince Mishari sent me a bowl of meat. Smiling, he signalled me to tuck into it. Eating with my hands in typical Arabic fashion, I picked up a chunk of meat and bit into it. The first bite was from me; the next five were of my jaw bouncing up and down on the tough meat within my mouth. It tasted fine, but it was tough. "Sultan, what meat is this? It's really tough."

"Oh Mark, it's camel," he answered. Enough of that, I thought. It wasn't that it didn't taste good, but my jaw ached from chewing it.

There was much animated conversation between the prince and the other men. Whether the conversation was of importance or not, I couldn't make out. As I sat cross-legged, I constantly made sure the soles of my feet didn't face anyone as I was told this would be insulting to them. I'd made two cock-ups already and didn't want to make a third. I didn't think it would go down well—not as well as the food was going down, anyhow. I asked Sultan, "What's this lunch all about? Does it have any particular relevance or is it just a social gathering?"

"Well, it's both. Anyone who has a grievance of some kind can explain it to the prince and he will offer them his advice. Others may want to join in with the discussions, or they may just want to meet the prince. They are all welcome and it's a good public relations exercise," he said.

When lunch finished, Prince Mishari stood up. As was expected, everyone else quickly stood up in respect. He made his way to the exit and everyone followed. After bidding their farewells, Majid opened the door of the air-conditioned Mercedes. Before the prince got into the car, he called Mohammed. He spoke to him briefly. Then the prince said, "Mark, I have told Mohammed to take you to the *souk* (market) and sort out some clothes for you."

"Yes, sir," I replied.

"I will see you later back at the house."

"Yes, Your Highness, take care," I said as he got into his car. Captain Mansour got into the front passenger seat next to Majid. Smiles and waves from the assembled men followed the prince as the car hastened away. Plumes of dust hovered in the air, kicked up from the sandy road by the tyres of the Mercedes.

With Prince Mishari gone, I could relax a little. Mohammed and I laughed and joked as we drove to the *souk*.

At the *souk*, I found it strange seeing the women covered from head to foot in their black *abayas*. I wondered if they helped keep the women cool as well as hiding them. Did the Saudi men consider their women to be that ugly that they had to cover them, I wondered? In reality, I knew that many of the Saudi women were beautiful and wondered if that were the real reason they were hidden from the men? As a mere infidel, what did I know anyway?

Mohammed told a shopkeeper what we wanted and then I stood still like a tailor's dummy while *thobes*, cotton shorts and long cotton under trousers called *sirwal* were held up against me. From the corner of my eye I noticed the *igals* (the classic black circular headbands), which sat on top of the Arab headdress. I wasn't about to make the same mistake that a friend of mine called Jack had made when he had been a guest of the Governor of Riyadh. I chose a normal black *igal* whereas Jack had chosen one of the flashier looking *igals* with the gold embroidered bands that you see worn elsewhere in Arabia. Wearing it, Jack had arrived back at Prince Salman's palace in Riyadh and stepped out of the car. He found King Fahd, Prince Abdullah (the Crown Prince), Prince Sultan (the Defence Minister), Prince Naïf (the Interior Minister) and Prince Salman dropping their playing cards as they stood up to greet the unexpected Arabian Ruler who had dropped in to see them! Then, as Jack got closer, they realised it was another crazy Englishman, and Prince Salman had ordered Jack to go off to an anteroom to change his *igal*. As he'd walked away, Jack had heard King Fahd and the other princes roaring with laughter. What Jack had not realised was that only the rulers of other Arabian countries wore this *igal*. The change had occurred after the assassination on the 25th March 1975 of the late King Faisal by his nephew Prince Faisal Bin Musaid—although children sometimes wear smaller 'flashy' *igal* these days at festivals or during *Eid*.

Eid ul-Fitr commemorates the month of Ramadan, marking the end of the month-long fast. *Fitr* means to break, and therefore symbolizes breaking the fasting period and of all evil habits. It is a joyous occasion with significant religious significance. Happiness follows from gaining spiritual uplift after a month of fasting. Muslims dress in holiday clothes and attend a special congregational prayer in the morning. After the service, worshippers greet and embrace each other in a spirit of peace, love and brotherhood and visit friends and relatives.

For Muslims, *Eid ul Fitr* is a joyful celebration of achieving increased piety. It is a day of forgiveness, moral victory and peace, congregation, fellowship, brotherhood and unity.

As I thought about this, I smiled, thinking that at least my minor cock-ups were nothing in comparison to Jack's *faux pas*.

* * *

Once back at Prince Mishari's palace, I sat on a step opposite the main house where the prince and his family lived and looked at the large wall that surrounded it. Perplexed, I wondered why there was a garage door in the middle of it. Suddenly, the door opened and I could see through it. To the left were some steps, which I thought must lead into the house. A Cadillac motorcar was parked in a large courtyard area. The car reversed out and momentarily stopped as the forward gears were selected. I looked at the windows, but couldn't see through them as they were blacked out. I remained sitting on the step, wondering who was in the car.

An hour or so later, Mohammed arrived and asked me if I was all right. I motioned for him to join me, and he sat down next to me. As he did so, the Cadillac returned, stopping in front of the garage door. Automatically, the door lifted and the car drove into the courtyard. Watching closely, I saw no movement at all as the garage door closed. "Mohammed, what was that all about? Why didn't the passengers get out of the car?"

"It was Princess al-Anud, Mark; she has been out visiting a friend. No one sees the women when they enter or leave the palace; only the cars when they come and go." His attitude had become one of seriousness; mine on the other hand had not. I recalled the times when the princesses came to the villa in Marbella. They had all swum and lounged about by the pool in their bathing costumes as I watched them. Smiling, I thought about how I had seen Princess al-Anud and her companions all but naked and now here she was hidden behind large brick walls and a black *abaya*. The princess was beautiful and had a figure to die for: what a waste, I thought. Mind you, a set of photographs of the princess posing came into my possession some time later, so I could always drool over them.

Later that afternoon, Prince Mishari walked up to me and said, "Mark, I want you to come over to the other house to say hello to the princess."

"That would be good," I said. I walked with the prince over to the garage door, which opened for us. We walked up the steps I'd seen earlier and entered the main house. Princess al-Anud stood before us and extended her hand for me to shake. She was wearing some fashionable clothes that she had bought from either Paris or Rome. "Hello, Mark, it's good to see you, how are you enjoying your stay with us?"

"Your Royal Highness, it is good to see you. I'm enjoying my stay greatly, thank you." I said. For a few minutes the prince, princess and I engaged in small talk. Afterwards, the prince escorted me to the garage door and let me out.

All the time, I was trying hard to understand some of the different contrasts that I was seeing in the Kingdom.

In the five or six weeks that I would spend in Saudi Arabia, I would see the princess just one more time. The only women I saw out and about were little black blobs out shopping in the *souk* or the malls. I found the segregation of men and women strange and very hard to get used to.

Chapter 21

Desert

Every day I saw the prince's young son, Turki. He was around five or six years old at that time. Like every other young prince, he was sometimes a spoiled brat; screaming and playing up to get his own way. One time in Marbella he spat in my face and asked why he was eating with the servants as he sat at our table eating lunch. At other times, he could be an absolute angel—a real pleasure to be around.

The day after I spoke with the prince and princess in the family house, Turki wanted to show me one of his cars. Walking by the servant's quarters, I saw a beautiful Chevrolet Day van. It was finished in metallic blue and silver paintwork and had chrome bright work all-round it. Inside, it had a television and video recorder, deep dark-blue velvet buttoned captain's chairs, a fridge and ice-cold air-conditioning. What a lucky little boy he was, I thought.

Later that evening, Prince Mishari joined us in the lounge. "Mark," he said, "how would you like to spend some time in the desert?"

I replied, "I would love it, sir."

"Good, tomorrow we will leave for the desert and stay for two days or so." Two days in the desert! No worries, I thought, as I styled myself the new Lawrence of Arabia.

The next morning I waited excitedly for departure. What's the first job you will do when you get into the desert, Lawrence? I asked myself. Set up camp and start a fire, I answered myself.

Within hours, we were pulling up in the Chevrolet 4x4 at the chosen site. The campsite was set up and dozens of National Guard soldiers and Bedouin Arabs milled around. Right, Lawrence, you won't set up camp then, I thought. Mohammed wandered over and said that he would look after me. No worries, I thought.

I stared out at the desert. You could see for miles. It was as flat as a billiards table. There were no bushes, no sand dunes and no

180

undulations. Not what I had imagined, but I could deal with it. Looking at the various tents, I turned and asked Mohammed which one housed the toilet. "What do you want, Mark?"

"Where is the toilet? *Fayn al-hammam*?" I repeated in Arabic.

With a large sweep of his arm from East to West, covering the whole horizon he said, "Here, Mark, here is the toilet."

Fuck that, I thought, Lawrence could keep his desert if a man can't even have a crap in private!

Two days, could I hold on for two days? I wondered. As it happened, I didn't need anything more than a wee.

I wandered over to the radio communications tent and started chatting with the operators. Their English wasn't up to much, but then again, neither was my Arabic. Between the two, and coupled with some hand gestures, we managed to communicate. Their names were Talal and Munir, and they were gay. They enjoyed teasing me with sexual innuendos but it did not bother me. I wasn't surprised that I had stumbled across some homosexuals, as Saudi Arabia was such a segregated society it was obvious to me that homosexuality would abound. In Riyadh, it was rumoured there were three gay clubs. I knew that one of Prince Mishari's brothers had died of AIDS. Also, the King's youngest brother, Prince Humoud Bin Abdul Aziz was gay: he'd tried to bed me at his house in Stanmore, North London, but had been unsuccessful. I was and have always been strictly a ladies man, but now and again, someone would try it on. Many princes showed feminine traits, too.

Noticing a fire burning brightly, I left the radio operators and joined the Bedouin by the fireside. I wondered if the National Guard employed them, not that it mattered. All the 'ordinary' Saudis I came across, including the Bedouin, I found full of kindness and hospitality. The problems I faced throughout my career stemmed from either members of the royal family or the sycophants that they surrounded themselves with.

Sitting by the fireside, I gestured and tried out my pidgin Arabic on the Bedouin, who laughed and laughed. Whether they were laughing at what I said or my gesticulations, I will never know. I was just another crazy Englishman who was a distraction in the desert for them. From my side, I found the Bedouin kind, warm, generous and hospitable.

I watched the flames flickering with gusto, their reds, blues and oranges glowing like the sunset. The embers at the base and sides of the fire glowed fiercely as they were caught by gusts of wind. I watched the Bedouin throw some rat type creatures into the embers. They passed me one and holding it in my hand, I asked what I was supposed to do with it. A Bedouin caught on to what I was saying and laughed as he took another rat thing from the fire. He began chewing the flesh off the charred remains. Oh shit, I thought, they want me to eat a bloody rat!

No way could I refuse their hospitality or cause offence, so I began to nibble on the small rodent, praying I would not throw up. I wasn't excessively keen on the meat and washed it down with several cups of *gawha* (Arabic coffee). As soon as I was able to make my escape, I set off to find Mohammed. I needed to know what rodent it was that I had eaten.

"Mohammed, Mohammed, they made me eat a small rat thing. Will I die?"

Mohammed burst out laughing; he loved it when I played the fool. "Mark, if they ate it as well then surely it is all right to eat, no?"

"Then tell me Mohammed, why do they eat rats?"

"Mark, they are not rats, they are *Jerboa*. We hunt them, and then after they have been killed in the *Halal* fashion we cook and eat them."

"Oh, that's all right then," I said as I remembered what a Jerboa was in English—a desert rat!

Shit, I've eaten a rat! I just knew I had.

After two days passed, I sat in the Chevrolet 4x4 with Prince Mishari as we made our way back to Dammam.

"Mark, did you enjoy your visit to the desert? Did you enjoy your experiences? Were the Bedouin good to you?" asked the prince.

Now we were on our way back and feeling safe, I said, "Your Royal Highness, it was a wonderful experience, one I will treasure forever, apart from the toilet facilities, that is. I would have liked to stay longer."

"Good, very good, we are going back in a few days, for another two weeks." Thud, my heart hit the floor; it sounded loud enough for me to hear, so I was sure he must have heard it, too! Was he joking with me, I wondered? Looking through the darkened windows of the 4x4, I saw the desert stretching out for mile after mile, flat and barren. Every so often, we saw camels with their herder and I marvelled at how they were able to tolerate the harsh conditions. I thought about the contradictions of the desert. Inhospitable conditions, hospitable people.

* * *

Some hours after arriving back in Dammam, Prince Mishari came to speak with me. "Mark," he said, "tomorrow we'll be going to Riyadh where we'll stay for a day and a night. Then we'll fly to Jeddah where we'll stay for another day and night before returning to Dhahran. Make sure you get anything you need ready."

"I look forward to it, Your Highness," I replied. He left and returned to the main house.

Looking over to a patio area, I saw the guy's playing cards. I went and sat with them. Squeezing between Majid and Sultan, I acknowledged Mohammed, Ghassim and Joha. Dressed in my *thobe* and headdress, I felt comfortable and no doubt looked like one of them, I thought, laughing to myself.

It was like a beautiful summer's day in the United Kingdom. We sat in a shaded area, it was a little cooler yet there was no obvious breeze. The sunlight for me at that time of year was a joy to behold. Normally, I would be suffering the cold, mainly wet, damp and darker nights in the UK and so the weather was pure bliss.

"Mark," Mohammed said, "We are going into Al Khobar later and we wondered if you would like to come with us?"

"Do you think it will be all right with the prince?" I asked.

"We'll ask him and if he says yes, will you come with us?"

"Yes, I'd like to have a look around." As they continued playing, I took my leave and went for a short sleep.

Bang, bang, bang came the rapping on the door. Drowsily, I got up and went to open it. It felt like only a moment or two ago that I

183

had laid my head down on the pillow. Sultan and Mohammed stood there excitedly 'geeing' me up. "Come on Mark, get ready, Prince Mishari said you can come with us. Hurry up, we want to get moving."

"Give me a minute," I said. With that, I went to the bathroom and splashed some cold water over my face. That did the trick and the drowsiness I had felt all but melted away.

Al Khobar was exciting, bustling, and I loved looking in the jewellers there. Gold shops abounded in Gold Alley in the old section of Al Khobar. Everywhere I looked, I saw a gold shop. I didn't think there was that much gold in the world: the street was swamped with the stuff. The evening was cool and the hustle and bustle of the traders and their customers livened the place up.

"Mohammed," I called, "Why is this gold and jewellery not properly secured? It seems crazy to me, what happens if someone steals something?"

With a shrug of his shoulders he replied, "No problem; the jeweller loses a necklace, the thief loses their hand."

"Sultan, why do you think Prince Mishari wanted me to visit the Kingdom?" I asked.

"Mark, I don't know, maybe he wanted you to get a better understanding of where we come from and what ordinary Saudi's are like. Just remember you are privileged to be his guest, which is an honour in itself, so just enjoy it."

"Mohammed, Mohammed," I called, "Come and see the necklace I've found." As he arrived, I exclaimed, "There is someone special I want to buy that for. How much is it?"

Mohammed spoke with the shopkeeper and told me the price, which frankly didn't mean a thing to me. "Mohammed, I have enough money. Will you buy it for me?"

Mohammed spoke animatedly with the shopkeeper. I watched and waited for Mohammed to finish his diatribe, by which time I felt sorry for the shopkeeper! The outcome of this banter was a sizeable discount for me; a victory for Mohammed and a beautiful necklace for that someone special back home in the UK.

I beamed a smile at Mohammed and slapped him on the back as I thanked him for the discount he had secured for me. This had been the first time I had seen bartering in action since my arrival and I would have loved to be privy to all that was said.

After a couple of hours looking around the shops, Sultan decided that we should be getting back as we had an early start in the morning. I felt content and got on well with the prince, his family and their staff. Only a few months later, I would see a different side to the princess and it would only be a matter of time before the grim reaper would come to call for me.

* * *

"Mark, Mark, are you up yet?" came the voice from outside the door. Opening it, I found Sultan standing there with a big grin on his face.

"Let me just get my holdall and I'll be right with you," I said. Briskly, we made our way out to the prince's Mercedes and found Majid already waiting for us.

"*Ahlan, ahlan yaa Majid* (Hello, Majid) *khayf il Haal?* (How are you?)" I said.

"*Il Hamdu lillaah* (Praise be to God) *Bi kayr* (Good)" he replied. I had found that nearly every sentence uttered in Saudi Arabia made some reference or other to Allah (God). I found this ironic given how rarely the royal family practised their religion. Where the royals would flout their religion and get away with it, the punishments meted out to 'ordinary' citizens in Saudi if they did so were severe, sometimes resulting in the death penalty. Often the punishments they received were for doing nothing more than the royal family got up to every day of their lives. If the royal family were penalised in the same manner as their citizens then they would have a significantly smaller royal family.

I noted the engine was running so the air-conditioning would have cooled the car before the prince arrived. My holdall and the other cases had been put in the boot of the Mercedes and another Chevrolet 4x4 behind it.

As Prince Mishari walked over to us, the guys greeted him with all servility. I greeted the prince in a more reserved manner. Majid relieved the prince of his briefcase and waited for him to get into his car. He signalled for me to sit next to him. Sultan sat next to Majid, in the front passenger seat. At Dhahran airport, we were ushered straight through to the waiting aircraft. Sitting in the lavish first class cabin, we awaited take off. I could detect some uneasiness in the prince and remembered he wasn't comfortable with flying.

The flight was uneventful, and within an hour or so, we stood in the airport at Riyadh. I walked behind the prince and Sultan. I carried the prince's briefcase and marvelled at the architecture of the airport. It was a beautiful building; modern and clean. As I took in the sights, I lost ground, which would prove to be an unhealthy move. Looking ahead, I noticed the prince and Sultan clearing a checkpoint manned by armed guards. I quickened my pace to catch up and as I passed through the checkpoint, I set the alarms off. I looked at the guards; the guards looked at me. I wondered what the problem was and so did they. As they were deciding what to do, I noticed their hands move on to their firearms. I froze and held my breath, hoping I would not be subjected to a barrage of 9mm rounds whizzing about my head. By this time, Prince Mishari had turned round to see what was causing the commotion. On realising I was the offender he fired off a command to the guards who then waved me through. As I walked past them, I could see the suspicions they held towards me glinting in their eyes. Catching up to the prince, I asked, "Your Highness, what was that all about?"

"Nothing, Mark," he replied, "It was just the detectors picked up on my gun in the briefcase you are carrying that was all."

That's all? I thought. Fuck that, he could have told me I was carrying his gun. I would have made sure I had stayed glued to him right from the start. I didn't expect him to carry his gun in Saudi.

I savoured all that I could. Sights, sounds and smells I took in; I soaked them up like a sponge. As we neared the exit, another official-looking person approached us and greeted the prince. He led us out to the compulsory Mercedes. The driver loaded our gear into the car.

"Mark, we are going to my villa in Al Nasiriyah, where my father's palace was situated. He had a villa built for each of his children within the palace grounds." I wondered if that were true, as I knew King Saud had fathered over one hundred children.

"Once we settle in we will go to Prince Mohammed's [Bin Saud] for lunch. Prince Mohammed is one of my older brothers, he was the former Defence Minister of Saudi Arabia when our father was King," continued Prince Mishari. This Prince Mohammed was not the one I worked for in London, and I'd not yet met him.

As we approached a massive gateway Prince Mishari said, "This gateway is all that's left of the pinkish block walls that surrounded the palace compound." The gateway stood about thirty-five feet high and about one hundred and twenty feet across its base. On either side of the gateway were two large openings. One was the entrance, the other was the exit. Both openings had pointed tops, and set within the centre upright column separating the two was the Saudi Arabian symbol depicting the palm tree and swords. Above that, it looked as though an engraving of the Saudi Arabian flag had been carved into the stonework. The whole gateway was ornately designed. The size of the grounds beyond it was phenomenal, stretching about a mile square. I could only imagine what this compound must have looked like when the outer block wall had been in place. It took my breath away.

The driver stopped at the kerbside and opened the car door for the prince. As he walked up to the doorway of his villa, a servant opened it. Sultan and I followed him, with me carrying his all-important briefcase. The driver busied himself as he brought our luggage into the hallway. The villa was built in a Mediterranean style and occupied a single floor. It was large but nothing special in terms of its decor.

I noted lush vegetation as we entered the compound, which surprised me given the climate in Riyadh. Obviously, a great deal of time and effort had gone into planting and propagating the area.

Sultan showed me the bedroom I'd be using and I picked up my holdall and took it into the room. I took a quick shower and went back out into the lounge area to await the others. Sitting on a sofa, I took a minute to reflect on how lucky I was to be experiencing this trip to the Kingdom. Given the state of my finances back home, I knew I had, at most, five weeks to enjoy it. As Prince Mishari's guest, I did not expect to be paid for the visit.

As I daydreamed, the prince entered the room. As soon as I noticed him, I stood. Sultan was noticeable by his absence. "Are you ready, Mark? If you are ready, we will leave now."

"Yes sir, I'm ready," I replied. The prince led the way. He got in the driving seat of the Mercedes and signalled me to get in the front passenger seat. We set off for Prince Mohammed's villa. On the way, he spoke a little about his father's history and told me a little more about Al Nasiriyah.

Chapter 22

Lunch with Prince Mohammed Bin Saud

The first thing that I noticed was that Prince Mohammed's villa was much larger than Prince Mishari's. As we stopped, a servant opened the prince's door. Prince Mohammed's secretary, Nabil, greeted us. This man stood about five feet eight inches tall and was clean-shaven. I thought he was Egyptian and time proved me right. Once Nabil had greeted the prince, he introduced himself to me. Nabil was quietly spoken, courteous and polite. He exuded an authority that was evident in the way the other staff related to him.

As we entered the hallway, Prince Mohammed Bin Saud greeted his younger brother with affection. Extending his hand to shake mine, he greeted me in perfect English and welcomed me to his home. I answered him with six words, "I am honoured, Your Royal Highness." I thought Prince Mohammed had a gentle side, but could detect an air of authority and confidence about him.

Nabil guided us towards the dining room. This room was tasteful and luxurious. Crystal chandeliers hung from the ceiling. Formal dinner settings were in place. To the left was a napkin with a salad dinner and dessert fork to the right of it. On the right hand side of the dinner plate was placed a dinner knife, two teaspoons, a soup spoon, and a cocktail fork. Above those pieces to the left was a bread-and-butter plate with a knife. To the right above the cutlery on that side was a crystal water glass. There were no wineglasses on the table for obvious reasons. Instead, a coffee cup and saucer was placed to the right of the crystal water glass.

While the princes talked, Nabil took the opportunity to speak with me. Singing Prince Mohammed's praises, he told me the prince spoke several languages including English and French, fluently. I was told Prince Mohammed owned properties in Paris and Cannes, as well as many properties elsewhere. If he were trying to impress me, that wasn't the way to do it: I was more interested in Prince

Mohammed as an individual. I watched how he conducted himself, how he ate, how he spoke, his mannerisms and the way in which he related to his staff—all came under the microscope. My conclusions were that here was a man with style and presence. He was cultured and attentive. I found it interesting that he was no longer involved in government. I felt he had more character, charisma and personality going for him than our own Old Etonian Member of Parliament, Jonathan Aitken. As I had met and studied Aitken several times over the years, I felt well qualified to make the comparison. The Saudi Government, I thought, was wasting Prince Mohammed, as he clearly had more to offer his country. It crossed my mind that nepotism rules in the house of King Fahd, whose sons were given powerful positions within government. I had come across many Saudis in my travels that I felt were more able to fulfil the positions occupied by King Fahd's sons. That's not to say King Fahd was the only person to practise nepotism in the Kingdom, as it is rife in one way or another throughout the House of Saud.

After lunch, our host bade us farewell. Prince Mishari got behind the wheel again and as he drove, he told me we were going to be taking a little detour. "Mark, we are going to stop at the palace of Crown Prince Abdullah for a short while," he said.

"Yes, sir," I replied. I liked experiencing anything new, so long as it didn't mean crapping in the desert where a thousand and one Bedouin could watch me.

We stopped in the palace courtyard and were told the Crown Prince would be arriving in a few minutes. I stayed out of the way, just watching. Within a minute or two, with sirens wailing and lights flashing, vehicles raced into the palace heralding the arrival of His Royal Highness Prince Abdullah Bin Abdul Aziz, the Crown Prince of Saudi Arabia.

I looked directly at the Crown Prince and watched as National Guard soldiers, Royal Guards and God knows who else swarmed all over the place like soldier ants. Organised chaos reigned for a time—with King Fahd, of course! As Prince Mishari was in Riyadh, it was his duty to stop by and pass his respects to the Crown Prince who is also the head of the National Guard. Prince Abdullah has the reputation of being both strict and fierce. He probably had to be since he wasn't of the 'Sudeiri Seven'. The seven sons of the first King's favourite wife Hussa Sudeiri rule the Kingdom, and even their sons have been given high profile positions within the country.

On our arrival back at Prince Mishari's villa, I found his plans had changed. We would take an evening flight to Jeddah instead of staying overnight in Riyadh. There goes our night out clubbing, I thought. I knew better than to ask why the change of plan. Their plans changed constantly and their minds changed even more than their plans! I never knew what was going on or what was going to happen next. I lived my life in a constant state of alert or in a mind-blowing state of boredom. I couldn't plan when to take a shower, when to use the telephone or even when to go to the toilet. Sometimes I would sit for hours doing nothing but as soon as I sat down on the toilet, someone would be banging on the door shouting that I was needed.

We sorted ourselves out and Sultan returned so we set off for the airport. I was looking forward to exploring Riyadh but the chance was snatched away. On noticing my loss, Sultan tried to cheer me up by declaring that he would take me to 'chop-chop' square later, so I could witness a beheading. I decided to forgo that one experience, though, as all I wanted to take away from Saudi Arabia were happy and fond memories.

During the flight to Jeddah, Prince Mishari asked me to visit the flight deck with him. I'd flown in various aircraft many times, and had even piloted a helicopter myself, so visiting the flight deck wasn't of real interest to me. The new and everlasting experience I was looking for would not come from anything on the aircraft but more from what I could see from it. Approaching Jeddah airport at night, I watched the shimmering, twinkling and dancing lights of the city from the flight deck. The night sky was clear and bright as we descended towards the runway. It appeared no one wanted to direct the prince or me to return to our seats. Just as the thought crossed my mind, the prince said, "Mark, I think we should return to our seats now."

I was sure I heard a sigh of relief from the Captain. As we took our seats the prince asked, "Mark, have you met Princess al-Anud's brother yet?"

"Which brother would that be, Your Highness?" I replied.

"Prince Khalid Bin Fahd."

"Yes sir, I had the pleasure of tucking him up in London one time," I said.

"What do you mean by that, Mark?"

"Do you remember John, the Hungarian guy, in London, sir?"

"Yes I do, why?"

"He works for Prince Khalid in London. He was unable to take care of him on one occasion and asked me to cover the job. I did so but on the last day, John arrived and told me what to charge the prince. The charges were excessive and I felt uncomfortable asking for them.

"I see," he said, "Well Mark, you may like to know that we'll be staying as Prince Khalid's guests in his villa tonight."

Oh, bollocks, I thought, just what I need. What reception I would get, I wondered. Maybe he would charge me an excessive rate to stay in his villa for the night.

As we exited the aircraft, I carried Prince Mishari's briefcase, only this time I stuck to him like glue. Officials fell over themselves seeing to the prince's every need while they escorted us through the airport. As we neared the waiting Mercedes, I wondered if we were coming or going?

Prince Khalid's villa was nothing special. The minor princes, it seemed, lived frugal lives in reasonably sized villas. In stark contrast, the major princes lived in the lap of luxury in multimillion-pound palaces. However, Prince Khalid's villa was well equipped, clean and comfortable. After entering the villa, the princes greeted each other. The formalities completed, I seized the chance and offered my apologies to Prince Khalid for the overcharging in London. I explained what happened and he accepted my apology. Saleh, his servant, showed me to the rooms I would be using. My holdall was already deposited on the bedroom floor. I unpacked and took a quick shower. I put on a clean *thobe* and my headdress and walked back into the lounge. Several guests had turned up. One of them, an old man, made a beeline for me. He reached up and kissed me on the nose! As he did so, he rambled in Arabic. I made out the first word he repeated, it was *towilumrak* (oh, long of life). This was a word I had heard many times when Saudis addressed the princes.

I glanced at the princes and their assembled guests and I felt annoyed. Not annoyed for me but for the old man. I thought they had played a joke on him. Later, I was assured the old man whose sight was failing had genuinely mistaken me for a prince and had felt honour-bound to greet me in the traditional way.

During the evening, I got on well with a Saudi chap called Faisal. He wasn't a member of the royal family. Standing about six feet two inches tall, he had a slim build and the compulsory black moustache. Faisal was passionate about his country and had many ideas about how it should evolve. Given the nature of the Saudi Arabian regime, I wondered if by talking about these issues he was doing himself a disservice. I found his points of view enlightening and he displayed a degree of foresight. I knew that several people who had shown these qualities and expressed their views ended in prison. They suffered torture and many lashes were dished out to people the government thought to be dissenters. Faisal, I thought, would do well to keep his mouth shut. He was, I believed, just another one of the educated and ambitious Saudis who were on the road to nowhere. For hours, I talked with Faisal; we connected with each other.

Once we had put the world to rights and all the guests had left, Prince Mishari spoke with me. "Mark, you got on well with Faisal. What was it you talked about that was so interesting?"

Now, this was a loaded question if ever I had heard one. I detected he was annoyed by the tone of his voice. It upset him as I connected with someone else. Diplomatically I replied, "Your Highness, I could see you were caught up in conversation yourself. I did not want to either interrupt you or intrude into your conversation. I therefore made conversation with the person sitting nearest to me. If I've unintentionally offended you, then I apologise profusely."

"Not at all, Mark, I just wondered what was of so much interest to you about Faisal."

"We discussed his days at university in America and the difficulties he faced with his syllabus." Prince Mishari left it at that, probably realising that he wasn't going to get much out of me. Even so, I knew he wasn't happy as I retired to my room.

After taking another shower, I made a couple of telephone calls to the UK. Because it was Prince Khalid who had bugged the conversation I'd had in London with his girlfriend, I was guarded in what I said. Saudi Arabia was high up on my list of 'big brother' states anyway, and I was well aware of the control they exercised over their citizens. A few wrong words said at an untimely moment could result in dire consequences.

My phone calls finished, I climbed into bed and shortly after my head hit the pillow, I was asleep.

*   *   *

Sunlight coursed through the windows and bathed me in warmth as I opened my eyes and welcomed the new day. This was much better than waking to a cold, damp, wet and windy morning in England. Jumping in the shower, I let the powerful jets of water revitalise me in preparation for the day ahead. As I dressed, I paid particular attention to how I fixed my *kufiyeh* (headdress) under my *igal* (black rope-type band). I wanted to get the centre point of it just right. Once I was happy with it, I wandered through to the kitchen.

I found Sultan and two of Prince Khalid's servants there. *"Sabah'khair, kayfak inta?* (Good morning, how are you?)."

"Al hamduliallah (praise be to God)," I replied.

"Would you like some *shakshuka*," asked one of the staff.

"Yes, please, that would be good, thank you," I said and sat down next to Sultan. I started chatting; not about anything in particular, just idle chit-chat. Later when Prince Mishari emerged, I noticed he seemed rather preoccupied but I didn't know what was troubling him. Nonetheless, before we made our way to the airport he decided to take me for a drive along the Corniche (coast road) in Jeddah. This city, I was told was the second largest in Saudi Arabia after its capital, Riyadh. It's a coastal city adjoining the Red Sea and this is the city where most of the pilgrims arrive to when visiting the two holy mosques. Several Embassies are placed in Jeddah and there is a more relaxed atmosphere there. After our lightning tour, the prince headed to the airport for the return flight to Dhahran.

* * *

While I was Prince Mishari's guest, I found myself experiencing a new phenomenon. From being the protector, I now found myself, to a degree, being protected. This was the only time I would encounter this feeling. There was a real connection between the prince and me. He described me as being like a member of his family. What he meant by this, I don't know. What I do know is that when a prince voices sentiments such as these it usually resulted in any connection you had with them being severed shortly afterwards. It would prove to be no exception in my case, and I faced various changes that summer.

After arriving in Dhahran on 13th February 1985, we went to Prince Mishari's palace. Why they described it as a palace, I don't know. In fact, he rented two large houses—one for the men and one for the women. Segregation was the order of the day in Saudi Arabia then and it still is today.

Later that evening, the prince asked me to go with him to dinner at Prince Mohammed Bin Fahd's. Of course I knew Prince Mohammed well as I'd worked for him often and had just recently completed a job with him in London; he was the prince who'd beaten up a young woman. Because of this, I didn't want to go to dinner and made an excuse in the hope I could get out of it. There was no way I wanted to enter the lion's den. I had heard rumours about the types of parties he held and I didn't want to find myself in the middle of one of them. Of course, I couldn't tell Prince Mishari of my fears, so I made up some cock and bull story in the hope that Mishari would let me off the hook. Thankfully I was excused. As Mishari left, I went to my room, picked up the telephone receiver and asked the operator to connect me to my home.

"I'm sorry, I can't do that," he said. "Prince Mishari has given instructions not to allow any international calls to be put through." I got pissed off and all but demanded to be connected. Still he

195

refused, which angered me further. That was it; I decided to confront the prince about this on his return.

Winding myself up, I cast my mind back to my arrival when the prince had asked for my passport. I had refused. He had said, "Visitors are supposed to give their passports to their sponsors." I had replied, "I'll hold on to my passport if you don't mind."

"Fine, but remember you need an exit visa to leave the country, too," he had responded.

I detected a sinister undertone in his comment and retaliated. "Your Royal Highness, if I want to leave Saudi Arabia, then I will do so, with or without an exit visa. I'll walk home if I have to," I said, naively. Holding passports, barring telephone calls, censoring newspapers, magazines and controlling television programmes were all tactics the Saudi government used to control their people. Now I was being blatantly subjected to that control and I didn't like it.

Late that evening, the prince returned. As the Mercedes stopped, I opened the door. As he stepped from the car, I greeted him and asked, "How was the dinner, Your Highness? Did it go well?"

"Yes, it went well, how was your evening?" he asked.

"Not so good, sir."

"Why not?"

"Because I wanted to phone the UK and you've put a block on all international calls."

"That doesn't include you," replied the prince.

"It would have helped had you told the operator that. If I can't call the UK when I want to, then I will have to cut short my visit and return home," I said. Prince Mishari was well aware that I was prone to speak my mind and was accepting of it. In fact, he put up with a lot from me when he clearly didn't have to.

"Don't worry Mark; I will clear up the misunderstanding in the morning. Now I will say goodnight."

"Goodnight, sir."

As I headed into the house, I wondered was it a misunderstanding or had the prince been intentionally spiteful because I did not go with him? The following morning my international telephone ban was lifted.

Chapter 23

Desert round two

My opinion of the prince changed during the visit. Seeing him work in his government position and watching the power he wielded woke me up with a jolt. He did not have to put up with any of my tantrums, but he did. Whether I entertained him or not I don't know but I would forever wonder why he allowed me to get away with so much.

We set off back to the desert and I wondered how I would occupy myself there. As we passed close to the Kuwaiti border, I saw a huge plantation. It stretched for more than half a mile. Hundreds and hundreds of date palms stood tall next to each other; the view was awe-inspiring. Later we pulled in to the campsite and several National Guard and Bedouin Arabs encircled us. They greeted the prince as I quietly got out and stood to one side. The prince signalled Mohammed to take care of me. He took me off in the opposite direction of my old tent. As we neared the tent last used by the prince, Mohammed said, "Here, Mark, you will stay here. Prince Mishari will stay in his trailer." I was left to settle in.

Opening the canvas flap, I leant forward and stepped through. There was a king-sized mattress on the floor. Crisp white sheets and several blankets lay on top. Towards the rear was a large American-style refrigerator, which made me laugh. I opened the door and the light came on. It was well stocked and ice formed on its sides. I noticed the sound of a generator humming away in the background. I noticed another canvas door on the other side of the tent.

I lifted it and found a shower cubicle and portaloo toilet installed. The shower unit had hot and cold running water servicing it. I could wash and use the toilet in comfort now. This threw a different light on the trip. I was as happy as a pig in shit! These creature comforts were the icing on the cake.

I set off in search of the prince to thank him for his consideration. Passing the rear of the tent, I noticed the generator and a large water bowser, which serviced my utilities.

National Guard vehicles were dotted around the encampment. Each one was painted in a dull greyish colour. Several fires were alight outside the Bedouin tents as they sat by them drinking mint tea or Arabic coffee. Tea sounded like a good idea to me, but I had first to thank the prince.

"Mohammed, Mohammed," I called as I noticed him chatting with a couple of guy's nearby. "Yes. Mark, what do you want?"

"Sorry I disturbed you, but I need to speak with the prince. Do you know where I can find him?"

"I will take you to him," he said as he led the way towards three large trucks with massive trailers. As with the other vehicles, they were painted in the same dull, greyish colour. I wondered if they were the command posts or something like that. Getting closer I found the trucks more separated than they had at first appeared. We stopped at the bottom of some steps, which led up to a door in the side of one of them. "You will find Prince Mishari inside."

"Thanks Mohammed. I'll come and find you soon and we can have some tea and a chat. Is that all right?"

"Yes Mark, that will be good," he replied. With that, I walked up the steps to the door in the side of the monster trailer. I knocked and heard the prince answer: "Come in." Opening the door and looking in, I felt like I had been hit with a baseball bat. Ice-cold air-conditioning enveloped me. Massive and luxurious leather sofas and chairs sat on beautiful, intricately woven Arabian carpets. Crystal chandeliers hung from the ceiling. Polished dark wood and glass-topped coffee tables were next to the sofas. On top of the smaller tables by the armchairs, I saw gold table lamps, adorned with crystal droplet shades. The decoration was more exclusive than many of the five-star hotels I had stayed in around the world. Sitting in an armchair opposite the doorway was the prince. "Hello Mark, come in, sit down," he said. "I love being in the desert," he exclaimed as he sent a servant off to bring us some mint tea. I could see why; he wasn't going to be slumming it, I thought. The other two mobile palaces were being used by Princess al-Anud and their children,

Turki and Hala. Overall, though, I was more than happy with the tent placed at my disposal and even felt some romanticism about camping in the desert.

After leaving the prince, I went back to my tent and savoured the sights and sounds that engulfed me. Bending over to open the canvas flap, I made sure, I held on to my headdress. After closing it, I tied it down. I felt at ease and yet strangely isolated from the surrounding encampment. The tent was about twenty-five feet square. The ground was covered with several dark maroon embroidered carpets, which overlaid one another. I went over to the mattress, and lay down. I studied the paisley patterned yellow and dark red lining. I took a mental picture of the glorious colours as the sun lit them up. These rare moments would be the jewels I would treasure later in life. I drifted off into a deep sleep only to be awoken by the sound of gunshots ringing in my ears. Catching me unaware, I jumped to my feet and ran out to see what the commotion was all about.

My sandals and headdress were left behind. I found Prince Mishari with his brother, Prince Badr. A silver Colt 45 pistol hung from one of Prince Badr's hands, while a large bird hung from the other. The shots I heard heralded Prince Badr's arrival and did not show any special or remarkable marksmanship that would have been needed to shoot the bird from the sky.

"I heard the shots and wondered what was going on," I said. After being introduced to Prince Badr, we walked over to Prince Mishari's Mercedes. Majid came dashing over and unlocked the car. Prince Mishari opened the boot and looking inside, I exhaled a large breath as I took stock of the veritable arsenal of automatic and semi-automatic weapons on display.

"Tonight, Mark, we will be going hunting!" exclaimed the prince.

Hunting, hunting! I laughed to myself as visions of us loosing off thousands of rounds from machine-guns at some poor unsuspecting animal flashed through my mind. It would be a bloodbath, a massacre, I thought.

"What are we going to hunt, Your Highness?" I said as I tried to keep a straight face.

"Jerboa, Mark, we will hunt Jerboa." I felt my knees go weak and my chuckle muscles contort as I tried in vain to catch my suppressed laughter.

"Excuse me, Your Highness, but don't you think it a little excessive hunting these desert rats with machine-guns?" I asked.

Crippled with laughter, Prince Mishari couldn't speak. "What's so funny?" I asked.

"Mark, you idiot, I didn't mean we would be hunting with these weapons," he spluttered, as he no doubt visualised the scene which had previously been dancing across my mind. Contorted with laughter, tears streamed from our eyes. The more we thought about it, the more we laughed. That was until a Bedouin brought me back to my senses with his exclamation that I was a 'crazy Englishman'.

During the early years, I shared several special moments with the prince and thought we got on famously. Once the Bedouin passed by, I started chuckling again. The princes left me to it as they walked back to Prince Mishari's palatial trailer. I was sure within minutes the joke would be shared with the princess. I set off in search of Mohammed and some lunch. My jaw and 'chuckle' muscles were sore from all the laughter, which had wracked my body.

As we sat eating *kabsa*, a lamb and rice dish, I decided to catch at least one Jerboa during the hunt. As we chatted, I decided to keep the joke I had shared with the prince to myself. I asked what tactics were employed during these hunts. Instead of using automatic weapons, we would be using automatic jeeps. "Mark. We wait until after dark and then set off in several vehicles. We drive with our low beam headlights on searching for Jerboa. When spotted, we put on the high beam headlights. This signals to the others that we have found one. With all the high beam lights on, we light up a large area. Everyone chases the Jerboa and when we get close the men jump out and chase it on foot. If we catch it, then it's killed by the *Halal* method. In other words, its throat is cut. When we get back to camp, we throw them on the fire and eat them." Thanking Mohammed for his enlightenment on the hunt tactics, I set off back to my tent. As the sun began to set, my adrenaline began to rise. I felt a real buzz of excitement and anticipation. I began to long for the moment that I would catch my first Jerboa.

Shortly after this, Prince Mishari climbed into the driving seat of the large jeep. His uncle, Sultan, sat next to him. I sat behind Prince Mishari and Mohammed sat next to me in the other rear passenger seat. As everyone else got into their vehicles, Prince Mishari gunned the engine of our 4x4. An air of expectation engulfed us as we set off to hunt. It was only minutes later when the first Jerboa was sighted. A hail of light shone bright as the high beams of the jeeps flooded the area. I had decided previously to watch the first catch so I could see exactly how it was done. After studying the tactics, I was sure I could catch one. Now I waited with bated breath for the next sighting. This was going to be my catch. Nothing would prevent me securing my trophy. Mentally, I already had a Jerboa secured in my hand. Now all I had to do was physically make it happen.

Without warning, the high beam lights again lit up the night sky. The chase was on. The prince accelerated into the melee. I prepared myself. Moving closer to the door, I placed my hand on the handle in preparation of an early exit. I wasn't about to let my newfound friends deprive me of my moment of glory. Drawing ever closer to the Jerboa, my heart raced in tune with the V8 engine. I was going to catch it. I could smell victory. Heart pumping, adrenaline flowing, the sweat beads formed on my forehead, I pulled on the door handle.

Prince Mishari swerved sharply to the right as he continued the chase. I exited the jeep a little earlier than expected and landed face down on the sharp sand of the desert. My headdress had come off during the fall and had landed a short distance away from me. I vaguely watched it as it fluttered in the wind nearby. My *thobe* had somehow slid up around my waist area exposing my long white cotton under trousers. Searing pain shot through the palms of my hands as they contacted the sand. I lay on the ground.

After my unceremonious exit from the jeep and semi-conscious, I slowly became aware that no Jerboa resided in either of my hands.

I was severely pissed off, and became even more so as I noticed several Arab faces looking down at me, laughing and grinning. Then, it had to happen, I heard the phrase "Crazy, crazy Englishman," emanating from the Bedouin who had dogged me throughout my desert trip. I knew he was right. After picking myself up, with a little help from my friends, I climbed back into the jeep. Everyone was laughing and having fun, probably at my expense. Not being psychic, I didn't know it would be me who would be laughing the following night.

An hour or so later we returned to camp. Leaving the jeeps, we made our way over to the campfires nearby. As sweet mint tea was served, I marvelled at the bright blue, orange and red flames licking at the logs on the fire. Tiny crackling sparks flew skywards, drifting away in the light desert breeze. I sat on the right-hand side of the prince. Several Jerboas were unceremoniously thrown on to the burning embers at the base of the fire. Neither the prince nor I bothered to eat any of them. Much laughter and merriment emanated from the men sitting around us. No doubt, my hunting expertise was high up on the agenda of their discussions.

After a couple of hours, the prince rose. As we followed his lead, he bade the men goodnight. The prince signalled me to walk with him. "Mark, did you enjoy yourself tonight?"

"Yes, Your Highness, I did. That's apart from my early exit from the jeep, of course," I replied.

"I have to admit, I thought you were just a little bit hasty, too," he said, laughing. After saying goodnight, I made my way back to my tent. I opened the fridge door and scraped some ice from the icebox, and placed it on the palms of my hands to soothe the sand burns. I climbed into bed and the crisp, cold white sheets sent a shiver through me. The nights were freezing and if the wind blew, it cut through you like a knife. I was fortunate to have been given a desert Sheikh's robe, which was made from heavy canvas material and lined with white fur. This robe shielded me from the biting wind.

I placed the robe on top of my blankets and tried to get warm. My thoughts wandered until I drifted off to sleep.

* * *

"Mark, Mark, wake up, I want to show you something," called Sultan, the prince's uncle, from the canvas flap of my tent.

"Give me five minutes, will you?"

"Okay Mark, but hurry up, I think you will like this." Not happy with the disturbance, I nonetheless dragged myself from my bed. After a quick wash, I got dressed and went outside.

"I know you like new experiences, Mark, so I thought you may like to witness this." Sultan steered me towards the tent where the cooks prepared the food. Behind it, I saw two camels. One was very young, a baby, I thought. They were both tied up with rope. This rope extended from one front leg to one back leg.

"Mark, we are having the young one for dinner today." I felt a thud in my heart. I had guessed that Sultan thought I would like to witness the ritual killing of the baby camel. "Mark, do you want to see it being prepared?"

"No way," I answered and walked away. I was pissed off with Sultan. My guess was that he just wanted to see my reaction to the killing. I wasn't about to give him any satisfaction. When Sultan caught up to me, I asked, "Who is coming to dinner anyway?"

"Brigadier Cocking is coming. He is English and on secondment to the National Guard."

An hour or so later Prince Mishari introduced me to this Brigadier. I found him to be a typical British officer who no doubt had attended public school back home. In my opinion, he was stand-offish and reserved.

Prince Mishari told me a bed had been made up for the Brigadier in my tent, as he would be staying the night. I nodded my acceptance, not that I had any choice in the matter. Neither the Brigadier nor I had anything in common, so apart from a few pleasantries, no meaningful conversation took place between us.

I felt the Brigadier resented my being with the prince. It probably didn't help when Prince Mishari said he wanted only me to go with him while he went for a drive in the desert that evening.

Dinner was a sombre affair. I couldn't get the thought out of my mind that Sultan wanted me watch the death of the baby camel. This was the second time Sultan had tried to entice me into watching a killing. Their capital punishment, they called justice. But it wasn't justice, not least because I knew too well that several princes had committed crimes which would have seen them facing the executioner's sword along with people they had condemned, were their justice meted out equally to all.

"Mark, Prince Mishari wants you to meet him at his trailer," said one of the National Guard soldiers.

"Thanks, I'm on my way," I replied.

Arriving at Prince Mishari's trailer, I knocked the door.

"Is that you, Mark?"

"Yes, sir," I replied.

"Wait for me by the GMC. We are going for a tour of the neighbourhood."

What neighbourhood? I thought, as we were miles from anywhere.

Chapter 24

Sea of Sand

Two or three minutes later Prince Mishari bounded down the steps of his trailer. As he jumped in to the drivers' seat, a smile beamed across his face. "Come on Mark, get in," he said. I wondered where this magical mystery tour was going to end.

The main beams lit up the desert ahead of us as we set off across the wasteland. I wondered if we were heading for somewhere in particular. Would there be a pleasant surprise at the end of the drive? As it happened, there was a surprise, but not one I expected.

The comfortable GMC Suburban careered across the desert taking it all in its stride. Its upper bodywork was finished in shiny black whereas the lower panels were finished in a dark red colour. Prince Mishari chatted away freely; happy, I felt, to be away from the confines of the camp for a while. When we were alone, I saw a different person. He was relaxed, warm-hearted and I enjoyed his company. As I viewed him at work or in the company of his brothers, I would see a change in his character. It was as though he were on stage and had to give a performance.

The further away from the camp we got, the more undulating the desert became. Now we positively flew over the ruts, mounds and small dunes as they appeared before us. Prince Mishari was in his element and drove even faster as he became more excited with the new challenge the terrain offered. The dunes became like a sea on land. As the GMC's lights lit up the waves, the prince dived head first into them. Laughing like two little kids, we climbed to the top of the dunes and then dived right in to the sea of sand. Then it happened. We became bogged down, and with wheels spinning furiously, we moved not one inch. We were well and truly stuck.

I got out of the GMC as the prince tried to escape the dune. It was then I noticed that only the back wheels were spinning. I couldn't believe it. We had been tearing along in a two-wheel drive GMC and should never have gone off into the dunes. The prince cut the engine and I tried to dig us out. No way was this going to work.

I looked skywards and appreciated the moonlight, standing in the middle of nowhere. One minute we were swimming and diving in our sea of sand. The next, we were in danger of drowning in it. Turning to the prince, I asked him, "What now, boss?"

Calmly he replied, "Its fine, nothing to worry about." He leant in through the window of the jeep and turned the ignition on. Every ten seconds or so, he flashed the headlights. A couple of minutes later, lights flashed back at us from who knows where in the darkness. We got back into the GMC and waited for our rescuers. Every thirty seconds or so, the prince flashed the lights of the jeep. This helped guide them in to our position.

Ten minutes later, a shiny blue and silver jeep stopped in front of us. The engine burbled away, sounding much like a large V8 engine. In front of the grille was our saviour, a steel cable winch. The driver stepped from his jeep and nearly fell over. At first, I thought the sand was giving way beneath his feet. I soon realised that he was, in fact, drunk. Standing on top of this dune in Saudi Arabia, I looked at our stranded jeep. I then looked at the drunk who had come to our aid. I glanced at the prince and wondered what his take would be on this. Being the Under Secretary of the National Guard for the Eastern Province, I wondered if the prince would be compelled to take some action.

Our drunken friend climbed back into his jeep and activated the winch. As the cable wound out, the prince picked up the end of it. As he went to place it round the towing hook on our jeep, the drunk suddenly reversed. Instead of dropping the cable, the prince held on to it and was pulled several feet through the sand. I couldn't help myself and burst out laughing. The scene was like a *Carry On* movie; it was surreal.

The prince wasn't amused. After securing the cable to the GMC, we got in. Again, the blue and silver jeep reversed, but this time it pulled the GMC clear of the soft sand. We thanked our rescuer and bid him farewell. Once we were on our way, I said, "Surely you must have noticed that guy was drunk?"

"Of course."

"Why did you ignore it?"

"Well for one, he helped us. Two, we may have been over the Kuwaiti border and that guy was a Kuwaiti. Three, he will wake up with a sore head in the morning and probably will not remember anything. As he had helped us, why should I add to his troubles? More importantly, why did you laugh at me when he drove off when I was holding the cable? I could have been hurt."

"I couldn't help it. Had you been hurt, then I wouldn't have laughed. In fact, I would probably have killed the guy," I said, laughing once again.

Now that I'd seen the prince in action in the desert, I didn't feel so bad about my recent antics. It appeared that if I wasn't the next Lawrence of Arabia, neither was he! Back at camp, I kept our escapade secret. In truth, I never disclosed anything about the prince to anyone, so it was business as usual.

"Did you enjoy the evening, Mark?"

"Your Highness, it was an adventure I'm not likely to forget," I replied with a grin on my face. I appreciated him wanting me to enjoy the whole experience of visiting his homeland. However, money worries nagged me and I knew my cash reserves would be running low in the UK. With this in mind, I would shortly have to broach the subject of my leaving. After the prince had retired for the night, I made my way back to my own tent.

Sitting on the edge of my mattress, I reminisced about the visit. I found myself surprised at how much I had enjoyed it.

My mind wandered again to my financial difficulties. No way would I tell the prince about them. I would not ask; maybe it was pride or something, I don't know, but I could never ask anyone for money, ever. Therefore, I had no choice but to return to the UK and get back to work. As I had been invited to Saudi Arabia, I never expected to be paid.

As I opened my eyes in the morning, light flooded through the tent lining. The rich colours and light beamed into my brain, releasing serotonin, making me feel good. I got up, washed, dressed, and set about finding something to eat. On the way to the food tent, I stopped and chatted as best I could with anyone I came across. Saudi Arabia had grown on me in such a short time and I would like to stay longer, I thought. As I walked, I was immersed in sunlight, which made me feel both warm and comfortable. The desert no longer seemed an alien place to me. Catching sight of Mohammed, I signalled him with a wave of my hand to come and see me. As he got closer, I said, "Hi Mohammed, where have you been? How are you today?"

Smiling he replied, "Good, good, *Al Hamduliallah*." (Praise be to God). Other words permanently imprinted on my brain were "*Allah'u Akbar*" (God is Great). If I unintentionally came across any Arabs praying, I would discreetly disappear, in case I offended them. Not being Muslim, I didn't pray with them but I was sensitive to their beliefs and I respected them.

"The prince is going to show you some falcon hunting later in the day. Will that interest you, Mark?" Mohammed questioned.

"Mohammed, everything interests me here and I look forward to seeing the falcons."

"Where are you going, Mark?"

"I'm going to see if the cook will make me some *Shakshuka*."

"Mark, I'll look for you again after you have eaten."

I left him and went to eat. I then mooched around the camp. When I saw Sultan, he said, "I've been looking for you. Prince Mishari wants you to meet him over by his trailer."

Like an obedient servant, I dashed off to see the prince. I found him next to the offending GMC. "Good morning Mark, how are you today? Have you got over last night's fiasco yet?" he said, grinning at me. Before I could reply he added, "Would you like to see falcons hunting?"

"I would love to," I replied. Maybe I would get some photos of the falcons, I thought. This trip got better and better, and I didn't want to leave.

Getting into the GMC, I was told it was only a short drive to the falconry settlement. "Do we have to negotiate any sand dunes on the way?" I asked the prince. Not appreciating the joke, he didn't reply. Even though we were alone in the jeep, I took it as a sign to keep my mouth shut.

Eventually the prince said, "The sport of falconry is very old and the home of Arabian falconry lies chiefly in the plains of northern and eastern Arabia. The favourite choice of quarry of the falconer is the Houbara Bustard. Did you know that, Mark?"

"No, sir, I didn't, but I do now," I replied. At the falcon site, we got out of the jeep. A couple of other vehicles had followed us. The head falconer greeted the prince. On his right arm was a beautiful small male peregrine falcon. Its wings were of a slate blue-grey colour and the back barred with black. The underside was white with light brown stripes. Its head was a dark, shiny black, which followed down each side. Under its beak, the colour was lighter; a creamy colour. The falconer placed a small leather hood, a *burqa*, over the head of the bird, immobilizing and quieting it. We walked over to the rest of the men assembled nearby. A few birds were perched on blocks (called '*wakar*' in Arabic) knocked into the ground. I held one of the falcons on my arm and a photo was taken. Excitement and expectation filled the air.

It was two hours later that a Houbara was sighted. The falcon chosen for the chase was immediately unhooded and slipped from its 'jesses,' these tie the falcon to its leash. Flying straight at its prey, its wings beat powerfully. Surprisingly, it stayed near the ground as it closed in on the large Houbara. Almost on top of it and at the last moment, the falcon threw itself up into the air. Screaming towards its target, it dived and seized its prey with its talons. This sight, I was told, was rare and I should treasure it.

On the way back to camp, the prince asked if I had enjoyed the spectacle. Indeed I had, I assured him. Thinking the time was right; I finally told him that I would have to leave in a few days.

"Why? Are you not enjoying your time here? Don't you want to stay with us? Is there a problem?" The questions came fast.

I replied quickly to him, "Your Highness, I have enjoyed my time. There is no problem. I would like to stay but I can't because I've commitments that I have to attend to back in the UK." I could tell the prince was upset by this turn of events. I felt he thought I was ungrateful, or perhaps he felt snubbed in some way.

I got out of the GMC back at camp and felt the conversation had not gone well. I walked away wondering if I could have dealt with the issue more sensitively. Back to my tent I trundled and secured myself inside. I piled up and patted down sand over the bottom of the canvas flap door. I was feeling pissed off. Pissed off because I wanted to stay, and pissed off because I thought I had upset the prince. Had my finances been secure in the UK then I would have stayed, but I had no choice. I had to return to the UK and find work.

As darkness fell, I remained in my tent but left on the light, which was powered by the generator, as was the fridge. I climbed between the sheets on the mattress and studied the shadows cast by the light inside. Two or three minutes later, I heard a rustling at the bottom of the canvas door. Something or someone was trying to get in. I watched intently not knowing what to expect. Could it be a *dhub*, a large desert lizard, or perhaps a Jerboa or even the family of a Jerboa? Maybe they were trying to get in and wreak some revenge on me after my display of hunting prowess. Letting my mind wander, I laughed. As the canvas flap door opened, a familiar face came into view. It was the prince, and he must have been on his knees crouching over to get his head into that position. Inwardly I smiled, wondering what he was up to. "Mark, Mark, are you sleeping?" he asked.

"No, I'm awake."

"Are you upset?"

"Yes, I'm upset," I replied, not letting on that it was because I had to leave.

"Mark, don't be upset, we've arranged a special evening for you. We have some of the local Bedouin girls here and we have set up some Michael Jackson music. We are having a disco and you are the guest of honour. You must come and join us."

"If you've gone to that trouble, then I suppose, I'll have to," I replied.

"Good, hurry up then. We'll wait for you in the main tent, the *majlis*." As soon as he left, I laughed aloud. What a nice gesture, I thought. Obviously, he did not want any bad feeling between us. He often showed a softer, more compassionate side of his character to me. Apart from my boss, he had become a friend. Was this a good or bad thing? I wondered. Freshening up and dressing myself, I thought about the disco. This was a first as far as I was aware. A Michael Jackson disco in the desert and local Bedouin girls invited too!

As I strode up to the canvas door of the *majlis*, I noticed it was quiet. Were they waiting especially for me, as I was the guest of honour? Holding the top of my headdress, I bent down and stepped through into the *majlis*. Crossing the threshold, I had taken the step of no return. Inside, I saw a hundred or more faces staring at me, and not one was female. No Bedouin girls were in sight. Prince Mishari, sitting alone on a sofa at the far end of the *majlis*, signalled me to sit down. As I did so, I scanned the tent looking for the music system. I couldn't see that either. Looking toward the prince, I wondered what was going on. He smiled and raised his hand slowly towards an old lizard skinned Bedouin sitting on the floor who sat with his back against one of the main poles supporting the tent. At the prince's signal, the Bedouin picked up an instrument and began to play it. He sang as he played it. A wailing and screeching like I had never heard before assaulted my eardrums. They were under a full-on attack. *Ting, Ting, Ding, Wa, Wa, Wah*, he wailed. I stared on in disbelief. *Screech, screech, screech*; it sounded like someone was flogging a thousand cats at once.

Hour after hour, it went on. I sat there frozen in my seat, knowing I couldn't leave. It would be considered unacceptable behaviour. Every so often, I caught the prince's eye and he smiled. The bastard set me up! There was no Michael Jackson. No girls. No fun. Just an ear-splitting racket from a leathery skinned, toothless Bedouin who looked over a hundred years old. He screeched like a cat being castrated and played his *rababa* instrument as well as he sang. Looking at the rectangular box covered with lambskin and the one or two strings that were attached to it, I marvelled at how anyone could create such a racket with so little.

The evening over, I waited to catch the prince alone. "You bastard," I said, "You set me up."

After laughing, he replied, "If I have to suffer it, then I don't know why you shouldn't too!"

Two days later and we were back in Dammam. I stood firm on my decision to leave and on the day of departure, the prince said goodbye and handed me a large envelope. On the aircraft, I opened it and found it contained five thousand English pounds in cash. Had I known this before, I could have transferred the money to my bank in England and then stayed longer. I was shocked by his generosity but it made me question why he couldn't have given me a pay rise before, when I asked for one. It messed with my mind. As it was, as soon as I landed back in the UK, I was on the phone, telling Bill at the office that I was back in town and available for work.

Chapter 25

Back in the UK, March 1985

Within days of getting back from Saudi Arabia, I received a call from the office: Prince Fawaz Bin Abdul Aziz had been burgled.

Prince Fawaz is one of King Fahd's brothers. He now wanted security. I thought he was a little late in asking. Nonetheless, I got my act together and made my way to his house in the village of Chiddingfold, Surrey. It was late March, it was cold, and I missed the warmth that had enveloped me in Saudi Arabia. I told the office that I would be at the prince's house within the hour. I knew the prince's wife was Lebanese and her brother acted as their secretary. Oh, and one other thing—they had lost £750,000 worth of cash and jewellery.

When I arrived, Harvey, another bodyguard, was already on site. We went over the details of the theft with the secretary, and from what we heard, both thought the burglary had the hallmarks of an inside job.

The alarm was raised after a grounds man had found a ladder leaning against a wall under the principals dressing room window. We found no signs of forced entry. There was no damage to the leaded light windows or frame, so we believed the thief was a professional. No one, we were told, had secured the window the previous evening. Had this been an accomplice, or just lax security? The thief had secured the two doors inside the dressing room with door wedges. The burglary had put the fear of God, or in his case, Allah, into the prince.

Now we had to put some security back into Prince Fawaz's life. We weren't surprised to find that he was a raving alcoholic. What frightened him more than the burglary was that he could have been murdered. He didn't make any mention of being frightened that his wife might be murdered, I noted. Like many princes, he was a coward. If faced with a problem, the princes got someone else to deal with it for them—just as they had when the Iraqis invaded Kuwait and threatened Saudi Arabia. The Saudis bought an army, an American one, to fight their war for them.

I was aware that Prince Fawaz's alcoholism had caused him to be sacked, in 1980, from his position as Governor of Mecca, the most important holy site in Saudi Arabia. I also knew that he used the services of prostitutes. No surprise there! This fact was revealed publicly in open court in Paris when his Lebanese 'fixer' said it was part of his job to find young women for the prince. He said Prince Fawaz used the prostitutes at both the Hotel de Crillon and Royal Monceau hotels. If the prostitutes were suitable, they would receive £1000.

We endured a lengthy briefing. I took note of all the main points about the prince. I was already aware of where the prince slotted into the family tree, as I had studied it thoroughly. I was there to do a job, not for the brother-in-law, who yearned to be part of the *Al-Saud* family, but for the prince. The brother-in-law waffled and waffled and I just wished he would shut up and let us get on with our business.

Another strange twist about the burglary was the secretary had reported it to the police: the Saudi royals never normally did this. In the experience of their bodyguards, they always hid behind 'front men' or 'front companies'. They were always careful not to leave any trails that may lead back to them, wherever possible.

Static guys arrived to take care of the house and grounds, and I made it a priority to meet all the staff.

Prince Fawaz himself turned out to be pleasant and amiable; he was well educated and smart in appearance. This last point was good news: it meant I wouldn't be embarrassed when I went out with him.

* * *

When the prince ventured into London, we kept close. I stayed just off his right shoulder, while Harvey took the left. Both of us walked a pace behind him. As usual, our standard procedure when we arrived at our destination, be it a restaurant, club or what have you would be to note the exit points and the toilets.

We used two cars, the compulsory Mercedes and a backup car. Both drivers stayed with the cars. Aware the prince wasn't popular, we kept our guard high wherever we were—especially since the prince was a target of minority religious factions. On several occasions, we told the secretary not to walk between Prince Fawaz and us. If something happened, we needed to act on it instantly. Harvey would have brought the prince down and shielded him while I moved on the threat and dealt with it. The secretary would have had to take potluck with his own safety. We would protect our charge.

The prince favoured The Elephant on the River restaurant, set on the north bank of the River Thames. Sometimes, he went on to a club. One night, when we visited Tramp nightclub in Jermyn Street, London, our attentions focused on Sylvester Stallone, the movie star, who was there. It had become normal to analyse the body language and various signs in the makeup of people, and that night was no different. It became such a reflex action that I found myself analysing everyone, family and friends included.

Our priority was the prince's safety, and we cosseted him because of the burglary. As I stood in the toilets waiting for the prince to exit his cubicle that night, I admired myself in a mirror, just like Ziad used to admire himself in Princess Rima's mirror in the hallway of her house in Belgravia.

I was wearing a sharply cut black suit with a white shirt and maroon tie. I looked almost like a prince myself, I thought. If I staggered like a drunk with a prostitute on each arm, no one would be able to tell the difference!

* * *

As the prince's visit neared its end, I thought how it had proved fortuitous that he had full insurance coverage. He was later fully compensated, not that he couldn't afford to lose the money. After the burglary, though, Prince Fawaz never felt comfortable again at his magnificent country house and so it proved as it was soon for sale on the property market.

The rest of his visit passed without a hitch. We accompanied Prince Fawaz to the airport. The Saudi embassy arranged for us to go airside and enter the Hillingdon VIP suite. Martini met us at the VIP lounge. As we entered the suite, a private Gulfstream jet adorned in the national livery of Saudia airlines was ready and waiting. Martini went into action and completed the necessary formalities. The VIP suite staff brought refreshments—although not of the alcoholic variety, I noted with a wry smile.

A couple of minor princes were also waiting in the suite for their flights. Both of them approached Prince Fawaz and in turn kissed him on the right shoulder, showing respect. Meantime, I watched Martini pass the VAT forms across to Customs and Excise to stamp. Martini then received an envelope containing cash from the prince to compensate him for his services and to tip the staff and pay for the services used.

We left the suite and got into the Mercedes, then followed an airport car which escorted us to the prince's Gulfstream. Approaching the aircraft, I noticed a flight attendant standing on the tarmac awaiting the prince. Stepping out of the car, my eardrums were instantly assaulted by the screaming engines of the little Gulfstream. Prince Fawaz and his secretary said goodbye to us. The prince spoke briefly with Martini and then climbed the few steps into the jet. The Gulfstream taxied away; the thrust of the jet engines blasted our eardrums even more than before. We watched the Gulfstream line up for take off. With a roar of its engines, the jet careered down the runway and rose serenely into the sky. This was another job well done, and I complimented myself—as no other bugger would.

* * *

March and April 1985

Just six days after Prince Fawaz had left, the office called again. I was pleased to have a steady stream of work. My bank balance was looking healthier now, especially after the cash injection from Prince Mishari. Bill said Prince Saud Bin Naïf, the son of the fierce Saudi Arabian Interior Minister, was due in the UK. Usually Prince Saud accompanied his friend and brother-in-law, Prince Mohammed

Bin Fahd: in fact, I'd never seen one without the other. I wondered why Prince Saud was visiting alone.

The prince stayed at Cleve Lodge, his house in Hyde Park Gate. This large white mansion had tennis courts along the left-hand side of the property as you faced the front door. These were a waste of space, as I never saw them used. This part of Hyde Park Gate was well hidden. No one would assume that at the end of this turning near Hyde Park lay such an exquisite building. This building had cost the prince £7,000,000 just for a seven-year short-term lease. Our security numbered four guys on days and four on nights. Jose, the butler, and his wife Maria, the housekeeper, lived on site in a cottage at the end of the driveway next to the main house. They were Portuguese. They took care of everyone, and were polite and respectful people.

Peter, Tony, Brummie, and I were on night duty. Peter was a lad; he liked the women a lot and liked to play the field. He was from the East End of London and was a confident chap. Tony, on the other hand, was quiet, polite and professional. He was of mixed race and spoke fluent Spanish. Brummie was a different kettle of fish altogether—where the office had found him, I've no idea. I would describe him as the joker in the pack.

While we were on nights, we heard that Prince Mohammed Bin Fahd and Prince Fahd Bin Salman had had a bust up. Prince Mohammed was the Governor of the Eastern Province and Prince Fahd, the deputy Governor. Prince Fahd resigned because Prince Mohammed had taken advantage of him. What was so unusual about this was that any arguments within the royal family never normally got into the public domain. But on this occasion, various accusations were flying about. This was the reason Prince Mohammed had stayed in Saudi Arabia as he was unable to leave without a deputy to stand in for him. We also heard that Prince Fahd was accused of dubious banking practices and the liquidators of the BCCI bank claimed back $397,000 owed to them. He had given a guarantee for the overdraft of an offshore company, Colchest Corporation N.V., and they were now calling it in. Scandal swirled in the wind for several members of the royal family. It would get worse.

For reasons unknown to me, Peter brought a stun gun with him one evening. (They were not illegal in Britain at that time.) As soon as Brummie saw it, he had to have it, no matter what. He kept on at Peter like a little boy and although Peter was loath to let it go, Brummie offered him a deal, which saw Peter making a cool £100 profit. After pocketing the money, Peter studied the form of the horse racing the following day. He was a sucker for horses—and one-armed bandits, too.

Later that evening, Brummie disappeared. We looked all round the house and grounds but there was no sign of him. Eventually Tony checked Brummie's car. He came back laughing and told us to follow him. Nearing Brummie's car, we ducked down and crept silently towards it. As we got close to it, we raised our heads slowly to peep inside. Brummie came into view and looked to be in a stupor. Tony pointed out the brain of Britain had tried the stun gun out on himself. What a prat! We fell about laughing. Brummie became the focus of some serious banter after that. Where had they found this guy, I wondered? But worse was to come.

During the night, Peter and I entered the main house. We went to relieve Brummie at the main door. We walked out of the lounge and into the hallway where we came across Brummie lying on a silk Chinese carpet with a cushion under his head. He snored heavily. Peter was so incensed he gave him a stiff kick. Brummie sat bolt upright, complaining he had been winded. Peter said he was bloody lucky he had not killed him while he slept. The rest of the night passed without incident. At 7am, we finished our shift, and I made off for home. After a sleep, a shower, a change of clothes and something to eat it was time to get back into London.

Back at Cleve Lodge, I wondered what the night would bring. It wasn't long before I had my answer. Mr Cool himself, Tony, got annoyed not with Brummie, but with Winston Churchill, the Tory MP and grandson of the Great Winston Churchill. He had parked his Jaguar on our private cobbled parking area. Tony said to Churchill, "I'm sorry, sir, but you can't park there. Our drive is in constant use and we are expecting someone back momentarily."

Churchill replied, "I am only going to be a few minutes, young man."

Tony, taking offence at being called a young man, said, "I don't care how long you're going to be, move the car."

Thinking this could get out of hand, I moved closer to Tony so I could calm him if needs be. I had recognised Winston Churchill and laughed inwardly. What were the chances of two Tory MPs standing on the property simultaneously who'd both had affairs with Soraya Khashoggi, I wondered?

"Don't you know who I am?" asked Churchill. That wasn't a remark Tony wanted to hear either.

"I don't give a fuck who you are—move the fucking car or I'll move it for you!"

With that, Winston Churchill realised he was on a loser and moved his car.

Shortly before this, Jonathan Aitken MP had arrived with yet another beautiful young woman. It was later alleged that he supplied prostitutes to the princes. There wasn't anything he wouldn't do to keep the princes happy according to the newspapers.

An hour or so later, Said Ayas arrived. He is the prince's secretary and personal assistant, and godfather to Jonathan Aitken's daughter, Victoria.

"Mark," he said, "I'm going to look at a couple of apartments for sale next door, will you come with me?"

"Yes, sir," I responded. Both apartments were spacious and filled with luxuries. Expensive French crystal chandeliers hung in each of the lounges. "What do you think, Mark?" he asked.

"Tasteful, sir," I replied. Said Ayas was so impressed he bought both. He was always polite, quiet and gentlemanly. However, I heard that when it came to business—either his own or that of the prince—he was like a shark in a pond. If you put your hand in, you didn't expect to see it again.

As we stood in the hallway of Cleve Lodge later we listened to Fahd El Athel, a business partner of Prince Saud's, recount a recent business deal of Said Ayas'. He had bought a sizeable piece of land near a supermarket in America. He turned the land in to a car park then sold it to the supermarket! He made a sizeable profit in a short time.

The Saudi princes respected Said Ayas. He made them fortunes; he made himself fortunes, and he made Jonathan Aitken fortunes, too. Therefore, everyone was a winner—although it would not always remain so. Jonathan Aitken would achieve an amount of political success, but his dealings with Prince Mohammed and Said Ayas ultimately resulted in a heavy fall for him: Aitken went to jail for eighteen months for perjury. Said Ayas was charged with him, but the charges were later dropped. This was because it was in the British Government's interests.

When Said Ayas was recalled to Riyadh to see Prince Mohammed, he was immediately put under house arrest. He would later escape from Saudi Arabia via the United Arab Emirates, disguised as a woman.

Aitken went on to face allegations in the newspapers that he:

- Procured prostitutes for Arab guests at Inglewood Health Farm in Berkshire.
- Falsely passed himself off as Inglewood's owner to hide the identity of the hydro's Arab buyers.
- Lied while a Director of TV-am, and covered up a plan to give Arab investors control of the channel.
- Hid his links, while minister for defence procurement, with a Lebanese arms dealer involved in an arms contract between a British firm and the Lebanese government.
- Became financially dependent on his Arab contacts, including Prince Mohammed, the son of King Fahd of Saudi Arabia.

I knew Prince Mohammed, Said Ayas and Jonathan Aitken had talked about British armament companies paying millions of pounds in commission through a Swiss bank account. I knew also that Aitken had got the deals off the ground as Minister for Defence Procurement. Said Ayas sorted out the commissions with the firms. One of those deals alone was worth up to £50 million. Proof again that corruption rules within the House of Saud, that is along with the King of course! I also think that Aitken was given the position Minister for Defence Procurement solely because of his Saudi connections.

Prince Saud Bin Naïf and Prince Mohammed Bin Fahd surrounded themselves with 'front men'—among others were Aitken, Said Ayas, Peter Custer, Fahd Al Athel and Roger Kraillion. Any one of the front men could have found themselves in a similar position as Aitken or Said Ayas because of the princes' underhanded dealings. This was especially true as Prince Mohammed is considered one of the most corrupt in the Al Saud family. Later, he bragged about how he made millions of dollars from feeding and housing the American troops sent to protect the house of Saud during the Gulf War. The profits estimated on this venture alone were around $14,000,000. He even had public lands confiscated so he could house the troops. The only other person greedier than him was his father, King Fahd.

* * *

Four days after the prince left, Martin called me. He needed a favour: someone had let him down and he wanted me to cover a series of surveillance jobs. I told him I'd take the series on purely as a favour to him. I also made it clear that it would be my last lot of surveillance work. Where I'd once got a buzz out of stealthily watching someone who was possibly up to no good, I now found myself becoming increasingly uncomfortable with it. These jobs went against my core beliefs and it was about time that I started taking notice of them once again. I preferred being transparent and open but on surveillance detail, I felt deceitful and sneaky so I decided I should get out of it. So, even though I didn't relish it, on Thursday May 2nd I started the first of the series and as usual an insurance company was trying to avoid a significant payout after someone allegedly injured himself at work.

As my first target left his house, he climbed aboard a pedal cycle. He set off at a fair pace, dodging in and out of the cars that were parked along the street. I snapped away, and then put my camera down as I set off in pursuit. He neared a McDonald's hamburger shop and slowed down. I pulled into the kerbside and aimed the video camera that I had lying next to the Olympus at him. He jumped from the bike and entered McDonald's as I filmed him. I wrapped up the surveillance—I had all that I needed. The insurance company would be pleased with my work, as it appeared the target had miraculously recovered from his recent cruciate ligament injury. This injury affects the knee and as the target had pedalled hell for leather down the street, he showed no signs of any knee problem, job done!

I deposited my film and video in the office and was issued the next assignment. For the next six weeks or so, I went from one job to another. I never failed to get a result. Sometimes it was good for the insurers, but more often than not, it was good news for the claimant. Then, around the 13th June, I stopped work. I finally did what I had promised myself, I pulled the plug on my surveillance career.

I knew I would be called soon to spend the summer with Prince Mishari's family, and I wanted to get at least a week at home with my family before I set off. For a while, I played happy families, and waited for the phone to ring. I knew I wouldn't have to wait long because other members of his family were already on the move.

Chapter 26

Rome, Italy: Summer 1985

Ring ring, ring ring. Lifting the telephone receiver, I answered, "Hello."

"Mark, how are you?" Before I answered, Prince Mishari continued, "I need you to meet my family in Rome on the 23rd June. Arrive the day before and liaise with Nabil at the embassy. They have made all the arrangements for the hotel, cars and luggage transfers. They must take you to the airport for the arrival. Do you have any questions?"

"No, Your Highness," I replied. Business completed, we chatted briefly. We ended our chat and I reserved a seat with *Alitalia*, the Italian national airline. I then checked the hotel reservations, making sure the rooms were confirmed. Because I was meticulous in my planning and careful about arrangements I made, I prevented many problems. This time the Embassy was taking the lead. This pleased me, as it should save me untold grief—as making arrangements for the family usually involved nightmares of one sort or another.

Since the time Joha lost the prince's son, Turki, in Marbella the previous year, I'd become much more involved with Prince Mishari's wife, Princess al-Anud, and their two children, Turki and Hala. As I made my way to Rome, I reminisced about my time in Saudi Arabia. I had enjoyed my time there. Perhaps it had been because I had been able to spend more time with the prince.

I stepped from the *Alitalia* jet at Leonardo Da Vinci–Fiumicino airport in Rome and was hit by a wave of intense heat. It felt like I stepped into a sauna. With my usual efficiency, I cleared both passport and customs control. With my suitcase, I hailed a taxi. "The Hotel Excelsior in Via Veneto," I said to the driver. 35 kilometres and twenty-five minutes later, we approached the hotel and I marvelled at its splendour. Directly in front of me was a square building with one corner adorned with a half circular column topped with a pointed dome. This column looked like the shape of a bullet. To both right and left the hotel spread out. It stood six floors high and held 319 rooms. The dome, column and balconies were lit up in the darkness. The hotel's name—Excelsior—was emblazoned in blue light halfway up the dome. The hotel looked like a cake with icing on it.

A porter took care of my bag as I paid the taxi driver. I went to check in and then headed to my room. As I walked through the lobby area toward the lifts, I noted that the decoration and furnishings were exquisite. Italian black-and-white marble tiles adorned the floor. Large crystal chandeliers hung from the ceiling. Columns at the edge of the large walls gleamed with gold leaf. Maroon and gold material covered the ornate chairs and sofas. A large plant in a white ornate marble vase was placed on top of a medium sized round table. The table itself had three or four griffin type creatures sitting on a base supporting a thick top, which again was ornately decorated. On top of the table but beneath the planter was a thick glass tabletop. The table was covered in gold leaf as well.

The porter unlocked my room and I gave him a tip. Looking round the room, I noticed that rich custom fabrics and Renaissance furniture decorated it. I called the concierge and asked for someone to show me around the princess' suite. It was a real masterpiece, with walls and ceilings hand-decorated by master artisans. I checked her suite and the other rooms we had booked. I felt the princess would be most pleased with them. Once back in my room, I ordered something to eat from the room service menu.

A rare steak and fries was soon winging its way to me. After eating, I walked over to the bathroom, ran a hot bath, and climbed into it. Leaning my head back, I closed my eyes and relaxed. It must be good to be the prince, I thought as I soaked.

I set my alarm for nine in the morning and settled down for the night. I awoke before the alarm went off. Feeling refreshed, I took a shower and got dressed. I turned on the TV and flicked through the channels. Nothing caught my fancy, but I left it on anyway. At ten o'clock, the phone rang. Nabil introduced himself and said he would meet me in the lobby at twelve thirty. This would give us enough time to get to the airport before the princess arrived that afternoon.

As I had nothing else to do, I went for a stroll along Via Veneto. The sun shone brightly. Slowly I walked, window-shopping as I went, killing a little time. Back at the hotel, I told the concierge I was expecting Nabil and asked him to point him in my direction.

At twelve thirty on the dot an Arab-looking guy approached the concierge. He wore a dark coloured lightweight suit, a white shirt and black tie, with polished black shoes. He looked like he was going to a funeral. Was this Nabil? The concierge directed him towards me; I stood up and met him halfway. I extended my hand and as he reached for it, I introduced myself. Exchanging pleasantries, we made our way out to the car. It was a Mercedes. Didn't they ever get fed up with these cars, I wondered. The other vehicles needed to bring in the entourage and their luggage had already been sent on to the airport.

When we got to the airport, we took the opportunity to grab a cup of coffee before our flight arrived. Nabil seemed a bit standoffish.

We finished our coffee as it was announced our flight had landed. We went to the arrivals gate and watched as the Saudia flight taxied to a halt just outside the large glass window in front of us. We walked towards the exit door of the arrivals building. As we neared the exit, Nabil dropped a bombshell.

"You're not sanctioned to go airside or to enter the aircraft. I will escort Princess al-Anud from the plane and meet you back here," he said. With that, he spun on his heels and walked out through the door guarded by two armed Caribinieri—State Police officers. I wanted to follow him, but the sight of the armed men deterred me. I sat down on a seat facing the window instead. I watched Nabil approach the aircraft. The engines had to wind down before they allowed the aircraft steps to be rolled into place. Because the first class cabin was at the front of the aircraft, I knew that it would be from the front fuselage door that they would exit. I'd experienced these arrivals several times and the ground crew and staff appointed to meet the VIPs performed meticulously.

The drone of the powerful jet engines subsided and the ground crew moved in. As they busied themselves, the large flight of steps was pushed into place against the forward fuselage.

I watched the forward cabin door open, just as I had predicted. Nabil and a member of the airport staff went up the steps and were shown on-board by one of the flight crew. I pictured them walking into the first class section of the aircraft and then introducing themselves to Princess al-Anud. As Nabil was from the Embassy, she would feel comfortable leaving the aircraft with him, although she would probably wonder where I was.

All I had to do was sit and wait for them to show up. What could be easier? I thought it would take four or five minutes for the princess and her entourage to get their gear together and sort out the kids. Five minutes later, Nabil walked triumphantly off the aircraft with the family behind him.

As he neared me, I noted a smirk on his face, which spread from ear to ear, giving the impression he had one over on me. This didn't ruffle my feathers at all, as I had seen it all before. His chest was puffed up as he walked to me with a confident swagger, but I had other things to worry about.

Fuck, fuck, fuck! The words screamed through my brain as the arrival went tits up. Nabil arrived next to me and gestured toward the woman shrouded in a black *abaya* and the children standing next to her. He introduced me to Princess al-Anud as though I had never met her before.

"I don't know these people, who are they?" I asked him. Dumbfounded, he shrugged his shoulders.

Fuming, I went on, "You've brought the wrong family off the aircraft." Looking over his shoulder, I saw the princess, her children and entourage making their way down some steps inside the terminal building.

"That's the princess and her party," I said as I pointed towards them. Unceremoniously, he dumped the poor family he had brought to me and dashed over to Princess al-Anud. I could hear him apologising profusely. I was fuming, as I knew this fuck up would look bad for me. After all my double-checking of the hotel reservations and the rooms, I had been well and truly shafted. Nabil had been bloody quick off the mark trying to look good, and had grabbed the first family he had seen on the plane.

Obviously he didn't know that when Princess al-Anud was out of Saudi Arabia she always wore the best iridescent French and Italian fashions.

I walked briskly over to the princess. Extending my hand to take the briefcase she held, I too apologised. "Your Royal Highness, welcome to Rome, I trust you enjoyed your flight? I must apologise for the mix up. Authorization wasn't given for me to go airside and meet you. We were therefore left in the hands of Nabil from the embassy, and I'm afraid as he has never met you before, a mix-up occurred."

She replied, "It's fine Mark, don't worry about it." I held her briefcase in one hand, and with the other, I held her son, Turki. Mouthing a hello to the staff who followed, I signalled the nanny pushing their daughter Hala in a pushchair to walk ahead of me. I wanted all three principals in front of me where I could see them. Nabil guided the princess towards the waiting cars. I felt like shit after this cock up, so I could only guess how Nabil must have felt.

Within minutes, we were on our way. All we needed now was for the cars to break down, I thought. The concierge booked everyone in and Nabil showed Princess al-Anud to her suite. His job complete, he took his leave. As usual the princess kept her hands out of her pockets. If anyone expected a tip or a bonus from her then they would be sorely disappointed. Her husband, Prince Mishari, regularly tipped and gave bonuses to people, but throughout the years that I worked with them never once did I see the princess financially reward anyone. Nabil probably thought he hadn't been rewarded because of the mix up at the airport.

My job was to make sure no other upsets occurred during the visit. If the embassy sent Nabil to meet Prince Mishari at the end of the week, I would make sure that he didn't fuck up again.

There was always a chance that something could go wrong and if it did and it was my fault, I could deal with it. What I didn't want was to pick up the pieces of someone else's mistake. I suffered from a bad case of perfectionism. I wanted everything to go well. I *made*

things go well and once the principals had experienced my perfectionism, they expected nothing less.

* * *

During the first few days in Rome, we did the usual things. The shops, parks and beach all took a hammering. The beach I found interesting, not because of the beach babes there, but because of the sand. It was black and had tiny silver grains in it, which shimmered in the sunlight. It fascinated me that such a beautiful sight should result from some volcanic eruption thousands of years ago. In fact, everything about Rome fascinated me. We visited the Coliseum and strolled along the Via Sacra in the Roman Forum. When we had visited the Basilica di San Pietro, St Peter's square and the Vatican, I bought some rosaries for loved ones back home. A couple of days after our arrival, the princess bought herself some clothes and decided to treat herself to a Rolex watch.

After paying $10,000 for it, she turned to me and said, "This will be a surprise from Prince Mishari." I smiled and wondered if the prince knew he had spent $10,000 on his wife. As he was arriving later that day, perhaps I would find out.

That evening, I went off to meet the prince at the airport. On the drive back, he questioned me about the mix up during the princess' arrival.

I knew the incident would come back and bite me in the backside. I explained what happened in detail; Prince Mishari nodded but made no comment. I sat stewing in my own discomfort for the rest of the journey.

I booked the prince in and escorted him to his suite, then followed him inside. He greeted the kids enthusiastically, kissing and hugging them. He said hello to the princess, then told the nannies to take the children back to their suite.

The princess showed the prince the surprise watch he had bought her. I could see it was a surprise for him, let alone from him. He was none too happy to hear of the princess' outlay.

Prince Mishari sat down on the sofa next to a coffee table and took out a wad of $100 bills from his briefcase.

"Mark, come and sit down. I want you to count out three piles of $1000," he said as he handed me a stack of money. I counted out the three piles and gave the balance to him.

"Mark, I want you to give each one of the nannies $1000 each."

"Yes sir."

"Mark, we're leaving tomorrow; can you get the concierge to make up the bill now? Any extras we'll pay on departure?"

"Yes, sir, do I need to arrange for transfer to the airport or for the flights?" I asked.

"No, the embassy has taken care of them."

With that comment, Prince Mishari left the lounge and went to the bathroom. Before I left the suite, the princess said that she would give the money to the girls. I wasn't about to argue with her and so passed the cash over. I was dismissed and on leaving their suite, I decided to go and see the children. The nannies had heard about the departure and were busy packing. After playing with the children for a few minutes, I went down to the concierge.

The next day on the 30th June, we made our way to Rome's international airport. I wondered if I would ever visit Rome again. I had enjoyed my time there and wished I could have shared the sights with my own family.

Even on board the aircraft, I couldn't relax. Apart from keeping an eye on the family, I had to collect the passports and fill out landing cards for each of our entourage. Customs wanted to know what currency was being brought into the country. As usual, I put $5000 on the form, this was the amount I was always told to declare. Of course, in reality the family always carried a much more substantial sum when they travelled.

The house manager met us at Malaga airport. He had all the arrangements in hand, which saved me considerable time and effort. It was pure bliss not to have to worry about anything other than the principals.

An hour later, we drove into the forecourt of Casa Tam. Water gushed from the fountains heralding our arrival. Once the family entered the villa, I wandered over to my own quarters and slouched on the couch. I savoured what little time I had by myself because I knew it wouldn't last long.

I picked up the telephone and dialled home. After a moment or two, an angel's voice answered it

"Hello."

"Hi, it's me, how are you, are the boys all right?" I asked.

"We're fine, but missing you," Sue replied excitedly.

"We've just arrived at the villa in Marbella. Do you have the number here?"

"Yes, it's next to the phone. Did you like Rome? What did you see; have you taken any photographs for us to see?"

We spoke for some time before I was called to see the prince.

"Your Highness, you wanted to see me?" I said, approaching him as he sat on a chair on the ornate Italian marble patio at the front of the house.

"Yes, Mark. I want you to take Turki and Hala to the arcade in town."

"Yes, sir," I answered.

"Mark, please take care."

"Of course."

"Do you need any money?" the prince enquired.

"No sir. What time do you want us back?"

"Six o'clock, Mark. I will see you then. Don't be late."

I went to the children and called for the nannies to get ready, too. Within half an hour, we were walking along the promenade looking at the sand sculptures on the beach.

"Mark, who was it that gave us the money in Rome, was it the prince or the princess?" asked Elena, the Filipino nanny.

"It was Prince Mishari, why do you ask?" I replied

"We just wondered that was all. Will you thank the prince for the $600?"

"Of course I will. Did you get the same amount?" I asked Elena.

"Yes we did, Princess al-Anud passed it to us but we know she never gives anyone anything so we were really surprised by it. That's why I asked where it really came from, because she has taken money from me before."

"When was that?" I asked.

"It was when I took Turki to say happy birthday to Princess Sultana, Prince Salman's wife. Princess Sultana gave both Turki and me an envelope each, which contained money. On the way back to the prince's palace, Princess al-Anud asked me for the envelope on the pretext that she had come out without any money and only wanted to borrow it. I never saw it again."

I was dumbstruck and as we walked, I fumed. I knew the princess had stolen $400 from each of them. She needed her hand lopping off. If it were one of her family's subjects, their hand would be lopped off, so why not hers?

Chapter 27

Marbella, Spain: Summer 1985

On our return to the villa, I searched out the princess; there was something I wanted to say. On finding her, I asked if I could speak to her alone.

"What do you want?" she replied.

"Your Highness, what I have to say is best said in private."

Looking decidedly uncomfortable, she signalled that we should move over to the patio area.

"What is it, Mark, what is so important?"

"Your Highness, an issue has arisen that casts a bad light on you. I don't want to think badly of you and know there must be some innocent explanation for it. I know I'm not in a position to question your actions but I'm sure you would not like for me to have a misguided opinion of you."

"Please go on, Mark," she answered.

"Your Highness, I've heard the full amount of money destined for the nannies from Prince Mishari wasn't given to them. Could you tell me why that is?"

The princess was flustered by my impudence. She couldn't believe that someone was questioning her integrity.

"Mark, you have to consider that Prince Mishari probably did not realise how much money he was giving to the nannies. Therefore, I adjusted it according to the amount I believed he wanted them to have."

"Now I understand," I said, "Please forgive me my ignorance, Your Highness."

"That's fine, Mark, thank you for bringing the subject to my attention. I hope you don't think badly of me now?" she said with a smile.

232

"Of course not, Your Royal Highness," I said, and then made my way back to my quarters.

As I walked across the drive I thought, that's the biggest load of bollocks I've ever heard!

I had seen the prince handle all different types of currency and he knew exactly what money he was giving the nannies. I wanted the princess to realise she had been caught out. I knew that I would have to watch my back now. If the princess didn't think I had swallowed her story then the knives would be out.

A little later Prince Mishari called for me. I wondered if his wife had spoken to him about our earlier conversation. With some anxiety, I went to see him.

"Mark, I want you take these trousers to the dry cleaners."

With some relief, I took the trousers from him and left. I had shown an aptitude for getting things done and because of it, I now found myself completing many menial tasks for them. The major things I didn't mind doing, as I got a buzz out of getting results that others couldn't achieve. However, the menial tasks ate away at my self-esteem. Again, I felt more like a slave than a trusted and valued asset.

For the next few days, I had little to do with the princess. I thought she was avoiding me. For the moment, I had more important things on my mind as I was feeling a little peckish, so I decided to make my way to the kitchen. With a little luck, I may be able to get a snack, I thought. As I neared the staff dining table behind the house, I found Elena sobbing her heart out. Elena did an excellent job of looking after Turki, which was a mammoth task in itself. She could often be found ironing the children's clothes at 4am, in preparation for the next day.

She did everything for the family and once complained that she didn't like washing the prince's underwear because he suffered from herpes. There wasn't anything that these nannies didn't know about the families that they worked for.

"Elena, what's wrong?" I asked as I passed her a serviette from the table to dry her eyes on.

Spluttering she said, "Prince Mishari has been nasty to me."

"Why's that, do you want to tell me?"

"It all started over a pair of white trousers. Because I didn't have them ready he started shouting at me."

"Hold on a minute Elena, are these the same trousers that I took to the dry-cleaners the other day?"

"Yes, those trousers," she replied.

"Elena, stop crying. Don't worry, I'll sort it out."

"Thank you, Mark," she said, drying her eyes.

I walked away, pondering how I should handle this upset. After witnessing abuses of staff by members of the royal family over the years, I had made a conscious decision not to stand by and do nothing as I had done before.

"Hey Carlo, what's cooking?" I said as I entered the kitchen.

"I'm cooking some Chanquete," he replied in his broken English.

Chanquete is a small fish, thin and of about two centimetres long, which taste exquisite. It was a side dish he was preparing for lunch.

"I'm starving," I said. Carlo shrugged his shoulders. Then Hudda, another of the nannies, entered the kitchen.

"Hello Hudda, how are you today? You look nice and bright," I said. Hudda beamed a smile at me and turned a deep shade of red, clearly embarrassed by my comments.

"Mark," Carlo said, "Can you speak to the princess for me?"

"What about?"

"She keeps cutting down the money for the food. It is getting harder for me to prepare enough to eat for everyone."

Bloody hell, what's going on with this family, I thought.

It appeared the trip was falling apart at the seams, and here was I trying to tie it all together, just to keep the show on the road.

"Leave it to me, Carlo," I said, aware that they usually shoot the messenger.

"Mark," Hudda said, "I've made some *shakshuka*, would you like some?"

"Hudda, you are an angel."

I tucked into the scrambled egg, onion and tomato dish and watched as Hudda again turned a deep beetroot colour.

I finished my snack and Zeinob, a maid, opened the kitchen door.

"Mark, the princess wants you. She's by the front door."

"Thanks everyone," I said as I left.

234

"Your Highness, you called me?" I said as I surveyed a van parked in the driveway.

"Yes, Mark, I've bought some cheese from this man and I want you to pay him. The bill is 7000 pesetas and I want you to get a discount."

I paid the bill and asked for a discount. The cheese man looked at me incredulously. Shrugging his shoulders, he knew I wouldn't give in and rewarded me with a 1000 peseta discount. I felt sorry for the guy, but had to follow the order of the princess who afterwards asked me if I got a discount. When I told her, I had secured a 1000 peseta discount she said, "Is that all?"

Bloody hell, I thought, did she want me to get a discount from him or did she want me to rob him? As the princess went back into the villa, the prince walked out. Seizing the opportunity I said, "Your Royal Highness, may I have a word?"

"Yes Mark, what is it?"

"I came across Elena sobbing her heart out."

"Why was she upset?" he replied.

"Apparently you had been nasty to her and had shouted at her over the white pair of trousers that I had taken to the dry cleaners. Elena wasn't at fault. If you were upset, you should have directed your anger toward me."

"Mark, I have so much on my mind at the moment. I did not mean to upset Elena, I will speak to her."

"Thank you so much, Your Highness," I said.

Later that day as Turki played on the amusement arcade machines, Elena approached me.

"Mark, thank you so much for speaking to the prince, he apologised for snapping at me."

"So is everything all right between you and him now?"

"Yes it is, thank you again, Mark."

"No worries."

Back at the villa, I went to my quarters and lay on my bed. I soon dozed off, only to be awoken with a start by one of the Spanish national policemen that we had on static duty.

"Mark, the prince wants you," he said.

"Thank you," I replied.

Hastily I made my way over to the prince who was standing by the main entrance to the villa.

"Mark, prepare yourself, we are going to Puerto Banus in half an hour."

"I'll be ready, Your Highness." This was no surprise as we went to Puerto Banus every night.

After dinner, we paraded up and down in Puerto Banus. Then the prince asked me to take the princess back to the villa. On the way, she said the prince was going to meet his brothers.

However, when I met the prince back at the port, I found him with a young woman.

"Mark, we are going to Regine's nightclub."

"Yes, sir," I said as I opened the car doors for him and his guest.

At the nightclub in the Marbella Club complex, I spoke with the manager. He prepared a table for us on the edge of the dance floor. An hour or so later the prince panicked as he noticed his brothers arrive at the club. Jumping up he said, "Mark, grab the girl and dance with her. Make out she's with you. I'm going to the toilet."

Before I could reply, he was gone.

Taking the woman by the hand, I led her away from the dance floor. I couldn't dance and wasn't about to make a prat of myself for anyone.

"Listen to me, I'm so sorry but some important people have turned up and Mishari will have to sit with them to discuss some business. Please ignore him for the rest of the evening. I'm sure tomorrow he will make it up to you."

"I think I will go back to Puerto Banus. Is that all right?" she asked.

"That's a good idea. Go and enjoy yourself. No doubt I will see you tomorrow," I replied. Prince Mishari never called her again. I lost count of the times he made me lie for him and clean up his mess and I lost count of the times Prince Mishari had liaisons with women other than his wife. Now and again, the princess still asked if I had seen the prince go with other women.

"Your Highness, I've never seen Prince Mishari 'go' with another woman." I used the word 'go' loosely to mean actually have sex with another woman. I had not actually seen him commit the act so this was how I justified my answer. Had she asked if I had seen him in the company of other women, I would have had to think very carefully about how to answer.

Prince Mishari returned from the toilets and sat with his brothers. A round of Jack Daniels whiskey was ordered for them as usual. And as usual it crossed my mind that they are Muslim and alcohol is forbidden. I laughed inwardly as I thought, I'm not Muslim so am allowed alcohol—the joke being that I'm teetotal and they are not! This had always caused me some amusement from the moment I began working for them, and watched them drink to excess.

"Mark," Prince Mishari called.

"Yes, Your Highness," I replied, as he took off his watch.

"Take a look at this watch. Crown Prince Abdullah gave it to me. It's made from moon rock. How much do you think it's worth," he asked.

Luckily, I had seen watches like this for sale in the UK. "Your Highness, I reckon it's worth about £5," I answered. All the princes laughed aloud; whether they were laughing at me or not, I didn't know. Over the next few hours, the princes drank much alcohol. We left at 4am and made our way back to Casa Tam.

The prince was in a bad mood and I wondered if Jack Daniels made him aggressive. Anyway, as he got out of the car and walked towards the villa he started ranting at me. He was upset over the way I had disposed of the woman he was with. That was enough, I thought, and as he disappeared into the villa, I set about packing my suitcase.

I called Iberia airlines at Malaga airport and booked the first flight out to London. I got the prince's belongings together, the .38 snub nose revolver I carried, the prince's passport and what was left of his money, and placed them all into a large envelope. Then I walked round the front of the villa and found Elena, who was ironing the children's clothes for the day ahead.

"Elena, please give this envelope to the prince as soon as he wakes," I said.

"What is it?" she asked.

"It's his passport and belongings. If he asks where I am, tell him I'm in England."

"You must be joking," she said.

"Elena, I've never been so serious in my life. The prince was aggressive to me. I won't put up with it, so I'm off. Take care of yourself and I hope everything turns out all right for you in the end," I said and then, I left her.

Back at my room, I called a taxi and told the static guy to call me when it arrived. By six o'clock in the morning, I was on the Iberia airbus. A couple of hours after that, I was standing at my front door. As I entered the house, plenty of hugs and kisses from Sue and my boys greeted me.

"What's happened? Why didn't you say you were coming home? Why didn't you call? We would have met you at the airport," Sue said.

"Let's sit down and I'll tell you what's happened. Prince Mishari was aggressive and I thought enough is enough. So I left and here I am," I said.

"What happens now?" Sue asked me.

"I've no idea, but I've a return ticket booked as it was cheaper than a one way ticket. I booked the return for next Friday but I don't see that I will be using it. In a couple of days, I will call Bill at the office to let him know I'm back and after some work. For now though, I'm going to have a sleep as I've been up all night."

"We'll come and sit with you," Sue said.

"Don't get upset if I fall asleep, will you?"

"No, I won't."

Sue held and massaged my hand as I watched the boys playing on the bedroom floor. Shortly afterwards, I dozed off.

About midday, Sue shook my shoulder and woke me.

"Mark, you're wanted on the phone. I think it's Prince Mishari."

"Didn't you ask who it is?" I queried.

"No, I was surprised they even bothered calling, so I was caught off guard."

"All right, tell him I will be there in a second." I got out of bed and went to the phone.

"Hello," I said.

"Mark, what are you doing there?" Prince Mishari asked.

"Your Royal Highness, when we arrived back to the villa last night you were rude and curt towards me. I will not let anyone speak to me like that, so I left."

"I want you back. If I were rude, then I apologise. I don't remember saying anything when we returned last night. So spend some time with your family, take your time and I will see you tomorrow," he said and then hung up the phone.

I couldn't go back then even if I wanted to, as I did not have the money for a new ticket. I called back. Mohammed, the prince's uncle, answered the phone.

"Mohammed, can I speak with Prince Mishari please," I said.

"Mark, he has gone down to the swimming pool."

"All right, tell him I will be back on Friday."

"No Mark, you must come back tomorrow. Prince Mishari says you will be back tomorrow."

"Mohammed, tell Prince Mishari I will be back on Friday and if that's not good enough then I won't be back at all," I said.

"He won't like it."

"If I don't hear from him, then I will be back on Friday. Is that clear?"

"Yes, Mark, I will tell him," Mohammed replied.

During the next week, I took the time to chill out. I spent as much time with Sue and the boys as I could. We had fun and laughed a lot but knew that time was running out fast. I was surprised the prince had bothered calling me. I believed I'd placed my head on the block one time too many and that he would cut it off. Loss of face is everything to them, and I believed by asking me back he would have felt he had lost face to the people at Casa Tam. For that reason alone I thought he cared about me.

Friday arrived and I left Sue and the boys at Heathrow airport. I questioned whether I had made the right decision. I felt bad leaving my family and apprehensive of what I would find back in Marbella. The taxi stopped outside the gates of Casa Tam and I got out. I paid the driver and got my suitcase. The static guards opened the gates and greeted me warmly. I wondered if they had any idea about our disagreement. I walked over to my quarters and placed my bag on the bed. I did not bother opening it, as I wasn't sure how long I might be staying. I took a Coke from the fridge and sat on the couch. I never told anyone I had arrived. I knew the guards would have told the prince of my arrival. Sure enough, within ten to fifteen minutes, one of the guards knocked on my door.

"Mark, the prince wants you," he said.

"Fine, thanks," I replied and walked over to see the prince. He stood by the driver's door of the Chevrolet Camaro. As I neared him, he smiled at me and I smiled back. Reaching out his hand to shake mine, he greeted me.

"You English bastard," he said. I didn't take offence at his joke and knew then that all was good—for the moment, anyway.

I looked inside the Camaro and saw the princess sitting in the front passenger seat. I climbed into the back seat. As I got in the prince handed me a bag. Looking inside, I found his passport, his revolver and 20,000 pesetas. I found the back seats cramped and hoped we were only going for a short drive.

At the bottom of the hill, the prince turned right and drove along the N-340 main road. Near the Mosque, he turned right and in minutes, we arrived at the front door of La Meridiana, the Moorish styled restaurant. As I followed the principals into the restaurant, a car jockey parked the Camaro.

The maitre d' showed the prince and princess to their table and I made my way to the bar. After ordering my Coke, I got in to a discreet position where I could keep an eye on them. After they had finished, the prince called me over.

"Mark, please pay the bill for us."

"Yes, sir," I replied, but I thought the bill was going to come to more than the 20,000 pesetas which I had with me. At the till, I was presented with a bill for 35,000 pesetas. I felt my heart thud as I tried to free myself, and them, out of an embarrassing situation. I asked for the manager and took off my Cartier watch.

"Sir, I'm afraid I've left my cash bag back at the villa. His Highness will be so angry. Would you accept my Cartier watch as security for the bill until I return in the morning to settle up?"

Graciously, he declined my watch, "I realise that these things sometimes happen. Do not concern yourself. I will see you in the morning."

"Thank you so much for your understanding," I replied, and went back with my tail between my legs to signal the principals that the bill had been settled. As they regally walked down the steps to their waiting Camaro, I followed them with head bowed in embarrassment. Why had I come back? I questioned. How much longer would I have to put up with them tightening the purse strings? I no longer felt like a bodyguard when I worked for them. I had become a glorified babysitter and Mr Fix-It for them. I had made a break from them but then, when they called, I'd let myself down: I went running back to them. I could have kicked myself, and I should have kicked myself. It was with these thoughts in mind that I climbed in to the back of their car and sat quietly as the prince drove us to Puerto Banus.

Chapter 28

Cannes, France, late summer 1985

The next morning I settled the bill at La Meridiana. As I left and walked down the steps of the restaurant, I came across Alaa, who'd arrived in Marbella with some of the French bodyguards who worked on the circuit. Alaa held dual French and Egyptian citizenship. He'd hoped to find some work but had so far been unsuccessful. I decided to speak with Prince Mishari to see if we could use him. My hope was that Alaa would work with the children, allowing me to return to work with the prince. However, Alaa was out of luck.

Later that afternoon as I played in the television room with the children, the prince walked in. I stood up.

"Mark, Prince Mohammed Bin Fahd has invited us to Cannes in France for a week or so. He wants to see if I will like the south of France. We will stay at the Carlton Hotel and Prince Mohammed has said that he will pay for this visit. He has arranged for a private jet to pick us up at Malaga airport and Alaa will go with us on this trip. I am not happy for Prince Mohammed to pay. Therefore, when we arrive in Cannes, I want you to meet with his representatives and tell them that I will pay my own expenses. Do not offend anyone and be diplomatic in your handling of the situation."

"Of course, Your Royal Highness," I replied. This put me in a difficult position, as I'd often worked with Prince Mohammed in London, and knew his representatives well. Therefore, when I entered negotiations with Said Ayas, Prince Mohammed's secretary, I would have to lift my 'game' from that of the security man he knew in London to that of Prince Mishari's personal representative. Now, I wondered what the score was between the prince and Alaa. Would he be working with us, I wondered? When I caught up with Alaa later that evening, I asked him what was going on.

"Alaa, I hear you are coming to Cannes with us. Are you going to be working with us?"

"No, I'm not," he said. "I told Prince Mishari I have no money and he said he would help get me back to Paris."

I smelt a rat. Something wasn't right about this, but I couldn't put my finger on it. I would have to wait for the game to play itself out before I would have an idea what was behind Prince Mishari's thinking. Meanwhile, I set about tying up any loose ends before our departure.

I collected outstanding dry cleaning and picked up photographs left at the processors. I changed some pesetas for French francs for the prince at his bank. I liaised with the house administrator, making sure all relevant transport arrangements were in place for the transfer of the family and their luggage to Malaga airport. I revelled in sorting out problems that others couldn't. When I put my mind to it, I could move mountains for the prince and his family.

* * *

On Thursday 8th August, I stood on the tarmac at Malaga airport looking at the triple engine Falcon jet that had arrived to transport us to Nice. It would not be able to hold much luggage so I arranged to have the excess baggage sent on the following day. Then I noticed Alaa remove a case from the aircraft and put another in its place. I went over to see what was going on. Alaa had taken off one of Prince Mishari's cases and had put his own case on board.

"Alaa, get your case off the plane now! Put Prince Mishari's case back on board," I said. Shrugging his shoulders, he did as he was told. I would have to keep an eye on this slippery bastard.

"Mark, what's going on?"

"Your Highness, we don't have enough space on the plane for the luggage. I was making sure the family luggage is all aboard, and then I was arranging for the rest of it to follow tomorrow."

"Very good, Mark. Will your case follow as well?"

"Yes, sir," I replied.

"Don't worry, Mark, I will sort out some clothes for you when we get to Cannes."

"Thank you, sir," I said.

As we boarded the plane I said aloud, "Now don't forget; I have to sit near the door so if anything goes wrong, I can get off first and help everyone else off the aircraft from there."

"Mark, don't joke about that," the princess said. "Don't you know Prince Mishari is nervous of flying?"

"I'm sorry, Your Highness, it was a little thoughtless of me," I replied, and then I kept my mouth shut. Once aboard the aircraft, I noticed the princess smiled at me as she noticed that purely by chance, I was sitting next to the door of the plane. I wondered if she thought I was getting ready for a quick exit.

We were soon airborne and the Spanish mainland fell far away beneath us. The stewardess attended the family. I wondered if I would see my luggage the next day. The interior of the jet, while plush, wasn't anything special; at least not as special as the other jets I'd been aboard owned by other members of the royal family.

After an uneventful flight of less than two hours, we landed at Nice International airport. After stopping, the stewardess opened the fuselage door and lowered the onboard steps. I could see Said Ayas waiting at the bottom to greet Prince Mishari. I wondered if he would notice me, but rather doubted it since I knew his mind would be occupied with other things.

As the baggage handlers unloaded the luggage, a familiar case caught my eye. It belonged to Alaa! The slippery sod must have placed it back on the aircraft when Prince Mishari had spoken with me about the luggage back at Malaga. So often, I helped the underdog only to have them come back and bite me on the arse. Would I ever learn? Some time later, I would learn, but it would take an incident with dire consequences to teach me.

For the moment, though, I wondered whose case it was that Alaa had removed from the aircraft. Inside the airport arrivals building, I noticed Said Ayas looking at me. I nodded my head in acknowledgement and he returned my nod with a smile.

Now I knew he had recognized me, I walked over and handed him the passports. As Prince Mohammed's official representative, Said Ayas had from the moment the aircraft landed become responsible for getting Prince Mishari and his family safely to the

Carlton Hotel. He handled the formalities masterfully, and soon we were winging our way towards the hotel some 25 to 30 kilometres away. On nearing the hotel, which is in the heart of Cannes on one of the most beautiful avenues in France, the famous Boulevard de la Croisette, I marvelled at its unique historical façade. The Carlton's exterior is tiered and glossy white, much like a magnificently iced wedding cake. Boasting panoramic views of the Bay of Cannes, the Carlton exudes luxury and features 338 rooms, including 36 suites, which provide the best in luxury and comfort.

Stepping from the Mercedes, I squinted as I looked over the palm-lined strip and was dazzled by the glaring sun reflecting off the Mediterranean Sea. The fronds of the palm trees waved delicately at me as the light breeze caressed them. I could see the tops of the blue and white umbrellas beyond the esplanade, which delineated the area of private beach owned exclusively by the Carlton. For one brief moment, I soaked in the surroundings of the Cote d'Azur as I found myself checking out the bystanders near the main entrance.

Once the principals were ensconced within their suites, the reins of responsibility were handed back to me from Said Ayas. I then set off to find my room. I would be sharing with Alaa. Mohammed and Sultan went off in the opposite direction. The first thing I saw when I entered the room was Alaa's suitcase on his bed. It was open and he was busy unpacking.

"How did you manage to get your case back on the aircraft without chucking someone else's off?" I asked him.

"After Prince Mishari's case was put back on the plane, I noticed a space and slipped my case into it."

Lying bastard, I thought as I walked into the bathroom. After undressing, I soaked in a hot bath and relaxed for a while. I knew it would not be long before I was called up to the prince's suite. After drying myself, I dressed in the same clothes I had taken off. Not half an hour later, the prince called me to his suite. Elena opened the door and showed me into their lounge.

Prince Mishari handed me a beige coloured windcheater jacket.

"Here Mark, this will do you until your case arrives," he said.

Great, I thought, a fucking windcheater. That's all I need in the hot Mediterranean climate.

"Mark, go with the princess and wait for me by the lobby. I will follow shortly."

Not five minutes after leaving the suite the princess eyed up an Arab walking towards us. She hadn't recognised him, but I had as I had worked for him on many occasions. The princess was paying too much attention to him, so I leant in closer to her and whispered, "Saud Bin Naïf." She immediately averted her gaze and looked towards the floor. If Prince Saud Bin Naïf, one of the sons of the fierce Saudi Arabian Interior Minister, noticed her interest then it would bring shame and loss of face on Prince Mishari. It didn't help that Prince Saud was our benefactor Prince Mohammed Bin Fahd's best friend and business partner. I hoped I had been quick enough with my warning. I sensed the princess' unease as her husband arrived next to us a couple of minutes later.

"Mark, we are going to take a short walk along the Croisette."

"Yes, sir," I replied as I fell in behind them. The beachfront Croisette is where everything happens. We strolled towards the Palais du Festival, where the films are screened each year at the famous Cannes film festival. I watched the elegantly dressed people mingling on the hotel terraces drinking cups of espresso or sipping Champagne. Although Cannes exuded both glamour and sophistication, I could tell that Prince Mishari wasn't enamoured with it. Twenty minutes later, I was knocking on my door trying to gain entry. Alaa opened it and begged me to go away as he had a prostitute with him. I walked away, cursing him in my mind.

Alaa was a total waste of space.

* * *

The following lunchtime, Prince Mishari called me to his suite.

"Mark, come with me. We will lunch with my brother, Prince Mohammed Bin Saud, at the beach restaurant."

I liked Prince Mohammed Bin Saud and his secretary, Nabil whom I had met in Saudi Arabia, and looked forward to seeing them. The maitre d' showed us to their table and the princes greeted each other. I then shook hands warmly with Prince Mohammed and Nabil. During lunch, I was careful not to impose on the princes'

conversation. As lunch ended, Prince Mohammed invited us to dinner at his apartment that evening.

I escorted Prince Mishari to his suite and found myself cursing yet again. My suitcase had still not arrived. At 5pm, the prince called me and told me to prepare for dinner at 8pm. At six thirty I sat in an armchair, waiting for their call. Time dragged by and I became anxious that we would be late for dinner. Leaving it as late as I could, I set off for their suite. Elena opened the door in surprise.

"Are they ready yet?" I asked.

"They left about half an hour ago; we thought you were with them."

"They left without me. Are the children fine, Elena?"

"Yes, we've settled them for the night. Do you want to come in?"

"No, thank you, I'll take a short walk and return to my room should you need me."

"Yes, Mark, goodnight," she said as I left.

I was pissed off with the prince for not having the decency to let me know that I would not be needed. Then again, he was the boss and he could do whatever he liked, which reminded me of the comment made by the princess one time. "We are Saudian; we can do whatever we like." The shame about this statement was that over the years it seemed that she was right, as they often breached rules, regulations, and laws with no obvious consequences.

The following morning saw me attending the children at a local park. They were happy and contented. The girls expressed surprise that I was left behind the previous evening, especially as the prince had been insistent that I would be going with them until the last moment. From this we assumed it was the princess that had persuaded him to leave me. Either way, I wiped the issue from my mind, only for it to come up again at lunchtime.

The children, their nannies and I were in their suite when Prince Mishari entered. He said we were going to lunch again with Prince Mohammed Bin Saud at the beach restaurant. I went to get ready. At 1pm, I met the prince and we walked across the Croisette and esplanade down to the beach. After greeting Prince Mohammed and sitting down, I was taken by surprise.

"Mark, where were you last night?" Prince Mohammed asked.

Instantly, I looked to Prince Mishari to answer for me.

"Your Highness, we were not aware Mark was invited," Prince Mishari lied. I was a pawn in a game once more. Prince Mohammed was older and therefore superior to his younger sibling. I felt decidedly uncomfortable as the conversation unfolded.

"Mark, before you leave I will hold a dinner in your honour. Mishari, you will bring Mark to the dinner." It wasn't a request; it was an order.

"Yes, Your Highness," Prince Mishari replied as I wondered how I would suffer for this monumental putdown.

After lunch, Prince Mishari and I went back to his suite. Neither of us spoke about Prince Mohammed Bin Saud's invitation. As the prince closed his suite door he said, "Mark, arrange for our departure on the 14th. The princess, the children, you, Sultan and the nannies will go to Los Angeles. Mohammed, Alaa and I will go to London."

"I will take care of it immediately, Your Highness. I will also contact Said Ayas and let him know."

"Good, Mark. Let me know when you speak with him and what he has to say."

"Yes, sir,"

Alarm bells rang after hearing Alaa was going to London. Something was going on, and I had a good idea what it was. The prince was looking to replace me with Alaa. Two important things Alaa held over me were that he was Muslim and he spoke Arabic. I wondered if my assumption was correct, but only time would tell, and anyway it was out of my hands.

I arranged our flights. Someone was smiling on me from above, as after booking and confirming the prince and Mohammed's seats I was informed that the flight was now full. Alaa would have to take the next flight to London. I smiled, knowing Alaa would be pissed off by this. I told the prince of this slight inconvenience.

"Did you book him on the next available flight, Mark?"

"Yes sir, it will arrive about two and a half hours after you."

"That's fine, he can get a taxi to the hotel from the airport," he said.

When I told Alaa, all hell broke loose.

"I'm not having that. I will call my wife. She works for a travel agency in Paris. They get preferential treatment for their customers. They will bump someone off the plane and get me a seat," he ranted.

"I'll leave it with you, then," I said and went to meet Said Ayas in the lobby.

"Good afternoon, Mr Ayas," I said, greeting him with a warm handshake.

"Good afternoon, Mark," he replied. "Prince Mohammed Bin Fahd is insistent that he will pay the bill for Prince Mishari."

"That's a problem. Prince Mishari says he will pay his own bill."

We discussed various ways in which we could break the deadlock and settled on an idea. I telephoned Prince Mishari and said Prince Mohammed would be offended if his hospitality was rejected.

"Perhaps you should accept his hospitality in good faith," I suggested, "and then repay it by giving Prince Mohammed a gift as a thank you, therefore redressing the balance."

"Mark, that's a good idea. Yes, do that."

I spoke with Said Ayas and said, "We have a deal."

"Good, Mark, a deal that's good for everyone. Let's leave it at that. I will call you later to confirm all is well." Said Ayas left the hotel.

I went to my room and found Alaa grinning like an idiot.

"What are you so happy about?" I enquired.

"My wife has got me a seat on the flight already," he replied.

Bollocks, I thought.

Chapter 29

Guest of honour

The night before we left Nice, Prince Mishari, Princess al-Anud and I took the elevator to Prince Mohammed Bin Saud's apartment in Cannes. As the door opened, I stood to one side, by the control buttons, to allow the principals an easy exit. Prince Mohammed greeted them and asked, "Mishari, where is our guest of honour?"

I leant forward into view, still embarrassed that Prince Mohammed was using me as a pawn in their game. At least, I thought he was. Perhaps he genuinely liked me; who knows? Prince Mohammed greeted me warmly and introduced me to the other guests. Prince Mishari just accepted it, but I knew Princess al-Anud would have her hackles up. Nabil, Prince Mohammed's secretary, wanted to entice me away from Prince Mishari. They wanted me to work with one of Prince Mohammed's sons, but my loyalty was firmly set with my own prince. It was a shame his loyalty wasn't set on me, but it would be a few days before I found that out.

The evening passed by well and I enjoyed myself. Back at my room, I found my suitcase waiting for me. Thank heavens for that, as I had visions of moving on to Los Angeles without it. Making the most of what little time I had, I jumped into the bath and had a good soak. Then I dressed in clean, fresh clothes. It was heaven and I felt a million dollars. An hour later, the phone rang and Alaa answered.

"Mark, Said Ayas is on the phone," he called out to me.

"Thanks, Alaa."

"Hello, Mr Ayas, what can I do for you?"

"Hello, Mark. I wanted to thank you again in helping find a solution to our little problem. I'm sure I will see you again in London soon. Have you concluded your arrangements for departure tomorrow?"

"Yes, Mr Ayas, everything is taken care of, thank you."

"Well, if you need me, just call."

"Yes sir, I will. Thank you, Mr Ayas," I replied and hung up the phone.

The following morning I escorted the principals to their car. I got into a car behind them and the luggage van brought up the rear. Everything was progressing smoothly; too smoothly, in fact.

I thought I had covered all the bases, but was to receive a sharp kick to the bollocks when we got to the airport. First, I guided the princess and children to the premiere suite. The prince busied himself with some people he knew, as I set off to check in the flights. The princess' flight plans went smoothly. However, it was when checking in the prince that I got my kick in the bollocks. He was bumped off the aircraft—and the culprits were Alaa and his wife!

"That's not possible," I said to the check-in clerk. "I had confirmed reservations for both Prince Mishari and Mr Mohammed. Mr Alaa was to take a later flight, so what's gone wrong?"

"Please wait a moment, sir, and I will try to sort the problem out," the clerk said.

"Please be advised if Prince Mishari doesn't fly then no one will. Either you give him back his confirmed seat or I will have no recourse but to call the Saudi Arabian embassy and cause a diplomatic incident."

"I understand sir, please give me a moment."

"Well, you have five minutes," I said in a tone of voice full of authority. In truth, I didn't know what my next move would be. I was just playing the game. If my luck held, then we would continue as scheduled. If not, then I would probably send out an SOS to Said Ayas. The prince wandered over to see what the fuss was about.

"Your Highness, Alaa's wife had you removed from the passenger manifest and Alaa added to it. Now, you do not have a seat on the aircraft. I'm sorting the problem and will let you know the outcome momentarily."

"Let me know quickly, Mark."

The prince walked over to his family as I let rip at Alaa.

"You fucking imbecile, why can't you keep your nose out of my affairs? I tried to help you with a job but all you do is think of yourself. We're here for the benefit of the family and for no other reason. You're a fucking liability, thank fuck you're not coming to Los Angeles with us!" Just as I finished my rebuke, the check-in clerk returned.

"Sir, I'm delighted to tell you that another passenger has stood down, thus allowing us to find seats for all your party."

"Thank you so much," I said and handed the clerk a thousand francs. If the princess knew I had given them anything she would most likely have a heart attack and then I would have another problem to fix! I went to the prince and told him all our seats were available.

"That's good news, Mark. Please take good care of my family. I will be in London for two or three days and then back in Saudi Arabia just in case you need me for anything."

"I will take care of them, Your Highness, you have my word on it," I said. I knew while I was taking care of his family, he would no doubt be taking care of some young woman in London as he usually did when I escorted him.

Soon we were called for boarding. Prince Mishari said his goodbyes and we were escorted off by one of the ground crew to find our plane. I felt envious of Alaa going with the prince, but I had no choice and had to get on with it. Taking care of business, that was what I was good at doing. I could fix anything for them but when it came to me, I wasn't so hot. I was too soft and too trusting of the people around me.

Our first flight was a short hop to Paris. Luckily, we didn't have to change aircraft for the next leg to Los Angeles. The first class flight was enjoyable, as much as any flight can be. I took charge of the passports, tickets and boarding cards. Then I filled out the immigration cards, declaring we only had US $5000. Why that figure was never questioned, I'll never know. It was obvious we were carrying an amount far greater than that.

As we careered through the sky, I smiled recalling what a friend had said about the princess and her sister Princess Nouf. He said, over all the years that he knew them; all he ever got from them was a smile. He was luckier than me! I had received smiles, but also a whole lot of grief.

We were going to be met at Los Angeles by Abdullah, the secretary of the princess' brother, Prince Turki. We were staying in an apartment complex at Marina Del Rey, which was 4 miles from the airport and could be reached in about ten minutes by car. The name Marina Del Rey sounded great; I just hoped the place lived up to its name.

On Wednesday 14th August, we arrived at our apartments in the luxurious Marina Del Rey complex. The princess, the children and nannies would share one apartment, while Sultan and I used the other. I looked out of the apartment windows and marvelled at the yachts berthed in the marina. I carefully chose the one I wanted.

"Mark," said Abdullah, "Prince Turki wants a driver/bodyguard for his sister while she is here. I've arranged an interview with a guy a bit later and I want you to okay him. Is that all right with you?"

"Sure, Abdullah, just tell me where and when and I'll be there," I replied.

"I'll call you in an hour or so and then we can meet."

"No worries, Abdullah, catch you later," I said as I saw him out.

* * *

An hour and a half later, I sat with Abdullah. I was keenly aware that the princess had a roving eye, so I knew the tanned, well-muscled man sitting before us would never do. I did not intend to put temptation in her way. It was a shame, as I liked the guy and he seemed eminently qualified. Therefore, with a heavy heart I turned down Jean-Claude Van Damme for the job. I don't suppose he cared though, as shortly afterwards he hit the big time in the movies.

Instead of Jean-Claude, we settled on one of Abdullah's friends—a Lebanese guy who was shorter and stockier than Jean-Claude. His name was Hossam. Although he was perfect in the looks department, he proved to be anything but when it came to punctuality. A couple of days later I overheard the princess impressing on Hossam the need for him to be punctual in the morning as the children had an important medical at a nearby hospital. The next time I saw Elena, I asked her what the medical was for.

"Oh, Mark," she said, laughing, "When the prince and princess took the children to visit friends in Saudi Arabia, they noticed Turki was quite a bit shorter than another child he was playing with of the same age. So they brought him to America for tests to see if he has a problem."

"You've got to be kidding me," I replied.

"No, they are very insecure and worried that he may be small."

"Well, they never cease to amaze me, Elena. Now, do me a favour and find out the name and address of the hospital and what time the appointment is."

"Yes Mark, I'll let you know shortly," Elena replied. Meanwhile, I got a road map for the Los Angeles area. A while later Elena gave me the information I had asked for. I memorised the route to and from the hospital and estimated the time it would take to get there. If Hossam was late, I wanted to take over the reins.

The next morning they waited and waited. The princess got more and more tense, which in turn caused tension among us.

Finally, when time ran out, I said, "Your Highness, we had better leave now. We are out of time."

"Do you know the way?"

"I studied the route last night."

At the hospital, we sat in the waiting room. The children were called for blood tests and the princess and I took them through.

I passed Turki to her, "No Mark, you hold them. I don't want to; I can't."

"No worries," I said. Back at the apartment, the princess thanked me. I was taken aback by this as she rarely showed any gratitude for anything at all. Then, when Hossam arrived two hours later, I heard the princess balling him out.

We left them to it and headed off in our Lincoln town car to the theme parks, as we were due to leave Los Angeles for Paris the following morning. After our visit to Six Flags Magic Mountain, we made our way back to our apartments in Marina Del Rey. On the way, I stopped at a toy shop and spent $50 on a couple of toys for Turki and Hala.

On our arrival the princess was waiting for us. She asked where the children had got the toys from. When I told her I had bought them she wanted to know how much I had spent. When I said $50, the princess went ballistic at me for spending the money. In response, I took $50 of my money and dropped it on the coffee table in front of her.

"If $50 means so much to you then have it on me," I said.

She fumed, "How dare you insult me in such a way!"

"You're the one making an issue of it, not me," I said as I walked back to my apartment. I wasn't naive enough to think I wouldn't pay dearly at some stage for yet another confrontation with the princess.

The following morning, the last day of August 1985, we stood at Los Angeles international airport. The princess grudgingly gave me $1000 to cover any extra baggage charges. She gave Hossam his bonus, which was a big fat zilch. I was then told by the baggage clerk that the extra baggage came in at around $2000. After some serious flirting with my lovely English accent, I approached the subject of the extra charge again with the clerk as I checked in for the flight to Paris. With a smile and a wink, she checked our luggage for free. It made my day.

After a long flight, we arrived at the Paris Charles de Gaulle airport. I'd already arranged transportation that would see us arrive safely at the entrance of the George V Hotel, a few steps away from the Champs-Elysees.

On Sunday 1st September, I looked at the entrance of yet another luxury hotel. The hotel stood eight stories high and had 245 guest rooms, all with unique architectural details. Many of the rooms featured private terraces overlooking the city. We would be in Paris for two or three days before the family returned to Saudi Arabia.

The family soon settled. They never seemed fazed by the moving around and I wondered if this was because of their Bedouin origins. Bedouin were always on the move.

I made sure everyone was happy and went to leave the suite.

"Mark, before you go, can you tell me how much money you have with you?" the princess asked.

"Your Highness, I have 2,000 French francs and the $1000 you gave me for the baggage in Los Angeles," I answered.

"You still have the $1,000? Didn't you have to pay for the baggage?"

255

"No, Your Highness, I got it through for free."

"Oh good, can you get it to Saudi Arabia for free, too?"

"I'll try, Your Highness," I replied through gritted teeth.

There was no thank you, no reward, no nothing. I knew I was only kept on for the moment because I was expedient. After the clashes, I wondered if I would see any of them again.

Within hours of arriving at the George V hotel, an aide to Prince Khalid—another of the princess' brothers—arrived. This guy's name was Pierre. As her brother paid his wages, she was happy to have him around. For the most part, I was happy to have him around too, if it kept the princess off my back. For the last few days, I concentrated fully on the children. We went sightseeing and visited the zoo. We went up the Eiffel Tower and cruised on the Seine. We took lunch outside the hotel and had a good time. Pierre, I was told, would take care of the departure when the family left. Thank fuck for that, I thought, let some other prat have the hassle.

As I waited by the door of the suite I heard the princess talking with the prince. I could tell they were discussing Alaa's performance in London. The prince said he was useless. I knew then that the writing was on the wall for me.

We stayed only four days in Paris. Then, on 5th September, we made our way to the airport once again and found another problem with the luggage. This time, French Customs wanted to go through all the princess' suitcases and trunks. As there were around fifty cases or so, to open them all up for inspection would have been a nightmare. The extra taxes on the goods she'd bought but not declared would have left the princess choking. Pierre couldn't get the extra baggage through free. Negotiations began. Pierre knew he would have to suffer the extra baggage charge. The negotiations took a sinister turn over the Customs issue. Seeing where these talks were heading, I walked away and stood by the princess and the children. Pierre bribed the Customs officers. I wasn't about to get involved with that, as I did not fancy the idea of time in a French prison.

Once Pierre returned, we got the family on to the plane. As the aircraft taxied away, I said to Pierre, "What the fuck do you think you were doing? If that stunt with the Customs went pear-shaped, we could have had an international incident on our hands. We could have gone to prison! Is this the way you do business for Prince Khalid? In fact, do not answer that. Just leave me alone. I will make my own way to the London check in desk. Goodbye, Pierre." I turned on my heels and walked away. I could hear him spluttering something at me but took no notice.

* * *

"Taxi, taxi," I called. I was at Heathrow airport and had no Mercedes to take me home. Forty minutes later, I walked through my front door. I hugged and kissed Sue and then chased the kids out the back door and into the garden. They squealed as they ran from me.

"You can't catch me, Daddy," they shouted, and of course, I couldn't. I had stayed in some of the best places in the world. I had seen and experienced so much more than most of my peers. Yet at that moment as I chased the kids, magic engulfed me. Nowhere was quite like home. I would make the most of it until the next assignment came in.

Chapter 30

Chaos - 1985 into 1986

I received an emergency call. Trouble had flared up at Sheikh Khalid Al Ibrahim's house in Hill Street near Berkeley Square. The Sheikh is one of King Fahd's favourite in-laws. Two incidents occurred, the first was serious. The Sheikh had brought home some young women the previous evening, one cried rape and the police were now looking into the allegations. Martini visited the house to 'fix' it. The rape allegation concerned one of the Gazawi's, whose father was then Saudi Ambassador to Germany.

Damage limitation was the order of the day. One woman claimed drugs were slipped into their drinks and they had raped her, the others were still too dazed to know what had occurred. Witnessing events like this with this family sometime later, I spoke out and found myself in a whole heap of trouble.

Martini paid the woman off. The police left. This wasn't the only time Martini paid someone off—the King (Fahd) got an Iranian woman by the name of Jamilah, who lives in London pregnant and he paid her off after she was forced to abort the baby.

Whilst the first incident was serious, the second, I found funny. A guy I worked with before, a serving SAS trooper named Mark, was working on a basement door when a Filipino servant came to him with a suitcase. She said she was to take the suitcase to the Sheikh's other house. Mark said he would call a taxi for her. He even helped her with the case. The problem was she wasn't going to the other house. She was running away.

Martini now had to contact the Foreign Office to report this woman's escape. I received a call to go in, sort out the security, and try to re-establish some goodwill with the housekeeper.

My friend Peter was on the job, so I decided to get his input on recent events. Peter told me the woman who cried rape told the truth, and that he witnessed drinks spiked for that specific purpose.

Then, on the 15th December, the Sheikh left two hundred and fifty thousand pounds sterling in cash in the boot of his Rolls Royce Phantom. The alarm was off and the driver had not been aware of the contents. Often, the complacency shown was despicable.

The Sheikh and his family liked Rolls Royce's, and yet they clashed with the company. This came about over the Al Yamamah commissions. The Al Ibrahim family issued a High Court writ against Rolls Royce, claiming they had reneged on an agreement to pay 15% commission on the engines of nearly 200 Tornado and Hawk aircraft. The Al Ibrahim's expected to take up to £90 million on the deal worth £600 million but was claiming Rolls Royce recognised only £23 million.

Al Yamamah was worth twenty billion dollars, or two billion dollars a year for the next ten years. Years later, Foreign Secretary Robin Cook called for a public inquiry into the deal following allegations that Mark Thatcher had received millions in commissions. The former Prime Minister asked for some favour to be shown towards her son, and through a Saudi/Syrian middle man and Prince Turki Bin Nasser, $12 million passed under the table. There were some princes and their 'associates' who raked off at least £2 billion from the deal. There were many accusations of corruption and dodgy dealing. I witnessed some of these deals.

On the 23rd December 1985, the Sheikh and his entourage left but he wouldn't be gone for long. He was going to the States for a brief visit and we expected him back around mid January 1986. I worked for him and his brothers numerous times over the years, and saw the Al-Ibrahim family continue to systematically abuse their privileged position.

* * *

On the 3rd of January 1986, I received a call to go to an apartment in Grosvenor Square, Mayfair. The Governor of Tabuk, Prince Abdul Majid Bin Abdul Aziz (another of the King's brothers) was due in. When I arrived, I recognised the house manager as she also worked for Prince Talal Bin Abdul Aziz, my very first charge.

The staff consisted of a cook and a cleaner, who were sisters from Poland. The house manager told them to look after me. When the prince arrived, I noticed three Westerners accompanied him. They were introduced as the family's travelling security, and each one was an ex-American police officer. The boss of their team was an ex-sergeant named Bill. I struck up a rapport with him and his crew. The prince's driver, Bob Elvins, was English and had worked with the family for some time. Bob was best of friends with my mate Bruce. Bob always dressed smartly—he sometimes looked better than the prince.

One of the Americans, a big guy called Irv, asked me if I would go down and get a package from the prince's Rolls Royce. As I walked out of the main door, the house manager was just getting out of her black Ferrari 308 GTS. I couldn't help wondering what I was doing wrong—I rather liked the idea of having a Ferrari. I wandered over to her. As we were alone, we were able to talk freely. I laughed as we chatted about Soraya Khashoggi, the wife of Adnan Khashoggi, and the old story of Prince Talal.

The house manager and I walked back to the apartment together and as we arrived, there was some commotion. As the servants unpacked one of the prince's suitcases, they noticed his *igal*—the black woven circlet that went on top of the headdress—was missing. They panicked, knowing the prince would wear his robes and headdress when he arrived in Saudi Arabia. No one knew of a shop that sold them in London back then.

I mentioned to the house manager that I had a full headdress at home. Although it looked like new, I had used it, I told her. They asked if I thought it would fit the prince and if so, could he borrow it.

The next day I brought in my *igal* and the prince tried it on. It fit him, but I, in truth, was reluctant to let it go, as it was part of my Saudi Arabian experience. Therefore, I put a condition on his borrowing it—I wanted it back once the prince had returned to Saudi Arabia. They agreed, and I gave them my details.

I never saw it again and knew if I had nicked it, I would probably have my hand amputated for theft. Again, one rule for them, another for us!

The prince and his son spent the four day trip either going to the movies or out to dinner. The rest of the time they sat round the apartment. On the 7th January 1986, the Prince left for Saudi Arabia. On the 26th January, Prince Abdul Majid was appointed Governor of Mecca. For me another job was complete.

* * *

Mid January 1986, as expected, the Al Ibrahim Sheikh was back in town. On this visit, he decided to stay in one house and party in another. One of his entourage turned up with a model from Los Angeles who was stunning. This model, Jamie, stood six feet tall. Not an ounce of fat could be detected on what was visible of her body. She was tanned and toned, had long blonde hair and piercing blue eyes. She complained because they promised her a special diet and she didn't get it. All her food was weighed, and the fish she ate was skinned. She was bloody awkward, I thought. However, if they promised her a special diet, then that's what she should have. Another deal reneged on by the Arabs—they were expert at doing that, I can tell you from my own experiences. They often promised you the world and gave you nothing.

The housekeeper Mohammed was from Morocco and his entire family worked at these houses. The houses were unclean and unkempt; I wondered how this was possible with almost the entire Moroccan population supposedly cleaning them. The Sheikh had his own team of bodyguard's from Morocco. They had been a gift from King Hassan of Morocco. They held First Dan black belts in Karate.

We provided the static security. The house was large and the basement contained a bar, a discotheque, and a swimming pool. The swimming pool looked like an oasis, and the discotheque had small, coloured under-floor flashing lights and looked professional, just as you would find in a top class London club.

Numerous bottles of spirits lined the shelves of the bar in the same fashion as a London club. The Sheikh was Muslim so he did not drink alcohol, although I often saw him drunk. Maybe he became drunk from the fumes of his guests' drinks! The entire place was used to corrupt the young women who turned up each evening. The Sheikh employed a pimp called Marwan, a Lebanese, who went round the nightclubs getting young women to attend the disco at the house.

One night a guy turned up and I wouldn't let him in. He left but arrived back shortly afterwards driving a black Corvette Stingray. This time, he was with an underage girl; I still wouldn't let him in. He went ballistic. He was an egotistical spoilt brat. Once he calmed himself, he asked to use a phone. This I allowed, and one of the aides came up from the disco and told me to let him in.

He was the son of a Jewish man who owned a few nightclubs and property development businesses. Within fifteen minutes or so this guy left but came back a little later, and this time he had his sister with him. After being told to let them in when they returned, I did so.

The Sheikh arrived shortly afterwards with some other young women. His driver, Brian, came in and sat talking with me—we spoke about the debauchery taking place. Marwan (the Lebanese pimp) arrived with even more women, followed by an erotic dance group. They were to perform for the Sheikh and his guests. The Sheikh paid them extra to give a raunchier show.

The women guests soon staggered about drunk, some of them also stoned out of their heads on the drugs supplied: cocaine was freely available. Marwan told me that very often, drugs found their way into an unsuspecting woman's drink. The drug placed in the drinks was called Rohypnol. Marwan said openly that the specific intent was to have sex with them while they were not in a position to do anything about it—to put it bluntly, the drugged girls were being raped.

After this revelation, Marwan disappeared into a toilet with one of the girls and the Sheikh banged on the door and shouted, "Let me in!" Marwan told me afterwards that as the Sheikh banged the door, the girl had given him, Marwan, a blowjob, and he wasn't about to open the door until he came. Marwan was a liability, too free with his tongue when stoned.

After his exploits in the toilet, the playboy reappeared, spraying champagne over a young girl. I thought he was perverted and preyed on underage girls. I had my suspicions that he was sleeping with the youngster. Then again, I think Sheikh Khalid and some of his brothers were perverted, too. I remembered the poor Filipino woman who Princess Fahda had beaten and stripped and then sent back to Saudi Arabia. I remembered the promise I made myself not to stand by and do nothing.

So I thought I would warn the women about their antics, but I soon found myself in the shit. One of them told the Sheikh; he called Martini, who in turn called the office. I was told and of course, I denied all knowledge of it. Bill called me in to the office and wanted me to explain my actions. I had a hell of a job getting out of that one and had to resign myself to the fact I couldn't even warn the young women because I would be the loser. Sometimes it's a sad world.

Later that night, a small old man turned up, his arm entwined in the arm of a tall young black woman with long legs. They made for the oddest couple I had seen that night. They were expected.

Later, Marwan introduced me to him. He seemed polite, handed me his business card, and asked me to contact him when the Sheikh had left. I never bothered.

His business card showed his name was Desmond Bloom and he owned six London nightclubs and a finance company. He was a multi millionaire and the father of the playboy I had stopped from coming in: the son was Baron, his sister was Beverley.

* * *

A new day guy called Justin Mayer was to start in the morning. I had heard of him before, but we'd not met. People referred to him as "Justin the nutter."

Using my usual diplomacy, I asked, "Are you the guy they call 'Justin the nutter'?" He spent forty-five minutes with his face two inches away from mine claiming he wasn't a nutter, by which time he had convinced me that he was.

Justin and I got on famously. I found him hilarious. Not many people took to him. Perhaps I was just drawn to the nutty ones and maybe I was becoming one myself! Justin did have a few surprises up his sleeve, however, and I soon saw two of them.

On the third morning after he started, he sat in a chair by the double front doors. I leant against a wall. Justin had both doors wide open. Outside was a covered porch, which had four steps leading down to street level. A driver, John, arrived and walked through while Justin and I were talking. As John was about to walk between us, Justin threw out a punch. It connected with John and he flew out and down the steps landing on his back. I wondered what it was I must have missed. Justin twisted his head from side to side, as though trying to free some stiffness from his neck, as boxers often do.

He then said, "Doesn't say good morning to me, that'll teach him." That was John's 'crime'. I made a mental note to make sure I said good morning to Justin when he arrived.

Another incident occurred a few days later. A van driver pulled up outside the house, blocking our parking space. Justin asked the van driver politely to move the van, as we were expecting the Rolls Royce. The van driver told Justin to wait. Justin asked once again and the driver ignored him. Justin went out to the van, and seeing the key in the ignition, got in and drove the van out into the traffic light controlled crossroad. Justin stopped in the middle of them, got out, and threw the keys away. He did have his own unique way of dealing with people! I later worked with him when some 'shady' guys hired us. Rumour was they had underworld connections. One payday, Charlie, one of the bosses, said they weren't going to be able to pay anyone until the Monday, as they had run into a small problem. Justin didn't accept that and said to Charlie, "I've done the work, I want my money."

"Tough. You will have to wait like the rest of them."

Justin said softly, "If you do not give me my money today, I will kill you." - Justin got his money.

I suppose it is just as well as some time later Justin surfaced on the television programme *Crime Watch UK* as one the ten most wanted criminals. The police accused him of murder. The name he was using had been given to him by the authorities after he had turned super grass against some of the gangsters in Liverpool. The police interviewed several guys who had worked with 'Justin' and tried to get a lead on him. Charlie had made the right decision.

On a cold wet morning in February 1986, I bade farewell to Justin as the job came to an end. I never saw him again.

Chapter 31

Megeve, France: March 1986

Rather unexpectedly, Prince Mishari Bin Saud called me again in March 1986. I had felt sure that after my recent confrontations with the princess, I'd be cast aside. Now it appeared that although the princess and I clashed at times, she didn't seem too concerned about it.

"Mark, I'm taking Turki skiing in Megeve. I want you to meet us at the airport in Geneva on Friday the 7th, can you manage that?"

"No problem, Your Highness," I said, "Can you give me your flight details?"

As I took them down, I noticed the princess and Hala were not on the list. I couldn't say I was too sorry about that.

"Mark," Prince Mishari continued, "Prince Saud Bin Fahd (another of King Fahd's sons) has offered us the use of his chalet at the bottom of the slopes. I have decided however, that we will stay at the hotel Mont Blanc. We will use the chalet during the day. My office has made all the necessary arrangements. Prince Saud has also arranged for us to have two of his ski instructors attend us."

"Very good Your Highness. May I ask, can you ski?"

"No, Mark, this is the first time for any of us here but Prince Saud has convinced me to try it."

I hung up the phone and breathed a sigh of relief. I couldn't ski either and had visions of careering down a mountainside, out of control never to be seen again with Prince Mishari waving me off into the great beyond.

Somehow, I couldn't envisage the prince on skis. I knew he wasn't the sporting type, so I wondered just how long it would take for him to pack it in. I also noted that it seemed the prince was spending more and more time with the sons of King Fahd since taking on his own position within the National Guard.

I was concerned about the prince's changing attitude since he settled into his job. I was concerned about my changing attitude, too. At least we would be a small group. Apart from me, there was the prince, his son Turki, the nanny Elena, and Abdullah. I didn't know if Abdullah was a family member or just a friend of the prince; either way it made no difference to me.

"Sue, I'm on the move again. The prince wants me to go to Megeve skiing with them."

"You know I've always wanted to go skiing, it's not fair," Sue replied.

"It's a hard life, what can I do?" I replied, laughing with her.

I was concerned because I couldn't break loose from the Saudis. It was as if I were entangled within a spider's web. I got a buzz mixing with the vastly rich and travelling the world with them, but I paid a price. On one hand, I revelled in my abilities to fix any problem I was faced with, other times I didn't. I looked after them as if they were my own family. I cared deeply for them. Yet in stark contradiction to this, at times they treated me with contempt. They had a knack of making you feel worthless while making you feel-good. Because of this, my emotions began to see-saw. I wondered if it was my imagination that made me feel this way.

I contacted Peter, who also travelled the world with the royal family to sound him out. Surprisingly, he felt the same way and spoke of the many times he felt like walking away. He felt trapped and couldn't free himself from the web, either. He too felt that he suffered psychologically. We felt like slaves at times. Why couldn't we free ourselves? What was the mysterious hold that these people gripped us with?

It couldn't be the money. We earned the equivalent of two weeks' salary of a person doing a normal job. Yet in each week, we worked at least double the hours. We enjoyed the prestige of working with a royal family and getting to see other parts of the world. However, what you got in one hand you paid dearly for out of the other. We were suffering low self-esteem, but more importantly, we had become hardened to other people's feelings. This went against my core beliefs.

I always prided myself on my softer, caring side. Because I was kowtowing to my bosses, I found myself suffering mood swings. I was deeply disturbed by the person I was becoming. I felt I was beginning to think and act like them, and I couldn't handle it. Perhaps I was just thinking too much.

*   *   *

I met with Prince Mishari and his group at Geneva airport and set off for Megeve, across the border in France. It was a journey of 40 or so miles. Our driver told us many famous people had stayed at the Hotel Mont Blanc. He reeled off the names—Marlon Brando, Marlene Dietrich and others—but I thought, "So what? What do I care?"

The hotel was in the middle of town at the foot of the Mont Blanc Mountain. The hotel was in the traditional alpine style and near the church. After we checked in, the prince ordered room service. This caused a problem, as the hotel didn't provide room service. For the first evening some food was provided in the breakfast room.

Shortly after eating, our lead instructor arrived and introduced herself to us. Maryvonne, was slim, wore thick glasses, and her hair was brown and curly. She spoke English well and said Prince Saud told her to make sure the family were well looked after. This was music to the prince's ears, and he set out the needs of his family. I feared Maryvonne had bitten off more than she could chew.

The prince stayed in his room for some time after Maryvonne's arrival, which suited me fine. I used the time getting to know Maryvonne and found out about our new environment. Maryvonne asked many questions about the prince and I answered her, so long as it was appropriate.

The next morning Maryvonne took us to the ski supply shop. Once we were kitted out, we made our way on to the nursery slopes. Maryvonne was joined by her colleague, Christophe. He was about 5'10" tall and slim, like Maryvonne. They both wore the blue tops with a yellow stripe running through them which showed that they were ski instructors. We were taken through the basics. Once they were happy with our progress, they asked for a volunteer to show

268

the technique. No one stepped forward, so the prince in his wisdom decided I should go first. Bollocks, I thought, I'll show them! I whizzed off down the slope. It was only a slight decline, but it felt like the steepest slope on the mountainside to me. The only other whizzing I did was into the air. I looked skyward momentarily and then landed on my backside. Skis went one way; I went another. Whoops of laughter followed me down the slope. When I found my feet again, I set off to find my skis. They had come adrift easily as they had been calibrated to do so to minimize injuries. One by one, the party tried their snowplough techniques. One by one, each of them careered along the slope on their backsides. Laughter followed them, too. The prince wasn't amused. Each time he tried, he scoured the slopes to see if anyone was looking at him.

At lunchtime, the instructors took us to a restaurant on the slopes. But Prince Mishari was agitated over the skiing, as I knew he would be. He became even more agitated when he noticed another influential prince dining opposite us.

Prince Mishari called Turki. I watched closely, as I had witnessed his games before. Looking out the corner of his eye, the prince lifted Turki on to his knee and the show began. He earnestly displayed his qualities as a good father, not for Turki, but for the benefit of the other prince. Prince Mishari rarely publicly displayed affection, unless he had a hidden agenda. I knew the prince well. He always used the same techniques. He was a showman, and turned on the charm instantly. This ability brought him to the attention of the senior princes in the royal family. All the junior members of the family tried to play the game at one time or another. They just weren't successful at it.

After lunch, we went on the slopes again. This time, we tried the button lifts. Trying to get on to one and stay on it was a feat in itself. We fell. It was then the prince gave up. He couldn't bear the thought others were laughing at him. The next few days only Turki, Abdullah and I skied. The prince and Elena followed us on foot. As none of us was any good, this did not prove to be a problem for them.

In the afternoons, we went to Prince Saud's chalet and relaxed. Turki and I would play on the games machines he had installed. One afternoon as we played, Maryvonne approached the prince and asked to speak. I watched and cringed as he curtly, rudely and arrogantly dispatched her. He clicked his fingers and waved her away as though she were worthless. Each time she opened her mouth, he waved his hand and said, "Go away, I told you go away." He was so rude; I had to console Maryvonne as she cried in the kitchen.

"I had to tell him that his wife needs to speak to him urgently," she said.

"Don't worry about it, he'll find out soon enough, you'll see." More and more, the prince acted this way after starting his job with the National Guard. I wondered if he was up to it, could he take the pressure of his position. Others who knew the prince commented on his changing character. I didn't like what I was seeing.

Two days later, I waved them off at the departure gate in Geneva. I felt the visit had been a waste of time. I couldn't wait to get home.

A few hours later, I sat at home in the bosom of my own family and recounted the tales of my great skiing adventure to them. I laughed until I cried, and Sue laughed with me. The problem was, she wanted to go skiing—now more than ever!

Chapter 32

April 1986

The next prince on the agenda was Prince Khalid Bin Abdullah—a racehorse fanatic and one of the biggest racehorse owners in Arabia. When I arrived at his house on the corner of Belgrave Square, an old friend, Owen, met me. This was a surprise, as I wasn't aware he worked 'permanently' with Prince Khalid. When he had time off, he worked on the circuit.

Belgrave Square is in one of the most exclusive parts of London. The house was massive, tastefully furnished, and beautifully decorated. It shouted out 'class', and gave me some insight into the prince. Most of the royal family had no idea about style or taste, but some stood far above the rest. Prince Khalid was one of those; he had exceptional taste. He was well educated, polite and regal, too.

Prince Khalid owned several properties, and had many staff—the waiters wore uniforms and white gloves, while the others were suited, booted, and smart. The staff performed their duties impressively. It was obvious the prince liked everything performed with precision.

These observations were helpful to me. I was the grey man, who stayed in the background. As the grey man, your principal knows who you are, where you are, and what you are doing—but there is no reason others need to know, unless situations dictate it. As Prince Khalid's grey man, I could pass myself off as an assistant, secretary, or some other member of the entourage.

I thought I'd be the prince's only bodyguard on this job, but was happy to spend time chatting with Owen, the prince's driver. He was professional. However, shortly after my arrival, there was a knock on the rear door, the tradesman's entrance. I walked with Owen to the door. As Owen opened the door, I peered over his shoulder. There was Bruce! It was good to have him on board. I knew it would make life easier for me. Bruce wasn't surprised to see me.

After introductions and some chat, Bruce and I went over our planned tactics with Owen as we needed to use a security backup car. It was a four-door high-powered BMW. Many times, the backup car was a BMW, as though it was a compulsory fixture, like their Mercedes. I drove and backed up Bruce. He was always up for a little fun, as he called it.

Owen gave us a brief on the places the prince would normally frequent. The prince was only staying for a few days and wanted to spend time looking over some of his racehorses.

A waiter told us the prince was about to leave. We prepared the cars and pulled up outside by the front doors. Owen stood by the rear door of the prince's Mercedes while Bruce waited near the front door of the house, ready to escort the prince to the car. I waited near the BMW, but on the pavement. While not too close, I was close enough to provide important backup should Bruce need it. Once the prince entered the Mercedes and the door closed, I jumped into the BMW. Bruce hopped in too, then we followed Owen's lead. This looked easy but timing was everything.

The prince was off to Juddmonte Farm the horse stud he had recently bought near Newbury in Berkshire. This was one minor part of his conglomerate.

Once Bruce and I were alone we got on with the serious business of catching up. I drove the BMW to position it in a way that no other vehicle could come between us. I had perfected this technique over several years. When Owen signalled his intent, I moved out into the outside lane, just before he moved across. In this way, if co-ordinated properly, we would free-flow into the position Owen had chosen. We needed to maintain a safe distance, but used different techniques to prevent others from entering our space. It was necessary to be on constant lookout for changes in road conditions as well as side roads and driveways. Good observation always puts you in a better position to act on any unforeseen hazard. On this trip, though, there were no complications other than some heavy congestion on the M4 motorway.

We turned off the M4 and drove down country roads, soon arriving at the main gates of the stud. We meandered up the driveway and stopped at the large double-fronted main doors. A butler waited for the prince. I stopped the BMW a little short, allowing Bruce to get out and up to the prince's door just as his car stopped.

Once the prince was safe inside, Owen took us to the staff quarters behind the house. Bruce and I were ready for a brew and, cups in hand, we wandered into the staff room.

We introduced ourselves to the guys, and a minute later Bruce caught my eye and signalled me to follow him. Outside, he asked if I had clocked the old boy's Regimental badge. He said some old guy in the driver's room was wearing the 'Who Dares Wins' Regimental badge of the Special Air Service on his blazer. Bruce wanted to question the old guy about his service. The old fellow was 'kosher' and had originally served in the Long-Range Desert Group. Years later, I found my father also served with them, going on to serve in Special Forces and the secret intelligence service (MI6).

We discovered the old boy had gone into the SAS at its formation and now stories started flowing. From everyone having been a bit reserved initially, talk now became animated; everyone in the room woke up and joined in. I dare say we were having a jollier time than the prince. As with most jobs, it was the same scenario, hurry up and wait. Once the prince completed his business in the house, they called us to the front door. We then strolled down to the stables following the prince discreetly. We could just hear the prince and his trainer discussing the horses. The paddocks were large, and the place must have been worth a fortune. Once the prince was satisfied, we walked back toward the cars. Owen was ready and waiting and some staff stood by the house, in case the prince should want anything. Prince Khalid got in his car and Owen stood back, allowing the trainer to say goodbye. The trainer closed the door. I watched as both Bruce and Owen rechecked the door. Slowly, we set off down the driveway.

The journey back to London was uneventful and we made our way to the Villa Dei Cesari restaurant on the bank of the River Thames for dinner. The car valet would secure the vehicles, which meant we would all be dining. The prince had an aide with him, and during dinner, they did not relax—it all seemed a bit too reserved for my liking. Bruce and I kept alert. I felt uneasy. I couldn't put my finger on it, but something wasn't right. Even so, nothing more came of this feeling throughout the visit.

After dinner, we returned to Belgravia and went over the schedule for the following day. The highlight, it seemed, would be a visit to the prince's country house, Fairlawns, in Plaxtol, Kent. Owen said this place would impress us—the prince bought it for £20 million. Anything costing £20 million was likely to impress me, I thought. Owen said it had a trout lake in the grounds. Bruce wondered what the chances were on doing some fishing—but we knew the answer already: no chance! This house, we were told, had one of only two remaining real tennis courts in England. The other one is in Hampton Court Palace. I was looking forward to getting a look at this place.

In the morning, the Mercedes parked by the front door, while we sat behind it. A few minutes later, Owen signalled the prince was on his way. Bruce and I took up our respective positions. The prince, his aide and a young woman who was not known to us, walked out. Once in the cars, we set off towards Maidstone in Kent; it would take an hour or so to near our final destination. As we arrived, large wrought iron gates welcomed us.

As we approached, a guy expecting us opened them and we drove through. I looked on in disbelief; the house was magnificent. Owen had been right; this place impressed me! Bruce, on the other hand, said it has nothing on Buck House! I wasn't sure Her Majesty would have agreed.

The prince got out of his car and spoke with Owen. After he went inside, we walked over to Owen. He said the prince had told him to show us round and that he would send someone to find us when it was time for lunch, which was thoughtful. It made a difference when you knew the principal took the time to think of you.

As we looked at the trout, a waiter came over and called us for lunch. I wanted to laugh; it was as though we were in a movie. Firstly, though, I had to have a quick look at that tennis court.

To think that apart from Hampton Court Palace, this private mansion was the only other place to hold such a feature! I wondered if it was true.

A waiter showed us to the main dining room. The prince and his party had already eaten. As we entered, my jaw hit my chest. It was indescribable—a wonder to behold. I hoped the prince was going to cherish this, our heritage. Dark wood with deep intricate carvings covered the walls. No amount of words could describe the awe this place instilled in you. At least the prince could afford the proper upkeep of the place. With his wealth, he could keep the properties he owned properly preserved. I stared in wonder, thinking that at least when I climb into my wooden overcoat; I will take some extraordinary memories with me. Good and bad!

When the visit ended, I realised how much good this prince was doing for the country in many respects. This side of the coin was one I had not experienced with any other Saudi. I held a respect for Prince Khalid.

While immersed in this room, I imagined the scenes the hall had been privy to, but too soon our call came. The prince was on the move, so we made our way to the cars and waited. As he emerged, I could see he was searching our faces for a reaction. I realised he must treasure the place and he got a kick out of people's reactions when viewing it for the first time, fair play to him. Down the road we went as Bruce said he would have enjoyed the visit more if we were able to drop a line in—he was still going on about the fishing!

It was strange to think that Prince Khalid's town house in Belgravia probably cost as much as the country mansion, including the refurbishments. To me, there seemed no comparison between the two properties.

Prince Khalid loved his horses and his houses and was always polite and thoughtful of his staff. The prince, I determined, was a good guy. Owen asked what we thought of Fairlawns. I said it was unbelievable, but Bruce said he couldn't find the fishing rods.

We drove the cars into the mews behind the house and parked up. Then we made our way to the drivers' room for another important task, to make another brew. Bruce told a few jokes, and I was chuckling away when someone in a *thobe* wandered in.

We looked toward the door; Owen was up on his feet. I still chuckled at the joke when I realised it was the prince who had entered. Immediately, Bruce and I stood up. The prince asked if

275

everything was all right and if there was anything we needed. We assured him we were fine. I detected a slight pause from Bruce, and wondered if he was going to ask where the fishing rods were at Fairlawns. I'm sure it crossed his mind, but he thought better of it. The prince had shown us again that he did not take us for granted—what a pleasant change!

Later that evening, Owen told us to prepare the cars: we were going out to dinner again. Round to the front of the house we went and positioned ourselves as usual. Some distance away, a group of youths approached. We noticed they were making some noise and a couple of them swayed a little, and not from any breeze. We knew they would arrive the same time the prince left— it was 'Sods Law'. We tried telepathically to hurry the prince, but it never worked! We watched, we waited, and we hoped they passed by before the prince emerged.

The prince stepped on to the pavement just as the group approached. Bruce and I moved in to cover him. We did not expect trouble, but we prepared ourselves nonetheless. We got the prince in the car and we were on our merry way. Bruce controlled himself but I think he wanted to give the youths a little dig because they pissed him off. I hoped no other surprises were in store for us. We escorted the prince inside the restaurant and noticed him nod at us; this we thought was an acknowledgment of how we covered him from the group. It was sad to see him leave but as they say, all good things come to an end.

These days it appeared that all I met were the big boys, as I called them. I started to think it was time to get away from the Saudis as I became more and more disenchanted with them. It was draining working for them, both physically and emotionally. Even so, there was many would-be bodyguards' knocking on the door trying to get into the business, although knocking was no guarantee the door would open. It is a notoriously difficult business to get into. But make a mistake, and it is a notoriously easy business to get out of!

* * *

Over the next couple of months, even though I had promised myself not to do it, I reverted to doing some surveillance. It gave me a break from the stress. Yet, I knew, when the Saudis rang again, I would be on my way. I couldn't say no to them. Maybe I was my own worst enemy, but I had to earn a living, and if it was Arab work that was available at the time then I took it.

Sure enough, in June, Prince Mishari called and I caught a flight to Malaga. A day after my arrival, I waited at the airport for his family. The prince would follow two weeks later.

The next two weeks were murder. Princess al-Anud tightened the purse strings like never before. It was ridiculous; it reached the point where I paid some of their expenses with my money! My self-esteem plummeted. The princess made me feel guilty asking her for money. I felt like a beggar.

"Please, Ma'am, can I have some more?" I said when I was given 2000 pesetas to fill up the Mercedes. I was Oliver Twist in a rare moment of humour. With that pittance, the tank would be lucky to hit the quarter-full mark. I had to pick up the prince from the airport thirty miles away and then return and I didn't fancy running out of petrol with him in the car. You would have thought I was asking for her life's blood.

After fetching the prince, he asked to be taken to Puerto Banus. Instead of going to his family, he went to see his brothers. The prince sent me to get the car and I found I didn't have the money to pay the fee. Embarrassed, I went to ask the prince if he had 200 pesetas, for the car park charge. Apologising profusely, I said, "Your Highness, Princess al-Anud will not give me enough money to pay for the family's needs." His response was a shrug of his shoulders.

The next day, the prince told me to take him to the mosque. The petrol light was on in the Mercedes and I said we needed fuel soon. No answer.

He, like all the other royals in Marbella, only attended the mosque on a Friday when Prince Salman, the Governor of Riyadh was in town. On any other Friday, you could go to the mosque and park 10 coaches in the car park. They were so hypocritical. I called

277

them 'fair-weather Muslims'. They preached to their people all the time, yet they broke all the rules of their religion on a regular basis.

A few days later, one of the static guys took me to the airport. The prince had sent me to pick up his Ferrari 400i saying, "Mark, please be careful with it. I have had it refinished. It is now perfect and I want it to be perfect when you get back."

I made sure he gave me enough money for petrol. The Ferrari would drink it and I knew when shipped it would be almost emptied. At the airport, I watched the Ferrari being unloaded from a pallet. There was an almighty crash as they caught the front underside spoiler on the edge of the pallet.

"Fuck, fuck, fuck!" I shouted as I ran over to it. As the damage was on the underside, I doubted the prince would notice it. I made a report for the insurance claim in a nearby office. When I returned to the Ferrari, I noticed a big puddle of oil. It was nowhere near the area of the car that had been caught on the pallet. I decided to give the Ferrari a good look over before moving it.

It was in a sorry state. Lights had been wrongly fitted after its respray. Oil leaked badly from the engine. Many faults existed. Was this the usual Saudi workmanship, I wondered, as I fired up the V12 engine and drove out of the airport? I stopped at the nearest petrol station and filled up. When I tried to start the car again, it wouldn't fire up.

"Bollocks, bollocks, bollocks," I said. After an hour and a half and several tries, it finally started. I got back to Marbella and had a mechanic friend take a look at it. After a diagnostic check, I was told there was an intermittent fault in the Ferrari's electronic control unit. This meant that you never knew if the car would start. My day just got worse.

The price of a new ECU? US$ 2000.

Once back at the villa, I went over the faults with the prince. He was livid. Unfortunately, he blamed me for it and banished me to my room and the Ferrari to the garage at the villa, where it remained throughout the visit. Two weeks later, Prince Mishari left Marbella and went back to Saudi Arabia. The princess followed him four weeks later. I received no bonus. I always got a bonus from the prince. The whole visit was a disaster. I couldn't get out of there fast enough. I was shocked at the change in Prince Mishari's manner on the trip. He wasn't the person I once knew. He had changed significantly since getting his job. I now wondered if they would ever call me again, and I no longer knew whether I wanted them to. I decided if I had work the next time Prince Mishari called, I'd turn him down, but if I had no work, then I would relent and try with him once again. I was prepared to give it one last shot, although I knew in my heart of hearts it would not improve.

* * *

Over the next 6 months or so, I worked mainly for the royal family of Abu Dhabi. I enjoyed working in the teams when I did close protection work: it was good having someone to watch my back. Trust was all-important, and I trusted the team implicitly. I had known some of the guys for a few years, and none of them ever let me down. Trust was the key. You watched their backs and they watched yours. Your life could depend on it!

* * *

On the third week of March 1987, I prepared myself for the imminent State visit of King Fahd. The official dates of the visit were the 24th to the 27th March 1987, but His Majesty would also spend a few extra days enjoying a private visit to the United Kingdom. Hundreds of courtiers attended him but the visit would prove memorable to me for a few reasons. One was that Pete Scholey, another ex-SAS guy, was placed as team leader. Two was the chaos that ensued. Three was that I noticed Janan Harb visiting the King. Fourth was that the King presented a cheque to his son, Abdul Aziz 'Azoozi' for the sum of $300 million as a gift for his fifteenth birthday!

Chapter 33

Paris, France: July 1987

Surprise, surprise—Prince Mishari called at the beginning of July, just when my other work dried up. What were the chances of that, I asked myself? He asked me to meet his family in Paris on Thursday 16th July. I agreed to do it. However, after hanging up the phone I discussed with Sue whether I should accept the assignment. This was unprecedented for me.

The family, the prince had told me, would move on to Marbella after five days and he would meet with them. I wondered what frame of mind Princess al-Anud would be in. Already, my mind was analysing. I was definitely thinking too much. It was curious, the stages you went through if you worked personally with one branch of the royal family.

Originally, you were hired as a bodyguard, and then you became a babysitter. From a babysitter, you became a gofer–go for this, go for that. Then you became a Mr Fix-It. Then you were welcomed as a member of their 'family' (if they liked you well enough). But this usually sounded the death knell and you were on borrowed time.

From there, you invariably became the used tissue they discarded when of no further use. And all the time this is happening, your self-respect and self-esteem are plummeting.

With these thoughts in mind, I waited for the princess and her children at the airport in Paris. As the princess came into view, I detected a twinkle in her eyes. Her step appeared more bouncy than before. She smiled more freely. My first thought was that she must be in love, but I dismissed the idea as quickly as it came. I greeted her and the children then nodded to the nannies and staff that followed. I escorted them to the waiting cars and we set off for the Royal Monceau Hotel, which is located near the Champs Elysées and the Arc de Triomphe. We arrived outside the hotel in the Avenue Hoche; I noticed that it was, as usual, first class all the way.

After a while though, one hotel seemed much like another. I settled the family into their suites and went to my room to unpack.

Now all I had to do was wait for the phone to ring and it wasn't long before Elena called me to the princess' suite.

"Mark, the princess wants us to take the children to the Menagerie du Jardin des Plantes."

"All right, Elena, we have to take the kids to the zoo, I get the idea," I replied, and laughed with her.

This zoo was modest in size and one of the attractions in the Jardin des Plantes. Outside the zoo, you could see a large building. This housed the Museum of Natural History, while the smaller building opposite housed the Palaeontology Museum. Without doubt, the best zoo is in the south-eastern outskirts of Paris. This zoo is called the Parc Zoologique de Paris and many of the zoo's animals live in settings similar to their natural habitats, hemmed in by rock barriers, not bars or cages, not that I suppose the Saudis noticed. I knew we would visit it in a day or two. The princess usually got the kids out of the way, so she could indulge in her favourite pastime, shopping! Again, I noticed the princess was more lively and bouncy and wondered why.

"Is everyone ready?" I asked.

"Yes, we're coming now," Elena, replied.

As Turki arrived at the suite door, I reminded him to stay close to me. Hala toddled out behind her brother with the nannies in tow. After leaving the hotel, I went in to protection mode but was careful as I didn't want the kids growing up with any signs of paranoia brought on by an overeager bodyguard.

I was pleased with the princess' change of mood and secretly hoped Prince Mishari would be in a like frame of mind. At six o'clock, we returned to the hotel. I stayed with the children as the nannies ordered something for them to eat from room service. Not long after, the princess arrived back from her shopping spree.

"Mark," she said, "I want you to escort me this evening. We will leave at eight o'clock."

"Yes, Your Highness," I replied, "Do I need to dress formally?"

"No, Mark, we are just going for a drive and maybe a walk."

With that, I left the family to enjoy their time together.

In my room, I ordered a fillet steak and put on the TV. Before dinner arrived, I took a quick shower. At five minutes to eight, my phone rang.

"Mark, are you ready?"

"Yes, Your Highness, I'll come to you now," I said.

I knocked the suite door and waited for one of the girls to answer it.

"Good evening, Elena. The princess called for me."

"Yes, Mark, she's saying goodnight to the children and then she'll be with you."

I wondered why the princess wanted me, as this was unusual these days. I opened the door of the Mercedes and the princess got in. I closed her door and jumped in to the front passenger seat.

"Driver, Bois de Boulogne," she said. Now I knew why she wanted me. We were on one of her tours of the "red light district" of Paris. She often toured them; she had a curiosity about prostitutes. The princess asked the driver to slow down and asked me to open my window. The driver advised her against it and so did I. She ignored us both. She eyed a prostitute standing on a pathway. I wondered if the figure before us was a man or a woman. As I looked out of the window the figure shouted at me from the pathway, "*Je suis le meilleure en Paris pour seulement deux cents francs* (I'm the best in Paris for only 200 francs)." No way was I going to find out if that were true and I ordered the driver to move on.

"Driver, take us to the Rue St Denis now," the princess ordered.

Oh bollocks, I thought, here we go again. It is difficult to explain what the Rue St Denis is like, because it is like another world. Hundreds of girls lined the street and the streets, which ran off the Rue St Denis. Girls displayed generous helpings of what they had to offer. The only thing that was taboo in the street was cameras. Every two or three steps you would find a girl standing, leaning, peeking out of a window, over balconies or occasionally reclining on the hood of a car. *Les Femmes De Le Nuit* (the ladies of the night) were all gorgeous and I couldn't understand why they had chosen this profession. As we walked down the street, laughter rang out. Someone was having a good time, I thought. I, personally, was having a nightmare. My eyes darted back and forth.

282

The girls appeared friendly but I wondered what dangers lurked behind the scenes. Even though my time with the princess had sometimes been rocky, I would protect her at all costs. Some of the girls fired questions at us. I was surprised the questions were directed more towards the princess.

"Where are you from?"—"You are beautiful, do you want to work here?"—"Can we borrow your man?"

The princess laughed or smiled and analysed them carefully. I often wondered what she thought, but she never told me. I also wondered if this was a cheap evening's entertainment for her. After all, we didn't sample the goods and looking was free.

I was nothing short of amazed that the princess let me view this evening's entertainment with her, though. Was it a test? Did she expect me to tell the prince? Did she have some hidden agenda? If so, she would be out of luck as I always separated the principals' interests. What he did, I didn't tell her about and what she did, I didn't tell him about. Over the years, each of them questioned me many times about the other's movements but I always told them not to ask, because it wasn't my business to speak about. Luckily, that had been enough to prevent them asking further.

Something was amiss about this trip; I could feel it in my bones.

Over the next few days, I reverted to traipsing around the usual attractions with the children. Nonetheless, the nannies enjoyed the sightseeing, as did I. We took a cruise on the river Seine and looked out over Paris from the various stages of the Eiffel Tower. We walked around Notre Dame Cathedral and watched the artists painting on Montmartre, which is the highest hill in Paris. We ogled the beautiful white Catholic Basilica, La Basilique du Sacre Coeur de Montmartre. During the evenings, I would escort the princess as she walked around the most beautiful avenue in the world—*C'est la plus belle avenue du monde*—the Champs-Elysee. This was the magic of the job for me. The downside was the times I wanted to share the experiences with my own family. I missed them. Being away during the summer months meant that I missed the boys' summer vacation from school. I would never shrug off the guilt I felt for missing so much of their free time.

Looking out of the aircraft window, I saw Paris recede below us. We were on our way to Malaga, where we spent most of the summer. I called ahead and spoke with Salvador, the house administrator. He arranged our arrival. I never liked Salvador or his wife. They struck me as devious and they upset the housekeeper many times. One time, Salvador took the gold and silver cutlery from the prince's villa and used it for a dinner party. They returned it scratched and blamed the housekeeper, Aurora, and her husband, Diego. This was one of many incidents. However, Salvador and Conchita, his wife, worked their magic on the princess and were firmly imbedded in the set up. At least they never interfered with my business.

Once settled, I noticed a telephone line light up. This light stayed on for hours. I knew it was the princess; no one else would be on the phone for such an excessive time. Although we had our upsets, I admired the princess for her intelligence and style yet I felt she was the proverbial 'bird stuck in a golden cage'. As a woman, her intellect was wasted in Saudi Arabia, as they were considered second class citizens by the hardliners in their country.

In three days, the prince would arrive. I looked forward to this and hoped he was in a bubbly mood. Meanwhile, I accompanied the children to the Tivoli World theme park in Arroyo de la Miel. Turki got me to take him on some of the most thrilling rides. If his mother had seen us, I would be shot. On one occasion, Hudda, one of the nannies, insisted on going on a ride. I tried to dissuade her. Two minutes later it had to be stopped. Hudda was hysterical. Medical attention was sought. Turki found Hudda's response to the ride hysterically funny. I wondered if the princess would hear about it. Once Hudda settled, she insisted we carry on with our visit. We sat by the enormous water flume, Tivoli Agua. As the water danced to the background music, coloured lights lit up the flume. I decided to give the Tivoli Dragon, Roller Coaster, Twister, Terror Passage, Mysterious Boat and Jurassic Adventure a miss. I didn't think I could handle any more excitement in one day.

The next day we went to the amusement arcade by the seafront. We watched a man making sculptures in the sand. Miraculously, a mermaid emerged from the beach and people threw coins to the sculptor in appreciation. I thought about picking a few of them up, so I could give them to the princess to help her finances. At the villa, I noticed the phone line lit up again. It was engaged for hours and hours. This never happened during any of our previous visits. I also noticed the nannies together talking secretly—this, too, was out of character.

The next morning, Elena asked me to take some photographs in for processing.

"Mark, whatever you do don't let the princess know I gave them to you," Elena said. There was something fishy here, I felt. Therefore, as I passed the film over, I asked for two copies to be processed. If the shit was going to hit the fan, I wanted to make sure my back was covered. I collected the photographs and gave a set to Elena, the other I put in my briefcase. She handled them like a bar of gold. Something was amiss, but I didn't get a chance to look at them until much later.

I drove out to Malaga airport to meet the prince. The sun shone brightly, as it did every day. I listened to the music player in the car and sailed along as I hummed away to it. I grabbed a coffee in the terminal building as I waited for the aircraft to land. I was pleased to see it was on schedule, as I didn't fancy hanging around for hours. I periodically checked the flight information board and when I saw the 'clearing customs' sign appear, I made my way over to the arrivals gate.

The prince walked through with Khairy. Bollocks, I thought. It must be the prince's turn to have him. He was passed between the princes like a plaything; a toy to keep them amused. He would play cards with them and make an ass of himself to keep them happy. The problem was he tried to make an ass of the staff as well, me included. There was a personality clash between us. I sorely wanted to give him a slap! I knew the rest of the visit was going to be crap. I took the prince's briefcase and shook hands with him. I could tell his mood wasn't up to much. Whatever happened to the nice guy I had met a few years ago, I wondered?

One word came to mind—responsibility. I believed the responsibility of his job weighed heavily on him. I drove them back to the villa. Khairy tried to jolly the prince and cracked a few jokes, but the prince's mood was sombre.

In stark contrast, the princess' mood was in the clouds. The Spanish National policeman on guard opened the wrought iron gates as we approached and I drove through. I could see the princess waiting on the patio. Whether she waited for her husband or not was another matter. As the prince walked over to her, I could see her manner had changed. She was quieter and reserved, kowtowing to her husband. This wasn't unusual; I witnessed such scenes often. I left them and went to my room. I left Khairy alone. For the rest of the day and early evening, the phone line stayed quiet.

I was called to escort the prince. "You called me, Your Highness?"

"Yes, Mark, we are going to Puerto Banus. Can you call Khairy and get the car ready?"

"Right away, Your Highness."

I rustled Khairy up and prepared the car. The prince came out and spoke to Khairy; he then got in the passenger seat of the Camaro. The princess walked over and went to get into the small back seat of the sports car. As she leant forward, her ample bosom bulged out of her dress. The prince was angered and sent her off with a flea in her ear. Two minutes later, she returned with a safety pin holding the neckline of her dress in a more suitable manner. I preferred it the other way.

I drove to the port and parked up. The prince walked alongside his wife and I followed. We came across some of the other princesses vacationing in Marbella. The prince sent the princess to sit with them. He told me to stay with him. We walked further down the port and came across Prince Sultan Bin Salman, the first Arab astronaut. The prince knew him well and we sat at his table. I shook hands with Prince Sultan. By this time, Khairy had joined us. He pushed in to sit next to the prince. I sat next to Prince Sultan. Soon, Prince Sultan and I were engrossed in conversation. We spoke of his flight on the space shuttle. We became lost in our conversation as the others chatted. Then I heard the words that put me firmly in my place.

"Mark, please allow us some time with Prince Sultan, too," Prince Mishari said.

"I'm so sorry, Your Highness," I replied, "It was thoughtless of me, please forgive me."

"Mishari, Mark and I are old friends, we were catching up," Prince Sultan interjected.

Once again, I had become a pawn in a power play and I did not like it.

"I wasn't aware you knew Mark," Prince Mishari replied.

I kept my mouth shut while the conversation continued between the princes. Half an hour later, Prince Mishari stood. We left Prince Sultan and his party and wandered along the quayside. Looking to my left, I saw a short portly character jump to his feet. He looked short, about five foot five, and was balding. Rosy cheeks adorned his face. I recognised him. It was the Saudi Arabian arms dealer, Adnan Khashoggi. He recognised Prince Mishari and came over to extend his greetings to the prince. Seeing Adnan Khashoggi cast my mind back to when I had first set eyes on his yacht. It was magnificent and he named it after his daughter, Nabila. It was so large it had to be berthed outside the walls of the port.

Helicopters constantly ferried people back and forth to his villa in the mountains. I had marvelled at it, not knowing Khashoggi would soon be in the shit with the American authorities. The word 'corruption' was bandied about. No change there, and I thought it a joke, as corruption is rife within Saudi Arabia.

As the prince spoke with Khashoggi, I took note of the gorgeous girls sitting at his table. I noted Khashoggi's secretary, Abdul Khoury, at the table, too. What I didn't know, was that the prince was taking more than a little notice of one of the girls.

The prince whispered, "Mark, go and find out about that girl sitting to the right of Abdul Khoury."

"Yes, sir."

"Mr. Khoury," I said discreetly, "Can I have a word?"

"Of course," he replied and moved away from the table.

287

"His Royal Highness has asked me to ask about the girl sitting next to you; can you tell me about her?"

"Yes," he replied, "Her name is Heather, Heather Mills, and she is English." With a smile he continued, "She is, how do you say, a hooker, a prostitute, and a favourite of Mr. Khashoggi's."

"I see, thank you for your candour. I will tell His Highness." As I returned to the prince, Khashoggi returned to his guests.

We then went in search of the princess. On the way, the prince asked about Miss Mills. We found the princess still deep in conversation with the other princesses. The prince said good evening to them and the princess stood up and said goodnight to them.

We left Puerto Banus and within five minutes, were back in the villa. The phone line stayed quiet. I took a shower. The phone line stayed quiet. I made up my accounts and tallied up the money I had left in my bag. The phone line stayed quiet.

The next day Elena called me over as I watched over the children swimming in the pool.

"Mark, please say you didn't tell anyone about the photographs I asked you to get."

"No Elena, I haven't spoken about them, why?"

"I'm worried, that's all, because the princess said, 'Don't let Mark see them; he mustn't see them at all costs!' Did you look at them?" Elena asked.

"No, Elena, I didn't." I never mentioned the copy I had.

"All right, Mark, that's good."

Now I felt distinctly uncomfortable. Why had Elena deliberately given me the photos for processing? What did she want me to see? What was going on? What had the nannies been furtively discussing before? Many questions filled my head. Was someone trying to load the gun and get me to fire it?

After the children finished playing, we went in to the villa. My mind spun wildly as thoughts engulfed it and then Khairy loomed into sight and everything else dissolved as I focused on him.

"Mark, the prince wants you. Get the car. Hurry up."

I wanted to tell him to fuck off, but I knew he would go crying to the prince so I held my tongue. I got the Camaro out of the garage where it was kept to keep it cool from the noonday sun. I drove it up to the main entrance of the villa and waited for the prince. He walked out wearing a short-sleeved shirt and light-coloured lightweight trousers. Dark shoes and sunglasses complemented his dress.

"Mark, I'll drive. Get in."

"Yes, sir."

"Mark, we're going on the *SHAF*, Prince Salman's yacht. We have been invited by Prince Sultan."

Prince Salman allowed his children to use his yacht as they saw fit. I fancied a cruise on the Mediterranean. The prince picked his nose throughout the short drive. When we stopped, he checked his face to see that no evidence of that fact remained and then asked me to double check as he always did. Once he felt comfortable, sure that no one would see him with a large bogey on his face, he got out of the car.

We walked over to the port entrance, where we met three of his brothers. They too had been invited on the cruise, which would take us to Gibraltar and back. We walked towards the *SHAF* and Prince Mansour, the prince's older brother, waved me away. I looked at Prince Mishari and he signalled me to follow. Three or four times we went through the same scenario. Prince Mansour was becoming angry with me as I ignored him. When we got to the gangplank of the *SHAF,* I noticed Prince Mishari talking with Prince Sultan. Just as Prince Mansour was about to wave me away, Prince Sultan leant over and said, "Hello, Mark, glad you could make it, welcome aboard!"

Prince Mansour's face was a picture. Another power game, I thought. This time the game was between Prince Mansour and Prince Mishari. The royal family was rife with rivalries and jealousies, and often brothers hated each other. We sat at a large table on the rear deck and helped ourselves to cold drinks. A little while later, I took my leave and went up to the ship's bow. There was a corner bench that straddled the yacht and I sat on it. After we had been at sea for a little while, I decided to take my T-Shirt off and sunbathe. A feeling that I was being watched came over me. I opened my eyes slowly to find Prince Mansour standing next to Prince Salman, the Governor of Riyadh!

I leapt to my feet, grabbed at my shirt, and quickly pulled it on. I didn't know Prince Salman was aboard. Fuck, fuck, fuck, I thought. Prince Salman is one of the Sudeiri Seven, the seven most powerful brothers in Saudi Arabia.

"Your Royal Highness, please forgive me, I wasn't aware that you were aboard," I spluttered. Prince Salman asked Prince Mansour in Arabic who I was. Prince Mansour had great delight in telling him that I was with Prince Mishari. In a soft calm voice, Prince Salman said to me, "Have you eaten yet?"

"No, Your Royal Highness," I replied.

"Dinner has been served, please go and eat." A polite way of telling me to fuck off, I thought.

"Thank you so much, Your Royal Highness," I replied and made a hasty exit. Luckily, nothing else was said about the matter, probably because Prince Mishari was well liked by the members of the Sudeiri Seven. I had been quick to get on the yacht but I was quicker still, getting off it.

The next few days passed by quietly. Still the phone line was quiet.

Sitting by a banana tree in the garden, I watched the children play around the pool. Gaily they ran about until there was a splash at the deep end. The nannies looked stunned, and never moved. I dived in as Hala, the prince's daughter, went under for the second time. As I surfaced, I held her and took her to the edge of the pool, where I placed her in Elena's hands. Hala spluttered and cried. Elena and the nannies panicked.

"Please Mark, don't tell the princess, please, please, please," they pleaded. "Don't worry," I said, "your secret is safe with me."

Zeinob and Hudda walked away with the children while Elena collected their belongings.

290

Chapter 34

Affair

Elena, overcome with emotion, blurted out to me. "Mark, they do whatever they like, but if we make a mistake we could be dead. It's all right for the princess to have her affair, but we can't have anything."

"What?" I said, not believing what I heard. "The princess is seeing someone?"

"Yes, Mark, he's from the United Arab Emirates and she is always on the phone to him."

Now the penny dropped—that was why the phone line was always so busy when the prince was away.

"Does anyone else know of the affair?" I asked.

"Yes, Hudda and Zeinob know, and so do several staff in Saudi Arabia."

"All right, Elena, calm down, relax and go back to the villa."

It made sense to me now, the furtive discussions between the staff, the phone line always busy, and the princess on cloud nine all the time. What did the photos contain that the princess didn't want me to see? This was a dangerous game the princess was playing, a game that could result in her losing her head, literally. Again, I questioned myself.

Why did Elena tell me this? Was it just emotion coming out? Did she have an agenda—did they want the prince to find out? Was she telling the truth? Next day, I contacted the telephone exchange to check the record of the calls made to and from the villa. The technology wasn't available then, so it drew a blank. I looked at the photographs and found they contained very promiscuous shots. These, Elena told me, were to be sent on to the princess' boyfriend. This was beginning to get out of hand, and too many people knew about it for my liking. What, if anything, should I do? The whole vacation had suddenly gone tits up right in front of me. Each time I looked at the prince, I found myself avoiding his eyes. There had been a time when we were close, and I still felt great loyalty towards him. I decided to say nothing and carried on as normal, or so I thought.

Days passed by, and the nannies spoke freely about the affair in front of me. I kept my thoughts to myself. But I knew that with so much talk, it would only be a matter of time before the shit hit the fan. It wouldn't be long before the trip ended, so I thought I would keep my head down to stop it being shot off. As the days rolled by, the atmosphere became ever more strained.

Apart from the normal activity, the telephone line stayed quiet. The princess' mood dropped and she took out her frustrations on the staff, me included. The prince ambled along in a world of his own, seemingly oblivious to what was going on behind his back.

Early mornings, I spent sorting business. In between doing these chores, I juggled money about because I never had enough to go round. After 10am, I took the children out and invariably we met up with the princess sometime in the afternoon. We returned at 6pm. Then I escorted the prince and princess on their late evening jaunt. I would return the princess to the villa and then go out again with the prince. By this time, he had stopped visiting the casinos. Therefore, we would end up in some nightclub or other. We would get back to the villa between three-thirty and four in the morning. Very often, I saw the nannies preparing clothes for the children to wear that day. They, like me, worked all the hours God sent. By half past eight, I was up and ready to go again.

As the trip was drawing to a close, I approached Prince Mishari and asked if I could speak with him.

"Yes, Mark, what is it?"

"If you remember, Your Highness, I took a salary cut three years ago. I dropped my wage from US $1000 a week to US $700. Now I would like to know if I can have an increase."

"No Mark, not yet, I am going through a difficult time, I am having another palace built in Dammam," he replied. "Perhaps in another year or two you can ask again."

That was it, no raise. Times were hard for me, too, but he didn't care. I walked away thinking, what a lot of bollocks; times are hard just now—fucking sauce, he's taking the piss.

My anger soon subsided, and I got on with the job. The staff continually moaned about the princess, and I could see, I was on a sinking ship. A couple of nights later, I sat with the prince in the same coffee shop, cum bar, where we had met Prince Sultan. My mood had dropped significantly and the prince noticed it.

"Mark, what's wrong with you?"

"I do have some issues playing on my mind, but I would rather keep them to myself," I replied.

"Come on Mark, aren't we friends? You're like one of my family; tell me what's bothering you."

Like one of the family, I thought. If that's the case, why didn't you give me a raise?

"Your Highness, I don't think this is the time or the place to discuss my concerns."

"Mark, you must tell me what is bothering you."

"As I said, Your Highness, this is neither the time nor place."

"Mark, you're like one of my brothers, you can tell me anything. I'm asking you as a brother—what is wrong?"

So now I'm Prince Mark, am I? You must be having a laugh, I thought.

"Your Highness, things have changed since you took your Government position. Several of the staff are unhappy, and so am I."

"Why are you unhappy?"

"Well, for one, I have to struggle to pay your bills and have often found myself subsidising you, with my own money. That's ridiculous. I asked you for a raise and you said no, as times are hard for you. Well, times are hard for me, too. Your attitude has changed dramatically, so much so you're not the person I first worked for. You take the side of Khairy over me constantly, even when you know I'm trying to look after your interests. There you have it; these are some of the issues that are bothering me."

"I didn't realise Mark, what else is there?"

"Your Highness, I've always been straight with you, and will continue to be, so long as I'm around. Therefore, don't ask me what else is wrong."

"You must tell me, Mark, I insist!"

"You don't want to know," I replied.

"We won't leave here, until you tell me."

"Your Highness, don't force me to tell. I don't want to tell you, and believe me; you don't want to know, so please, let's just leave it at that."

"Mark, I ask you as a brother, you should tell me out of love; tell me, just tell me!"

Oh bollocks, I thought, if you want to hear it so much, then hear it.

"Your Highness, it appears Princess al-Anud has been seeing someone else."

As soon as the words left my lips, I regretted saying them. The prince jumped out of his seat and darted off through the crowds. I ran after him. Finally, he sat down in another bar and I sat next to him. His mind was out of control. I deeply regretted the pain I had caused him. I knew his loss of face would be causing him great shame. I said nothing.

"Mark, who else knows about this?"

I told him what I knew.

"Take me to Ghassim's apartment."

Ghassim was another of their staff. He had been seconded to the prince when he was a young boy. Although slavery had been abolished in 1962 within the Kingdom, many of these people were slaves in all but name.

"Mark, wait here, I will go alone," the prince said.

Five minutes later, he returned. I could see he had been crying.

"Ghassim says he knows nothing of this. He bent down and kissed my feet; he was crying. Do you believe him?"

"Your Highness, if Ghassim says he knows nothing, then he doesn't."

"Take me back to the villa."

"Yes sir," I replied.

"Now tell me everything."

"Your Highness, the first thing to keep in mind is there may be no truth to the rumour. For the moment, I think it best to see what you find out by your own means."

Prince Mishari got out of the car and told me to walk with him. We headed to the laundry, where the nannies prepared the clothes

294

for the children. Elena jumped out of her skin when she saw the prince. I raised my eyebrows, trying to signal as best I could, that the shit had hit the fan. Whether she understood my warning, I do not know.

"Elena," he said, "I am going to ask you a question. You will answer it truthfully and honestly."

I could see that Elena had caught on, as fear etched itself across her face.

"Is the princess seeing someone else?"

I fully expected Elena to deny any knowledge of any affair. Nevertheless, to my surprise she answered, "Yes, sir, she is."

"Who else knows about this?"

"Zeinob, Hudda and several others," she replied.

"What about Ghassim?"

"No, Your Highness, he knows nothing."

"Who took the photographs of the princess, and where are they now?"

"I took the photos, sir, I think she may still have them," Elena said.

"I am going to look into this and find out what is going on," the prince said as he spun on his heels and made his way back in to the villa.

"Did you tell him, Mark?"

"Yes," I replied, "but I wish I hadn't, it was reckless."

I knew for sure he would find out more when he got back to Saudi Arabia. It would have been much worse for him to learn of it there. Somehow, I did not feel any better for knowing this. I knew the girls had hoped I would tell him. In a roundabout way, they were trying to protect the prince. Either way, I went to my bed and lay down. Sleep eluded me.

Early the next morning, a knock on the large patio windows of my room disturbed me. I looked out and was surprised to find not a Spanish police officer but the prince himself. I quickly went out to him.

"Mark, I am going to Malaga to check the phone records at the telephone exchange. You stay here. I have seen the photographs of the princess and have taken them."

I waved him off, knowing he would find nothing. I knew he was looking to save face, and I knew too, what he would say to me on his return.

A few hours later, the prince returned and called for me.

"Mark, I checked the records and everything is fine. The numbers check out."

I knew he was lying, but replied, "I'm so pleased, I told you to see if it were a rumour first."

"You were right. Now go and bring Elena to me."

I went and got Elena. We stood in front of him waiting for judgment day.

"Now we know the truth, I don't want you to discuss or mention this business again; not among yourselves or with others. Is that understood?"

"Yes, sir," we replied. The prince walked away. We looked at each other. We knew the prince was lying through his teeth and the truth was out.

Within two days the prince was on his way back to Saudi. The phone line crackled once again. No doubt, the princess was warning her 'friend' of recent developments. I knew before the prince left Marbella he had his office get the telephone records from their exchange in Dammam. The technology was there for him to check what calls were made. He wanted to see them and the quickest way he could do it was to fly back to Saudi.

Within days, the prince recalled the family to Saudi Arabia. The princess made no comment about recent events. No bonus was left, not that I expected one. As I watched the family board their aircraft, I knew it was finally the end of the line.

Now I had to reconcile my own thoughts and emotions. I needed to be honest. Had I told the prince out of genuine concern for him or was I just being bloody-minded? After all, over several years they had fucked me over many times—was this my way of getting back at them? After much soul searching, I realised I did not have it in me to stoop so low. My concern had always been for my boss, who was also my friend.

However, I would never again tell a friend their partner is cheating on them. I made a serious error in judgement and as the saying goes, "They shoot the messenger, don't they?"

Chapter 35

Late 1987

Three weeks later, I headed for North London, wondering what riches were in store for me this time. It was a bitterly cold, late October night. The prince I was awaiting was King Fahd's youngest brother, Prince Humoud Bin Abdul Aziz. He was already en route from Heathrow airport. I had not met this prince before. As it turned out, he caused me all sorts of problems—not least because of the attention he attracted.

On approaching the property, my awareness levels and observation skills went into overdrive. Darkness had fallen and I noted the street wasn't well lit. I cast an eye over the property as I drove past it. I parked a hundred yards or so away. Removing my basic kit from the boot of my car, I made my way slowly towards the house. No vehicles parked in the street. Every property had its own driveway with entry and exit points. I searched the bushes, trees and likely hiding places in which a person could hide. I did not expect or find anything out of the ordinary. Later I'd retrace my steps, if necessary, with my 500,000 candlepower halogen hand-held searchlight. For now, I wanted to draw as little attention to myself as possible. The nearer I got to the property, the more switched on I became. My awareness levels increased and on entering the grounds, I searched any nooks and crannies I came across. I used my searchlight on site, which was just as well as I probably wouldn't have noticed the swimming pool as it was covered in green slime and algae. What a disgusting sight that was—it looked like it hadn't been cleaned for years. You couldn't see the bottom and I wondered if someone had fallen in and died. If so, you would never find them; gone forever, I thought.

The house was dirty and unkempt. It was disgusting.

Inside the house, I checked the windows, doors, and entry and exit points. I spent time checking the alarm and noticed no installation of CCTV cameras. There was however, a large safe in the lobby area, and I wondered if they bothered using a bank. Moving upstairs, I checked the house thoroughly. Under beds, inside cupboards—I searched everywhere as the place had been empty for some time. I did not want the principal to come face to face with a potential attacker or even squatters. That wouldn't be good form, old boy, I thought. Once satisfied, I decided to have a cup of tea before he arrived. One problem, I couldn't find a clean cup. Dirty, yes!

I found some cleaning materials and set about degreasing the cleanest one, which proved to be a mammoth task. For good measure I disinfected it, bleached it, and poured boiling water over it, even then I was apprehensive about using it. Never before or since had I seen one of their houses in such a disgusting state. Time was getting on and I knew the prince's arrival was imminent. Finally, a car drove in. No one forewarned me what I would be facing. I suppose they thought I would find out soon enough, and I did!

It took my breath away—what a monstrosity! The front end of the car was from an Aston Martin Lagonda and the rear from a Mercedes Benz 500 SEL. It had all the bells and whistles, including TV and video. The windscreen leaked, where it did not fit properly. Mercedes Benz would not carry out any work or servicing on the car. This monstrosity was going to attract so much attention.

My gut was in turmoil; it did somersaults. I considered running off down the road! Worse was to come. Two cars followed with the prince's entourage. The monstrosity stopped by the front door. I opened the door and stepped to one side so the prince would pass between me and the open door. This offered my charge cover from both sides in case of attack.

It looked good, anyway! Most assassination attacks occur when the intended target is either entering or leaving a building and getting into or out of their car. As the prince passed by, I searched the vicinity.

Was the prince wearing women's perfume? I followed him into the house, positioning myself off his right shoulder; it gave me something to do.

I went to close the door but several young men tried to follow us in. I directed them to the rear door. The less time the front door was open, the less time the prince was a target, I reasoned.

Prince Humoud turned to face me. He said hello, introduced himself, and my jaw hit my chest. The prince not only wore women's perfume—he also wore women's Paris fashions!

He had on a black silk trouser suit and thickly plastered makeup—eyeliner, mascara, and rouge with eyebrows pencilled in. I was gob smacked. I never thought I would see one of the King's brothers looking like this. I tried to conduct myself in a way not to cause the prince embarrassment. He was an embarrassment himself, and I felt like I had the breath knocked out of me. The boys followed through one at a time. What had I let myself in for, I thought?

Obviously, the prince was 'different', and he did not care what people thought. Given his position and the strict Arab background he came from, I couldn't believe what I was seeing. The boys who accompanied him were his mobile harem, and I wondered if he was the 'Saudi Queen'. I had not met such blatant behaviour from anyone in the higher echelons of the royal family, and admit I found it hard to cope with.

The prince said he spent most days sleeping. I did the night duty. He said he kept cash and jewellery in the safe. I wondered who else knew this and what potential risk it posed.

I contacted Peter, as he would be doing the day duty. I discreetly explained the evening's events to him; he scoffed in disbelief.

When I arrived the next evening, I asked if he had met the prince. "Not yet," He said, and I breathed a sigh of relief. I had hoped to introduce them.

When the prince emerged from his room, he turned down the heating thermostat. Just the chance I needed. I quietly said, "That's the prince." I went to introduce them.

Peter said, "Oh, no!" Were my fears about to materialise?

He said they met at dinner. The boys went to eat in the dining room and Peter assumed the prince would eat in his room. The boys invited Peter to join them. The prince entered and sat next to him. When Peter couldn't reach the salt, he had nudged the prince and asked him to pass it. Worse, the boys bitched among themselves and

Peter had joked about it with the prince, saying they acted like a bunch of poofters!

Peter said he wasn't sure if he could do the job. I don't know if he was homophobic, but he said everything was so dirty and because of their sexuality, he was afraid he might catch AIDS. I must admit the thought had crossed my mind more than once. Peter said he would stay for a couple of days to see if his fears eased. At least he was up front with me.

I laughed aloud when I realised the prince had not taken offence at Peter's dining etiquette! Peter was quick to say he would not go out of the house on protection duties with the prince in case he was seen with Prince Humoud. I laughed at that too, though it brought to mind my own predicament.

Surely the prince would go to town and as the Arabs all visited the same places, this caused me concern. I was acutely aware I could lose some professional credibility if I was seen with the prince. News soon travels round the circuit and this was news I could do without.

Prince Humoud was soft in nature. I found him sensitive, warm and considerate. His main interest was his vast video collection. I went out of my way to be helpful, polite, and understanding of his situation. I felt the prince recognized my efforts. During my shift, the prince said I could watch videos if I wanted. I appreciated that, as it cut down on the boredom.

So one evening, I decided to take him up on his offer and put on a videotape. While I waited for it to start, I went to the kitchen to make a cup of tea. The hygiene was still revolting. I went through the routine of decontamination.

On my return to the lounge, I saw two young bodybuilders having sex—on the videotape, that is. This vision jolted me. Caught off guard, it shocked me. My concern was that if one of the occupants of the house entered the room while the bodybuilder entered his mate, I would have been a marked man! I rushed to turn off the tape before anyone saw me and drew the wrong conclusions.

It had not crossed my mind that there would be gay pornographic videos in the prince's collection. Perhaps the prince wanted me to view the videos, getting some thrill out it? If that were the case, I never found out.

Prince Humoud spent much of his time watching his videos. He had a major fixation with his collection, most of which were, thankfully, normal action type movies. On the times we did venture out, we got a mixed reception. A few times incidents flared up, and it was my job to fix them.

On one occasion, we were in Leicester Square and as we walked near Chinatown, two youths approached. They both looked European, and I could smell trouble long before it came. Looking them up and down, I naturally weighed them up and looked for the edge.

Hoping that nothing would kick off, I just knew in my heart of hearts that it would. The leading youth swore at the prince and called him a transsexual misfit and threw in a few rather choice expletives. He lunged forward, making a grab at the prince's chest. Whether he was aiming to strike the prince or steal his brooch, I didn't know!

I shot out a ridge hand strike. I caught him a perfect strike to his throat, he gasped for air, grabbed at his neck and dropped to the floor. It would take him a few minutes to recover, by which time we would be long gone. The other youth pushed aside the prince's 'friend' and kicked out at the prince. Missing him, he went off balance. An opportunity to sweep his legs away and deflect the attack from us presented itself. Unfortunately, as I took his legs away he spun in the air and came down face first towards the ground. His nose ruptured on impact and blood gushed forth. I wasn't ecstatic, but that was the luck of the draw.

The princes do not like any confrontation. My intent was to deflect the attack away. Either way, we were out of there.

We flew along in our motoring monstrosity. If anyone took notice of the car and gave details to the police, they wouldn't have much trouble finding us. Prince Humoud looked like a clown when he ventured out. It was obvious he would draw attention. He loved dressing up in flowing silk trouser suits, gold chains, and brooches, and he piled on his makeup so thickly I wondered if a builder's plasterer had applied it. When I knew we were going to town, I would cringe and pray. Prince Humoud's visit was for two weeks and I thought I could just about handle that after the night's events.

However, when we arrived back at the house his secretary was waiting for us and told us the prince's stay had been extended to six weeks. I wanted to cry. What else could go wrong? The rain lashed down and the wind blew, perhaps in sympathy with me. Maybe God was crying too.

The rain and wind picked up that night; it was becoming rough. I felt a real storm was brewing and I wasn't wrong.

Suddenly in the night, there was an almighty crash. Jumping up, my adrenaline gushed and I moved deftly to the prince's bedroom. Checking he was safe, I stayed by his side, my first duty that of protecting my charge.

The noise died down a little but the sound from the wind and rain made me think half of the house had gone. Moving the prince to a more secure position out of harm's way was my priority. I shouted to the driver and secretary to check if anyone had suffered injury and after that, to check the extent of any damage if it was safe to do so.

My mind raced—who would want to dispose of Prince Humoud? Perhaps his own family, disposing of a liability, I wondered. The mind plays tricks with you at such times. The driver called me, shouting it was safe. I marked the driver's card for future reference as he conducted himself well.

Prince Humoud and I emerged from our hideaway. Behind the house on the far side was the offending article. A tree had uprooted and fallen through the roof of an upstairs bedroom. What a prat, I thought. Nonetheless, safety and security come first. This time a tree, next time who knows what? Rain and wind lashed through the roof.

The prince told the secretary to get the insurers out and get the damage fixed. I didn't think he would concern himself with insurance issues, as the secretary would normally deal with that. This provided an amusing tale as events unfolded over the next few days.

The following evening the insurers sent a representative. He and the secretary looked over the damage. After inspecting the mess, the agent said, the policy's a month out of date! The insurers were not going to entertain the claim, even though the secretary said he would pay any amounts due. The agent said that wasn't possible.

The secretary, sensing he was in trouble, tried a bribe. That did not work either, and the agent left. The secretary had to tell the prince he'd made a mistake and forgotten to renew the policy. Prince Humoud asked the secretary to call the manager of the insurance company and ask him to come to the house the following evening.

When the manager arrived, the secretary tried to cajole and convince him to support the claim. He said they'd used their insurers for several years and had made no claims against their policy.

The policy should have continued and would have done so, if not for a clerical error. The manager said that was the point, because of the error they had reason not to honour the claim. In effect, he backed up his agent. I enjoyed this banter while it went on. Game over; checkmate! The secretary now had to tell the prince.

The prince smiled and told the secretary to call the manager back to the house again, this time to speak with the prince. I was thinking, Just let it go; the insurers are not going to back down. The prince has money; he should just pay for the repairs.

The next evening, the manager arrived and the prince left his room and went to the kitchen. I followed him; I wanted to hear the gossip and used my guise as his bodyguard to get in there.

I listened intently, keen to know where this saga was heading. The prince explained about the tree and the damage. The manager explained about the lapsed policy. The prince asked how long the manager had worked in the office and if he enjoyed it. The manager replied 18 months at the office and yes he enjoyed his work. The banter went back and forth, and then the prince served an ace. He said the insurance company would sack him. The prince was serious, and the manager asked Prince Humoud to explain himself. The prince sent the secretary to his safe to fetch some business papers. On his return, the secretary gave a large brown envelope to the prince.

He opened the envelope and showed the manager the documents. The manager's face drained and became devoid of all colour. I wondered what the hell was going on. The prince asked the manager what he found in the papers. The manager said loud enough for me to hear that the owner of the insurance company was the prince!

What an ace; served better than Pete Sampras, I thought! I had been just as shocked as the manager had been. The prince asked the manager if there was a way he might find to repair the damage and save his job. The manager, being a bright chap, said he'd arrange the repairs, apologized and saved his job.

Money is power and once again, I had been reminded of the fact. Despite the prince's lifestyle and his idiosyncrasies, it proved even he knew that it was useful to throw your money where it will be heard.

I did not know if I were coming or going; it was all becoming so farcical. Then I was told the prince's son and daughter-in-law were flying in the next day from Italy. This was a shock so I asked some of the lads about it.

The prince, they said, had met the son in Italy. The son was begging in the street and the prince felt sorry for him. Prince Humoud found out who this boy's parents were and then arranged with them to adopt the boy. This was how he came to have a son.

It was strange to see the prince with his son and daughter-in-law. He adored them both; there wasn't anything he wouldn't do for them. In turn, they adored him—it was surreal. The son had an interest for all types of gadgets. He was twenty-two years old, and I nicknamed him Mr Gadget. His wife was twenty-one and attractive. It seemed the prince also longed for a grandson.

The prince bought them two apartments, one in Paris, France and one in Rome, Italy. He was generous to them. His son was reclusive and rarely ventured out. The prince was protective of them just as a biological father would be.

The next evening, the prince decided to go to town—Piccadilly, to be exact. This instilled dread in me, as I knew the place to be full of drug addicts and people of questionable character. Just like him, I suppose. I believed a night of action was in store and surprise, surprise, I wasn't wrong. When the monstrosity pulled up in Piccadilly, we were immediately in trouble.

A gang surrounded the car and peered in through the windows. The doors were locked. Shit, if I got out and tried to move them on,

I would probably get the crap kicked out of me. As the car provided a safe environment, I thought it was best to stay in it.

I thought I would play it cool and see what developed. I told everyone to stay put and keep calm. The gang became bored and moved on. We drove off towards Leicester Square and I breathed a huge sigh of relief.

We got out the car and walked over to the Statue of Eros. There were a few strange people out and about—but no one took any notice of us! I looked at the prince. His jet-black hair was long and wavy and was shoulder length. His face had makeup plastered all over it. He also wore his usual dark flowing silk Paris fashions. Plenty of gold jewellery adorned his clothes—chains, brooches and the like. He was the perfect target for pickpockets and robbers. We wandered around enjoying the sights for an hour or so.

Then we turned a corner, and there lined up along the street were about twenty motorbikes. Standing next to them were the bikers. My heart sank, we were clearly in the shit. My first concern was the prince, and my next concern was ME! My mind raced. Then I heard one of the bikers say, "Hi, I like your gear, where did you get it? I want something like it for my woman," and the bikers laughed. This broke the ice, and the prince spoke with them. We must have chatted for about half an hour. The evening ended on a peaceful note and I thanked God that it had.

Then to spoil it all, the prince said that he wanted to bring his children to town for dinner the next evening. I could have died. Did I need this, I thought?

In the morning, I went out and bought a groin protector and a gum shield. I thought we had been lucky so far; however, I thought I should get some insurance for the family jewels. My family jewels, that is, not his!

That evening found all the boys bubbly and ready for the night ahead. Four cars were ready to take us to town—safety in numbers; that's good, I thought. None of them would be any use if we got in to trouble, of that I was sure. When the prince finally emerged and walked by me on his way to his son, I swear I nearly collapsed. He was surely taking the piss now; he was wearing a tiara!

I tried to cry off ill and called Peter to come in and cover me. He swore, saying I must be fucking mad to be going out with that! He refused to cover me.

I cannot be having with this, how can I get out of it? This has to be a wind up—how did I end up on this job? I asked myself. Never again, I thought. This was extremist stuff.

I knew this guy was the King's brother, but considering his position, I thought he was a disgrace. The house was never clean and the dishes were filthy; the conditions were bloody awful.

Before going out the prince retired to his room. He called me in, and as I entered, he was half lying on his bed. He patted the side of the bed and asked me sit. There was a large screen stereo TV and video recorder on a unit at the base of his bed. The pop video 'Relax' by Frankie Goes to Hollywood was playing. He told me this was the uncut version from Paris; I hadn't been aware there was an uncut version. There was one scene he wanted me to watch, but I wasn't having any of it. Later, I found out the scene was one of some men ejaculating over the backs of some others.

The prince asked me many personal questions and I answered them. I have a knack of talking a lot and saying nothing, which was useful on many occasions. Prince Humoud seemed excited and asked if I ever had sex with another male. "No," I answered. He asked if I'd be open to try it, and I said no. He said he would like me to go to bed with him. I said I have no problem with other people's sexuality, and I was okay to a degree with his. However, I told him I wasn't into men. He said he liked to take it rather than give it. I explained that either way, I had no interest in a sexual relationship.

Looking at his tiara, I stifled a laugh. I told him I did not understand why he wore those types of clothes and jewellery or why his car looked the way it did. We had a real in depth conversation. He explained his love of Fantasy and Fantasia. His reasoning wasn't bizarre at all. Everyone around him accepted it without question. I explained it wasn't my scene. After our chat, the prince decided not to go to town. I couldn't begin to describe my relief. He put it off until the next night—perhaps I spoiled his evening. Whatever it was that had changed his mind, it was fine by me.

I started to question myself and my mind would not rest. The question I asked was will I genuinely feel able to take a hit for this guy? This question became more and more difficult to answer.

Then, as though someone had turned on a light, the answer came to me and it was short and to the point: the answer was NO, and therefore it would not have been right for me to continue the assignment. I contacted the office and told them I was pulling out at the end of the shift, and gave a brief explanation why this was so. They accepted my reasons.

Now I always ask myself, how far am I prepared to go for my charge? If I cannot give my all, then I walk away.

They brought in another bodyguard to cover the duration. I wondered how he would get on with the prince.

Within two days, the prince packed up and left; he went back to his beloved Paris. Perhaps he would feel better now, as he had told me before that Parisians were much more accepting of Fantasy and Fantasia.

When Prince Humoud Bin Abdul Aziz came back to England on more visits, he always asked for me. After getting a negative response several times, he finally gave up asking.

Chapter 36

Early 1988

It was early 1988 and two months since my last Saudi job. Money had become short so I went back to surveillance work. I kicked myself but it was a case of needs must, so I'd kept busy process serving and carrying out more surveillance work. The surveillance jobs I completed proved to be challenging. A couple were based in Leeds and Bradford, deep within the Indian, Pakistani, Muslim and Sikh communities. Not being from an ethnic minority, I didn't blend in well. No grey man here, I thought.

The process serving had gone well. The two surveillance jobs I did there were for the benefit of insurance companies. The first target was a Pakistani who had significantly damaged his right ankle. I was told he should be on crutches and finding it difficult to walk. He lived in a terraced house and I parked my car four doors away. Then I went to the offside front wheel and let the air out of the tyre. Behind the car, I opened the boot, and then I leant against a wall by the car. If anyone took notice of me, I pointed at the flat tyre and moaned about it. If they spoke to me, I told them I'd called the breakdown services but there was some backlog before they'd get out to me.

Now all I had to do was wait for the target to surface. Two hours later he came out, which was just as well as I had overstayed my welcome. He struggled to get down the step outside his front door. His wife supported him and helped him struggle down the street to the corner on his crutches. As they walked away, I grabbed my video camera and filmed them. Once at the corner, they turned round and made their way back. I wandered over to them.

"That looks bad," I said.

"Yes, it is very painful," the target answered. Good, he speaks English, I thought.

"How did you do it?"

"I got it caught between two machines at work and when I tried to pull it out, it twisted and snapped." The poor sod looked to be in tremendous pain. With his wife, I helped him to his front door. I drew up my report for the office and placed it in my folder.

Time to move, I thought, and then went to the boot of my car and got out my electric pump. Twenty minutes later, my tyre was firm and I set off after target number two.

This second target owned a minicab company. He'd fallen from a chair at work and severely damaged his back. I had his home address and opted to check that first. There was no sign of any movement and the area wasn't one in which I could hide myself, so I moved away. I drove to a local telephone box and called his office. I asked for the owner and was told he wouldn't be in until 2pm.

"I was told he has a Mercedes for sale," I said

"No, you are mistaken; he drives a BMW convertible."

"Sorry to have troubled you, I've just realised I've got a digit wrong in the phone number I have." Hanging up, I smiled. I drove by his house again. I noticed a dark blue BMW convertible parked outside, which led me to believe he was still at home. I drove back to the cab office and parked some way up the road and waited. I was doing a lot of waiting about these days, I thought.

Just before 2pm, I saw the dark blue BMW turn the corner and park up. The boss got out, I checked him against the picture I had been given by the office. I had a Positive ID. Outside the office, I watched as an English looking guy painted a new sign above the door. I assumed the inside was being redecorated, too, as several items of furniture were on the pavement outside the office. I lifted my camera and zoomed in. As I checked the focus, the owner of the cab office bent down, lifted a sofa on to its side, and then stood it up on end. I couldn't believe it, what a stroke of luck!

I rewound the film and checked it through the viewfinder. I had captured it and was over the moon. Then I felt a presence next to me. Looking up, I noticed the painter standing next to my car.

"You do know there is a law about invading someone's privacy," he said.

"Do yourself a favour, mate, and fuck off while you still can," I replied.

310

He turned away and walked back towards the cab office. I did myself a favour, started my car, and fucked off while I still could.

Leeds and Bradford were a success for me.

Two days later, the office called. Bill told me Princess Fahda was back in town. She was the second wife of Prince Salman Bin Abdul Aziz. This visit could be lengthy.

I hoped the princess wasn't going to beat a Filipino servant again, as she had previously on our return to the Intercontinental Hotel from a shopping trip. As we'd approached her suite, the princess happened to spy a servant on the telephone. The princess called her into the corridor, where she slapped her about the face. The servant screamed, causing a commotion, and rightly so. The princess yelled back and dragged the servant by her hair to another room. She called for her other staff to come. They locked the windows and stripped the bedding from the room. Then they stripped the servant in front of us, disconnected the phone and locked her in. I couldn't believe it.

Two security guys stood guard outside the door. Arrangements were made to return the servant to Saudi Arabia on the first available flight in the morning. I have always been a supporter of the underdog, but I stood by, did nothing, and am ashamed of myself. I made a promise that I would never allow such a terrible event to happen before me again; not without trying to do something to help the victim. I did call the police to the hotel to investigate. If they attended the scene, it did no good, for on my next shift the servant was back in Saudi Arabia as planned.

The Saudi royals never failed to surprise me. These are the people I felt honour-bound to take a bullet for. Yet I'm sure that had I been killed on duty, their attitude would have been to say, "Move that mess out of the way and get another one." I was that expendable.

On this visit, she would stay in private apartments. Either someone was trying to keep costs down or perhaps the hotel wouldn't let her back again. A stretched Rolls Royce was put at her disposal, along with numerous staff consisting of cleaners, a cook, someone to take care of the shopping, a chauffeur, static security guards, and two bodyguards.

Princess Fahda's younger sister was due to have an operation. She was eleven years old and had a curvature of the spine.

Before her sister's admission, they did a little sightseeing. Then they went shopping with a vengeance, too. The shops took such a hammering and so many bags came back, there was nowhere in the apartment to put them. The problem was so bad, suitcases were bought by the dozen, packed up and flown back to Saudi.

The parking was a nightmare, and one of our cars suffered damage when hit by a delivery van. If any cars got a parking ticket, the drivers would have to pay for them out of their own pockets. The Rolls Royce drew so much attention that it was a liability. When the day of the youngster's admission arrived, nerves became frayed and the princess snappy, but we expected this.

We set off for the Clinic with the youngster in good spirits. My partner, Paul, a former Royal Marines sniper, and I escorted the princess and her sister inside. The chauffeur, Bill, stayed with the Rolls Royce. A clinic representative waited and met the princess as we entered the building. Before they entered the suite, I performed a sweep. We placed a static guard outside the door.

The princess entered the suite as I exited. The curve in the sister's spine was severe, but expectations were high and everyone looked forward to the youngster shrugging off her disability. The operation would take place a few days after admittance. Until then, our lives consisted of shopping and more shopping and then going to the Clinic during visiting times. Apart from the Rolls, we had a security car. Bill, the chauffeur was well trained and considerate. It was good to have a professional team working well together.

We became aware a group of protesters against the Saudi Arabian regime were staying nearby. So we were careful to keep the princess' presence under wraps.

Traipsing around Harrods during the morning, we received a call saying the operation was about to take place on the youngster. We dropped everything and made our way to the Clinic. The princess went in to see her sister and when she emerged, it was plain to see she had been crying. Princess Fahda stayed, while the operation took place. Time dragged by. It was traumatic for the princess. She had some of her entourage to keep her company. No doubt they tried to reassure her, too.

A surgeon arrived and said because of complications they had to transfer the youngster to the Middlesex Hospital, also in London. Panic set in and tears flowed. The complication was serious and it was necessary to transfer her to a national health hospital that was far more able to deal with the situation, the surgeon said.

We shot over to the Middlesex. The youngster was in theatre. Princess Fahda learned they had accidentally punctured her sister's bowel at the clinic and the surgeons at the Middlesex were trying to repair the damage.

We waited for hours before hearing the youngster was out of theatre and in the recovery room. Later from there, she would be moved to the Intensive Care Unit. We went to the ICU to await her arrival. Her condition was very, very serious. As the youngster arrived at the ICU, we saw just how serious it looked. She was clearly bloated and jaundiced, and tubes emanated from her every orifice—she was a shocking sight. Nothing we could do could help to ease the pain the princess was feeling. It was so sad. Even with all of their money, power and possessions, there wasn't anything they could do, except pray.

We went back and forth each day, waiting for signs of progress. Sometimes there was a slight change for the better and sometimes it was a slight change for the worse. George, one of Martini's staff members, attended and telephoned any updates to his boss.

I was on duty outside the ICU when Paul came up. I noticed a concerned look on his face.

He said he'd watched a drunk wandering along Mortimer Street outside the hospital. The drunk approached the hospital entrance, stiffened up and steeled himself, then wandered into the hospital. Paul joked that with our luck, he would probably enter our floor and create a problem. Just as he finished saying that, a flash passed the window. We ran over to see what it was.

The drunken guy had jumped off the roof. I told Paul to stay put and I ran downstairs to see what, if anything, I could do. There, lying on the ground was the drunk. Blood oozed from his nose, eyes and ears as a doctor attended to him. The guy was obviously dead, and his shoes lay on the floor next to him, the soles torn from them. The impact had ripped them apart. The police arrived and some screens were placed around the body. A young woman police constable had to walk away from the gruesome scene, and she started to cry. I comforted her. She said this was the first suicide she had attended. We spoke at length, and she settled a little. As we walked back, the suicide victim lay on a trolley with a sheet placed over him. On top of the sheet, someone had placed his shoes.

He had to be transported to a casualty hospital where death could be certified. It was a terrible shame; perhaps he would have felt differently when he sobered up. I returned to the ICU and reported to Paul. There was no change in the youngster's condition. Days on end we waited, a gloomy sense of doom hanging over us like a cloud of depression. The princess received important visitors, as members of the family became aware of the youngster's condition. I recognised many of the princes and princesses that visited, as I had worked for them previously. Some of the other visitors, I would work for later in my career.

The princess moved out of the apartments and into the Intercontinental Hotel. Martini visited every day and left George there to attend the princess. The princess because of her depression, was unable to sleep. The King sent his personal doctor, Dr Kharter, hoping he could be of help. The King brought in the top specialists from Pittsburgh to see if they could help the youngster. Slowly the youngster improved, but it took a long time. The poisons seeping in from the punctured bowel slowly poisoned her entire system, and this in turn caused extensive damage to several of her organs. Each day dragged by, exactly like the previous one. Only slight changes in her condition occurred, yet the youngster was a fighter and wasn't giving up. Then came the fateful day we had all been dreading. The youngster died. The poor child had not been able to rally from the extensive damage caused to her vital organs. As was the norm, the youngster's body left on a Saudia flight shortly after her death. The princess and her entourage accompanied it. It was a sad day for all concerned. We had hoped the child would come through the operation successfully. Now we were in shock and upset that this sweet child had lost her life.

Spring 1988

Some ten years or so after starting with the Saudi royal family, I found myself in an unenviable position. Madame Sara arrived. She was a young mother with two young children, the wife of the King's private secretary, Sheikh Mohammed Al Suleiman.

Madam Sara strolled up the pathway towards the large front door of Prince Mohammed Bin Fahd's town house at 2 Bolney Gate, Knightsbridge. She was tall, slim and elegant, with long flowing blonde hair. Two Filipino nannies walked behind her with her delightful little girls. I guessed the older daughter was three years old and the younger two years old. Sheikh Mohammed, perfectly dressed, followed them all with a sombre look etched into his face. He was somewhat older than his wife.

Madame Sara had cancer and the prognosis was bleak. I resolved myself to treat her normally and to take care of them, especially the children, as best I could. I hoped my small input would take at least a tiny amount of grief away.

King Fahd had ordered the house opened to the family—no doubt, Prince Mohammed had been happy to comply with his father's wishes. The King made available a Lear Jet for Sheikh Mohammed to commute back and forth to Saudi.

The King ordered the Saudi Embassy to cater to the family's needs. Martini visited often and Prince Mohammed's complement of staff serviced the family's daily needs. The house manager, Yasser, took charge of the household. We had the usual drivers, George and Anil. The housekeeper, Mary, was an Irish woman. She neared retirement age and had a soft, caring, and sweet nature, which was perfect for this assignment.

Within two days, Madame Sara began her treatment at the Charing Cross Hospital. For a time, she stayed as an in-patient and each day we visited her with the children, spending hours in her company. Other visitors came and went, offering their support and trying to keep Madame Sara's spirits high.

Sheikh Mohammed still had to attend the King, and therefore travelled back and forth as often as he could to check on his wife. The Sheikh's sister, a medical doctor, came to stay and spent many an hour at Madame Sara's bedside. The Sheikh, for his part, seemed ill at ease with his situation but had no choice; he had to attend the needs of the King. When he visited, it would be for only a day or two. He made the best of a bad job.

After a while, Madame Sara came home but she attended hospital for regular chemotherapy. On a stopover, Sheikh Mohammed had a visitor. Salem Bin Laden was a close family friend. Sheikh Salem offered his country house to the family, when they were able to escape from London. Sheikh Mohammed accepted his offer. We would now spend our time moving like Bedouin between the two homes.

It was summer, the sun shone brightly and the children played contentedly. Madame Sara, by this time had lost both weight and her long blonde hair. She had taken to wearing a headscarf to cover her baldness, and I felt rather sad for her. Often in the garden, she spent time with the children, if she felt well enough. The nannies and I would sit with them, play, and sometimes chat. I could sense Madame Sara felt comfortable around me. Usually we stayed for three or four days at Salem's house before making our way back to London.

Back at Prince Mohammed's house, I sat in the foyer. It was small, perhaps ten feet square. Directly opposite the front door was a mirrored glass door, which led into a small elevator. Long glass coffee tables were placed along the walls. In each corner there was a chair, where the drivers would sometimes sit, if they got the chance. Behind my chair, a few steps led down to a small cloakroom.

On a fine sunny day, I heard the sound of voices approaching the front door; I looked through the spy hole and saw the visitor was Salem Bin Laden. Looking past him, I noticed his white Porsche 928 sports car parked by the kerb. Salem had two people with him, one I recognised as Lindsay, who worked for Salem, the other, I had not seen before. Lindsay was a friendly guy, and both he and his wife Lynn worked for Salem at his house in Luton.

Salem was in an upbeat mood. He was gregarious—even more so than usual today, I thought. He had passed by to see how Madame Sara was faring and to check on her progress. As Salem waited in the foyer for permission to ascend the stairs to the lounge, he engaged in conversation. Salem spoke animatedly about an upcoming trip to San Antonio in Texas. He was going to catch up with his agent Jim Bath, who he said invested money in Arbusto, a company owned by George Bush on Salem's behalf. I remember smiling as I recalled an advert on the television for gravy, which had the catchphrase, "Ah Bisto!"

Salem was much too open in his discussion, I thought. He spoke of funds paid through BCCI bank to Harken and how George Bush had been grateful for the investment. Sheikh Salem spoke of his friend Khalid Bin Mahfouz, and discussed issues to do with his BAC 111 aircraft. Salem said he would playfully 'buzz' the King's palaces while he was in residence. I asked him how this was so, as I thought the security controls would have put a stop to it. He said he was such a good friend of the King that he allowed it. I rather doubted this, but found out later that he was telling the truth. Salem Bin Laden said he and Rafik Hariri had invested $20 million for King Fahd's wife Janan Harb, in Saudi Oger, which was the King's 'front' company. The King had given instructions for Janan Harb to receive the investment, should anything happen to him. Salem said, with a laugh, it was to keep them safe from the King's beloved 'Azoozi' and the family. By now, I had seen Janan Harb but only from a distance, when she visited King Fahd around the time of his State Visit. I kept this snippet of information to myself. I loved hearing the gossip, but I thought Salem was too loose lipped for his own good. I wondered if he had been on cocaine or speed as he seemed so high. Later, I heard about the funds transferred through BCCI to George Bush and Harken once again. This time, Ghaith Pharoan had said it as he visited a prince I was working with. I walked away as I had more important things on my mind—I wanted to check out Pharoan's Mercedes SLC sports car.

A few days later Madame Sara and her menagerie, that is, the rest of us who by now I had named the Bedouin tribe, moved back up to Luton. Although close to the airport, we never suffered from any aircraft noise. Salem's house was large, but sparsely furnished. The installed music system surprised me; it was a superb piece of equipment. Salem was obviously a serious music lover. As I walked through the lower part of the house at night, I would either walk on tiptoe or take my shoes off. All the floors were polished oak and made such a noise. I did not want to disturb Madame Sara.

The day after we arrived at Salem's house, news came through that a microlight aircraft that he piloted had crashed at an airfield in San Antonio. Salem was killed, and the consensus was that it had been no accident. Saudi embassy officials visited and I overheard a conversation in which they said Salem had been deliberately killed. They said he knew too many things about Bush and the BCCI affair and that he was talking too much! I wondered if he was done away with, but gave it no further thought. Instructions from the Embassy officials to the Arabic staff were given, to remove any articles about Salem's death in the Arabic newspapers, which the drivers brought in daily. They were concerned that Salem's death would hinder Madame Sara's recovery. Madame Sara was smart and spoke several languages. Soon she confronted 'Soapeh', the waiter whose Arabic name none of us were able to pronounce, and demanded to know what was going on and why her newspapers had holes cut in them. He would not say but quickly told the Embassy of the confrontation. Shortly afterwards, Martini arrived to break the news of Salem's death to her. We moved back to London.

The next day their older daughter 'lost' one of her diamond earrings upstairs. We suspected the older nanny had stolen the child's earring, and we couldn't find it. Madame Sara seethed and sent us to Harrods to find a matching one. We found a perfect match but the price was a hefty £3000 so we went back with the bad news. Madame Sara was hopping mad and made sure that everyone in earshot knew she was. After she completed her treatment, the family returned to Saudi Arabia. However, before she left, she kissed me on the cheek. Mary saw it and quickly reported it to Martini. I was called in to the office, as I was in the shit again.

It would be two years before Madame Sara returned to London when she would appear to be doing well and looked as though she was well on her way to full recovery.

Chapter 37

May 1988

Princess Nora Bint Sultan, the daughter of the Saudi Arabian defence minister, was about to descend on us, and she had her seven children with her. We therefore had a large security contingent to take care of them. Various drivers on the job came courtesy of Reg and his Iranian friend's car hire company. The drivers paid a percentage of their salaries to them. We lost a percentage of our salaries to Martini, Bill and Reg, too, as he wanted a commission from our office for using us.

The princess' husband, Prince Turki Bin Nasser, was due to arrive a couple of days later. I would be looking after her. We would go to her usual haunts. She liked the cheap material and clothes shops in Eastcastle Street. She was a regular Jekyll and Hyde. On one side, she was cautious of every penny she spent; on the other, she was a spendthrift. Her driver, Reg, was an old colleague and he drove the Rolls Royce bought for her as a birthday present, courtesy of one of Britain's biggest arms companies, BAE Systems, formerly known as British Aerospace. Reg's French wife, Josette, ran the household. Reg and his wife skimmed money off from wherever they could.

Top of the range Rover and Range Rover cars were supplied to the family by BAE, and replaced every six months. It amused me no end that Reg and his Iranian partner hired out the cars supplied by BAE. Even the princess' Rolls Royce was for hire when the family were not in residence, courtesy of BAE.

I noticed if the princess put her hand in her own pocket, she found nothing but if she put her hand in the 'pocket' of BAE, she found millions. Nothing on this assignment was as it seemed—it was all smoke and mirrors; a deception.

I was in for a treat—not, as we went off to a trade show at the Olympia exhibition centre. The princess' friends owned a shop and got passes for us. The show consisted of all things domestic. No doubt she was after a bargain or two. I waited outside their large corner house in Sussex Square, behind the Bayswater Road. Looking down into the basement area, I nodded to Gus, the static security guy. As the front door opened, I caught Reg's attention, signalling to him that we were moving. I shadowed the princess to the car as Reg held her door open. Once she was secure inside, I got into the front seat. The princess said "Olympia exhibition centre", and on her command, we set off.

We spent hours wandering around the trade show as the princess ordered all sorts of things as though they were going out of fashion. Perhaps BAE was picking up the tab for this too. My feet ached as I marvelled at how these people could shop, but I couldn't wait to get out of there. I was going brain dead wandering round and round looking at the same things over and again. My head ached as I focused my attention on the princess, watching her every move, but it ached more so when watching every move of the people who got near to her. On leaving the centre, I couldn't wait to get back to the house, rest my weary feet, and take some headache tablets. Therefore, as I sat back in the Rolls, I was stunned to hear the princess order Reg to take her to Harrods. My God, more shopping; we were going on to round two!

We turned into Kensington High Street and drove down towards Knightsbridge, turning right when we got to Trevor Place. We then turned right into Montpellier Square just as Lionel Blair, the dancer and television celebrity was exiting it in his Rolls Royce. We turned left into Brompton Road as the princess called out "James Bond! James Bond!" I looked round wondering what she wanted. Was she calling me James Bond because she did not know my name, or maybe that was how she saw my job, as some James Bond character? Not knowing what I should say or do, I spun back round in my seat to look forward again. I then saw, perched on the bonnet of the Rolls Royce, Timothy Dalton, the actor who was the current James Bond. He had a big smile on his face and a beautiful woman on his arm. Reg's claim to fame was how he almost killed James Bond, where the Russians had failed.

I was team leader and escorted the princess. Others would deal with her children, Faisal, Abdullah, Abir, Arij, Lamia, Rima and Haifa.

I assigned Bruce to Abdullah, while Peter took care of Arij and Abir, since they were close in age. Gus and Clive, I put on static duty. Alan, I put with Lamia, Rima, and Haifa, as they were all within a manageable age group and had nannies with them. Both Gus and Alan were ex-Royal Marines and, over the years, I clashed with them several times. Some grief on this job came about, too, as Reg's wife, Josette, took a fancy to Gus, which affected his duties.

Shortly after the family's arrival, the princess' husband Prince Turki Bin Nasser joined them. He was a major player in the al-Yamamah arms deals negotiated with Saudi Arabia, which were worth billions of pounds. People from BAE Systems fell over themselves throwing money and gifts his way so he would continue to favour their company. Reg brought the prince into town in one of the new BAE Range Rovers. Three people accompanied Prince Turki, they were Tony Winship, a former Royal Air Force Wing Commander; Peter Gardiner, and Edward Cunningham. They had to keep the prince happy at all costs. Edward Cunningham also looked after any young Saudi air force pilots that visited.

I went to Peter Gardiner's travel agency, Travellers World, a few times with Reg when he booked his travel arrangements, probably at the expense of BAE. Gardiner's company blossomed after BAE channelled over £7 million a year through it, paying for all the luxuries Prince Turki expected. The prince cheated on his wife with a regular hooker, whom he had deposited round the corner from the family home in Whites Hotel, Lancaster Gate—also at the expense of BAE. The benefits extended beyond the prince and encompassed the princess and the rest of their family. Other people from the Embassy, Military Attachés office and Reg also got in on the act—as far as they could, that is.

The amounts of money spent were beyond understanding as the family raided the BAE vaults. At one stage, they paid for the charter of a Boeing 747 jumbo jet to fly home their shopping. The son, Faisal, went skiing in Colorado and BAE got a bill for almost £100,000. A three month holiday for the family landed a £2 million bill on the desk of BAE. Gambling debts, prostitutes and nightclubs were all funded by BAE Systems—there was no end to it.

For a driver and housekeeper, Reg and Josette enjoyed a lifestyle which was above their station—with properties in Denver, Colorado and the south of France. They jetted back and forth at the drop of a hat with their travel arrangements always made through Travellers World. Even officials at the Saudi Embassy got in on the act, claiming gifts of gold cutlery sets. A massive free-for-all went on; only the security guys were not getting any of the cream—I can assure you of that.

The children did the usual activities, as on all their visits, such as ice-skating, horse riding in Hyde Park, going to the cinema and eating fast food. Their mother shopped and shopped and shopped. When she wasn't shopping, she visited the Richoux restaurants in either South Audley Street or Piccadilly. She sampled their goods, dined out in other places, or visited her friends. The prince did whatever he wanted. He also 'did' the hooker he visited at Whites 'BAE' Hotel.

When it came time for departure, the security team, as usual, became removal men and carried hundreds of cases and trunks down from the upper floors out and on to the line of trucks assembled outside. The drivers would transport the luggage to the waiting Boeing 747 Jumbo jet.

After all this hard work, we were given zilch. In fact, we were lucky if we got a goodbye from the departing royals as they made their way to some exotic destination to carry on plundering the coffers of BAE Systems.

* * *

June 1989

I was asked to work for Prince Mashour Bin Abdul Aziz, another of the King's brothers. The last time I'd worked for him, I was left sitting in a car in the freezing cold. I made it clear; no way would I work in those conditions again. The prince's Egyptian secretary, 'Jimmy', whose real name was Mohammed Ramadan, assured me the job was different this time. The prince specifically asked for me.

This made no difference to me. I agreed to do it but made clear if I were not happy at any point, then I would be off.

Prince Mashour arrived at his recently bought house in Holland Park. The house was large and situated in a tree-lined avenue with other multi-million pound properties. Almost directly across the road lived Sir Richard Branson, the entrepreneur. The prince's beautifully decorated house was furnished exquisitely. It contained a gymnasium, sauna, and a swimming pool, which had a wave-making machine. These toys sat in the basement area of the property.

His wife, Princess Nora, followed him with a couple of staff. These staff kept themselves out of the way in another part of the house. Jimmy had an assistant and I felt uneasy about their partnership.

Something was wrong with the prince. Each day he stayed in the house and most of that time he spent asleep on the sofa near the swimming pool. It was obvious to me that he was suffering a deep depression. I never saw him taking medication. The Saudi royals live an insular lifestyle and often suffer the effects of it.

Princess Nora, on the other hand, was bubbly. Perhaps between them they had manic depression; he had the lows, she the highs! I took care of Princess Nora and soon found we got on famously. We even raced down the road at times. Escorting this princess was a pleasure. It was such a rare occurrence to find any Saudi royal who was not centred on themselves. Her personality and bearing was inconsistent with what I was used to.

During the day, we went shopping. No surprises there.

One evening we strolled along as a drunk staggered towards us. As he got closer, I checked the locality in case he was just a distraction vying for my attention.

I guided the princess into a recessed doorway. Three walls protected her while I faced the danger. My senses heightened and I switched on to any slight movement he made. I stepped a little closer, removing any threat as much as I was able. The princess stayed safely confined behind me. I reached out toward the drunk, handed him a five-pound note, and told him to disappear. He took it and thanked us. Even so, I kept him at a distance from the princess and some distance from me, as well. Princess Nora grabbed my arm as she was scared. The following day, the princess bought me a watch as a thank you. It was a designer model and expensive. I later gave it away to someone in my family as I usually did. As the princess carried on living normally, the prince on the other hand suffered and found it impossible to cope. Jimmy said Prince Mashour had sex with young boys and I wondered if that was what caused him problems. Many of the Saudi royal family were off their heads for one reason or another. I believed they were beginning to affect me, too, as I became more withdrawn. As I've said, I found over the years that they eroded my self-confidence and self-respect. I felt for the prince and his suffering.

Princess Nora sent word that we were going to dinner in the evening, two days after our meeting with the drunk. We drove to the Fakhreldine restaurant in Piccadilly. I was fond of Lebanese cuisine, and my mouth watered in anticipation.

The princess ordered several dishes and soon a good selection sat on the table before us. Jimmy and Linda, a friend of the princess, accompanied us. I detected a glint in the princess' eye. What was she up to, that was the question? I tucked into the exotic dishes and was enjoying the meal and conversation.

The evening became more pleasant by the minute. Jimmy passed a dish my way, and I took one of the meatballs and bit into it. I ate it and enjoyed it. The princess passed some salad dressed with Tabasco sauce. I had never tasted it before. I tucked into the salad and leapt out of my seat. I grabbed the glass of water on the table. My mouth felt scorched—it was bloody boiling! The princess and the others laughed; they thought it hilarious. I didn't—not for a while, anyway.

That wasn't the only joke—the meatball I had eaten was a sheep's testicle. They stitched me up good and proper. There was plenty of fun with the princess, but this time it was at my expense. They had me this time; next time I would be the one laughing, or so I hoped.

Even though we had fun, I never forgot my priorities. I kept the princess safe. The following morning, a couple of hours after arriving for work, I received an emergency telephone call from my brother. His wife had just given birth to twins—one was gravely ill, and they didn't expect him to live more than a few hours. My older brother cried. I never heard him cry before. It was traumatic for me, but not as traumatic as the situation facing him. I told him I would be there within the hour. I told the princess, who was understanding and let me go. This was the only time I ever took time off an assignment. I had to support my brother.

On my return to work, I had a shock when told the princess wanted to go and see dog racing. Jimmy arranged a table so we could have dinner and watch the races, while sitting in the warmth. I had been to the Wembley dog races before, and realised it was easy to lose your car in the car park. I planned that we would lose ours. I owed them one after all. As we pulled into the car park, I distracted everyone. Even while playing silly buggers, I kept a close eye on the princess and kept her close to me. If the others got into difficulty, it would be tough for them—my concern was for my charge, and that was that. A member of the restaurant staff met us at the entrance and escorted us to our table. The princess was excited. I was pleased to see her enjoying herself. We laughed, cheered on the dogs, and enjoyed the meal. The evening was successful; we hadn't had any problems. When we got to the car park, it was another story.

"Where's the car?" asked Jimmy.

I shrugged my shoulders, "I don't know!" Jimmy couldn't remember where we left it, and of course the princess had no idea either. I had them all looking for it. If they got close to it, I would direct them away. After a half-hour, I guided them to the car. The princess was first to spot it, she shouted out and was so excited you would have thought she had won the lottery.

We were about a hundred feet from it when I said, "I'll race you." As she took off, she shouted back, "All right!"

I ran up close behind her, and she squealed and laughed as I chased her. I was sure these were the best times she had experienced in years. When I told them I knew all along where the car was parked she told me off, wagging her finger at me. She still laughed and was a real sport and good fun to be around.

The prince still suffered. I was concerned and suggested to Jimmy that he get some professional help. What I wasn't aware of was that Jimmy had a hidden agenda. Jimmy cajoled the prince, who was in no fit state, to look at brochures of expensive property. When Jimmy was away, his assistant carried this on, so their barrage was relentless. The house they peddled was called Mandalay, and was on the market for five million pounds.

Now it became clear that Jimmy and his assistant were swindling the prince. They got the prince to pay the full asking price for the properties and then pocketed any discounts and commissions they had negotiated, too. Meanwhile, the prince stayed on the sofa, complaining of money worries. It was no surprise as Jimmy was bleeding him dry while the prince was ill.

By now Jimmy was on a roll, and announced to the prince that his brother, the Defence Minister, Prince Sultan Bin Abdul Aziz, was visiting England in a couple of days. Jimmy said that Prince Mashour was duty-bound to go and greet his brother at the airport. Jimmy sent word to Prince Sultan's aides about the prince's financial plight. Jimmy was told Prince Sultan would give substantial funds to Prince Mashour when they met. Jimmy became excited by this and told the prince. The prince's financial problems, real or imagined, were at an end. Prince Mashour was out of it and didn't care one way or the other.

The day of Prince Sultan's visit loomed, but the prince stayed on the sofa. No matter how much Jimmy egged on the prince, he just dozed on the sofa—nothing could move him. In retrospect, I believe he should have gone into hospital. Prince Mashour never went to the airport to meet his brother on his arrival in June of 1989.

The princess told me their daughter Princess Nouf was arriving in a day or two. The princess said she wanted me to look after her when she arrived. I knew then our "honeymoon" period was over. The princess would now stay at home. I found this odd, as the princess loved shopping, dinner, and even the movies. I wondered if she felt she had to conduct herself in a more fitting manner while her daughter was here. Like most princesses, she now became that bird trapped in the gilded cage.

Jimmy told me the daughter was a horrible child. She was fifteen years old, and travelled with a friend and a servant. He said she couldn't stand her father, as she had caught him with a young boy one time. After he finished his stories, I was dreading meeting her so I thought some reverse psychology might be in order.

When Princess Nouf arrived, I got to work. Although she was young, she had a full figure, she was attractive, and she knew it. The first day we went to see a movie. I gave her space, kept a close eye on her, and kept my mouth shut. I had the feeling if I opened it, she would jump down my throat. From the movies, we went out to eat. I noticed Princess Nouf loved to be the centre of attention. The people round her fawned about and fell over themselves to keep her happy.

When we got back to the house, Princess Nouf dismissed me for the night. She said I should be back at the house at ten in the morning. I said it would be my pleasure and I think the stories I heard about her were untrue. I turned and walked away. I had cast my line, would she bite?

She called me and asked me what I meant. I told her that before her arrival, I'd heard she was a horrible, spoilt young woman and was warned she treated her bodyguards badly. I said how nice I thought she was. She swallowed what I said hook, line, and sinker, and thus I became the next best thing to sliced bread. It probably only worked because she was so young. I didn't care; it worked, and all I wanted was a peaceful life. A good bodyguard doesn't want any trouble. Not from a foe and certainly not from his charge! Many times a bodyguard will sense a potential problem developing and steer their charge out of harm's way with the charge not even aware of what's happened.

The next day, I faced the biggest smile from Princess Nouf as she emerged from the house; she even talked to me. She loved going to the Trocadero at Leicester Square. It was always stressful moving around the Piccadilly and Leicester Square areas, and once my shift finished, I always had a headache.

Jimmy asked how Princess Nouf and I got on. Fine, no problems whatever, I told him. I don't think he believed me.

The princess' mother said she and Prince Mashour were pleased that I got on so well with their daughter. She said it took the pressure off them; she never elaborated further. I found it hard to believe the prince was aware of anything. He still slept on the sofa and no one went near him unless he called them. That sofa was home to him.

I spoke to Linda, Princess Nora's friend about my concerns for the prince. Linda said the prince had suffered like this on and off for years. Linda also said the princess was going to ask me to go with them to Cannes, in the South of France, as they were going to continue their holiday there. This would prove impossible for me as I had long-standing commitments that I couldn't get out of, here in the UK.

The next day Princess Nora called me, and as expected she asked me to go to Cannes. I reluctantly turned her down and I suggested another bodyguard go with them. I asked Bill at the office for a replacement.

He suggested Pat Baker, a known mercenary, and asked me how I thought he would get on. Pat, I knew would run into problems so I suggested, East End Peter. I felt Peter would fit in much better but Bill decided to go with Pat Baker. I gave my advice; they didn't act on it, which was their concern, if it all went pear-shaped, tough, I thought. I still had a few days to take care of them before they left.

After leaving the princess, I came across Jimmy who said he had a three-piece suite he was selling. It sounded the type the princes would have bought themselves—it was off-white with gold thread running through it. I liked the sound of it and arranged to view it but Jimmy wanted me to promise two things. One, not to mention to anyone at the Holland Park house about the suite; the second, wasn't to tell anyone what his house was like. I agreed. When I went to see the suite, I liked the look of it straight away. It was from Harrods and the description Jimmy had given of it did not do it justice.

Jimmy's house was in Hampstead and of the Georgian style. It was large and had a fair amount of grounds. It was an expensive place. Now I understood where the money had come from to buy it. He was embezzling the prince and taking advantage of his illness. He had a Mercedes and a BMW. The BMW was his wife's. Jimmy drove to work in an old Ford Granada. I wasn't the brain of Britain, but even I could tell something did not add up.

I discovered what Jimmy's hidden agenda had been. I was right all along. No wonder he wasn't vocal in getting medical intervention for the prince. The chef at the house had been a staff nurse before making a career change, and I approached him with my concerns.

He said he would look into it, but I doubted he would, as any interference would inevitably lead to a walk down the road into unemployment. Jimmy, the bastard, annoyed me no end. What a disgusting swine.

The princes seemed more comfortable surrounded by their own kind. They knew they were robbing them blind, but the royals always had a chip on their shoulders about us 'infidels'. I spoke to Bruce about it at one time as he worked the bodyguard circuit too. His thoughts were enlightening. He thought the princes knew the other Arabs were robbing them—they saw it and knew what they took. Because of this, they knew where they stood with them. However, with the Western 'infidels', the princes were wary. Although the Western guys didn't steal from them, the princes thought they did. The problem was that the princes thought the Western 'infidels' were cleverer than them, because they didn't know *how* they were doing it.

Numerous times I saw our guys with large amounts of cash and jewellery, and as far as I am aware, none of it went missing. Maybe if it had, the princes would have felt more secure! I saw Jimmy in a different light, and I didn't like what I saw. The princess and other staff, including me would not dare call a doctor for the prince without his permission. I soothed myself with the thought that soon they would be off to Cannes and maybe a change of scenery would do the prince some good, I genuinely hoped so.

I wondered how long Pat would last and gave him a maximum of two weeks. As it turned out, I got it wrong. Bill introduced Pat Baker to the family himself, which pleased me, as I wanted to dissociate myself from his choice. I took Pat to one side and briefed him. I asked him if he was sure that he wanted to take the position. I was giving him an out if he wanted it but Pat decided to take the assignment.

Pat went to Cannes, and four days later, he was home. He said he couldn't put up with that 'bitch', referring to Princess Nouf. I knew very well that if Princess Nouf was handled carefully, she was not a problem. I also knew Pat did not have a personality that would compliment Nouf's, and that was why I'd told the office I thought he wouldn't be suitable for the job. My instincts had been proved right.

Pat, who was an ex-Queens Irish Hussar, came to my attention again a few years later—along with Alan Boydel, an ex-Royal Marine who also worked often on my team. They had both gone out to Surinam in South America to help overthrow its government. Pat soon fell out with the other mercenaries and returned home. Alan Boydel and the other mercenaries, on the other hand, turned on their superior, John Richards, and shot him in the head after binding him to a tree. Alan Boydel confessed to the killing on ITV's Cook Report television programme, aired in 1995. This incident is also reported in *A Mercenary's Tale* by Karl Penta and Mike Ridley (John Blake Publishing; see pages 171 and 174).

Chapter 38

Princess Luluah, Part 1: 1989

The sun shone brightly, and I sweated profusely. My muscles ached and my eyes stung as sweat dripped into them. I was in the middle of a Karate session, when my phone rang. Bill asked if I could make it to Champney's, the health farm in Tring, within the hour. I couldn't do it, but if he gave me two, I would have a crack at it.

Martini had called the office, Princess Luluah Bint Fahd, the King's daughter, had gone into the health farm. He wanted to impress on her secretary that she should have security. In reality, he was trying to set up another earner for himself.

I quickly showered, dressed, left the sports stadium and headed home. Darting upstairs, I made for my wardrobe. I got suited and booted and studied myself in the full-length mirror, I looked the business.

I rushed downstairs and jumped into my BMW. Running short of time, I pressed on towards the health club, taking care as I negotiated the country roads.

As I entered the gateway, I phoned Bill to let him know I was on site. Martini the secretary and I would meet at the main desk. I drove up to the large Rothschild mansion, which kept its period style. I got out the car and marvelled at the surroundings. The mansion sat in one hundred and seventy acres of parklands.

I found Martini and the secretary waiting for me. After the introductions, we went through to a light and airy morning room where we had some privacy. I studied the secretary, noticing that although smart in appearance, his clothes were not of the high standard I had come to expect of such a retainer. He was fifty years old, with grey throughout his hair, moustache, and beard. He wore heavy glasses, a checked jacket, and dark trousers. He was quiet and studious. Something didn't add up to me. It would be some time in the future before I was to find out what it was.

It didn't take long to convince the secretary they would need security. Once agreed, Martini went to discuss terms with the general manager.

As the princess occupied two suites and several other rooms, they decided we would be booked in as part of the entourage. This was a coup for us, as it gave us full use of the facilities, dining included.

Martini told me to call Bill and get him to secure the other members of the team. I was team leader. Bill was ecstatic that I'd managed to pull the deal off. I stayed on site and waited for the secretary to introduce me to the princess and her companions.

There were two princesses, Princess Luluah and Princess Haifa. Princess Haifa was the organiser. One of Princess Luluah's cousins also attended her. This cousin had no royal status. There were a couple of other women who were the maids, one of whom was called Hussa. They also had a tea boy (actually, an adult man).

I met Princess Lulu (as I came to call her) and thought I had been caught in an explosion—an explosion of cellulite, that is! She was tall, but at over twenty stone, she was still very, *very* big. She had long, dark hair and looked like her father, King Fahd, so she had nothing going for her in the looks department either. I wasn't sure how old she was. But I knew she was divorced from Prince (General) Khalid Bin Sultan, son of the Saudi Defence Minister.

After retiring from the introductions, I looked around the complex. The main suites and rooms we occupied sat on the upper floor of a recent addition to the health farm. I wondered why Champney's was the favoured choice of health resort when her brother, Prince Mohammed, owned Inglewood health farm in Kintbury near Newbury in Berkshire. Was it because he was embarrassed about her? Maybe it was that he did not want her to hear of the frolics he got up to there? I decided on the latter.

Walking into the corridor, I looked right but turned left. Next to the main suite was a manager's office. I introduced myself to the staff. The general manager had already briefed them. By the office, was a flight of stairs, which I descended to the ground floor. Turning my head to the right I saw a double glass door, our entry and exit point? I turned right and walked along the corridor.

A little way down on my right-hand side was a storage cupboard. I checked it was kept locked; it was. I wandered down to the end of the corridor, where I came across another flight of stairs. It took me back to our floor and I walked briskly along the corridor, noticing another storage cupboard. It too, was locked. It was clear to me: the extension contained three flights of stairs with a mid-point combined entry and exit. On the ground floor, two half-glassed fire doors led to the main complex area and mansion. I continued my tour, taking note of the toilet areas, entry and exit points, and other facilities.

In the morning room, staff served up tea, coffee, and other drinks. After getting the general layout of the place, I had a cup of Earl Grey tea and went back to the suite.

Bill phoned to say Martini was putting the ocean blue, armour-plated Rolls Royce at the princess' disposal. Anil would drive it. George would back him up in a stretched Mercedes. Bill said the princess was staying for three weeks and then she'd return to Saudi Arabia for Ramadan. Then, she would return to Champney's for a further three months. We were in for a long haul. I wondered if she would survive three weeks.

My thoughts turned to security. Communications were priority. I worked out schedules for the static guys which encompassed lunch, dinner, toilet, and relaxation breaks. By breaking up their twelve hour shifts, it would keep them alert and relieve stress. We would take advantage of the facilities, so long as the assignment wasn't compromised in any way. I asked the office for a floater, too.

The team consisted of 'Timber', Mark, Peter, Malcolm, and me. Mark and Malcolm were on days. Malcolm, I noticed, had a habit of running his fingers down the crease of his trousers when he sat down. He would then flip the bottoms over. He continually fussed over his clothes and constantly brushed his ever-thinning hair. I wondered if anyone had noticed any unusual quirks about me. Maybe these people were slowly driving us all crazy, I laughed.

I escorted the princess, who was no exercise freak and who would not venture down to the dining room, either. Champney's management organised a regime for her and had some of the beauty salon staff attend her in her suite. Beauty treatment! I thought someone was having a laugh—although in fairness, they were trying to instil some confidence in her. Meanwhile, Anil, George and I sat around waiting for something to happen. Eventually, the princesses decided to take a stroll in the grounds. I escorted them.

We wandered out towards the back of the complex, walking past a large garden chess set and I noticed a few guests staring in our direction. Rumour had gone round the King of Saudi Arabia's daughter was in the health farm. It wasn't too long before the stroll had taken its toll and we returned to her suite.

Princess Haifa called me and asked if I could get her the men's magazine with the nude pictures of Pamella Bordes in it. All the women in the entourage ranted on about them. Pamella Bordes was a 'high class' prostitute who was notorious for her many affairs, which included ones with the Saudi arms dealer Adnan Khashoggi and a Conservative Member of Parliament. This femme fatale was a hunter of men who had married and then split from Henri Bordes, a convicted arms dealer. I found all the magazines containing pictures of her. When I arrived back, there was such a commotion! Why the interest? I was missing something, but I did not know what it was.

As I wandered to the morning room, a tracksuit caught my attention in the boutique window and I decided to take a closer look at it. At that moment, the princess' cousin walked in and noticed me eyeing it up. She asked if I liked it, and if so, said I should get it. Looking at the price tag, I passed on it.

That afternoon, Hussa told me the princess was going to go to the art room. I made my way to her suite. The princess emerged and smiled at me, I smiled back. Standing to one side, I let her pass and then followed her. When we reached the stairwell, I moved in front of her and walked down the stairs. She was put out by this. I expected the question that would inevitably come later.

When we reached the bottom of the stairs, I moved to one side and let the princess pass. Turning to the left, we made our way towards the art room. I opened the door for her. I searched the room in an instant, just as I had done in the corridor as we passed along it.

They sat at the tables and prepared some paint, water and art paper. The princess motioned for me to take a seat near her and told me to paint or draw as well. I watched the princess as she painted her scene of a house with people standing on the grass outside. She painted a clear blue sky overhead with the sun encompassed within it. You would have thought an eight- or nine-year-old had painted it. My guess was she had a limited education. Being a woman in Saudi Arabia had not done her any favours.

Nonetheless, she had a soft nature and a good heart from what I could detect. I drew a picture, which I thought wasn't up to much, but the princess liked it, so I gave it to her. The princess made me feel sad—she was an unfortunate product of the society she had been brought up in. After completing our masterpieces, we set off back to the suite. I searched out the corridor and stairway, as we approached them, not that I expected problems.

This time as we climbed the stairs, I stayed behind the princess. I noticed odd glances from her entourage. Shortly afterwards the princess' cousin came looking for me. She asked why I was so rude to walk in front of the princess when she was going down the stairs. I assured her I meant no offence, explaining that I had walked in front of the princess down the stairs because if she tripped or fell then she would land on top of me. Therefore, I would protect her should she fall. When going up the stairs, if she toppled backwards she would land on top of me, once again protecting her. I never mentioned that if she were to fall, she would almost certainly crush me to death.

I must have done something right, as the following day the tracksuit I had admired was given to me as a gift from the princess. A few days later this gift came back and bit me on the backside when Martini visited. He checked on the princess. On his way out, he said George had told him about my gift. Martini checked how they paid for it. He was none too pleased to find the princess had booked the tracksuit on her suite. Therefore, the Embassy would foot the bill. He wanted to keep the costs down.

Meanwhile, Timber found himself a new friend, a young woman. She was smitten with him and stalked him constantly. Although this caused him some grief, he was well able to handle it. When we dined in the evenings, this girl and her sister would come and sit with us. She was posh and rude to the waiting staff, which did not endear her to me. We found their mother had recently died and their father put them into Champney's for a while because he did not know how to deal with them.

A couple of days later their father came to see them. I was at the front of the main building, when I noticed a black convertible Jaguar XJ6, which had a dark crimson leather interior. I was having a good look over it when its owner showed up. It was the girl's father and it turned out he was the heir to the Hertz car rental company. We spoke for some time; I felt he was a little lost over how to deal with his and his daughter's grief.

Then, almost as soon as the job began, it ended! They were packing up ready for their return to Saudi Arabia. Everything I had said or done in front of the cousin was relayed to the princess, which would prove fortuitous for me. The princess asked if I would be at the airport to meet her on their return. I said I would, but in truth I didn't expect to see her again as I felt sure the last place she would want to return to was a health farm.

*　*　*

Princess Luluah, Part 2 Summer 1989

"Aunty Luluah will be here shortly," said Martini in a mocking fashion as we stood outside the main entrance of the Hillingdon VIP Suite at Heathrow Airport. Bill had told me to report there after a personal request from Princess Luluah to the Saudi Embassy. This ruffled a few feathers and upset some people. For some reason, I often had various royals take an interest in me. Sometimes the women took a fancy to me, and sometimes the men! Obviously, an impression was made on the King's daughter. Just how and when I had made it was a mystery to me. Now, I would have the spectre of Martini looming over me throughout the visit.

Anil sat drinking tea and munched on biscuits with George in the morning room. Anil drove the Rolls Royce, George the long wheelbase Mercedes.

The princess arrived on a Boeing 707 jetliner from the King's royal fleet. Thinking about it, her father, the King, was a large person too, so maybe that explained why he travelled aboard his own Boeing 747 Jumbo jet. I tried to keep a sense of humour—and believe me, working with the Saudis, you needed one. It also came in handy that I studied Arabic and spent enormous amounts of time listening to the Arabs around me, often picking up snippets of information. Some of the other guys picked up bits and pieces of Arabic but I wanted to take it further. It helped me at times when at work and I wanted to mix in a little more with the staff. My attempts to emulate the guttural sounds was comedic, too, and at times had the principals' staff in fits of laughter.

I was expert at waiting, but soon the waiting ended, as the airport staff told us that we were to follow the airside car to the parked jetliner. Bill had just told me, I had to provide both the bodyguard and security driving duties for the princess. I had no idea how I was going to cope with this debacle. I wondered if this was Martini's way of punishing me. They would claim for a security driver's salary too, which would increase their profits. As the princess hardly ventured out during her previous visit, they assumed I would not have to perform the secondary duty. They did not know what the princess had in mind. The assignment was going to prove a nightmare for me. Apprehension hit me, and I wondered how I could carry out my duties effectively.

Anil headed out first in line, I followed in my BMW. Anil had the pleasure of Martini's company, while I had the pleasure of my own. George brought up the rear in the Mercedes.

We meandered slowly between the driveways, luggage trucks, and various utility vehicles with their orange flashing warning lights. Appearing before us, growing ever larger, was the aircraft containing the princess, decked out in the familiar livery of the Saudia airlines even though it was in fact a royal flight aircraft. The telltale sign was the registration mark adorning the fuselage. Saudi airlines registrations begin with HZ-A; however, the King's aircraft begin with HZ-HM, standing for His Majesty, followed by a number. Princess Luluah arrived on HZ-HM3.

I was troubled on our slow and methodical approach to the aircraft. I could hear a clanking metallic noise, which I thought emanated from one of the cars. I crossed my fingers and hoped it was inconsequential, as it was too late to do anything about it. I watched as the wheeled steps were placed by the forward door of the

337

aircraft fuselage. Martini was out of the lead car and ready to climb them in preparation of greeting the princess.

At the bottom of the stairs stood two officials and an airport police officer, and as the door opened, Martini in all servility welcomed Her Royal Highness. I stood near the Rolls and looked up towards to the VIPs about to disembark. Martini moved to one side as the princess descended the steps. Princess Haifa followed and then all hell broke loose as someone noticed she had a Yorkshire terrier dog. Blue lights flashed and speeding vehicles approached. Then I noticed a small quarantine van. The offender taken into custody stood about six inches tall and wore a long fur coat. This terrier dog caused a major incident and Princess Haifa cried.

As we drove to the VIP suite, I distinctly heard the metallic sound again, although I still couldn't detect where it came from. After parking up, I went over to the suite and as I entered, found one big upset. Princess Haifa cried loudly and anyone who had an opinion voiced it. Martini conferred with the officials attending this farcical scene.

One tiny dog caused the start of what I thought, was going to be World War 3! Various choices were put to the princesses. These consisted of the dog going into quarantine for six months; or, if they wanted, they could have it put to sleep; or, lastly, they could put it back on the aircraft and have it flown back to Saudi the following morning. After many tears and much discussion, they decided this tiny dog would go back to Saudi at great expense to the royal family.

I knew something was wrong, but that wasn't it!

This assignment had the hallmarks of becoming a comedy of errors. Thinking everything could only get better, I couldn't have been more wrong. This was only the first evening of a three month stay. I considered doing a runner, yet I knew I wasn't going anywhere.

After completing the formalities, the tears dried up. The princesses made their way to the Rolls Royce. Mohammed, their tea-maker and general dogsbody, climbed into my BMW. He was a little naïve and not educated, but he had a good heart and helped me no end with my Arabic.

George we left behind to sort out the entourage still waiting at the suite. He would catch up to us—sooner than we expected, as it turned out. Making way for the exit, I noticed that dreaded metallic clanking again. I was sure it was coming from the lead car. Each time the Rolls Royce quickened, the worse the noise became. It made a terrible din. As we drove through the underpass leading towards the M4 motorway, the extent of the problem was obvious. I decided on a course of action which could prove embarrassing to Anil and, more importantly, to Martini.

I asked myself—do I do my job or do I keep my mouth shut and get on with it? I flashed my lights to gain Anil's attention, and signalled them to pull over on to the hard shoulder of the motorway. I dashed up to Anil's window and said I wanted the princesses to change cars for their safety. He was aghast and couldn't believe I was commanding him to give up his passengers. I told the princesses they must change vehicles. George arrived and I commandeered his car for the princesses. The secretary joined Mohammed and me in the BMW.

The other women stayed with Anil while he found the best solution to his problem. Once the principals had transferred, we were off and the others would have to fend for themselves, as they were of no concern to me.

I couldn't believe it—what a mess! First the dog, and now this! I was in a world of shit. Martini would go berserk when he heard about this. God only knows what the princesses thought. The Mercedes now became the lead car and I tagged along behind them. I rejoiced as we got nearer and nearer to Mayfair. I hoped we would have no more upset this night. However, the closer we got to the apartments, the more uneasy I felt. Something just had to go wrong; I was sure of it.

We cruised through Hyde Park and reached Park Lane. Then we headed for Carlos Place. Within seconds of us arriving, Martini was on scene. He must have driven like a crazy man to reach us so soon. The look Martini fired my way could kill a person stone dead. Was I a dead man walking?

Martini escorted the princesses up to the apartments in this plush and expensive area. Two minutes later he was back out again.

Seconds later, Princess Haifa followed with a mobile phone in her hand. She passed the phone to Martini, I heard ranting from the handset, and Martini cowered as the tirade went on.

Yes, World War 3 had begun. Prince Faisal Bin Fahd gave Martini an almighty bollocking. The line went dead in his hand; he looked towards us sheepishly. Princess Luluah would not stay there. She wanted to move to the Intercontinental Hotel in Park Lane. Martini made the fatal mistake of saying she couldn't as he needed to keep the costs down. The princess took exception to this and bawled him out and then followed that with a phone call to her favourite brother, the King's oldest son, Prince Faisal. He bollocked Martini, and told him whatever his sister wants, she gets—whatever the cost. No doubt Martini saw his commission on the rental flying out the window. The rental was to run alongside the Champney's visit, which was to last three months. He faced losing a substantial sum. Hastily, arrangements were made for the transfer to the Intercontinental Hotel. This booking would also cover the three months the princesses were staying.

While this was going on, Anil drew up in the Rolls Royce and dropped his passengers off. He and George removed a wheel. Once it was off, they gave it a good shake and the metallic noise became audible again. Anil replaced the wheel and the problem was solved.

Martini ordered that the wheel be inspected in the morning. No doubt, he wanted the facts before giving me the 'good news'. I was pleased Martini received a bollocking in public, albeit on the end of a mobile phone. It was a welcome change for us, as we were usually on the receiving end of his diatribes.

The princesses and their cousin got into the Rolls Royce, and I shut the door behind them. I noticed Princess Luluah sat in the same seat she had occupied previously, above the broken wheel. I wondered if there was any significance in that, as I allowed a smile to cross my face.

The secretary and Mohammed already sat in the BMW, so I moved off as soon as the lead car was underway. A few minutes later we turned into the main entrance of the Intercontinental Hotel. Martini took care of the procedures as the duty manager showed us to the suites and rooms. We had a room earmarked for us, the security and drivers, which was another costly addition that Martini would have been tearing his hair out over—if he had any, that is.

I was team leader again. I placed Peter and Alan on static duties at the Intercontinental hotel; "Timber", Gill and I were in place at Champney's. Mark, who had served with Princess Luluah on her first visit and had caused raised eyebrows because of his physical condition, had since died of leukaemia, which saddened me.

Although the guys at the health farm would have use of all services, including the dining room, Peter and Alan would have an allowance of just ten pounds a day for food, courtesy of Martini and the Embassy! If we went to the hotel at any time we too would have the ten pounds allowance for food. Martini decreed that I could only claim parking allowance on my BMW if I followed the princess in it during the day. If not, then I had to set my food allowance against the car-parking fee in the hotel for that day.

When Anil arrived the morning after the princesses' arrival, he brought in some sharp metal shards. He said they were only a small part of the metal fragments which had been found inside the wheel of the Rolls Royce. The car had special run flat tyres in case they became holed and burst; thus, the car would remain mobile.

Part of that system included a metal band that ran around the centre of the wheel. This band held the tyre on and prevented the car from stopping. The cause of the metallic clanking I had heard had been the shattering metal band, which could have proved extremely dangerous. Therefore, my actions the previous evening proved justified, and I knew this for sure when I heard nothing further from Martini.

As we prepared to leave for Champney's, I fetched my BMW from the car park and stopped behind the Rolls Royce on the frontage. George parked behind me. Now I left my car and went up to the suite to escort the princesses. Why I put up with this ridiculous situation, I don't know, but I just got on with the task.

The princesses left their suite and I walked behind them. The entourage followed me and we made for the lifts. I pushed the button. I knew only the princesses and I would enter. The others would follow as soon as they could, and this presented me with a problem. As soon as the princesses got into their car, it would signal

Anil to move. I knew the secretary and Mohammed would go with me. If they weren't quick, I would be in difficulty. Anxiety was the order of the day, and I wasn't pleased about it.

Trying to adjust the pace, I hoped the entourage would make haste behind me. Across the marbled foyer we walked, the princess drawing attention from the clientele sitting on the sofas placed to one side. Instead of receiving my full concentration, I felt the princess was being short-changed by the manoeuvres of Martini. Nearing the steps leading to the main doors, I caught sight of the entourage to my right making their way towards us. I breathed a sigh of relief and knew now that we would leave as one unit.

Uneventful as the journey proved to be, I would soon be making a right idiot of myself, or so I thought. As we walked into the hallway of the annexe at Champney's, Princess Luluah held her head and swooned as though she was going to faint. What should I do, how could I help her?

As she weighed over twenty stones, I couldn't hold her up. Then again, as a man, I wasn't allowed to touch her anyway. Throwing caution to the wind, I pushed my shoulder into hers and pushed her up against the wall in an attempt to keep her on her feet.

Then in an empty hallway, I asked if she needed a chair to sit on! She shook her head from side to side, while I thanked God for letting me off the hook. Hussa, one of her maids, walked up to us and took one arm of the princess while I held the other and together we guided the princess towards her suite. Waiting in the hallway, I wondered what it was that made me ask if she wanted a seat. I felt a right prat. A few moments later, Hussa came out of the suite and handed me three hundred pounds, saying it was a thank you from the princess. I laughed as I realised this prat had just made three hundred pounds.

Visions came to mind of the princess and me crumpling to the floor in a heap as we slid down the wall, while I tried to support her in vain. As she was a very big woman, why I made such a futile attempt to prop her up, I will never know. However, I made an impression on her—and no doubt the wall, too!

Malcolm, one of the day guys, was his usual dapper self; he was perfectly dressed and groomed, reminding me of a tailor's shop mannequin. He drank too much in the evenings, but was always sober on duty. Malcolm stood all of six feet tall, had a normal build and had fair hair. I knew him to be reliable and he never caused problems.

'Timber', the other day guy, was of a similar height and build to Malcolm. He had a good sense of humour and a thinning scalp. He was excellent at his job and had been a former Royal Marines Commando. I had no qualms about either and was confident in their abilities.

The guys on night duty at Champney's were Gill and Pat. Gill was quite short and rotund. A former soldier who had dark hair and a moustache, he looked Indian but spoke with a broad Scottish accent. As he didn't look the part, I often wondered how he managed to get on the circuit. His standard of work was professional and warranted no criticism. Pat, I had doubts about. He stood about five foot ten inches in height, had a medium build with short hair and often worked as a mercenary with the two night static men at the hotel, Gus and Alan. Gus and Alan were ex-Royal Marine Commandos and were father and son, Gus being the father. I thought both of them slippery and devious. Alan stood the same height as his father, about six feet, and had a normal build. His father had a wirier, sinewy build. Gus had a thick moustache while Alan was clean-shaven.

The day statics at the hotel were Peter and Cliff. Peter was about six feet one inch in height and had a thickset build. He had thick, mousy hair and a moustache. He originated out of the East End of London. His abilities were well known to me and I was confident in him. Cliff was about five foot ten inches in height and of heavy build, but he wasn't fat. He had short hair, was clean-shaven. I was happy to have him on board. This was my team, and my only concerns were of the night static men, at the hotel—the father and son, Gus and Alan.

I had occasion to pull Alan up a few times because of his cunning behaviour. Even on this job, he would try to ingratiate himself with George, the driver who was Martini's spy in the camp, at the expense of the other men on the job. George reported daily to Martini. Alan did not care who he upset, so long as he curried favour with the 'bosses'. Alan was the weak link, with his father not far behind him. Both would have to be watched carefully.

Anil, an Indian chap, had come to England when Idi Amin had evicted all the Asians from Uganda. He drove the princess, was professional and a real gentleman. George was Martini's eyes and ears on any assignment, so we kept a close eye on him. He would readily drop someone in the shit if he thought it made him look good. I covered his back a couple of times when he made mistakes and also helped him when he suffered marital problems. Even so, I knew I would have to watch my back with him. The drivers worked independently of the security but still through Martini. Now and again, their actions proved damaging to the security of the principals and when that occurred, I confronted them. When it came to the smooth running of the security, I took no prisoners and would stamp down hard on the offenders, whoever they were or whatever position they enjoyed with Martini. Overall, though, I was happy with this team, with whom I would spend the next three months. And at least the young women that had stalked 'Timber' on the last visit were nowhere to be seen.

A major disadvantage was the covert operation we put in force each day when the princesses and entourage ordered McDonald's hamburgers and fries from the local fast food restaurant. This was a farce with the security guys acting as spotters, making sure the coast was clear when Anil pulled up in the Rolls Royce with the forbidden cargo.

A mad dash from the Rolls, through the glass entry doors, up the stairs past the manager's office, and directly to the suite would then take place. As Anil ran through, a security guy would run behind him spraying air freshener in an attempt to mask any odours that emanated from the offending McDonald's bags. Nearly rumbled a few times, we made out the security guys had eaten McDonald's for lunch or dinner. By the end of the visit we perfected the masquerade and would have done any special forces team proud!

We laughed so much. Special arrangements were made for the princesses and their entourage to eat in their suites. As the carefully calorie-counted meals arrived, we would take them into the room reserved for us and eat them. Many times, we coerced Mohammed into eating them. He was slender and he needed a little feeding up, we had decided. In exchange for his excellent sweet mint tea and the Arabic lessons he provided me, I would make sure he got whatever he wanted. He had a good heart and was a good person so I enjoyed spending my time with him. He was loyal to the family and so he loyally ate as much of the rabbit food we put in front of him!

Chapter 39

Princess Luluah, Part 3: 1989

While we waited for the princess to decide what she wanted to do, Anil, George, Malcolm and I decided we would play some pool. Anil was good, George was of a similar standard, I was hopeless, and Malcolm showed signs of a misspent youth.

We settled into our game. Then, I noticed Princess Haifa peering round the doors. She called me over. She was a good person; laid-back and caring, too. The princess told me we were going for a walk. I went to the suite.

Putting on my officious look, I waited for Princess Luluah to emerge into the corridor. Looking down at my shoes, I wondered whether to change into a sturdy pair of walking boots. The arrival of her maids interrupted my thoughts. The princess sauntered out of her suite. Mob handed, we made our way to the stairs. I pushed forward to the front and descended in front of the princesses. Each time I did this, I knew that Princess Luluah would be thinking that I was there to protect her should she stumble and fall. Each time I did this, I knew that if Princess Luluah should stumble and fall I would die, crushed to death.

We exited the doors leading to the extensive grounds. Looking forward to some fresh air and a brisk walk, we set off. After fifty yards or so, we turned around, and strolled back to the suite, job done.

Looking back in the poolroom after this exercise, I found the guys had not finished the game yet. They continued, while I sat down to watch and recover. On completing the game, we sat with our Earl Grey tea near the sauna area, as we found it a relaxing place with its tropical fauna. As befitted a keen protection officer, I kept a close eye on the more attractive members of staff who wandered by.

The communications we had in place worked throughout the buildings, which allowed us some freedom and enabled us to take advantage of some services provided. I often covered the duties of one or other of the static guys, so everyone benefited.

It was important to keep the team members happy and their morale high, as this benefited the principals as well as me, as team leader. I tried to foster a happy working environment for the guys, even though conditions on some jobs were revolting. We were lucky not to have any Saudi guards on this assignment, as it would have changed the relaxed environment for the principals and for us too.

Over the next few days, life became ever more tedious. Playing pool, snooker and working out in the weights room tired us out. If I were lucky, Princess Luluah would venture out for her fifty-yard dash. Our daily covert operations continued unabated with the McDonald's hamburgers. Mohammed continued feasting on the healthy food delivered to the suites, and looked much fitter and healthier for it. Often I ventured down to see him while he made his tea. Chatting to him in my pidgin Arabic was one of the highlights of my day. George tried to dissuade Mohammed from teaching me Arabic, but he continued nonetheless. Knowledge of our chats soon reached the ears of Martini, but he made no comment.

Each day Anil ventured to the newsagents on his way in. Then he hit McDonald's two or three times a day to collect the burgers. Those hamburgers were the safest in the country as they travelled back to the princess in her armour-plated Rolls Royce. On the other hand, once the burgers reached the hands of the princess, they became the least safe burgers in the country as she devoured them almost whole.

Management and staff became ever more frustrated as they tried in vain to coax the princess to eat in the dining room. They became even more frustrated at their inability to impose a healthy exercise regime. Therapists arrived at the suite each day, and if they were lucky, they would manage to apply a facial treatment. Sometimes they managed a manicure or pedicure. If they were unlucky, they didn't make it through the door.

As time went by, some of the team got braver and went swimming, had a massage or a sauna. I was always ready to move at a moment's notice. Boredom must have set in deeply with the guys at the hotel as they stood guard over several suites and empty rooms.

347

The costs of security and drivers must have run into tens of thousands of pounds, and who knows what the cost of the McDonald's burgers. However, Prince Faisal said whatever Princess Luluah wanted, it was Martini's job to make sure she got it. What toll it took on the princess, who knows? Then some retail therapy was in order. They did not need any therapist to show them how to engage in retail therapy, they were expert at it. Once it became known we were going shopping, George contacted Martini. I was told, when they bought anything, I must collect the VAT forms. This related to another swindle certain people had going on.

As the principals were foreign nationals, they could claim back any tax paid on items they bought over here. Customs and Excise officers stamped the forms when the principals left and the tax was repaid into an account of their choice. A duty of Customs and Excise was to inspect the goods to make sure they left the country. However, I never saw a single inspection carried out, and many of the principals didn't know they could claim the tax back. Therefore, masses of VAT was paid directly into an account belonging to the 'boss', but only after the Customs and Excise stamped the forms.

With that in mind, at midday on the Thursday we were told we were off to Edgware Road. Adrenalin was the drug of the day as extra pressure was put on as the secretary decided to hitch a lift with me. Everything went tits up now. I would jostle for a car parking space as close to the Rolls Royce as possible. Once I secured the space, I would have to get the secretary out of the BMW and secure it. Then I had to get to the lead car before the princess stepped out.

It was ridiculous—putting me in a position over which I had no control. There was no way I could do my job properly. Four scenarios plagued my mind. The first was I could get away with it. The second, I'd get a parking ticket, for which I would be liable. The third, they could clamp the wheel and leave me stranded, looking like a prize prat—and I would still be liable for the costs. The fourth, they might tow the BMW, again leaving me stranded and I would have to find the car, too. I would reclaim it and *still* be liable for the costs. All of this was courtesy of Martini and the Saudi Embassy. Not content with me being the princess' bodyguard, they wanted me to be a car jockey, too.

Anil, bless him, did his best to help me—taking his time when stopping and making his way to the princess' door slowly, giving me valuable seconds in which to catch up. I found out it was impossible to secure the BMW as it simply took too much time. Therefore, I left it unlocked. Anil kept watch on both cars as far as he was able, but if the police, a traffic warden, or the clampers showed up, then it was tough luck on me. He had to take care of the Rolls Royce.

The blood coursed through my veins and I felt my anxiety levels heightening as we bounced from shop to shop. It didn't help when the princesses walked between several of them, calling for Anil to follow them as they did so. When the princesses got into their car to drive off, I would have to sprint back to my car and then speed down the road to catch up. When I called Bill to complain he said, "Tough; either get on with it or fuck off." Needing the money, I kept my mouth shut. I knew that if I left, no more work would come my way, so it was checkmate to them.

We stopped at an electronics shop; the princess took a fancy to some gadgets. She wanted one each for her brothers Prince Faisal, and Prince Mohammed. Other electronic gadgets she bought as gifts for friends and family in Saudi. The bill mounted rapidly. Remembering my instructions, I asked the shopkeeper for the VAT forms to reclaim the tax. While I watched the princess, I tried to also watch my car from the window, and then I had to watch what they bought to make sure the shopkeeper included everything on the Customs and Excise form.

Oh, how I wished we were back at Champney's where I only had to struggle with the dreaded fifty-yard dash now and again! Having enjoyed a wonderful time there, it was obviously payback time now, and I was paying back big-time—or so I thought. Bigger payback was to come.

Jewellery! It must have come to them in a flash as they left the electronics store. Anil took care of several bags while I took care of the VAT forms. An animated conversation between the princesses closed with one word—"Kutchinsky". The princesses were safely deposited in the Rolls, as I sprinted off to find my BMW. I heaved a sigh of relief as I found the car where I had left it.

No parking ticket on the windscreen. Catching my breath, I thought someone was playing a joke and I was the butt of it with all this mincing around.

Playing out my Michael Schumacher impersonation, I sped off in pursuit of the lead car. We met each other as we rounded Marble Arch and turned into Park Lane heading toward Hyde Park Corner. I appreciated the density of the traffic. I moved in close behind the Rolls and relaxed a little as it was slow going and I was adept at keeping vehicles from coming between us. I mastered the defensive driving courses well and stuck to the lead car like superglue.

Once we reached Hyde Park Corner, I pulled alongside the Rolls on its right-hand side. Pushing myself forward, I blocked the flow of traffic, allowing Anil to pull on to the roundabout. I then slid in behind it. We circled the large monument of Queen Bodicea on her chariot and as we all but completed the circle, we turned left towards Knightsbridge. Further on, we pulled into the left-hand side directly outside Kutchinsky's jewellers. We caused an obstacle to other road users, and they blasted their car horns in anger, making a bad situation even worse for us should they catch the attention of any nearby traffic wardens.

The princesses exited the Rolls looking like children ready to raid the cookie jar. I looked to Anil as he smiled at me and shrugged his shoulders; he too knew the shop was about to take a hammering. Both cars were parked on double yellow lines and were proving to be a nightmare for the rush hour traffic. Did the princesses care? Not a lot. As with all members of the royal family, all they cared about was themselves. They never gave away anything of significance, unless it benefited them in some way. Having said that, the King *did* give away tonnes of dates to the people of one region in Saudi Arabia, although it escapes me what they did with them. It was back to the serious business of shopping. Looking in their eyes, I noticed they sparkled in anticipation as much as the diamonds they were about to see.

Walking through the door, I noticed nods of acknowledgement, directed at me. I also noticed the looks of horror on the faces of the staff as they witnessed their closing time pass by. They and I knew they had a long evening ahead of them.

As the children–sorry, princesses—and their entourage sat down, the shop security staff secured the main doors and the security grille as the safe door was opened. The excitable women cackled in unison as various pieces of jewellery landed on the table before them. Many of these pieces would be presents for other members of the royal family. One necklace Princess Luluah chose had one link of gold and the next link encrusted with diamonds continuing all-round it. The cost amounted to the same as the mortgage of my house, a bargain that she placed to one side. Now I wondered how I was going to pay my recently arrived electricity bill. Dozens of watches—yellow gold, white gold, and diamond encrusted—she also placed to one side. Necklaces and chains followed, not to be outdone by the bangles and bracelets. I could hear the princess saying, "Faisal would like this; Mohammed would like that; Khalid would like this; Sultan would like that, and Abdul Aziz, 'Azoozi' could have that," and on it went. As hard as I tried, I did not hear that Mark would like this or that.

Even at six thirty, the cars were not safe because they were parked on double yellow lines, which meant they were still parked illegally. Kutchinsky's thought Christmas had come early. I had learned the culture of the royal family revolved around corruption. Greed was good, but only good for them.

Would I have to pay my electricity bill in instalments? I wondered, as an attractive assistant brought me a cup of tea and a small plate of biscuits. My eye again caught the gold and diamond encrusted necklace put to one side. I could see my house sitting there! As hard as I tried, I couldn't hear anyone say Mark would like that. Therefore, I shut my mind to it and tucked into my tea and biscuits. Finally, at eight thirty in the evening, the princess stood up and made her way towards the secure doors. The door attendant opened them and waved us off. The cars were still there. God must have smiled on me, and I was grateful for that.

The next place on the princesses' agenda was the Richoux restaurant in Piccadilly. Doing a U-turn, we caused yet more upset to the other drivers. We drove towards Piccadilly and stopped by the kerbside outside Richoux's. Pulling up sharply, I jumped from the backup car and hastily made my way to the door of Princess Luluah.

The secretary and Mohammed could make their own way, in their own time; it was of no concern to me.

Opening her door, I extended my hand to help her out. As she exited, the rings she wore on her right-hand fell into the gutter. I bent down and picked them up. I grovelled; saying how wonderful it was she was losing so much weight her rings didn't fit her any longer. I surprised myself with the crap I dished out, as it was embarrassing. The princess beamed and positively floated over the kerb and pavement toward Richoux.

The princess invited Anil in, which made a change for him and gave me some company, too. Given the princess was floating on air over her supposed weight loss, she decided to treat herself. A large plate of cream cakes arrived at her table, ready to be devoured. Often the princess smiled at me, as she was so ecstatic about her dramatic weight loss. After all, her rings had fallen off her fingers! The more ecstatic she became, the more she treated herself, making short work of the cream cakes placed before her.

Champney's may have been one of the best health farms in the country but they did not provide either of the therapies that Princess Luluah needed—food and proper retail therapy.

Once the group had eaten the Richoux stock, they waddled out to the cars. We told the guys at the Intercontinental that we were on our way. We spent so little time there we did not want them to be caught off guard. It would make a change for them to have something to do. As much as I admired Champney's, they couldn't compete with the princess' extracurricular activities. Striding briskly up to the door of the Rolls, I reached out to open it. Anil graciously stepped to one side and allowed me to do so. Both princesses exited by the same door. Anil took care of his other passengers. The doorman tipped his head at the princesses as he held the hotel doors open for them. Princess Haifa dropped a five pound note into his hand.

Walking across the marble-floored lobby, it seemed we had never been away. We entered the lift area and I pushed the call button. As the doors opened, the princesses entered the empty lift. The secretary and I followed.

Once we reached our floor, I checked it was safe for the principals to exit. Peering down the corridor, I could see Gus and Alan standing erect and looking smart, a credit to the team. Moving to one side, I dropped behind the princesses and followed them to their suites.

Once they were tucked up safely, we waited for a brew to arrive from room service. We had to pay for it. Unfortunately, I still felt uneasy with Alan and Gus and so was careful with my rhetoric. Feeling drained after the day's antics and needing some sleep, I left them.

I slept peacefully. The next day would be a nightmare.

*　*　*

Waking refreshed, I jumped into the shower and washed the cobwebs away. The drive into London proved a little tedious, but that was nothing unusual. I used the time productively listening to my Arabic language tapes. Driving down Hamilton Place, I turned right and descended into the hotel car park. I parked my aged BMW next to the new Rolls Royce's, Bentleys, and Ferraris. I hoped their owners would be careful not to bang their doors on my car. Walking through the car park, I shielded my eyes from the dazzling array of metallic pieces of art. I entered the car park lift, which took me directly to the lobby. I made my way to the breakfast lounge. The team were waiting. I began the briefing. The guys had several issues they were not happy about. I promised I would take care of them.

Alan asked why I wouldn't allow the drivers to attend the briefings. I already saw him and his father as snakes in the grass and I didn't need any others around. Alan had struck up a friendship with George and anything we discussed was already finding its way back to Martini at the Embassy. George manipulated Alan and I wasn't about to let the fox into the chicken run. George was a thorn in my side and before the day was out, it would be proved to me how much of a thorn he was.

On the way to Kutchinsky the previous day, the princesses had noticed a women's fashion shop just past Sloane Street on the Brompton Road. Today they wanted to visit it. They would shop until they dropped. This would to prove an enormous problem. All the cars would have to sit on double yellow lines close to a traffic light controlled junction. We hadn't even turned a wheel and the apprehension had begun. I knew the day was going to be bad; I just didn't know *how* bad it would become.

The princesses were late sleepers so we wouldn't make it out of the hotel until well after lunch. As I was using my car it meant I could send out for a sandwich on the ten pounds generously granted by Martini.

They were on the move, so I dashed to the car park and brought the BMW round on to the forecourt. I went to the suite and waited, trying to relax as I waited for the women to emerge. I contacted the office and suggested one of the static guys back me up when we went out. They wouldn't listen.

The women came bounding out of their rooms, blocking the corridor in the process. Peter and Cliff kept an eye on them, while we waited for the principals. The secretary sauntered along the corridor towards us. He entered the suite, spoke with the princesses and then came out. He wandered away, clearly content he wasn't going to be joining us.

Princess Luluah emerged, a smile on her face, and Princess Haifa followed. The entourage parted in the middle like the Red Sea and the princesses passed through unhindered. I pushed through and placed myself behind the principals. I peered over their shoulders and checked the corridor. The women jockeyed for position behind me.

'Déjà vu,' I thought as we crossed the lobby. Anil opened the door for the princess as I watched a guest arriving outside. The women got in the BMW and Mercedes. I would be chauffeuring today as well, what a bloody joke. But that would prove to be the least of my problems.

We drove down Knightsbridge across Sloane Street and pulled up on the left-hand side outside the fashion shop with the double yellow lines glaring at me, positively shouting 'no parking'.

I dashed to the princesses' door and escorted them into the shop. Seconds later, their entourage hit the shop like an exploding bomb.

For a while, Princess Luluah walked around looking at the clothes and trinkets on display. Then after choosing hundreds of pounds worth of the fashion jewellery, she asked for a chair on which to sit.

I stood near her as the women went on their rampage, inspecting every piece of clothing and every single accessory the shop held. Several customers entered the shop and it became crowded. I told the women to be aware of pickpockets. Whether they understood me or not, I don't know, but I had my hands full at this end of the shop. Princess Luluah pulled her seat closer to a circular railing, as she wanted to look at the clothes that hung on it. I felt decidedly uneasy about it and moved in as close as I dared.

A few people moved towards us, and it made me feel more uncomfortable. The group, although separate, had the look of South Americans, possibly Colombians. They moved about all over the place. One went round the other side of the circular railing. They crouched down as though examining the clothing, and, feeling something wasn't right, I crouched down and pulled the clothing apart. As I did this, the person stood quickly and moved away. Looking at the princess, I saw a slash mark across her handbag.

The adrenalin hit me so hard I thought my heart would burst. All sorts of thoughts rushed through my mind in a millisecond. Part of me wanted to catch the offender; another part of me said no, it could be a decoy. I stayed with my charge and made sure she was safe. Feeling dejected and a failure I pointed at her bag. She calmly checked it and found that it had not been slashed right through. Nothing was missing, and she asked for another bag from a maid. The gang may not have taken anything from her, but they certainly took something from me.

Chapter 40

Princess Luluah, Part 4: 1989

The shit hit the fan shortly afterwards. Leaving the shop carrying the slashed bag was the catalyst for George to contact Martini. I knew the airwaves would be crackling. I was severely pissed off about the incident. I shouldn't have let anyone get so close to the principal. Perhaps I had let my guard drop momentarily; maybe not, but no one could have made me feel any worse than I already did. In my defence, I had noticed them and made a move, chasing them off. But I should have moved earlier.

After climbing back into the cars, we drove all of a hundred yards into Hans Crescent and stopped outside Harrods. The adrenalin still coursed through my veins, mixing with the anger I felt. After parking up, I escorted the princesses into the emporium. The bill soon ran into the thousands of pounds as they bought bags of cosmetics, perfumes, and anything else that caught their fancy. One large bag shortly became two, and then three and four. They passed bags to me to carry and this presented another problem—I needed my hands free. I had been down this road before with other guys but when I discussed it with Bill; I was told to stop whinging. Do what we tell you or piss off, was the answer I received.

Often I felt the jobs were a game we played, for one reason and one reason only, to make serious money for Martini and Bill. The fact was, some serious players were making serious money, but it wasn't us.

Becoming buried under an ever-increasing pile of green and gold Harrods bags, I placed myself next to an adjoining counter. The top of the counter was off and some plywood leant against it. Work carried on. This became the storage point for the continuous arrival of even more bags. My eyes ached. I focused intensely on Princess Luluah. I didn't need another fuck up. I telephoned Anil for help. Within a minute or two, he and George arrived and took away as many bags as they could carry. Then they came back and took away some more. Finally, the princesses stopped for the day. Grasping the bags quickly beside me, in the hope of a quick escape, I caught the back of my hand on the edge of a plywood sheet and scratched it. I cussed and wondered what else could go wrong.

Hussa noticed blood oozing from the scratches. Was it cut the same time as the princess' bag, she asked? I showed her the sheet of wood on which I had scratched myself. Hussa pointed out my hand to the princess and pointed at the sheet of wood that caused the scratches. Exiting Harrods, I placed the princess safely in the Rolls, and as I did so she asked to see my hand. She poured some perfume over it and dabbed it with a tissue.

George was straight on the 'phone. I didn't have to guess who he was calling. Within seconds of getting in my car, my 'phone rang. Bill swore at me and asked what happened to my hand. Martini had told him I suffered the injury during the attempt to rob the princess, but I told him I'd scratched my hand on some plywood. He wanted me at the office in the morning. A day I thought couldn't get any worse, had just done so. Looking at George, I remembered how his wife left him and how distraught he was. I helped them get back together, and this was my payback.

When I got to the office, Bill asked to inspect my hand. I left the office shortly afterwards. Bill seemed satisfied with my explanation. That day the princess stayed in, which allowed me some time to myself. God knows I needed it, as my mood had dropped significantly. They were due to depart in two days and given recent events I looked forward to it. As I sat in the lobby, George told me that Martini had said no security guys are to escort Princess Luluah to the airport when she leaves. I didn't care one way or the other.

That night we went out to celebrate the princess' birthday. The Villa Dei Cesari in Grosvenor Road opposite Dolphin Square on the riverbank was the setting. Even this news did not lift my spirits. Apart from the static guys, everyone else had to attend. I would take Mohammed and the secretary in my car. The secretary was rarely around and was quiet and elusive. I wondered what his story was.

As notice came to prepare for departure, I made off for the hotel car park. Then I hastened back to the suite. The entourage waited in the corridor, dressed in their finery.

Mohammed stood next to the static guys in the drabbest clothes imaginable. He smiled like an excitable little kid going on his first picnic. I looked at my reflection in a nearby window and checked myself out. Feeling reasonably content with the results, I waited in line for the princesses. Soon we descended in the lifts to the lobby. Princess Luluah gave me a huge smile, so I knew she was still comfortable with me, which made me feel better. We set off for the restaurant.

My mood was depressed as we walked in to the Villa Dei Cesari. The princesses and their female entourage sat at a large table, a level higher than the lower floor. The views from their table, over the river, with the lights reflecting on the water, were beautiful. I thought it odd the secretary sat with them. Anil, George, Mohammed and I sat quietly by the dance floor. Everyone ordered dinner and the evening got underway. The lights dimmed and the band played while we ate, everyone enjoyed themselves—well, everyone apart from me.

As time passed, I listened to the music and munched on my medium-rare steak. I relaxed, my mood soared and this made me feel uneasy. Some time later, a waiter took a birthday cake up to the top table, and we sang 'Happy Birthday' to the princess. I told the guys at our table that I should take a rose from the vase, present it to the princess, and ask her to dance. This had the guys in stitches. Something inside me would not allow the idea to pass. My mood still soared—perhaps my drink was spiked; I just don't know.

I reached for the vase and took a rose. The guys laughed, thinking I was playing up to them, but quickly slid down in their chairs as I went up to the princess. When I looked back, I saw Mohammed almost having a heart attack and George fumbling for his beloved phone, no doubt trying to warn Martini before the place erupted. As I neared their table, the women looked at me. Seeing the rose in my hand their chins hit their chests—even the secretary looked aghast.

358

I stood by Princess Luluah and passed her the rose. I then asked her to dance. She stumbled over her words, and pointing to Hussa she said, "Maybe Hussa; maybe she dance."

I replied, "all right," but Hussa wasn't having any of it, so I went to sit down with the guys.

Shortly after this, Princess Haifa came down and called me to one side.

"What do you think you're doing?" she asked.

"Is Princess Luluah upset?"

"Yes, she is, but her psychiatrist is talking with her, trying to calm her down,"

"Her psychiatrist?" I asked.

"Yes," she said, "the man sitting with us."

I was told Princess Luluah suffered extreme mood swings to such an extent that a psychiatrist travelled with her. Oh dear, what a cock up! I was truly in the shit, yet still my mood soared and soared.

I floated on air. The people on the dance floor twirled in slow motion. With celebrations complete, we returned to the hotel. The fallout I expected over this stunt would be more than both the atom bombs dropped on Japan during the Second World War. No one spoke a word as we exited the cars and went to the suites. We deposited the principals and I positively danced like Fred Astaire to my BMW and drove home. I was floating on a magic carpet.

Arriving home, I found the house in darkness and unlocked the door, switched on the lights, and made my way straight to the bathroom where I took a shower before stumbling into bed.

Enjoying a fitful sleep, I awoke feeling refreshed and ready for the day ahead. Vaguely, I remembered the previous evening. Perhaps a dressing down from Bill or Martini was on the way, or maybe a call telling me I should stay home. Any number of things could happen and yet I did not care; I did not give a shit. This was an unusual departure for me as I was by nature a conscientious person and prided myself on my professionalism. I needed to understand why I acted in such a way the evening before. I didn't bother with a briefing at the hotel. I heard nothing from the office, and Anil and George were ominously silent.

We went through the routine of getting the principals into the cars and drove to Old Bond Street. Princess Luluah heard the jewellers calling, "Come to us; buy our goods, we're waiting!"

The princesses, Hussa, their cousin and I entered the shop. The princesses eyed up the goodies placed before them. Their cousin approached me. This was the time of reckoning I had been dreading. She asked what I was thinking the night before.

I said as it was such a special occasion and the atmosphere was so pleasant, I thought Princess Luluah might like to dance. Knowing no one was going to ask her, I thought I would, giving her the choice. If she wanted to dance, she could do so; if not, that was fine, too. At least she had the opportunity given to her.

The princess was upset by it, but the cousin said she now understood my motives. That was cool, as I still did not understand them myself but hoped the blurb would be enough to quell the storm.

It must have worked, because shortly afterwards, I was again the next best thing to sliced bread. As I collected the VAT forms, the princess asked me why I did this in all the shops we visited. I didn't want to lie, so I explained the procedure to her. The tax, I told her, would be refunded to the account number shown on the form. The princess said, when at the airport, she would speak to me about something. Why at the airport? Martini had stopped me going to the airport. I later spoke with Princess Haifa and mentioned the predicament I was in. She told me not to worry, and said she would sort it.

Back at the hotel, Princess Haifa told George that Princess Luluah wanted me to escort her to the airport. Once she left him, he called Martini. I was told to make up some excuse. I knew this would become a power play between them. Yet again, I was to be the pawn caught up in the middle. I explained to Princess Haifa what was going on behind the scenes and she said not to worry. They telephoned Martini. As a result, George begrudgingly told me I had to escort the princess to the airport.

Although the princess won the battle, I was sure to lose the war. I would have to soothe each ego in turn, not wanting to upset either of them. Martini made the necessary arrangements to allow me airside at Heathrow Airport.

Bill called me, asking what the hell I was playing at and demanded I go and see him as soon as I left the airport the following day. Sometimes I felt like telling them to fuck off, but if I wanted the work, I had to put up with it.

At least the hotel porters would deal with the luggage, even putting it on to the trucks. The princess was heading for one of her father's properties in Geneva, Switzerland. As final preparations took place in the suites, I stood on the pavement outside the hotel chatting with the guys. A taxi drove slowly by and the driver lowered his window, started swearing at us, and told us to get the BMW out of the taxi rank. I told him to sod off and he responded by saying he'd call the police. I shrugged my shoulders and told him to piss off and to do whatever he likes. This incensed him. He picked up a fare and drove away.

Anil said he heard Martini was upset with me over this airport affair. What was I supposed to do? I'm only a pawn in their game, I told him. I had to go with the flow.

After dropping his fare, the taxi driver returned. He shouted some more obscenities at us and went in search of a police officer. I carried on chatting and paid him no attention. He came back with not one, but two police officers. Pointing at the BMW, he launched into his diatribe and I could plainly hear him say he told us to move the car and how I told him to sod off. The taxi driver was excitable. I watched him and the police officers until he finished his tirade.

One of the officers told me to move the BMW, but I refused to do so. He threatened to have the car clamped, I told him to do it. He said after clamping the car, if I had not paid the correct fee to unclamp it within half an hour, then he would have it towed away. I told him to do whatever he liked with the car. I didn't care, and said it's not my car anyway and for me to move it would be illegal. The officer laughed and saw the lighter side of the prank, as did his colleague. The taxi driver did not. Playing the game killed some time while we waited for the off.

George walked over and told me they wanted me at the suite. Outside the suite, Hussa met me and gave me a Rado watch from the princess. I asked her to thank the princess for me.

Hussa asked if I were going to the airport, as the princess wanted to know. Assuring her I would be, she left me and went back into the suite.

Soon, the princesses emerged. Princess Luluah looked at me and smiled. I took this to be a smile of victory as she had won her little game with Martini. I knew it was a game she couldn't lose. Martini knew it, too. Nonetheless, it made her happy for the moment. One last time we made our way out of the hotel towards her waiting armour-plated Rolls Royce.

An air of excitement always accompanied the departure of royal family members, and I often wondered if the relief of getting rid of them brought this on. But I had grown fond of Princess Luluah, whose heart had proved to be a large as she was.

The journey to the airport proved uneventful, which was just as well as the next hour or two would prove to be anything but. Departure was from Terminal 4's Spelthorne VIP suite.

Martini stood outside the suite waiting for the princess. Anil drove up to the suite; I parked my car out of the way. George moved up to allow access to the lounge for his passengers.

Martini opened the princess' door, but she refused to get out. After some great persuasion, she finally went through to the lounge. Within a couple of minutes, she was out again with Martini chasing behind her. Sitting in the car, door open, she waited for Martini to close it. As he wasn't going to, I moved forward to shut it and as I did so, Princess Luluah passed me a roll of fifty-pound notes. Thanking her, I backed away, noticing the glare Martini cast my way.

On our left, an airport car with its orange flashing lights pulled over in readiness to escort the princess out to her aircraft. As I walked back to my car, Martini called me. He told me to get into the airport car with him. I wondered what was going on. He didn't say one word to me as we drove out to the jetliner. Looking behind us, I saw Anil driving the princesses' car, while George followed him in the Mercedes, and Martin (who drove Martini) followed in yet another Rolls Royce.

The airport car slowly passed the aircraft steps and slowed to a halt, leaving space for Anil to pull up alongside them. Everyone got out and the princesses climbed the stairs. I wandered over to Martin, who said: "What have you done to make Martini mad? You are going to be drowning in shit soon." With those words ringing in my ears, he passed me an envelope saying Martini had told him to give it to me.

Peering inside the envelope, I saw some VAT forms. Even with a quick glance, I could see many were missing, so someone skimmed them off and I was confident I knew who the culprit was. Martini must have had a coronary. As I tried to digest this information, Martin told me Martini was calling me over to the aircraft. Once I reached him, I was told the princess wanted to speak with me. I went to see her in the cabin; she said if she called in a day or two would I come to Geneva.

I said yes, and thanked her for the VAT forms, not mentioning that many of them were missing. The princess passed me her phone number in Geneva and told me to call her, should I get any trouble from Martini. I said I would, knowing I would not. As I left the cabin, I paid particular attention to Martini behind me, just in case he should decide to push me down the steps I had just climbed.

I went back to Martin, who said Bill had been on the phone and asked Martin to remind me to stop in at the office.

I watched them remove the steps from the fuselage after the cabin door closed. As the aircraft taxied away, we made our way back to the suite and awaited confirmation the aircraft was airborne. Not once did Martini acknowledge me; he obviously saw me as the villain of the piece.

What reception would I get from Bill? He already knew about the airport fiasco and demanded an explanation. All I could say was that I had been a pawn in their game—no more, no less. He asked to see the VAT forms they gave me. I showed them to him. I noticed their total value was only a few hundred pounds and the large value jewellery ones had gone walkies. On the way home I tore them up and threw them away because there was no way I was about to get involved in any Customs and Excise fraud.

I wondered if I would ever get any more work from the Saudi Embassy. I was pleased to get a break as the hours I worked were killing me. I didn't get enough sleep and often, I felt as though I were suffering from exhaustion.

Chapter 41

Abu Dhabi Royalty: 1989

Two weeks later, I was at Gerrards Cross in Buckinghamshire. This time I was with the Abu Dhabi royal family. I drove to the main gates of a large mansion that sat back a little from the road. The wrought iron gates were black with the spiked tops painted gold. I could see through them and noticed a large expanse of land stretching out before me with a driveway that I presumed meandered towards the main house. I walked over to the intercom system set in a large brick pillar. Announcing my arrival, I waited for the gates to open. I got back in the car and set off down the driveway, taking note of the layout of the grounds, paying attention to the large trees and rhododendron bushes where intruders could hide should they gain entry to the property.

As I approached the main house, I was directed down another small driveway. Several cars were parked on the right-hand side in front of some small outbuildings and I parked alongside them. Martin, a security guy, met me. I could see he took particular pride in his appearance. He was ex-military, and I noticed his shoes gleamed in the sunlight. I noted over the next few days that he spent ages cleaning them when sitting around waiting for his charge. I wondered if he had a shoe fetish as he applied so much love and attention on them.

Martin took me through to the security room and introduced me to the guys, some of whom I knew already. Several guards patrolled the grounds. Bodyguards looked after the principals. There were a few drivers assigned to either a group or an individual. Off to one side of the room was a bedroom, where three Nepalese guys slept. These guys were general dogsbodies who helped the housekeeper and her husband. Their main job was to keep the grounds in order and they did a remarkable job of it, considering there were fifty acres.

Martin briefed me on the security and took me on a detailed tour of the grounds and main house.

The house was built in a Gothic style. I found it reminiscent of a castle. The walls were block stone with large arched sandstone doorways. The doors were thick and solid, made from lightly carved oak and adorned with heavy metalwork furnishings. The floors were dark polished wood, covered with tasteful Persian rugs. The rooms had leaded light windows set in arched and carved stone surrounds. Back outside, it was a beautiful summer's day. This job was an easy touch for me. On the first day a static guy cried off. The bosses asked for a volunteer to take his place, to give them a few hours breathing space in which to find a replacement. I volunteered. My ego wasn't that large, I would happily work a static position. Over the years, I found you had to be careful of some security guys' egos; some were downright dangerous, and that included some Special Branch officers I'd worked with. I logged those characters in my memory bank and always kept them at a distance.

The Sheikh and Sheikha who owned this property were of a different class to the Arabs I usually served. They showed us respect and recognised what we did for them. When the Sheikha emerged from the house, black flowing robes, an *abaya*, covered her from head to foot. She wore a *yashmak* that covered her face. Her eyes were beautiful!

We were told that the Sheikha was having marital problems and to keep that in mind. As with most influential Arabs, the Sheikha had a large entourage that travelled with her. One of the young women could only whisper. Her name was Ayshea. She was fifteen years old and wore the *abaya,* but no *yashmak*. She was beautiful. I supposed it would not be long before someone snatched her up and married her; it's usual for Arabs to marry young in their culture.

After taking note of the royals and their entourage, I focused my attention on the security team. There were a few new personalities on this job and I made it a priority to find out more about them. One guy named Eddy didn't come up to the mark, in my opinion. He was sneaky and devious and I felt had an inferiority complex. He hadn't a Special Forces background and it bugged him. Eddy, I determined, was best kept as far away from me as humanly possible.

The Sheikha liked her staff to feel comfortable and happy, and that included us. Each day she walked around to our room and made conversation. I believe I may have caught her eye!

The Sheikha had a female manager whose husband was Sheikh Surooha's (the Sheikha's husband) manager. The Sheikh gave his manager a black Rolls Royce Silver Spur. He collected it with a smile on his face. If I received it as a gift, I would have a smile on my face too. In the Sheikh's garage there was a Daimler Double Six Vanden Plas and a Lamborghini Countach 5000 QV. Although I chose the Lamborghini and waited for it patiently, I never got it. The Sheikha's manager got it instead. How she got it was a story in itself!

The Sheikha decided one morning that she wanted to take the Lamborghini for a drive around the estate. The Sheikha's first name was also Sheikha, so everyone called her Sheikha Sheikha. The Sheikha, wearing her *abaya* and *yashmak*, climbed into the low sports car with one of her female companions. She turned the key and the engine roared with a sweet burbling sound erupting from the exhausts. It was an orgasmic sight and sound for a young man. The car emerged from the large garage and off she set. We got reports from each of the guys round the estate as she went by. Our communication system bristled. The Sheikha drove across the beautifully manicured lawns, but it was when she appeared at the front of the house that the trouble came. She decided to change gear! Into second gear she went, and off she sped. Out of control, she shot across the drive, bottomed out on a kerb, flew over that and smashed into a tree. The car suffered severe damage; the Sheikha none.

Her manager arrived, surveyed the scene, shrugged her shoulders and went to the house. After a time, she emerged, dangling the keys of the car in her hand. The Sheikha had given it to her. So what, I thought, it's no bloody good now! The manager thought differently. She had a low-loader take the car to her house and placed it undercover in her garage. The Sheikh did not claim on the car insurance. The manager insured the Lamborghini and left it for a while before putting in an insurance claim. They paid out. What a fraud. As usual, someone was on the make.

The women, like all Arab women, were well schooled in the art of shopping. If there were ever an Olympic sport of shopping, these people would win it easily. As we patrolled the grounds, we often came across the younger women wandering about. When they noticed us, they went all coy and ran off, laughing. They appeared shy and dignified, yet you could see they were expert in exploiting their femininity and no doubt that was how they courted their men. Ayshea, the young girl and her mother had been brought to England by the Sheikha to allow the youngster to get medical treatment. They went to Harley Street, the London Clinic, and others, but to no benefit. I think they had all but given up hope of her ever speaking properly again. I thought it an endearing quality myself, a woman who couldn't talk above a whisper. Heaven, I thought.

A few weeks into the job, one of the drivers mentioned that a funfair had set up at Eton near Windsor. That was it—as soon as the women heard about it they wanted to go. From then on, each evening the women went to the funfair; they adored it.

Meanwhile, Ayshea still attended various doctors and hospitals, yet nothing helped. None of them had any idea of how to treat her. One evening as the women set off for the funfair, they called Ayshea. They wanted her to go with them. The Sheikha and the women spent ages on the bumper cars. Ayshea merely stood nearby and watched, yet it was obvious she wanted to get on them.

The Sheikha, noticing this, called her on to the ride and had her sit next to her. Ayshea and the Sheikha took turns on steering it. When Ayshea drove, her face beamed. She laughed so softly no one could hear her. Repeatedly, they all spun round the track having fun. Suddenly a bumper car hit Ayshea's car, catching her off guard. She was so shocked she let out a scream. The Sheikha stopped and all the women ran over to Ayshea; they laughed, they cried, they cuddled. From that moment, Ayshea's voice returned to normal. The Sheikha spent much money trying to cure her, and yet a cheap bumper car ride solved the problem. The women were ecstatic, and threw a party for her back at the house. Surprisingly, the next day Ayshea and her mother prepared to fly back home to Abu Dhabi.

A couple of days later, the Sheikha and her entourage moved into their house in The Boltons, London. We, the Sheikha's security and drivers moved into town with her. We felt like Bedouin Arabs at times, as we moved around. We had two guys on static, day and night; one at the front of the house the other to the rear, alternating hourly. Two days after arriving in the Boltons, the Sheikha decided to spend two days in Kent. She asked me to go with her—which surprised me. I knew I had caught her eye and must have made an impression on her! As we arrived back in the Boltons from Kent we were told the Sheikha's husband had arrived and moved in to Gerrards Cross. Another team of security and drivers moved into the house at Gerrards Cross with the Sheikh.

Now the reason we moved into London became clear. The principals were going to be staying in separate properties. The bosses told us to expect the Sheikh within a day or so as he attempted to save his marriage. And so it proved as the next day he did in fact arrive to see his wife. From then the Sheikh would visit each day, and each day he looked very sombre.

The Sheikh had decided that he would stay in the Gerrards Cross property and showed no concerns that his Lamborghini had kissed a tree. One wondered if it had been an accident after all. Maybe the Sheikha was trying to escape from him permanently. The Sheikh used his Daimler Double Six instead. The royal family from Abu Dhabi had a softer and more caring nature. Now all he had to do was remind his wife of that.

After three months, their relationship started to look healthier. They started going to dinner together and on their return, the Sheikh would stay a while. Sheikh Surooha took the children out during the days and this proved to be a milestone in getting their relationship on course. Their marriage back on track, they returned shortly afterwards to Abu Dhabi.

As I drove home on my last day of working for them, I thought about my mother. I tried so many times to help her, but nothing worked. She caused me so much grief because of her drinking, promiscuity and overdoses. Of course, I still loved her and would always be there for her. I decided to pass by and see her the next day. I couldn't wait to get back home. I had missed my family. What little time I had been able to get at home was spent sleeping, bathing, or eating. There was never enough time. Various jobs kept me busy, but by now, I came to believe I was in the wrong business. This bodyguard lark wasn't all it was cracked up to be.

Chapter 42

1990

I waited patiently for Prince Ahmed Bin Salman and his wife, Princess Lamia Bint Mishall. Prince Ahmed was one of Prince Salman, the Governor of Riyadh's sons. I'd often worked with the Salman family over the years.

Prince Ahmed had recently sold his house in Wilton Crescent, Belgravia, as it was too small for him and his new wife. On this visit, they would use the Salman family home in Hill Street, Mayfair. This was one of many homes the family owned throughout the world.

As I waited, I recalled how Price Salman named his multimillion-pound super yacht after his *'first'* family's names. It was called *SHAF* and berthed in Puerto Banus. Their initials made up its name, Salman, Sultana, Sultan, Hussa, Ahmed, Abdul Aziz and Faisal. After my time with them, I thought it should be called SHAF 'TED', because of all the people they shafted along the way.

Not to be outdone, Prince Salman's younger wife, Fahda was jealous of his, *'first'* family's yacht so he bought another super yacht for her to use as well, and called this one TUEQ.

I thought too, about the times when Peter and I had carried Prince Ahmed from his car when he was out of his head on drink and drugs. How they enforced and carried out such strict and barbaric penalties against their people when the royal family carried on in such an unseemly fashion was beyond understanding to me. If he were anyone else, not a member of the royal family, they would probably have lopped off his head! At least Prince Ahmed was fortunate enough to make it into a rehabilitation clinic—many others didn't make it that far.

We had rooms in one of the houses they owned in South Street, round the corner from the main house in Hill Street. Below our rooms lived Elly and his wife, a Filipino. Elly was a waiter and general dogsbody who was meticulous and thorough when it came to his duties. He was a long-time retainer who would later be 'shafted' by the family. I got on well with Elly, although he had funny ways—like all of us, I suppose.

There was a large garage under Elly's quarters, which housed the family's limousines—Mercedes, Jaguars, and suchlike. We would while away many an hour in South Street as we waited for the principals. It was here I waited for their Highnesses to arrive.

Jack, Prince Ahmed's driver was bringing them in. I wondered why Prince Ahmed and Princess Lamia still had Jack working for them. The princess positively hated Jack. Mind you, I stood in awe the prince and princess were still together.

I wondered if the prince was sober, and if he'd recognise me. He was a close friend of Prince Mishari and knew I worked closely with him. He wouldn't want his business getting back to Mishari.

I thought it best to play at hide-and-seek, staying out of his way as much as humanly possible. I was detailed as the security backup car driver. Peter would escort the principals as their bodyguard. He went with Jack to the airport. Jack was driving a Rolls Royce. I would be in the driving seat of a high-powered BMW. This made a change for me. I could concentrate on something different and it would prove a challenge, too: Jack was a driver who showed no consideration to his backup cars.

I waited with anxiety, wondering what this visit would bring. One never knew what mental state the prince would be in. He could be positively evil at times. As I sat drinking a cup of tea, the telephone rang. It was Jack, telling me they would be arriving in about five minutes. Everyone got ready with the house staff waiting by the main entrance, while the security staff positioned themselves discreetly.

The Rolls Royce stopped outside the big imposing house. Jack and Peter jumped out and opened the doors for the bosses. They got out of the car, ignoring Jack and Peter. They made their way in to the house. Bishara, the family secretary, was the first to greet them in a suitably servile manner. Elly was next and took the attaché case Prince Ahmed was carrying. The principals went through to the drawing room. Jack stopped at the house, speaking with Bishara as

Peter and I left the static guy, Eddy, to carry on with his duties. Both Peter and I knew we would have a long wait ahead of us.

Half an hour later, we were called to the front door. We laughed as we had been conned. The luggage truck had arrived, and as usual, we had to muck in and unload.

On manhandling a trunk through the main doors, I noticed a familiar face peering round the top of the stairs. Her name was Kathi Jo. We had first met in Marbella some years earlier and we got on well. She first came to my attention one evening when I left Regine's nightclub in the Hotel Puente Romano. I was with Prince Mishari and Prince Mansour Bin Saud, when I had heard a couple of women calling out 'fucking Arabs'. As it annoyed me, I telephoned the room where I thought the abuse had come from. The two women sharing the room were Kathi Jo and Tamara, both from California. I asked if they were the ones throwing abuse at the Arabs and they laughed at me. They said they were in Marbella with an Arab family, too. They mentioned Prince Ahmed to me. I knew the prince but had never come across them before.

Kathi Jo worked for the prince and he thought highly of her, as did the princess. When she noticed me, she came down the stairs to say hello. She pointed at the boots I wore and complimented me, as they were fashionable. She asked if I still worked with Prince Mishari, as she was aware he'd retained me for some years now. She knew Prince Ahmed was aware of that fact, too. She wondered what Prince Ahmed's reaction would be if he saw me on this assignment.

I told her that while Prince Mishari was in Saudi Arabia, he gave me the green light to work for the royal family to supplement my income. Nonetheless, she and I both realised I was in a precarious position. Therefore, she conspired with me to keep me both on the assignment and in the shadows. Maybe Prince Ahmed would not have cared, but he was so unpredictable you never knew which way he would react.

Bishara told us we would stay in London for two or three days and then move on to Cambridge for a few days. We would stay at the Cambridge Garden House Hotel, which bordered the River Cam. I wondered why the secrecy, and tried to think what Cambridge could offer them. I wondered if one of them was going to enrol at the university. The prince had a degree from the University of California at Irvine, so I thought it must be the princess who was going to further her education. I couldn't have been more wrong.

Peter and I were with the prince. I was backup driver, Peter the bodyguard; Nathan and Ken were with the princess. Nathan was backup driver, Ken the bodyguard; and Eddy and Clive were on static duties.

We spent the first couple of days quietly at Hill Street with the occasional shopping outing, restaurant visit or stroll around the block. This, we guessed, was a quiet, reflective time for them. Now and again, Kathi Jo and I managed to catch up.

Then the principals made a change in the security arrangements. Peter was going with the prince and would ride in his car alongside Jack. I looked after the princess and Nathan was my backup driver. Eddy would do the static security at the hotel. Ken and Clive stood down during the Cambridge visit. It helped that I would still be able to keep out of the prince's way. It was ridiculous, but I needed the job. Anyway, it gave me the chance to catch up with Nathan. I trusted him—a trust that would later come back and bite me on the arse with plenty of venom.

Jack, Peter, and the principals were in the Rolls on the drive up to Cambridge. Nathan, Eddy, Kathi Jo and I followed in Nathan's Rover 8 series backup car. We made steady progress towards our destination. Nathan proved to be an accomplished backup driver in the underpowered car and did well to keep up with Jack. During the journey, we laughed and joked. We were sure Jack and Peter were not enjoying their journey as much, sitting bolt upright as though covered in starch. I was warned about the princess. If she turned on you, then any loyalty she had towards you disappeared in a flash. I would watch myself carefully on this job. I had to avoid the prince and had to avoid being bitten by the princess. It was getting better by the minute.

Finally, we turned into Mill Lane, which led into Granta Place and there was the hotel. Looking through the car window, I could see the river meandering past and the setting seemed idyllic. Jack had telephoned ahead to inform the hotel of our impending arrival, and the baggage carriers and concierge waited for us. For once, someone else was going to be carrying the baggage—what bliss!

The duty manager escorted the principals to their suite, and we followed like lemmings. We deposited Eddy outside the suite. We sorted ourselves out. Jack and Kathi Jo had a room each while Peter shared with Nathan and I shared with Eddy. The rooms of the hotel were well furnished and comfortable, enjoying beautiful views over the River Cam where we watched the punts drifting by. The hotel lay within its own secluded gardens and just a few minutes' walk away were the city's historic sights and universities, including the famous King's College.

Jack knocked our door and called us to meet him in the bar. This was an excellent idea, and we darted from the room and made haste along the corridor, almost bumping into two guests. On apologising, we noticed it was the comedy duo Little and Large, whom I'd often seen on television. Conducting ourselves in a more seemly fashion, we strode out purposefully towards the bar.

Now Eddy, who was on duty, did not take kindly to this turn of events. It was unfortunate that his was the static duty. Had I been doing stag duty then I would have accepted the limits it imposed on me. In fact, often I was on the unfortunate end of a static duty and just got on with it. But Eddy was a pain in the backside. It was a shame one of the other more settled guys had not accompanied us; it would have made life a lot more bearable. After a couple of drinks, we settled at a table in the restaurant, making small talk as we studied the menu. There was no doubt that Ahmed's personal secretary, Kathi Jo, was close to them. She got on famously with them. The Arab men working for the principals did not like her. They were jealous of her. I think it had everything to do with their culture and upbringing and the inherent insecurity that's inbred.

Even though Eddy could stand down at six o'clock in the evening, he was still not happy. His hours had dropped significantly and we relieved him often, but he thought he was missing something. Even though we had a fair amount of free time, we were still tied to the hotel in case the principals decided to venture out.

The following morning we were called to get ready. Peter and I escorted the principals from their suite, although I stood well back out of detection range. I sensed they were very tense. Peter was aware that I was staying in the background.

We strode down the corridor in convoy towards the waiting cars. Both principals got into the Rolls Royce and Jack and Peter followed them.

Stepping back to our car, I noticed Nathan already inside. As I jumped in, we sped off, catching up quickly to plant ourselves behind the lead car. Jack made off at speed without any consideration of poor old Nathan, who was trying to solidify himself to their car. It would have been helpful to have some idea where we were going, but no; no one bothered to convey such a helpful message to us.

We moved away from the university area. It now became a magical mystery tour to me. Looking at the road signs, I noticed a place called Bourn kept cropping up. Why Bourn would be so special to them, I had no idea. Driving at a fair pace, we soon arrived at the High Street.

The Rolls Royce slowly drifted to a halt, by which time I had already decamped and was alongside the princess' door. No one moved in the car, as they were deep in conversation. Jack and Peter remained rigid in their seats. I wondered what the discussion was about, but Kathi Jo striding up towards us caught my attention. She gave a look which asked me what was going on. I shrugged, as I had no idea. We waited patiently as I looked over towards the building. A sign caught my eye, which read Bourn Hall Clinic.

I was still none the wiser, apart from realising that we were here on some medical mission now and not an educational one. I thought last-minute nerves brought on the discussion. Not that it was any of my business; I did wonder what the problem was and why it couldn't be sorted out in London.

What had all the secrecy been about? What was so special about this place? Would I find out or would I have to rush back to the backup car if the principals decided on a quick exit?

Eventually the car door opened slightly, and I stood back as Jack got out and opened the door for the princess. Peter opened the prince's door as he too stepped out. We walked up the pathway toward the main entrance.

Television cameras were set up in the entrance and they sent the principals into a panic. We steered them away and into another room, away from prying eyes. After assurances the cameras were nothing to do with their visit, they relaxed. As they waited, I went over to ask the camera operators what they were filming. They were making a documentary on this pioneering clinic, which they revealed specialises in IVF (In Vitro Fertilisation) treatment. The secret was out—the principals were here for help in producing a child. The prince suffered from a low sperm count. I considered what the attitudes of the Muslim world towards IVF treatment might be. I'm sure there would have been a loss of face for the prince if it were known he couldn't father a child naturally. In Arab society, children are a man's claim to pride, honour, and standing.

The princess would not stop having children until she produced a boy and it proved fortuitous for her that she did. We spent the next week or so in Cambridge as the couple underwent tests and procedures, all in the hope of conceiving. The doctor, Patrick Steptoe, took care of the principals and he was attentive of them.

Back at the hotel, I wandered down to the main town and watched the students as they rode by on their bicycles en masse. I thought how privileged they were to be able to attend such universities and marvelled at the students when they went punting down the River Cam. Something seemed romantic and exciting about learning in such an environment to me. When all the tests and treatment had been concluded, we set off for London. So much tension was released from of our charges. I hoped that this would allow them to relax a little more once we descended on Hill Street.

That evening we went to the Haymarket to see Sir Andrew Lloyd Webber's stage play *Phantom of the Opera*. I wasn't sure if I would appreciate the play, but then again, I had no business in even having an interest in it. As it was, it was taken out of my hands as they were a ticket short and I was the unfortunate one who missed out. I still wonder what I missed, but that's the way it pans out sometimes.

While waiting for the principals to enter the theatre, I stood on the corner watching. A metallic blue Mercedes 560 SEL drove up and as it manoeuvred the corner, I noticed the driver as the window was down. He looked straight at me and I could tell he knew I had recognised him. It was Frank Bruno, the British heavyweight boxer. He drove down Jermyn Street and I continued watching. Shortly afterwards the Mercedes approached again. The window was still down and Frank Bruno looked at me again, but this time he nodded his head slightly. I waited now, thinking he would pass again. He made it to two rounds, but he never made it to round three. Later, I noticed his car outside Tramp, the nightclub in Jermyn Street. He had obviously been looking for a parking space and had found it during round two.

Once the principals were inside, Jack suggested we go back to the apartment. As there was nothing else I could do, I agreed. On the way, Jack booked up a table for us at the Wembley dog stadium for the following week. The prince loved gambling—so did Jack and Peter. The prince's first love was his racehorses. He was fanatical about them as well as the whole horseracing scene. He loved his horses more than his wife. The prince always took care of Jack, and in turn, Jack was like a surrogate father to the prince.

Soon we were on our way back to the theatre. When they emerged, their faces sparkled with excitement. They said the show was magnificent, yet I still wondered if it would be a show that would impress me. There was no more time to think about it as we ushered the principals to the waiting cars. Our only concern now was getting them back to Hill Street safely.

Chapter 43

Funding fundamentalists?

The following day it was business as usual with the compulsory shopping trip. We were aware this visit was ending soon and as much shopping as was humanly possible had to be done before departure. That day we hit Oxford Street, Bond Street and all the major shopping areas of the West End of London. I knew the princess was careful with money before her marriage, but now she spent money like it was going out of fashion—the prince's money. She reminded me a lot of Prince Mishari's wife, Princess al-Anud, who also happened to be her best friend. Their spending habits were similar.

Later, Bishara called me to see him. He told me to go to Lloyds Bank in Berkeley Square to collect £385,000 in cash ($500,000). The Bank knew I was coming and all I had to do was sign for a holdall containing the cash. This was unusual, but I had no problem carrying it out. I collected the cash. I knew Bishara had lied to me. I gave Prince Ahmed the money and he passed it to Abdul Wahab, the 'mad mullah', as we called him. Prince Ahmed financed Muslim fundamentalists, who were later branded terrorists.

That evening Nathan went out clubbing with Peter. He brought in his Mercedes sports car, which he had up for sale at £14,000. As nice as it was, none of us had the money to buy it. The following day Nathan brought in another car, a Jaguar XJS, which he was selling for £10,000. No one bit on that car, either. Nathan told us he bought and sold cars on the side to supplement his income. We believed him.

As darkness fell the principals descended the stairs ready for an evening at the dog racing. We had a large table set out for us at Wembley and the prince gave everyone £50 to bet on the dogs. He had still not noticed me, and I continued to blend into the background. I soon lost the money the prince gave me. I've never been a gambler and the loss of the money proved the point of why I had not become one. Jack gambled every day and so did the prince. Many times, Peter was the bookie's runner. The bookie's shop in Park Lane loved it when the prince visited, as their takings escalated dramatically. Considering the Saudi royals never gamble, they did ever so well out of this one. Peter would sit with £50,000 in his pocket and wait for the prince to call. He would be told to put £5000 on this horse, £10,000 on another one and so it went. When he ran out of money, he would go back to the house and receive another top up. Then it would all start again.

We had a day or so left of the visit and I wondered if I were going to pull off my illusion of being invisible to the prince. It wasn't going to be too long before I found out as the evening drew towards a close.

As we walked to the lifts, I held back. However, as the prince entered the lift and spun round to face the open door, I caught his eye. For a millisecond, I was sure there was a flicker of acknowledgement but hoped I was wrong.

After the night out we deposited the principals safely at home. As I went to go back to our quarters, I heard a voice calling me back. It was Kathi Jo and she told me I had been rumbled, the prince had recognised me. The prince got into his car and said to Jack, "That's Mark who's with Mishari." The princess had asked Kathi Jo if she knew I was there and she had said yes she knew. I thanked her for the warning and walked away wondering if there would be any fallout.

It was obvious, they would wonder if I would mention their IVF treatment to Prince Mishari. Therefore, I expected them to ask for assurances that I would keep this information to myself. I waited with bated breath for my summons, but it never came. The principals left London without acknowledging me in any way. Perhaps they thought it best to bury their heads in the sand and pretend nothing had happened. Whatever the case, they had five children over the next few years. One boy and four girls, all by IVF and delivered by caesarean section conducted in New York, as the treatment in Cambridge proved unsuccessful.

* * *

Controversy followed the family in the coming years, as Prince Ahmed was linked with his father and others to the Al Qaeda terrorist network. Two books linked Prince Ahmed to Al Qaeda, the terror group. This of course reminded me of the unusual cash donation which was made to Abdul Wahab, the 'mad mullah'. It was well known by many connected to the family that an agreement was reached between the Saudi royal family and Osama Bin Laden. This agreement provided him with secret funds so long as he refrained from promoting attacks within the kingdom. We saw this as no different from the protection rackets, which are run throughout the world. Others saw it differently claiming that the Saudi's (including Prince Ahmed) financed terrorists.

The author of one of those books, Gerald Posner, judged that the Saudis had effectively had Osama Bin Laden on their payroll since the start of the decade. I believe he is correct. He also made an assumption that Prince Ahmed was murdered because of his 'terrorist' connections. However, I knew that Prince Ahmed had been in hospital undergoing liposuction surgery, as he had become despondent over his weight gain. He had been idle after the surgery, defying the doctor's advice to move around to aid his recovery. When he made the effort to say goodbye to his brother Prince Faisal after his visit, he collapsed with a heart attack. Both Prince Faisal and Prince Ahmed's American security guy, Howard Brown, (HB) were with the prince.

My belief is his death may have been the catalyst for the sudden deaths of two other Saudi princes alleged to have been involved with Al Qaeda. They were Prince Sultan Bin Faisal Bin Turki Al Saud and Prince Fahd Bin Turki Bin Saud Al Kabir. A few months later, the Pakistani official caught up in the allegations also died, although in an aircraft crash, which nicely tidied up the loose ends.

Later, Prince Ahmed's widow, Princess Lamia Bint Mishall Bin Saud made a statement against Gerald Posner's assertions. Contained within her statement were the following words:

> Prince Ahmed was an honest, kind and generous
> person who was loved by many people in both the

United States and Saudi Arabia . . . He strived to live a life of sincerity and decency, ideals our family has always cherished and lives by. Mr. Posner does Ahmed a great injustice. He cannot appreciate and apparently does not care about the pain he has inflicted on Prince Ahmed's family. "We believe that decent people everywhere will see through this deceit and that justice will be served. Honesty and decency demand that, for the sake of our five small children and the rest of his family, as well as his many friends in the United States and elsewhere, these false accusations be addressed by Mr. Posner.

"We will, God willing, always remain committed to protect Ahmed's good name and carry forward his bright legacy. We will not allow his reputation and a lifetime of good work to be tarnished by sensationalism or outlandish lies such as those of Mr. Posner."

When I read her statement, I had a different take on it: I knew Prince Ahmed well. I found him dishonest, unkind and mean. His life of supposed sincerity and decency was a life I saw to be anything but. He was a drug addicted alcoholic gambler who slept around and did evil many times. The princess says that Posner does not care about the pain inflicted on Prince Ahmed's family. Did the prince worry about the pain he inflicted on his wife, when he had her in tears every day of their two month honeymoon?

The princess says that "He strived to live a life of sincerity and decency, ideals our family has always cherished and lives by."

But does she consider the pain she inflicted on Prince Ahmed's retainers by laying them off, often owing them large amounts of back pay? In particular, Howard Brown, who was with the prince when he died and who is now suing her for back pay? And Elly, a retainer of twenty years, whom she took through the courts to evict from the apartment he lived in? Elly, the prince's valet-waiter-retainer of twenty years so-called crime was that he tried to warn

Prince Ahmed about a swindle taking place on the insurance on his racehorses. The prince responded by sacking him and denying him the back pay, he was owed. Princess Lamia followed through on Elly's eviction after Prince Ahmed's death.

Given my knowledge of Princess Lamia, I find her comments rather unseemly especially in the context of certain events I recall. A couple of incidents which come to mind concern Jack Rusbridge. He was a retainer of the family for thirty-two years. When he saw Princess Lamia after Prince Ahmed's death and passed her some photos of his grandchild, she did not even have the decency to look at them and passed them back immediately, snubbing him in the process. She went on further with her assault on Jack when she found out that he had been deposited in a house by Prince Ahmed that the prince had bought for him. When she had it checked out she found it was still held in one of the several companies the prince owned. Princess Lamia had a secretary by the name of Khadija, telephone Jack saying that they wanted the house back and gave him notice to leave. Jack, by now seventy-two years old, got cancer through the shock and worry and died not too long afterwards.

And can Princess Lamia explain why she snubs her late husband's family? When Prince Abdul Aziz and his wife entered the Lainsborough Hotel in London, Lamia noticed them, got up, and walked out, ignoring them in the process.

In addition, although Princess Lamia is in fact a Saudi royal princess, she is in my opinion a Queen of double standards and hypocrisy who also carries a ruthless streak. Princess Lamia, it should be said, loves to gamble in Las Vegas; she loves the slot machines. When she wins significant amounts, to avoid paying tax on the winnings she gets her English security guy to sign for them. This way she benefits from the cross-country agreement that allows the Americans and the English to keep any winnings they have free of tax. I wonder if this would be deemed criminal behaviour–defrauding the American government and their taxpayers?

She says Posner does Prince Ahmed an injustice. Well, her husband the prince did me an injustice by denying me justice, when he refused two of his retainers to give evidence in court on my behalf. He even threatened them with the sack and eviction from their tied homes if they did so. Kathi Jo, another retainer of 15 years was owed $50,000 in back pay and a promised gift. Prince Ahmed's secretary Bishara made her an offer of $25,000 and wanted her to sign a privacy clause. Kathi Jo's comments were "Are you kidding ME? You bastards have all the money in the world and you want to cheat me!" Finally, Princess Lamia's response to a falling out with her friends of many years, Princes al-Anud Bint Fahd and Princess Nouf Bint Fahd, was to cut up their photographs and throw them in the bin. This all comes from a princess who says her family ideals are of sincerity, honesty and decency. I think not.

Within the space of a year, two of Prince Salman's sons were dead. The first, Prince Fahd Bin Salman died at 46 years of age in Riyadh on the 25th July 2001. His death was attributed to a heart attack. However, it appears Prince Fahd took his own life while suffering from depression brought about by family issues that he was unable to resolve. The second son, Prince Ahmed Bin Salman died at 43-years-old on the 22nd July 2002. He suffered a heart attack after undergoing liposuction cosmetic surgery.

Chapter 44

Madame Sara and the Gulf War: 1990 to 1991

As the end of 1990 loomed, I considered starting my own security business and discussed plans with friends, including a Special Branch police officer. There were unsavoury characters in the security business and I thought it best to hide my intentions from them. I spoke to one of my most trusted team members; he suggested I open a company but that I should also use a false name to hide my identity. His advice made sense at the time. Meanwhile, a client I worked with a few times before arrived in London.

I'd first worked for Madame Sara when she was diagnosed with cancer and had come to London for treatment. She was now clear of the disease. I got on well with her and her family. The Embassy arranged for her and the children to stay in a large apartment in Kingston House South, Ennismore Gardens.

I shouldn't have taken the job, as I suffered a depressive bout. My mood dropped significantly and was a concern to those around me. My doctor prescribed medication, but it didn't help. If anything, it made me feel drunk and woozy. It caused me to forget things, which happened only hours before. I later found out this drug was often used in date rape incidents. Of course, I thought I was able to function normally. Luckily, the job I took on only involved static duties.

During one of my night shifts, I received a call from Nathan—a team member I'd worked with previously. I liked him a lot, trusted him completely, and always felt he watched my back.

"Mark," Nathan said, "Are you still starting up on your own?"

"Yes, I am. I don't know how much longer I can handle working on the circuit myself. Why do you ask?"

"Well, you'll need a bank account, right?"

"Yeah, I guess so, why?" I replied

"Well, I've got some documents, which you can use to get started. Give me your address and I will send them to you."

"All right, mate," I said. A day or so later they arrived. I signed them and foolishly opened a bank account with them.

My intent was always to use the account honourably. I was pleased to have the account opened. Within a few days, a chequebook and paying in book arrived. I deposited a £1000 of my money, and carried on working at Kingston House South.

The hours took their toll on me and I felt tired all the time. I continued my medication and tried to carry on. I didn't know I was on meltdown. Sue tried to get me to pull off the job, but I wouldn't. I muddled through, thinking I knew best.

Christmas came and went, and I carried on. I became increasingly drained. My mood got lower, but I persevered. Over the Christmas period, there was much talk about the impending Gulf War. Iraq was given a deadline to leave Kuwait and the West waited for Sadaam's response. A few weeks after opening my account, around the 9th January 1991, I started hearing from Nathan more often. At around midnight on the 16th January 1991, the air war started against Iraq. I watched the scenes unfold on the TV in the lounge in Madame Sara's apartment.

I walked down the hallway and called one of the Filipino maids. I told her to let Madame Sara know the war had begun. Minutes later, everyone apart from the children sat in front of the TV. Concern was etched on their faces. I, on the other hand, was high on medication.

The war raged on the following day, and so did my depression, although I still wouldn't give in to it. The next few nights were consumed with Madame Sara and the rest of us at Kingston House South watching the live news reports on the Gulf War.

On the 24th January, Nathan called me again. He told me he'd sold his car, the blue Rover 800 he used on the Cambridge job. He asked if he could pay the cheque into the account I had opened, as he didn't have one of his own.

"Of course, Nathan," I said, thinking I owed him a favour anyway. I thought no more about it. He said the cheque was for £5000, which sounded about right for what I thought the car was worth. I never felt uncomfortable about this transaction and trusted Nathan implicitly.

On the 26th January, Madame Sara and her family suddenly shipped out.

I went home. All I did was sleep. I put it down to the night shifts catching up with me. For the next few days, I caught up on my sleep and settled back into family life. Everything, I thought, was going fine. My family did not think it was, and they would soon be proven right.

* * *

On the 29th January, I went to the garage. The mechanic was a friend I had known for years. When I arrived, he told me Nathan had phoned for to me. I was surprised and wondered how he had the number, so I called home. Sue told me he had phoned there and she had given him the mechanic's number. I called Nathan from the garage.

"Hi Nathan, how's it going?" I asked.

"Yeah, fine, and you?"

"All right, mate. My wife said you called—what can I do for you?" I asked.

"Mark, have you called to see if the cheque has cleared yet?"

"No, not yet, I'll give them a ring and get back to you."

"Yeah, that'll be fine, thanks Mark."

"No worries, I'll speak to you soon."

"Hey, Tony," I said to the mechanic, "Can I call my bank?"

"Sure," he replied.

I called the bank and asked if the cheque had cleared. It had, so I asked for the balance on the account. The cheque totalled around £35,700! Stunned, I asked the balance again. "That's cleared funds, is it?" I asked.

"Yes, sir," the bank officer replied.

I hung up the phone. What the fuck is going on? I was so surprised; I even mentioned it to Tony. Normally, I kept things like this close to my chest, but I couldn't help myself.

"I need to call Nathan, is that all right?" I asked.

"Sure,"

I rang him and as he picked up the phone, I shouted at him. "What the fuck's going on? They say there is thirty-five odd thousand pounds in the account!"

"Has it cleared?" Nathan asked.

"Has it cleared? Has it cleared?" I was amazed. "Who gives a fuck whether it's cleared? What's it doing in there?" I asked.

"Well, Mark, you know I had three cars, well, I managed to sell all of them. That's what I got for them. I didn't think you would mind me paying it in, after all it will make your account look good for your business, won't it?"

I knew Nathan had the cars and the figure deposited would represent the rough value of the cheque. After an angry exchange, he managed to calm me down and convince me that everything was fine. As the bank cleared the funds, I believed what I was told. Nathan asked me to collect £11,000 from the bank, which I agreed to do.

"Hey Tony, what a cheeky fuck, I guess you heard all that?"

"Yeah, what's going on?"

I told him.

"At least you know it's all right because the bank's cleared it," Tony said.

"Maybe so, but what a bloody cheek, he wants me to collect £11,000 and meet with him. What a nerve," I joked. "Can I call the bank again, Tony?"

"Sure, feel free."

I called the bank and arranged to collect the money. Later that day, I met Nathan and gave him his money. A colleague, Elly, witnessed the meeting.

On the 30th January, Nathan asked if I would collect another £15,000. I was fucked off with him now, but still trusted him implicitly. I just thought he was taking the piss, that's all. I called the bank and arranged to collect the money.

I told Sue what was going on, and she begged me not to go. She said she could 'feel' something wasn't right. I ignored her. I went to the bank. The manager asked to see me. As I sat in his office, three men entered. One was another bank official; the other two were

Criminal Investigation Department Police Officers. I was told the cheque had been stolen! I nearly fell off the fucking chair!

"Hold on a minute," I said, "I don't know anything about a stolen cheque. In fact, the money belongs to a friend of mine." I gave them his name and said I was going to meet him. I suggested they come with me and they could question him about it. They declined and I was arrested! After keeping me in the police cells for thirty-six hours, I was released on police bail pending further enquiries.

* * *

I co-operated fully with the police, and they later arrested Nathan and his uncle. They were lucky to find him, as I couldn't get hold of him for love nor money. He had done a disappearing act on me. Once the police had completed their investigations, formal charges were laid against all three of us. After attending Magistrates Court, Nathan's uncle had his charges dropped on a technicality. Nathan's and mine still stood, though, and we were bailed pending trial.

What upset me most was when the officer in charge of the case approached me and Sue and said that they knew I had not been criminal but just foolish. However, he continued the only way they could get Nathan was through me! Oh, that was all right then, was it? On top of this, I received a phone call telling me one of my brothers had been diagnosed with cancer and had six weeks to live. My mother was poorly, and I was going through a major mind fuck. I prayed everything would be all right and knew justice would prevail.

As a result, I was a walking zombie when the next call came through for an assignment. Sue pleaded with me not to take it. It was no use; I wasn't listening to anyone. How I managed to work, let alone convince others I was in a capable state, I'll never know. I was a robot on autopilot when Prince Mashour Bin Abdul Aziz became my next charge, in Bishops Avenue, North London.

As I drove down Bishops Avenue, on the 14th February, I passed one of King Fahd's houses, Kenstead Hall, which he'd bought from Ravi Tikoo, the shipping magnate, for £3 million. The King spent another £30 million refurbishing it. I had worked there for King

Fahd twice before, once when he stopped by for a couple of days before his state visit to the USA and then again on his state visit to the UK in 1987.

When I got to the house, they asked me in and Jimmy introduced me to the prince. Why he had chosen to use the name Jimmy escaped me. Prince Mashour was visiting with his wife. I should have known this job was too good to be true, and of course, it was. Everything in my life was fucked up—except my marriage: Sue supported me fully. I should have listened to her. I was a prat.

Jimmy told me the prince wanted me to sit in the driveway in my car, keep watch on the house, and patrol the garden area every so often. It was March and freezing. So this wasn't a bodyguard assignment? I had mixed feelings. I needed the money, but I didn't want the job. I said if I stayed out all night I was liable to freeze to death! He spoke with the prince, who said that once he retired for the night I could come into the house. I could also get a hot water bottle to help keep me warm should I need it. How considerate.

"This is crazy," I thought. "Why it is when you need to get some money together, a crap job comes along?" As it turned out, apart from the intense cold, it was the best job I could have had at the time. All I had to do was sit there, and because of that, I managed to pull it off even in my fragile state.

After the first night, I saw what I was facing. Sue bought me thermal underwear, socks, and gloves to help keep me warm. Often Martini visited, presumably to see if the prince was all right.

Throughout the night, I patrolled the grounds and perimeter. I did jumping jacks, jogging on the spot, and anything else I could think of to try to produce some body warmth. In truth, as my moods swung higher, I became hyperactive and couldn't sit still. At any other time, if I had been in a different frame of mind, I would have chucked the job in.

I never once saw the prince again in the time that he stayed. I found it strange when Jimmy said the prince liked me and wanted to use me again when he came back to England! I couldn't wait for the job to end. I thought it would take me six months just to thaw out. But if I thought that was cold, I was in for a rude awakening.

It was a cold time of year and I hadn't expected to see another Arab for at least a couple of months. No such luck. Maybe I was being punished for something, as another assignment came in. My life was falling apart, and yet I still carried on. As I answered the phone, I was told Prince Saud Bin Naifs' mother, Princess Jauhara, (the wife of the Interior Minister) was on her way through the VIP suite at Heathrow. It was now March of 1991, and the princess would be staying at her home in Totteridge, North London. This was going to be a big affair with half a dozen drivers and a dozen bodyguards. There were four cleaners, a butler, and a housekeeper. The house was large and had extensive grounds with a summerhouse and swimming pool. The arrangements were all co-ordinated through Princess Jauhara's son and Prince Mohammed Bin Fahd's London office, Al Bilad (UK). The person responsible for making sure the visit ran smoothly was Jonathan Aitken—the MP Prince Saud had 'in his pocket' according to a conversation I'd overheard in Cleve Lodge. I accepted the job against Sue's advice, as usual.

On the first evening, Jonathan Aitken showed off the new Jaguar motor car Prince Mohammed had bought him. We were told not to mention it to outsiders.

All the guys knew Jonathan Aitken was a notorious ladies man. One of his conquests was Carol Thatcher, and when Aitken dumped her, this upset her mother, Margaret Thatcher, the former British Prime Minister. She stuffed Aitken because of it.

Apart from the bodyguards, the rest of us had to perform patrolling duties. This house was large and had once been the property of an old English actor named Jack Hawkins. I would be working on the night shift and doing a static duty. Boy was I pissed off about that, but in fact, it turned out to be very fortunate for me as it kept me out of the way.

Totteridge is on top of a hill in North London and because of this it was even colder than the previous job. I can safely say I had never been so cold, either before or since. One of the guys on with me, Cameron, was a good friend who served in the Military Police Special Investigations Branch, and he secured balaclavas for us. We wore thermals and plenty layers of warm clothing. I tucked a hot water bottle up inside my coat and on to my chest. I also wore Wellington boots to keep my feet dry from the dew and frost on the grass.

After the princess and her entourage had eaten, the housekeeper would call us to eat. We went through to the dining room two at a time. The principals ate first and then we had the leftovers. This caused unrest among the new guys, as they did not understand this was the Saudi royals' custom. There was always plenty to eat and the food was good. The Portuguese housekeeper Jose and his wife Maria went out of their way to make our shifts as pleasant as possible for us.

A couple of days before this job, I buried my mother after a long illness, so it was an emotional time for me. I spent a lot of time during my patrolling talking to her and used the time to say many of the things I felt I wanted and needed to say. This helped me with her death—it also helped distract my mind from the intense cold and other problems that I was facing.

One particular evening as I patrolled, a Mini motorcar caught my attention in the garage block. This Mini, a Margrave, was commissioned especially for Prince Saud. The bodywork was finished in Rolls Royce Caribbean Blue and it had electric windows, an electric glass sunroof, and special deep-buttoned navy blue velour seats. The headrests on the seats had built in radio speakers. Although it sounds over the top, it was a nice car.

After a few days, a small caravan was placed on site for us to use and electricity was connected to it. This was like heaven. We were able to make hot drinks to help ward off the cold and could refill our water bottles more often. I would look at the house and wonder if the princess or other occupants even gave a thought to us being out in such severe conditions.

Until the caravan arrived, our only source of heat other than the water bottles had been an extractor fan at the back of the house that blew out warm air now and again. We took turns standing by it. What a sad state of affairs that was.

We had a couple of electric heaters installed in the caravan as soon as we could. We worked out a system of two guys in the caravan, two patrolling the front of the house, and two patrolling the rear, and every hour we would change about. I was taking whatever work I could get, be it static or mobile. The cold got into my bones and even after a few hours of finishing my shift, it was still impossible to shake it off.

Each evening Jonathan Aitken visited in his shiny new Jaguar to make sure the princess was happy and then he'd be on his way again. During the days, the princess went shopping in London and once there, didn't return until the shops closed.

The guys with her paid particular attention to pickpockets, as the South American teams were over and on the prowl. This was unusual for the time of year. They usually favoured the summertime when there were more tourists about. They roamed in packs, which made the job more difficult; you needed someone watching your back.

We had a surprise development one day when Princess Jauhara went shoe shopping in town and took only one bodyguard, Derek Pringle, with her. This guy was an ex-policeman who had a drink problem. Perhaps he had mixed too much with the Saudis!

Princess Jauhara was in a shop when Derek decided to have a smoke and he went outside—a stupid thing to do, and inexcusable.

The princess spent ages in the shop, then finished and left. Having his smoke outside, Derek didn't notice her leave. After finishing his cigarette, he went back into the shop to take up position again. Inside, he realised the princess was gone and panicked. He called for backup and the search began. Princess Jauhara was furious her bodyguard had gone missing. Nonetheless, she kept calm and continued checking out the shoe shops.

The team arrived and deployed. The princess was sighted and picked up within a matter of minutes. She dismissed Derek and had another bodyguard take his place. Once the princess got home, the shit hit the fan. Her secretary called in Martini and Jonathan Aitken. They wanted a breakdown of the afternoon's fiasco. Bill was summoned and told he may lose the contract. It was clear should another incident occur heads would roll. As Martini was, in reality, our boss, he wouldn't lose out. Being shrewd, he had a front man, Bill, handling the day-to-day running of the security. All he would have to do was change him.

Chapter 45

After the Gulf War: 1991

Over the coming months, I muddled through as I waited for the trial date. I was confident the truth would emerge and that I would walk out of Court a free man, without so much as a stain on my character. For the moment, I kept watch on the Saudi royal family and was amused to hear that General Prince Khalid Bin Sultan was under the illusion he had won the Gulf War on his own. He upset his family with his holier-than-thou attitude. His family also brought him to book over his indiscretion in questioning the King.

Another indiscretion by Prince Khalid soon followed—this time with a Hollywood star. This was the big-busted, tall and blonde Hollywood actor, Brigitte Nielsen. She left Europe to seek stardom in America and found it. She married Sylvester Stallone, the star of the *Rambo* movies. Prince Khalid became infatuated with her and it was alleged he offered her $1 million to sleep with him. A painting of her and her naked assets hung above the prince's bed. An English Sunday newspaper found out and printed an article about them. The article displeased the Saudi royal family intensely. This was another hypocritical attitude of those in power, who themselves, as I knew, were just as bad, if not worse, than Prince Khalid.

Every prince I met proved to be vain. Some had hairdressers and masseurs that travelled the world with them. Every day, the hairdressers would coiffure the prince or princess' hair. The masseurs massaged the princes, and probably massaged their egos as well.

The King and his full brothers from Hussa Sudeiri looked after their own, and invariably the good government positions went to them and their sons. In my opinion, nepotism reigned supreme with the King in Saudi Arabia. This caused a great deal of unrest and dissent in ordinary Saudis, and there was a major problem with Shi'ite Muslim factions in the eastern province. These factions were kept under a tight rein, but some rebelled and suffered severely for it.

Sometimes significant events occurred while I travelled with the royal family. Two such incidents concerned the Hajj in Mecca. One occurred in 1988 and the other in 1989. In the first incident, a riot in Mecca caused many deaths. Thousands of Iranians rioted after the repulsive treatment they received from the Saudi authorities. The police fired on the rioters, killing around four hundred and wounding around another six hundred.

Another incident was at the Hajj religious festival in Mecca the following year. Stupidity and recklessness by the Saudi authorities resulted in a problem occurring in a tunnel. This caused a stampede that killed around four thousand people—again mainly Iranians. A prince I was with immediately received information about the incidents. As I was aware of their significance, I passed the information on to the Special Branch. They found it hard to believe at first because of the sheer number of casualties and people killed. The Saudi authorities put news blackouts into effect immediately. The Al Saud family tried to keep the news from the world, fearing the incident may be the start of a revolution.

The Saudi royals ran riot. Alcohol, drugs, boys, and girls were just some of the things they abused—apart from themselves, that is. The younger the child sexually abused the better, they thought.

Many princesses paid for sex, and even more had sex with their servants. Many princes were gay, and several princesses were lesbians. The things they got up to were available in Saudi, too; however, they were more discreet about them there. Some years ago, Prince Mishari Bin Abdul Aziz, one of the King's brothers, who died in 2000, suffered imprisonment after shooting dead the British Consul in Jeddah, Saudi Arabia. The British Consul, Cyril Ousman, would not give the prince any more whiskey to drink. There was talk of the Consul messing around with the prince's wife; either way, the prince killed the Consul. The King paid the British Consul's widow seventy thousand pounds in blood money. Prince Mishari, instead of losing his head like any other murderer, went to prison instead. The Saudi royals released the prince after a few months—no surprises there! The British Government chose to let the prince off and looked the other way, even taking a dim view towards any journalists that tried to research the killing.

The King paid for a palace to be built for the prince, maybe as a reward, and gave him the money to pay the contractors, the Al Fayez group. The prince promptly stole the money. After the father, the head of the Al Fayez family, died, one of his sons went to petition the King to ask for payment. The King paid the money. No action was taken against the prince.

Another of the King's brothers, Prince Nasser Bin Abdul Aziz, distilled his own alcohol, and when he served it to four visitors it killed them. Despite this, his son, Prince Turki Bin Nasser, later went on to receive millions from BAE systems.

When I visited Saudi Arabia, I found whiskey and drugs freely available, for those who knew where to get them. The cost of a bottle of whiskey was $100.

To get an idea of the Saudi mentality, one only has to look at the beginning of King Abdul Aziz's reign. One prince confided to me that the King had several hundred virgins and was in the habit of deflowering young girls and giving them away as presents. Servants suffered sexual abuse and beatings regularly, and unfortunately, I witnessed some of the brutality the Saudi royals dished out. Amnesty International recorded an incident of one prince whose servant worked eighteen hours a day and then suffered beatings from him. Many foreign servants committed suicide because they couldn't escape the royal family.

King Saud Bin Abdul Aziz had young boys supplied to him by the CIA. The Saudis eventually sent the King into exile, and in one month in Athens, he spent $10 million. There was never a shortage of money for the major Princes, and their corruption knew no bounds. One of my charges, Prince Faisal Bin Fahd (now deceased), murdered his male lover.

Because of the things I saw, I seriously considered giving up working with the Saudis. I didn't think I could take much more of them. It was my choice—go or stay. Events soon took overtook my decision.

* * *

The Trial and Beyond: 1992

During the trial, I took thirty to forty diazepam tablets a day. Nathan Thompson put the blame on me. I told the truth. The police lied under oath.

Of the eight witnesses I was relying on to give evidence on my behalf, only one arrived at court. Two principal witnesses worked in Sardinia with Prince Ahmed Bin Salman. They were refused permission to come back and give evidence on my behalf. They were under threat of being sacked and losing their tied homes. Another witness was living in Cyprus and didn't receive notice of the trial until after it was finished. And a Special Branch police officer's superiors refused him permission to give evidence for me. Whatever could go wrong did go wrong. I was mentally destroyed by it all.

On the 23rd July 1992, Nathan and I stood as the jury foreman handed out the verdicts. They had been out twenty-five minutes. Nathan was found guilty of theft, attempted theft, using a false instrument with intent, and handling stolen goods. The jury couldn't reach a verdict on me, so were sent out for further deliberation.

Three times they came back without a decision. One juror had left the trial, claiming to be sick. Finally, the verdict was in. A majority verdict of ten to one found me guilty of theft and attempted theft.

Nathan and I were sentenced to six months imprisonment. I was so high on my medication; it wouldn't have mattered to me at the time if I had been sentenced to sixty years. I was out of it.

On the 7th August 1992, I was taken to the medical wing of the prison: my system had crashed from coming off the diazepam. I was transferred to a hospital near my home. While Nathan went through the prison system, I went through the hospital system. My wife and boys visited me daily, as did my friends. I had the freedom to wander anywhere I wished on the hospital grounds, and that was where I stayed until the end of my sentence.

My belief in British justice was shattered forever. My belief in the police force was shattered, too. I learnt a tough lesson. I've never claimed to be an angel, but what had happened to me was undeserved. I slipped in to a deep depression with thoughts of suicide haunting me.

* * *

When I got home, I spent time appreciating what I had. Slowly, I began to feel like my old self-again. Then I received a phone call that would get me back on my feet. The ruling family of the UAE had been having trouble with vandals at a property they owned not far from where I lived. I was asked to take a look and see if I could sort it out.

As their property was empty and no one else would be involved on the job, I took it on. I reasoned I could use the time to convalesce. I would not have to deal with any Arabs or face the stresses of my usual work, so it seemed perfect for me.

Therefore, I made my way to the Sheikh's empty house near Reading in Berkshire. I was told I would only be needed for two or three weeks. By this time, I'd decided this would be my last Arab job.

The house sat on an island surrounded by a river. The grounds stretched for thirty-two acres and a run-down cottage and outbuildings adjoined another part of the river. When I first went into the property, I could see signs of vandalism. There were smashed doors and windows, and broken glass littered the ground.

Two weeks came and went, and I was still there. I dealt with lots of fishermen and a few vandals who entered the property. Sue and my boys would come and visit, and we had barbecues by the river. Overall, it was idyllic and peaceful, just what I needed. Weeks went by, and then months. I was told the Sheikh had put the house on the market and I would stay there until it sold. As the house and outbuildings would need substantial refurbishment, I hoped it would take some time before it would sell. Life progressed. I still couldn't get my head around the court case and resulting events that enveloped me and haunted me.

* * *

One dismal grey morning, on 26th April, a brown envelope came through my front door. It contained an affidavit from the bank's solicitors. They were claiming back from me the money Nathan had stolen, with interest.

I went to see my lawyers to file a defence and counterclaim. Just when I thought life was getting a little better, the Court case had come back and bitten me on the backside. We filled out their form, stating:

> I dispute the claim because it arises out of the payment by the Plaintiff of a cheque, which was later found to be a forgery. The payment was made by the Plaintiff to me by way of a credit to my account with the Plaintiff. After seeking an assurance from the Plaintiff that the funds had cleared, I drew against them in favour of a third party. When the Plaintiff notified me that the cheque paid into my account was a forgery it was too late for me to retrieve the funds from the third party. I thereby incurred a loss equivalent to the Plaintiff's claim by reason of the Plaintiff's negligence and breach of contract.

I counterclaimed against them for the full amount they were seeking from me. My claim read:

> I wish to counterclaim against the plaintiff the equivalent of the Plaintiff's total claim by way of damages in negligence for breach of the Plaintiff's duty of care to me and breach of an implied term of the Plaintiff's contract with me as my banker; namely, that it would use a reasonable skill in the performance of its duties.

399

After three Court appearances in the County Court, the Judge presiding dismissed the bank's claim against me. This ruling, in effect, saved our home, as we would have had to sell it to repay the money that I had given Nathan.

I had not stopped working whilst this latest course of events took place, as before; I got on with the job. However, all too soon after breathing a sigh of relief and putting this latest upset behind me, I got caught off guard yet again. At one time, I had prided myself at being able to see the unexpected coming. Now, I wasn't able to see a thing. I was sure if a big red double-decker London bus drove straight at me, I probably wouldn't notice it!

Chapter 46

A New Beginning: 1994

Out of the blue on the 25th August 1994, I found myself with a new sworn affidavit made by Nathan Thompson. It covered many points about our case. The points that most interested me said:

29.　After Mark Young and myself had been found guilty, the Crown Prosecution Service barrister stood up and asked for compensation for National Westminster Bank. The judge then asked the barristers if either of us had any money. They said "no". The judge then decided that National Westminster Bank would not be given any compensation, then he said he would make an order that the bank could not take proceedings because he had taken the compensation point into account when sentencing Mark Young and myself.

30.　Mark Young was a totally innocent party and should never have been arrested or charged. I feel very bad about this and don't want it on my conscience any longer.

31.　I have not seen or spoken to Mark Young since being in prison. I was contacted with a third party and was told that Mark Young wanted to speak to me, a meeting was arranged that day, Monday 8th August 1994. Mark Young and his friend Terry Walters met with me at the Excelsior Hotel at Heathrow at 4:30pm.

32.　I told Terry Walters about Mark Young wanting to run his own security company, about the threats that he had received from ▀▀▀▀▀▀▀ and that I had advised him to trade in another name and to open a bank account in that name.

33.　I told Terry Walters that a cheque for about £36,000 was paid into the Gerald Vincent account. I told him that Mark Young had no idea that the cheque was stolen. I also said that Mark Young had personally given me the £11,000 out of the Gerald Vincent account. I also told him that Mark Young protests of innocence at the trial had been true.

34.　I have attended Mark Young's solicitors on three separate occasions.

sworn at 23 High Street

this 2ⁿᵈ day of Aug 1994

before me

Solicitor/Commissioner of Oaths

R. C. FLOATE
23 HIGH STREET

SOLICITOR

Armed with this new information, a barrister's opinion was sought. His opinion filled me with hope. After such a long black period, I finally saw some light at the end of the tunnel.

R V Young

GROUND OF APPEAL

The convictions of the Applicant on each count of the indictment are rendered unsafe and unsatisfactory by the evidence now supplied by his co-accused Nathan Thompson. Such evidence is to the effect that the Applicant acted innocently throughout and was deceived into acting as he did by the said Nathan Thompson and was not available to the Applicant at the time of his trial.

John Coveney
1/x/94

My lawyers made an application to the Court of Appeal in London. While we waited to hear from them, the Sheikh managed to sell his house. I had worked for the Arabs from 1979 until the day I broke free from them on the 10th November 1994, some 15 years or more later.

A week later on Friday 17th November 1994, my family and friends accompanied me to finally see justice done. I wondered if Nathan Thompson would show up, as he was putting his neck on the line.

In making the new affidavit, which cleared me of any wrongdoing, Nathan was admitting that he committed perjury during our trial. For this, he could be looking at a prison sentence as long as seven years!

My heart beat as though it was going to burst at any moment as Nathan Thompson showed up to face the judges on the bench. To everyone's dismay, they said they would not hear his evidence. They said he had no credibility now! Why didn't they listen to him and then decide? Why wasn't he charged with perjury? The evidence was before them but they discounted it.

For that reason and that reason alone my convictions stand.

Happy Christmas? I don't think so!

During the trial, I found out the cheque was reported stolen on the 7th January 1991 and a 'stop' was placed on it on the same day. The cheque was deposited into my account on the 24th January 1991. I drew against it on the 29th January 1991; three weeks after the 'stop' had been placed on it, and only then after the bank had cleared it to draw against. Now, I do not consider myself the brain of Britain. However, I do think that had the bank done their job properly, I would not have been able to draw against the cheque and therefore would not have faced the charges that I did!

Therefore, take a tip from me, if a bank says a cheque has cleared—don't count on it!

* * *

I managed to grasp my dream: I became a bodyguard, and a very successful one at that. When I'd first had the chance to work for an Arab prince, the memories of watching movies about the Caliphs of Arabia had come flooding back. They were exciting and romantic times, so I found myself diving into my newfound profession with great fervour.

I imagined how much good the Saudi Arabian royal family could do for me as well as others with the vast wealth and power they controlled. Instead, I found almost all the Saudi royal family self centred, corrupt and selfish. They treated people with contempt, merely corporeal chattels to do with as they pleased. Girls and boys were often drugged and raped. Alcohol and drugs were widely used and hypocrisy ruled their country alongside them. After people outlived their usefulness, they were discarded like used tissues. Disillusionment set in because of what was revealed to me, and I questioned my own integrity. I had suffered over the years as it just became impossible to ignore the drink and drug fuelled rages displayed by certain members of the royal family. The beatings and mental torture meted out to the 'menial' members of staff also caused real distress to me and my colleagues. And knowing that young women were plied unsuspectingly with 'Rohypnol' type drugs and then raped; well that just ripped me apart.

How could I legitimately protect these people, I questioned, when I had come to disagree with most of what they stood for? Long hours, sleep deprivation and months spent apart from my family brought on depression and mood swings. My family suffered, but supported me throughout. I found myself corrupted by the Arabs' first class world, and the belief that I, too, would become wealthy off the back of them. I wanted what they had—expensive clothes, cars, boats and houses. I dreamed of giving my family all the things I never had. Prince Mishari had promised to buy me a house; dangled carrots in front of me to chase—and like so many before me, I fell for it. For that reason, I stayed with them when I should have walked away.

When I found myself in trouble with the law, my whole world came crashing down. I could have stolen huge sums of money or jewellery over the years, and yet the authorities believed I had put my position and family at risk for a few thousand pounds. It made no sense to me. It had been inconceivable to me that it would be one of my bodyguard team and not the Saudis who would in the end cause me the most grief. I had made an enormous error in judgment by watching too closely what was going on in front of me with respect to the safety and well being of the Saudi royals, when obviously I should have been watching even more closely the person covering my back. Nathan eventually showed remorse for what he had done to me, but it was far too late. I felt destroyed by not just the Saudi royals but by a member of my own security team as well. And yet out of this quagmire of hurt and desperation the sun began to shine for me. I remembered who I was and what was important to me. Through my work with the Saudis and other Arabs, and also through my misfortune with the law, I learned the real value of my own family. I learned to rebuild my integrity and self-esteem and, most importantly, I learned that I was rich already and had always been. I had just been too blind to see it!

After my time with the Saudi's, I was in effect headhunted by my new employer. As a result, I was working back with an English 'celebrity', in a security role, and I had never been happier. For once, it appeared 'Lady Luck' was shining on me.

Addendum:

* * *

As I sat with friends at their kitchen table in May of 2002, a picture of Paul McCartney and Heather Mills flashed up on the television screen with the headline, "McCartney and Mills To Wed". I had known Terry and his wife for over twenty-five years and had surprised Terry many times with my revelations about Mark Thatcher, Jonathan Aitken and others.

"You must be joking—I don't believe it!" I blurted out.

"What are you talking about?" Terry replied.

"That's a bloody shock to me; I bet it will all end in tears," I commented.

"What do you mean?" said Terry.

"I've just seen a picture of Paul McCartney and his bride-to-be on the television, did you see her?"

"Yes, it's that model that lost part of her leg in a motor accident."

"Well, I've news for you. Heather Mills was a prostitute who serviced Adnan Khashoggi and members of the Saudi Royal family. Prince Mishari showed much interest in her when we were in Marbella. You'll see, it'll all come out in the end."

"You must be joking. I wonder if he knows about her past?" Terry replied.

"No, I'm not joking. Had Mishari followed through in his interest in her and said something to Khashoggi, he would have made a gift of her to him; that's how it works with the major players."